THE ITALIAN INFLUENCE ON EUROPEAN LAW

Drawing on expertise from across the worlds of the judiciary, the bar, and legal academia, this book provides fascinating insights into the role of a key Member State and how its legal influence informs the wider Union's development.

This collection sheds light on the Italian influence on European law by examining the judicial biographies of Italian judges and advocates general during almost five decades of the European Union. It explores the national ties of judges and advocates general to their Member States, to better understand the continuous relationship between the members of the EU judiciary and their Member States' governments and how they practise the principle of judicial independence, a central pillar of the ECJ's rule of law jurisprudence.

Volume 10 in the series EU Law in the Member States

We would like to express our sincere gratitude to Alfredo Calot Escobar, Greffier of the European Court of Justice for allowing us to use and reproduce the official portraits of the Italian judges and Advocates General in this book.

EU Law in the Member States

Located at the cross-section between EU law, comparative law and socio-legal studies, *EU Law in the Member States* explores the interaction of EU law and national legal systems by analysing comparative evidence of the impact landmark EU measures – from CJEU decisions and secondary legislation to soft-law – have had across different Member States. The nature and operation of EU law has traditionally been analysed in a highly 'centralised' way, through the lenses of Brussels and Luxembourg, and in terms of the Treaty and its interpretation by the Court of Justice. Beneath this orthodoxy, however, lies the complex world of the genuine life of EU law in the Member States. Judicial and administrative practices across the Union's 28 Member States considerably qualify and sometimes even challenge the long-standing assumption that doctrines such as the direct effect and supremacy of EU law ensure a uniform and effective application of its provisions.

Each volume brings together leading academics, national experts and practitioners in order to draw conclusions both for EU law generally and the specific area in question on the basis of Member State reports and broader horizontal papers, and will be of interest to generalist EU lawyers and specialists in each field across the Member States. Academic audiences will benefit from the tight integration of national case studies and doctrinal analysis, whilst practitioners and policy makers will find systematically presented comparative evidence and commentary.

Series Editors
Jeremias Prassl
Michal Bobek

Volume 1: *Viking*, *Laval* and Beyond
Edited by Mark Freedland and Jeremias Prassl

Volume 2: Central European Judges under the European Influence: The Transformative Power of the EU Revisited
Edited by Michal Bobek

Volume 3: Air Passenger Rights, Ten Years On
Edited by Jeremias Prassl and Michal Bobek

Volume 4: The Eurosceptic Challenge
Edited by Clara Rauchegger and Anna Wallerman

Volume 5: The Impact of European Institutions on the Rule of Law and Democracy: Slovenia and Beyond
Matej Avbelj and Jernej Letnar Cernic

Volume 6: The Effectiveness of the Köbler Liability in National Courts
Zsófia Varga

Volume 7: The EU Charter on Fundamental Rights in the Member States
Edited by Michal Bobek and Jeremias Prassl

Volume 8: EU Soft Law in the Member States: Theoretical Findings and Empirical Evidence
Edited by Mariolina Eliantonio, Emilia Korkea-aho and Oana Stefan

Volume 9: Free Movement of Persons in the Nordic States: EU Law, EEA Law, and Regional Cooperation
Edited by Katarina Hyltén-Cavallius and Jaan Paju

Volume 10: The Italian Influence on European Law: Judges and Advocates General (1952–2000)
Edited by Daniele Gallo, Roberto Mastroianni, Fernanda G. Nicola and Lorenzo Cecchetti

The Italian Influence on European Law

Judges and Advocates General (1952–2000)

Edited by
Daniele Gallo
Roberto Mastroianni
Fernanda G. Nicola
and
Lorenzo Cecchetti

•HART•
OXFORD • LONDON • NEW YORK • NEW DELHI • SYDNEY

HART PUBLISHING

Bloomsbury Publishing Plc

Kemp House, Chawley Park, Cumnor Hill, Oxford, OX2 9PH, UK

1385 Broadway, New York, NY 10018, USA

29 Earlsfort Terrace, Dublin 2, Ireland

First published in Great Britain 2024

A catalogue record for this book is available from the British Library.

A catalogue record for this book is available from the Library of Congress.

Library of Congress Control Number: 2024940199

ISBN: HB: 978-1-50996-776-6
ePDF: 978-1-50996-778-0
ePub: 978-1-50996-777-3

Typeset by Compuscript Ltd, Shannon

Foreword

The Italian Legacy to a Multifaceted Court

To write a foreword to an innovative book, as the one I now present to readers, means to be responsible and cautious at the same time: responsible because there must be objectivity in describing both the methodology and the contents, cautious in order not to appear too partisan.

I openly admit that, having taken both tasks very seriously, I find myself in the position to combine objectivity and caution and to merge them into a clear-cut positive consideration of the efforts undertaken by both the editors and the authors, as well as of the final result achieved.

I also want to express my personal pride – as an Italian scholar and for nine years as a constitutional justice – in reading stories of success and competence in the Luxembourg Court, ever since its inception. Respect for such a prestigious institution is thus combined with appreciation for the Italian legacy over the years. What we now discover, in reading this book, is that there is a coherent commitment in enhancing European law, despite differences in the professional backgrounds of the Italian judges and Advocates General covered in the study. Such a legacy is grounded on sound historical research and presented to a wide audience of scholars and practitioners, as well as – and this is the auspice I want to express – to students in law and in parallel fields.

The remark on an Italian legacy appears even more perspicuous if we take into account the well depicted different 'generations' or phases in the history of the Court of Justice, which correspond to the three sections into which the editors have divided Part I: the generation of the 'pioneers' (from 1950 to the 1960s), the second with the 'innovators' (from the 1960s to the 1980s), and the third with the 'EU constitutionalists' (from the 1980s to 2000).

First of all, during this period of time, legal education has undergone significant changes in Italy. No doubt the study of European law brought fresh air into the classrooms of law schools throughout the country. Furthermore, the expertise of Italian diplomats and of leading figures operating within European institutions strengthened the playing field in which integration was being pursued.

I often quote Tommaso Padoa-Schioppa, a leading figure at the European Central Bank in the 1990s, who brilliantly portrayed in his writings the original and outstanding Italian contribution in pursuing European integration.

Part of that contribution can be better understood by looking at the intertwining of economic and monetary policies with culture and politics, so that national history in all these fields became a significant part of the European project. In the promising institutional context of the time, Europe is presented as a harmonious example of international cooperation, as opposed to disharmonious equilibria in other parts of the world. To behave in a European way – it is argued – must be a stimulus from within the country rather than from outside (T Padoa-Schioppa, *Europa, forza gentile*, Bologna, Il Mulino, 2001, 123).

A positive and pragmatic approach, equal to the one I just recalled, emerges among the characteristics of the figures outlined in the book. In order to draw such unique portraits of judges and Advocates General, the volume adopts a methodology which blends interdisciplinarity with a 'law in context' approach. In this respect, it is worth highlighting the comparative legal, sociological, institutional, and methodological studies on the 'Italian influence' on European law carried out in the seven chapters of Part II of the volume. Overall, the authors underline how the history of European integration is also the outcome of 'contextual practices, and institutional processes that take place at particular times and in determinate settings', which are the outcome of individual commitments. All these special prerogatives are traced back, looking at the style displayed in drafting decisions and in exploiting the stimulating environment of a multilingual and multicultural Court, as well as taking advantage of the expertise and passion of the Italian members of the Court and their collaborators.

The relevance of many of the decisions to which the figures at the centre of this volume have contributed – which continue to be quoted by the Court in recent cases as leading precedents – is confirmed and further elucidated in academic writings and in textbooks on European law, which have become relevant in the legal training of several generations of students and – then – practitioners, judges, and academics.

In this context, I would like to mention the importance, which can hardly be overestimated, of the *continuous* legal training of national judges, which is at the heart of the activities carried on by the Italian *Scuola Superiore della Magistratura* (High School for the Judiciary). Those activities – organized under the supervision of the Board of Directors, composed of judges, academics and practicing lawyers, which I have the honor to chair – are a vibrant example of how European law is a fertile ground for laying the foundations of a community of courts in the European legal space.

Indeed, if Italian legal culture has enriched the Court of Justice over the years, this volume also points out that that expertise has, in return, been spread across the country with the dissemination of decisions, bringing about a more knowledgeable commitment in enhancing mutual trust and furthering cooperation among courts in Europe. This is not a marginal achievement, if one thinks of the skepticism, cultivated in some Italian circles, with regard to the process of constitutionalization driven by the Court of Justice and on the parallel spreading, through its case-law, of a culture of fundamental rights.

I can add to this my personal experience as a Professor at the European University Institute (EUI) in the late 1990s, where that process was intensively encouraged and even promoted. In such a lively academic environment interdisciplinary and comparative research led to innovative teaching and to fruitful fallouts among doctoral students, coming from different legal traditions. That extraordinary time in my life as a law professor and the privilege I had in following the professional paths taken by the EUI PhD students, convinced me that the history of institutions – be they academic or judiciary or political – is constructed on individual stories, as much as on collective and shared efforts. The importance of individual stories and of the way in which such stories have intertwined each other – creating robust professional networks – emerges clearly from the bibliographies of the Italian members of the Court. Similarly, the interest in comparative legal studies and different legal traditions has been shared by several members of the Court of justice at the core of this analysis.

History becomes an evocative part of institutional communication, which implies exploring the origins of institutions and focusing on their perseverance in looking ahead, capturing and interpreting social changes. Institutions have indeed a duty to communicate and to do so in a trustworthy and authoritative way. I refer once more to my personal experience in the Italian Constitutional Court, where efforts to make known an institutional message consisted, among other things, in setting up an archive and starting a series of interviews with former justices. This allowed for the dissemination of the activity of the Constitutional Court, the tracing of individual contributions and the emergence of different personalities.

Hence, I want to emphasize that judges and Advocates General who, through the pages of this book, speak with their own individual voices, notwithstanding the collegiality of the judicial body they are part of, are 'agents of transfer' of European law back home, as the authors suggest. In their words, the Italian judges and Advocates generals have 'served as a potent transmission belt for reintegrating European law and its principles into the judicial and academic fabric of Italian law'. In so doing, they have, in turn, expanded the horizons of what John Henry Merryman described as the 'Italian style' – somehow implying critically that legal formalism was a still dominant characteristic of the judiciary – because they have acted as innovators, each of them with his own 'Italian style' (JH Merryman, 'The Italian Style III: Interpretation' (1966) 18 *Stanford Law Review* 583).

We should no longer speak of 'a faceless Court', as we read in the concluding remarks, neither of a Court hidden away in the Duchy of Luxembourg, as Eric Stein described it in a well-known recollection of the early days of this institution (E Stein, 'Lawyers, Judges, and the Making of a Transnational Constitution' (1981) 75 *American Journal of International Law* 1). Historical investigation, combined with research in social sciences, reveal the image of a judicial body which constantly evolves, building on its own legacy and yet creating new frontiers in European law. In an ever-lasting circular communication of knowledge and expertise, we discover that Italian legal scholarship contributed to confirming the primary goals of the Court of Justice, particularly in ensuring the protection of individual rights conferred by Community (now EU) law, including human rights, and in strengthening the principle of effective judicial protection, as emerge from reading the volume. Such a heritage – to whose formation the Italian judges and Advocates General have played a pivotal role – contributes to strengthening a judicial body frequently called upon to act as an interlocutor with other institutions and to face unexpected challenges and threats to democracy and the rule of law.

In my attempt to be responsible and cautious, as I initially announced, I hope I have conveyed my admiration for this academic endeavor. It represents a commitment to coherence and an imperative for respect in judicial cooperation.

Silvana Sciarra
Emeritus Professor of Labour Law, University of Firenze
Emeritus President, Italian Constitutional Court
President, Scuola Superiore della Magistratura

Acknowledgements

Our initial idea to shed light on the personalities of the Italian judges and advocates generals at the Court of Justice of the European Union (CJEU) began with a conference entitled 'Italian Judges and Advocates General Shaping European Law (1952–1990s)' jointly organised by Luiss Guido Carli University (Luiss), American University Washington College of Law (AU WCL) and University of Naples Federico II, and held at Luiss University on the 24 and 25 of June 2022. The conference was organised with the support of the *Erasmus+* Programme, in the framework of the Jean Monnet Chair on 'Understanding EU Law in Practice: EU Rights in Action before Courts', held by Professor Daniele Gallo at Luiss University.[1] We would like to express our acknowledgements to the European Commission (Education, Audiovisual and Culture Executive Agency) for its support and co-funding, as this edited volume is one of the resulting publications of the Jean Monnet Chair.

The conference brought all the authors involved in this volume to Rome, where they presented a preliminary version of their research on the biographies of the Italian judges and advocates general at the CJEU, which resulted in Part I of our book. On that occasion, each of these presentations was followed by a comment by a 'discussant' who aimed at complementing and contextualising the biography of the judge or advocate general presented at the conference. Each author was asked to undertake their biographical research on a judge or advocate general according to the sets of research questions that we outlined to clarify our research agenda. A concluding roundtable provided leading experts in EU studies, as well as former and current judges and advocates general, with the opportunity to engage in discussions concerning legal traditions, comparative law methodologies, and their impact on European law. Most of these presentations are now included in Part II of our book.

We are grateful to all the participants in the Luiss conference who contributed with their support and their ideas to the shaping of this volume, especially to Mr Vincenzo Amendola – at the time, Undersecretary for European Affairs at the Italian Government's Presidency of the Council of Ministers – who offered his opening remarks at the conference. We are also indebted to the panelists of the first roundtable, Professors Sergio Maria Carbone, Lucia Serena Rossi, Silvana Sciarra, Gaetano Silvestri, Francesco Viganò and Antonio Tizzano, who discussed the evolving relationship between the CJEU and the Italian Constitutional Court. The purpose of this roundtable was to honour the memory of Professor Giuseppe Tesauro, one of the most influential Italian jurists of recent decades, who passed away on July 6th, 2021. The conference was dedicated to his legacy.

[1] Project Number 620360-EPP-1-2020-1-IT-EPPJMO-CHAIR.

In the same spirit, we wish to dedicate this edited volume to the memory of Professor Giuseppe Tesauro, who was advocate general from 1988 to 1998, President of the Italian Competition Authority from 1998 to 2005, and finally judge of the Italian Constitutional Court from 2005 to 2014, serving as its President in 2014.

We extend our heartfelt gratitude to all the speakers, commentators and moderators who presided over the various sessions of the conference, and to all the participants who contributed to the lively debates during the conference. Most notably, we are grateful to the following participants: Luiss Rector Professor Andrea Prencipe for his opening speech, Professor Enzo Moavero Milanesi for his introductory remarks, and Professors Robert Schütze and Nicola Lupo, who kindly agreed to chair the panels of the conference along with the editors of this volume.

We would like to express our gratitude to Professors Francesco Bestagno, Daniela Caruso, Claudia Massa, Morten Rasmussen, Ornella Porchia, Adelina Adinolfi, Daniela Amodeo, Síofra O'Leary, Paolo Mengozzi and Fabio Ferraro for their generosity in serving as discussants of the draft papers on the biographies of Italian judges and advocates general at the CJEU, and to Professor Tamara Perišin for her presentation in the concluding roundtable. Their expertise and insights have greatly enriched this work.

Finally, we also express our gratitude to the Department of Law of Luiss University, notably to its Dean Professor Antonio Punzi, for the financial support received for this project, and to Professors Michal Bobek and Jeremias Adams-Prassl, co-editors of the series 'EU Law in the Member States', and to Hart Publishing for the opportunity to publish this volume in their series. We are indebted to AU WCL students Karen Reitan, Alejandra Ureta Malcon and Teddy Mantovani for their invaluable research and editing assistance.

Last but not least, we would like to express our deepest gratitude to our families for their unwavering support, love, and understanding throughout the writing process of this volume.

Daniele Gallo, Roberto Mastroianni, Fernanda G. Nicola
and Lorenzo Cecchetti
Rome, Naples, Washington – August 2024

PRACT
EU Rights before Courts

With the support of the
Erasmus+ Programme
of the European Union

The European Commission's support for the production of this publication does not constitute an endorsement of the contents, which reflect the views only of the authors, and the Commission cannot be held responsible for any use which may be made of the information contained therein.

Contents

List of Contributors

Chiara Amalfitano	Professor of EU Law, University of Milan 'La Statale';
Amedeo Arena	Professor of EU Law, University of Naples Federico II; Visiting Fellow at the Historical Archives of the European Union
Antonio Aresu	Officer, European Commission
Michal Bobek	Justice, Czech Supreme Administrative Court, Former Advocate General, Court of Justice
Lorenzo Cecchetti	Postdoctoral Researcher in EU law, Luiss University
Laure Clément-Wilz	Professor of European Law, Paris-Est Créteil University
Massimo Condinanzi	Professor of EU Law, University of Milan 'La Statale'
Filippo Croci	Assistant Professor of EU Law, University of Milan 'La Statale'
Luigi Daniele	Professor of EU Law, Università degli Studi di Roma Tor Vergata
Vittorio Di Bucci	Registrar, General Court
Vera Fritz	Marie Skłodowska-Curie Postdoctoral Fellow, University of Copenhagen
Daniele Gallo	Professor of EU Law, Luiss University
Edoardo Greppi	Professor of International Law, University of Turin
Celestina Iannone	Director, Research and Documentation Directorate of the CJEU
Roberto Mastroianni	Professor of EU Law, University of Naples Federico II and Judge, General Court
Fernanda G Nicola	Professor of Law, American University Washington College of Law
Tommaso Pavone	Assistant Professor of European Politics, University of Toronto
Ezio Perillo	Former Judge, General Court

Siniša Rodin	Professor of EU Law, University of Zagreb, Judge, Court of Justice
Lucia Serena Rossi	Professor of EU Law, University of Bologna, Judge, Court of Justice
Silvana Sciarra	Emeritus Professor of Labour Law, University of Firenze, Emeritus President, Italian Constitutional Court
Eleanor Sharpston	Arthur Goodhart Visiting Professor in Legal Science, University of Cambridge; Former Advocate General, Court of Justice
Antonio Tizzano	Emeritus Professor of EU Law, La Sapienza University of Rome, Emeritus Vice-President, Court of Justice
Antoine Vauchez	CNRS Research Professor, Université Paris 1-Sorbonne
Joseph H. H. Weiler	Joseph Straus Professor of Law, New York University
Jacques Ziller	Honorary Professor of the Universities of Paris-1 Panthéon Sorbonne and of Pavia

1

Introduction: Tracing the Italian Influence on European Law Through Judicial Biographies

DANIELE GALLO, ROBERTO MASTROIANNI, FERNANDA G. NICOLA AND LORENZO CECCHETTI

1. THE VOLUME IN CONTEXT

TRADITIONALLY, MOST OF the scholarship that focuses on European integration in political science and law has produced a grand narrative of integration driven by law.[1] This has been done through a thorough investigation of the key legal transformations that resulted from the activity of the Court of Justice of the European Union (CJEU or the Court). Most notably, with few exceptions,[2] political scientists dived into quantitative accounts of the Court's case law to identify the real drivers of European Union (EU) law. At the same time, doctrinal lawyers were busy explaining the different steps through which the Court unearthed the contours of this new *sui generis* legal order.[3]

However, this scholarly scenario has recently experienced some important developments. Indeed, scholars have undertaken new avenues of research on the CJEU through historical lenses, including a case-oriented approach that has delved into descriptions of landmark cases,[4] socio-legal studies of Euro-lawyers' networks central to the fabric of EU law, and law-in-context approaches to map

[1] M Cappelletti, M Seccombe, and JHH Weiler (eds), *Integration Through Law: Europe and the American Federal Experience* (Berlin-New York, de Gruyter, 1986).

[2] KJ Alter, 'The European Court's Political Power' (1996) *West European Politics* vol 19 p. 458; K Alter, *Establishing the Supremacy of European Law* (Oxford, Oxford University Press, 2001).

[3] P Craig & G de Búrca, *EU Law: Text, Cases and Materials* (7th edn, Oxford, Oxford University Press, 2020).

[4] FG Nicola and B Davies (eds), *EU Law Stories. Contextual and Critical Histories of EU Jurisprudence* (Cambridge, Cambridge University Press, 2017); B Davies and M Rasmussen, *Towards a New History of European Law* (2012) 21 *Contemp. Eur. Hist*. 305, 309; M Rasmussen, 'Rewriting the History of European Public Law: The New Contribution of Historians' (2013) 28 *Am. U. Int'l L. Rev.* 1187, 1197.

the evolution of law through political, economic and social influences.[5] These theoretical challenges and methodological innovations have suddenly re-opened long-routinised research questions about the individuals responsible for legal decisions,[6] to some extent encouraged by the EU institutions themselves.[7] As regards the CJEU, socio-legal, historical, and empirical studies into the 'legal community' of EU lawyers[8] have highlighted the role of specific individuals working at the Court, such as Advocates General,[9] the Presidents of the Court,[10] and their partnership with *référendaires*.[11] Moreover, by venturing into the

[5] See, *inter alia*, E Stein, 'Lawyers, Judges, and the Making of a Transnational Constitution' (1981) 75 *American Journal of International Law* 1; R Zimmermann, *Roman Law, Contemporary Law, European Law: The Civilian Tradition Today* (Oxford, Oxford University Press, 2001); A Cohen, *Constitutionalism without Constitution: Transnational Elites Between Political Mobilization and Legal Expertise in the Making of a Constitution for Europe (1940s–1960s)* (2007) 32 *Law and Society Inquiry* 109; A Vauchez, 'The Transnational Politics of Judicialization. Van Gend en Loos and the Making of EU Polity' (2010) 16 *European Law Journal* 1; P Grossi, *A History of European Law* (New York, John Wiley & Sons, 2010); B Davies and M Rasmussen, 'Towards a New History of European Law' (2012) 21 *Contemporary European History* 305; F Bignami, 'Rethinking the Legal Foundations of the European Constitutional Order: The Lessons of the New Historical Research' (2013) 28 *American University International Law Review* 1311; M Egan, 'Towards a New History of European Law: New Wine in Old Bottles' (2013) 28 *American University International Law Review* 1223; A Vauchez and B de Witte (eds), *Lawyering Europe: European Law as a Transnational Social Field* (Oxford, Hart, 2013); Morten Rasmussen, 'Revolutionizing European Law: A History of the Van Gen en Loos Judgment' (2014) 12 *Int'l J. of Const. L.* 136; A Vauchez, 'Brokering Europe. Euro-Lawyers and the Making of a Transnational Polity' (Cambridge, Cambridge University Press, 2015) 116–146; Rasmussen (n 3); T Herzog, *A Short History of European Law: the Last Two and a Half Millennia* (Cambridge: Massachusetts, Harvard University Press, 2018); W Phelan, *Great Judgments of the European Court of Justice. Rethinking the Landmark Decisions of the Foundational Period* (Cambridge, Cambridge University Press, 2020) 31–57; T Pavone, *The Ghostwriters: Lawyers and the Politics Behind the Judicial Construction of Europe* (Cambridge, Cambridge University Press, 2022) 129–196.

[6] See H Schepel and R Wesseling, 'The Legal Community: Judges, Lawyers, Officials and Clerks in the Writing of Europe' (1997) 3 *European Law Journal* 165; T Tridimas & G Gari, 'Winners and Losers in Luxembourg: A Statistical Analysis of Judicial Review before the European Court of Justice and the Court of First Instance (2001–2005)' (2010) 35 *European Law Review* 131; M Rask Madsen, FG Nicola and A Vauchez (eds), *Researching the European Court of Justice Methodological Shifts and Law's Embeddedness* (Cambridge, Cambridge University Press, 2022).

[7] Suffice it to think to the opening of its historical archive on the hills of Fiesole at the European University Institute, see FG Nicola, 'Waiting for the Barbarians: Inside the Archive of the European Court of Justice', in C Kilpatrick and J Scott (eds), *New Legal Approaches to Studying the Court of Justice* (Oxford, Oxford University Press, 2020).

[8] Schepel and Wesseling (n 6).

[9] N Burrows and R Greaves, *The Advocate General and EC Law* (Oxford, Oxford University Press, 2007); I Solanke, *Independence and Diversity in the European Court of Justice* (2009) 15 *Columbia Journal of European Law* 1, 89–121; L Clément-Wilz, *La fonction de l'avocat général près la Cour de justice de l'Union européenne* (Bruxelles, Bruylant, 2010); I Solanke, 'The Advocate General: Securing Trust in the CJEU of Art 13 TFEU' (2012) 14 *Cambridge Yearbook of European Legal Studies*, 698–721 (2012); G Butler and A Łazowski (eds), *Shaping EU Law the British Way: UK Advocates General at the Court of Justice of the European Union* (Oxford, Hart, 2022).

[10] Colloque: La Cour de Justice de L'Union Européenne sous la Présidence de Vassilios Skouris (2015), https://curia.europa.eu/jcms/upload/docs/application/pdf/2015-11/actes_du_colloque_2015.pdf.

[11] I Solanke, 'Stop the ECJ? An Empirical Assessment of Activism at the ECJ' (2011) 17 *European Law Journal* 6.

analysis of professional networks, sociologists have revealed how the work of Euro-lawyers has been a powerful engine for the integration and liberalisation of the single market.[12] In turn, picking up on some of these insights, historians have provided further empirical exploration using new archival sources, facilitated by the recent opening of the archives of the Court. The findings of the new legal historians have brought to the surface legal and political resistance to the process of *constitutionalisation* driven by the CJEU.[13] The joining of forces among these different interdisciplinary approaches to legal research has borne fruit, for example, in narrating the jurisprudence of the CJEU through its case-law.[14] Rather than a necessary evolution, this interdisciplinary approach to legal research has shown how European jurisprudence develops through individual decisions, contextual practices, and institutional processes that take place at particular times and in certain settings. This emerging body of scholarship not only challenges the traditional functionalist paradigms of EU legal integration,[15] but also introduces a range of innovative methodologies for studying EU case law and its underlying narratives.[16] Furthermore, it broadens the spectrum of pertinent datasets, archival resources, biographies, and translation documents that scholars specialising in EU law can no longer overlook.[17]

2. AIMS AND RESEARCH QUESTIONS

The goal of the edited volume is to show how a legal tradition from a Member State of the Union has enriched EU law through the contributions of its judges and Advocates General who contributed to shape the jurisprudence of the CJEU

[12] A Vauchez, *Brokering Europe: Euro-lawyers and the making of a transnational polity* (Cambridge, Cambridge University press, 2016); A Vauchez, 'The Force of a Weak Field: Law and Lawyers in the Government of the European Union' (2008) 2(2) *International Political Sociology* 128.

[13] See B Davies, *Resisting the European Court of Justice: West Germany's Confrontation with European Law, 1949–1979* (Cambridge, Cambridge University Press, 2012); A Boerger and M Rasmussen, 'Transforming European Law: The Establishment of the Constitutional Discourse from 1950 to 1993' (2014) 10 *Eur. Const. L. Rev.* 199–225; M Rasmussen, 'Rewriting the History of European Public Law' (2013) 28 *Am. U. Int'l L. Rev.* 1187; Rasmussen (n 5); Bignami (n 5).

[14] See Davies and Nicola (n 4).

[15] See K Tuori, *Empire of Law: Nazi Germany, exile scholars and the battle for the future of Europe* (Cambridge, Cambridge University Press, 2019).

[16] See A Bailleux 'Beyond Judicial Activism. Europe's Judicial Narratives and the *Polity-cal* Role of the Court of Justice', in D Gallo, R Mastroianni, FG Nicola, and L Cecchetti (eds), *The Italian Influence on European Law: Judges and Advocates General (1952–2000)* (Oxford, Hart Publishing, 2024); A Bailleux, E Bernard, S Jacquot, Q Landenne, *Les recits judiciaries de l'Europe: Diffusion, reception et coproduction*, Tome 3 (Bruylant, Paris, 2023).

[17] See T Pavone, 'From Marx to Market: Lawyers, European Law, and the Contentious Transformation of the Port of Genoa' (2019) 53 *L. & Soc'y Rev.* 851; V Fritz, *Juges et avocats généraux de la Cour de Justice de l'Union européenne (1952–1972): Une approche biographique de l'histoire d'une révolution juridique* (Frankfurt, Klostermann, 2018); K McAuliffe, 'Hidden Translators: The Invisibility of Translators and the Influence of Lawyer-Linguists on the Case Law of the Court of Justice of the European Union' (2016) 3 *Language and Law/Linguagem e Direito* 5.

and to the development of European law for almost five decades (1952–2000). Most notably, our volume sheds light on the *Italian* influence on European law by focusing on the biographies of the Italian jurists at the CJEU. It provides a transversal discussion of the merits and limitations of researching the extent to which a network of Italian jurists, sharing the same national tradition, were key to the creation of innovative EU legal concepts, including narratives and doctrines. Furthermore, it analyses the impact of Italian jurists on shaping legal practice within the CJEU in Luxembourg and their role in the reception of European law in Italy. In this respect, the volume dwells on how these Italian jurists influenced the relationship between EU law and Italian law, during and after their return to Italy from their tenures in Luxembourg as academics, judges, high-level public servants, or attorneys.

To accomplish this multifaceted objective, our project engaged scholars and legal experts who had direct experience working alongside the judge or Advocate General in question. Additionally, we collaborated with individuals who had access to primary archival and biographical sources. Through this collaborative effort, we were able to vividly portray the Italian jurists in Luxembourg, and to provide a comprehensive understanding of their contributions. In this context, we have identified three sets of research questions that served to establish a coherent narrative underpinning the whole book.

The first set of research questions revolves around the Italian judges' and Advocates Generals' legal education, background, and professional career – before joining the Court in Luxembourg – and how such experiences impacted on their work at the Court. This part of the research can be understood within the context of the studies on judicial biographies, which are certainly not new in the Unites States[18] but are less frequently analysed in the EU.[19] In this regard, judicial 'biographies' should be understood, as claimed in the literature, not as 'a goal in themselves, but rather a means to craft primary material that can be explored to study different aspects of the functioning of the Court'.[20]

The second set of questions examines the relevance of each judge and Advocate General during their time at the Court, and their contributions to the

[18] See, *eg*, J Biskupic, *American Original: The Life and Constitution of Supreme Court Justice Antonin Scalia* (New York, Farrar, Straus & Giroux, 2010); M Hartnett *et al.*, *My Own Words* (New York, Simon & Schuster, 2016).

[19] Although legal historians like Vera Fritz have created an impressive collection of biographical materials in order to study the European Court of Justice through the lens of its main actors, see Fritz (n 17); A Boerger-De Smedt, 'La Cour de Justice dans les négociations du Traité de Paris instituant la CECA' (2008) 14 *Revue d'histoire de l'intégration européenne* 7; M Rasmussen, 'The Origins of a Legal Revolution – The Early History of the European Court of Justice' (2008) 14 *J. of Eur. Integration Hist.* 77.

[20] Fritz (n 17). For instance, Vera Fritz demonstrates that since the appointment mechanism was exclusively in the hands of national governments, the European judges of the 1960s and 1970s were generally well-connected to national politics, see V Fritz, 'Judge Biographies as a Methodology to Grasp the Dynamics Inside the CJEU and Its Relationship with EU Member States', in Rask Madsen, Nicola and Vauchez (n 6).

'*grands arrets*'. We asked the authors to comment on their work in Luxembourg from both a quantitative and a qualitative perspective, in so far as some legal concepts, stylistic or rhetorical formulas, and expressions recurred throughout the case law they were involved in or methodological approaches deriving from their national background, political affiliations and professional legal culture, could be identified. Moreover, the analysis encompassed the composition of the Italian judges' and Advocates Generals' cabinet, by looking at who the *référendaires* were and whether or not they were maintained from the cabinet of the previous Italian judge or Advocate General.

The third set of research questions concentrates on the formal and informal networks created by each jurist in both Luxembourg and Italy. In doing so, we solicited the contributors to the volume to pay closer attention to the connections of the Italian jurists with academic, political, and professional ties back home. In this way, we sought to understand how, during or after their careers in Luxembourg, they succeeded in becoming a bridge or a sounding board for the reception of the jurisprudence of the CJEU in the national context. For instance, we asked each contributor if the Italian judge or Advocate General continued to deliver lectures or speeches at universities *et similia* during their mandate. Additionally, we asked the authors to address if 'their' jurist played any role in designing the relationship between Italian and EU law after his mandate in Luxembourg. It would be fallacious to conceptualise the 'Italian influence' on European law as if it operated in 'one direction' only, ie, from the domestic legal order to the EU legal order and not vice-versa. We therefore asked all contributors to bring to life the links that each jurist leveraged to maintain their connections to the judiciary, the bar, and to legal academia, to illustrate how these Italian judges and Advocates General in Luxembourg were able to re-translate EU law in their Member State.[21]

In light of this structure, which aims to put flesh to the abstract notion of influence, the similarity with the other volumes published over the years in the series 'EU Law in the Member States' is evident. As a matter of fact, while this edited volume relates to Italian jurists, the main idea behind it could be extended to the judges and Advocates General of all the twenty-seven Member States to explore analogous or different ways in which they have established a dialogue between Luxembourg and the legal professional realm of their respective countries of origins.

A final note: in addition to the chapters dedicated to biographical analysis of the Italian jurists, the volume also includes several chapters that compare these biographies and the data derived from them, employing a law-in-context, comparative, and methodological perspective. This decision has influenced the structure of the work, as outlined in the next section.

[21] See, eg, LS Rossi and G Di Federico (eds), *L'incidenza del diritto dell'Unione europea sullo studio delle discipline giuridiche* (Naples, Editoriale Scientifica, 2008).

3. SCOPE AND STRUCTURE OF THE VOLUME

The volume consists of two parts. Part I collects the biographies of the eleven Italian judges and Advocates General who have served at the CJEU from the very beginning of the European integration process in 1952 until 2000 and ends with the conclusions offered by Professor Antonio Tizzano, whose mandate is beyond the scope of our book as he became Advocate General in 2000, judge in 2006 and finally Vice-President of the CJEU from 2015–2018.

Part II consists of seven chapters authored by former or current judges and Advocates General, as well as by leading experts in EU studies. Their analysis relies on comparative law, and sociological and institutional arguments, and draws on data collection provided by the biographical portraits in the volume. This approach has enabled the authors to better assess and define what we mean by the 'Italian influence' on European law. Professor Joseph H. H. Weiler's *Epilogue* further extends the reflections presented in Part II.

Part I: The Biographies of Italian Judges and Advocates General

Part I is divided chronologically into three Sections, which – adopting the three sets of research questions explained above – investigate the profile of each Italian judge or Advocate General across what we considered to be 'three generations' of jurists. The first spans from 1950 to the 1960s, with the 'pioneers' as Vera Fritz calls them; the second section runs from the 1960s to the 1980s, with the 'innovators'; and the third section covers the 1980s to 2000, with the 'EU constitutionalists'. Each chapter engages with a different member of the CJEU, ordered based on the year they took service at the Court. Such a tripartite chronological structure allows us to understand better if the influence of the Italian legal culture on EU jurisprudence has changed over time and whether or not this has impacted the different phases of the European integration process.

The first section, devoted to the 'first generation' of Italian judges and Advocates General, comprises Massimo Pilotti (1952–1958), Nicola Catalano (1958–1961) and Rino Rossi (1958–1964). It opens with Vera Fritz's chapter, which delves into the life and career of Pilotti, who, as first President of the Court of Justice of the European Coal and Steel Community (ECSC), held this role from its inception in 1952 until 1958, when the ECSC Court was transformed into the Court of Justice of the European Economic Communities. By relying on materials from national archives and the Historical Archive of the EU, Fritz gathered all the *dossiers de procédures* of the case law in which Pilotti was President. The chapter first sheds light on Pilotti's professional trajectory as an Italian diplomat and a judge prior to his appointment to the Court. It explains why Italy was tasked with the Presidency of the Court as a political compromise for not getting an Advocate General, as only France and Germany had one. The chapter then highlights Pilotti's initial aspirations and outlook for the Court as a supranational actor – emerging from his solemn address delivered during the inaugural ceremony of the institution – as well as on his contribution to setting up the Court and its procedural rules, and to shaping the foundations of the rising European integration project.

Subsequently, Tommaso Pavone examines the figure of Nicola Catalano, a judge at the Court of Justice of the European Economic Communities from 1958 to 1961. The author shows that, although Catalano is rarely included in the pantheon of Europe's founders, he made fundamental contributions to developing the European judicial order. Indeed, Catalano was crucial both as a member of the Legal Service of the High Authority and as one of the legal architects behind the Rome Treaty. In fact, the preliminary reference procedure set out in its Article 177 (today Article 267 TFEU) is said to be the 'brainchild' of Catalano, 'inspired' by the Italian constitutional system of judicial review. The chapter also traces how this institutional development was highly uncertain, contingent, and dependent on the chameleonic agency of legal entrepreneurs like Catalano. Leveraging archival, interview, and secondary evidence to retrace Catalano's professional life, Pavone brilliantly demonstrates that the development of the European judicial order rested to a significant extent on the tireless entrepreneurship of 'Euro-lawyers' determined to erode resistances to Europeanisation while fostering economic liberalisation within Member States.

Amedeo Arena's chapter brings to life the figure of Rino Rossi, judge at the Court of Justice from 1958 to 1964. The chapter digs into the life and career of Rossi, which brought him from the Alpine valleys, where he was born, to Luxembourg. Arena points out that, during his tenure at the Court, Rossi held firm to an ancient Italian dictum stating that judges should speak only through their rulings, thereby profoundly differing from the approach of the other Italian judge, Catalano, serving at the Court during the same period. Moreover, although the few statements made by Rossi revealed an internationalist conception of the European Communities – which once again departed significantly from Catalano's supranationalism and overt-federalist approach – this did not preclude him from taking part in the 'legal revolution' that occurred on the *Kirchberg plateau* in the early 1960s, as he sided with Alberto Trabucchi and Robert Lecourt in favour of the direct effect in *van Gend & Loos* and acting as rapporteur in landmark cases such as *Plaumann* and *Acciaierie San Michele*. According to Arena, Rossi's biography can be understood as the search for 'practical solutions' to keep pace with the intriguing complexity of the European integration process and to cope with (and react to) its various crises.

Included in the second generation of judges and Advocates General that we defined 'innovators' are: Alberto Trabucchi (1962–1976), Riccardo Monaco (1964–1976), Francesco Capotorti (1976–1982), and Giacinto Bosco (1976–1988). The biography of Alberto Trabucchi is sketched by Ezio Perillo's chapter, which, after having outlined Trabucchi's educational and professional background, focuses on the pivotal role he played in leveraging the effective protection of individual rights in the Court's decision in *van Gend & Loos* (and *Costa v Enel*). Amongst the different biographical aspects stressed by the author, Perillo highlights the contribution of the civil law perspective that was underpinned by Trabucchi's legal education and professional career as a Professor of Private law in Padova. Additionally, Perillo shows the impact on Trabucchi's career of his previous experiences in Community litigation as a consultant for the ECSC High Authority through his former pupil, Giulio Pasetti Bombardella, in high profile cases such as *Meroni*. Finally, Trabucchi was the first Italian jurist to be appointed as Advocate General and the first member of the Court to have the possibility to exercise the two different functions, serving as a judge from 1962 to 1972 and as an Advocate General from 1973 to 1976. According to Perillo, the experience already acquired during the years as a judge at the Court explains why Trabucchi was assigned to deliver Opinions in several significant cases, such as *Rewe Zentralfinanz*, *Dassonville*, *Centrafarm*, and *Defrenne*.

Edoardo Greppi's chapter explores Riccardo Monaco's biography, who served as a judge at the Court from 1964 to 1976. Greppi focuses on Monaco's – to some extent turbulent – career trajectory, and on his research on the legal nature of the European Communities imbued with international law dimensions and features. The author also highlights Monaco's inclination, first as a Professor of Public Law in Turin and Rome and then as a close advisor to the Ministry of Foreign Affairs, to consider theoretical speculation in international law as being inextricably linked with praxis. Indeed, his commitment to the creation and development of scientific associations aimed at studying international and European law is remarkable. During his two terms in Luxembourg, Monaco was involved in a considerable number of cases that dealt with staff regulations of EU officials, common agricultural policy, and the coordination of social security regimes connected to the free circulation of workers. Greppi's analysis of some of these cases emphasises the attention devoted by Monaco to the 'doctrine of supranationality' and to the position of private parties in the European *sui generis* legal order, notably in its judicial system. As is apparent from the foregoing, some of the former Italian members of the Court, such as Trabucchi, shared these interests.

Luigi Daniele's chapter delves into the biography and legacy of Francesco Capotorti, first judge at the Court of Justice for a short period in 1976 and then Advocate General from 1976 to 1982. After having outlined Capotorti's brilliant career in academia as a Professor of International and European law that began in Naples and culminated at La Sapienza in Rome, the Chapter focuses on his life and work at the Court after his appointment in Luxemburg. First, Daniele stresses Capotorti's strong independence of thought during his term as an Advocate General, showing an attitude that was rooted in his past experience as an influential academic in Italy and beyond. Second, the author recalls Capotorti's innate ability to build solid working networks and friendly relationships with other members of the Court as well as with his *référandaires* and staff in Luxembourg. Daniele shows how Caportorti nurtured his academic network by continuing to actively take part in the academic life of his Italian and European colleagues during his time in Luxembourg. Third, Daniele examines his work as an Advocate General, which is found to be impressive from both a quantitative and qualitative perspective. Indeed, Capotorti delivered more than 150 Opinions, mostly on cases that raised new and very delicate issues and are still quoted in the canon of European law today, such as *Defrenne III*, *CILFIT*, *Cassis de Dijon*, and *Hoffmann La Roche* – to mention a few.

In the last chapter on the 'innovators', Jacques Ziller carries out an in-depth biographical analysis of Giacinto Bosco, judge at the Court from 1976 to 1988. The chapter illustrates Bosco's academic and professional career, marked by his strong political ties with the Italian Christian Democracy Party, which led him to serve, *inter alia*, as a member of the Italian Parliament, as a Minister in several Cabinets, and as the Vice-President of the High Council of the Judiciary. Particular attention is devoted to his publications before, during, and after his term in Luxembourg and to the ways in which his previous political activity impacted his appointment and work at the Court. Most notably, Ziller argues that Bosco showed a remarkable capacity for hard work, a constant search for consensus as judge-rapporteur and chamber president, and a firm belief about the need to undertake a reform of the Court, showed through the creation of the Court of First Instance.

Finally, the four 'constitutionalists' of the 'third generation' of Italian judges and Advocates General are Giuseppe Federico Mancini (1982–1999), Giuseppe Tesauro (1988–1998), Antonio Mario La Pergola (1994–2006) and Antonio Saggio (1989–2000). The chapter on Giuseppe Federico Mancini, Advocate General from 1982 to 1988 and then judge from 1988 to 1999, is written by Vittorio Di Bucci, who examines both the career that led him to the *Kirchberg plateau*, the Court's location in Luxembourg, and his legacy through the Court's case law. Di Bucci points out the active role played by Mancini in legal academia as a Professor of Labor law, first in Bologna and then in Rome, by developing an informal network of labour lawyers active in different jurisdictions. He contributed to the emergence of a common legal thinking on the European social law in the Single Market and pushed toward a constitutional vision for the European legal order. The chapter also explores Mancini's actions beyond academia, most notably as an active participant in the Italian political and cultural life. In the same vein, Mancini's acute interest in judicial activities – matched by his election as a member of the Italian High Council of the Judiciary – allowed him to maintain long-lasting connections with some members of the Italian judiciary even during his period in Luxembourg. The chapter then explores the influence exercised by Mancini on the development of EU law; this is done by delving into some cases concerning the internal market and then focusing on two topics that were particularly dear to Mancini, namely social law and institutional law. In this regard, Di Bucci stresses the importance that Mancini attached to the interplay between the full effectiveness of EU law and the advancement of the integration process as a fully-fledged constitutional and federal project, to some extent 'anticipated' in his academic writings.

Roberto Mastroianni's and Massimo Condinanzi's chapter delves into the biography of Giuseppe Tesauro, Advocate General at the Court from 1988 to 1998, and begins with Tesauro's legal education, academic career, and professional experience. The chapter concentrates on his career in Luxembourg, stressing the impact of his academic background, as a Professor of EU law first in Naples and then in Rome. First, the authors clarify that Tesauro's approach to his role as Advocate General was typical of an academic who would delve into each case by looking not only into CJEU precedents but also into the scholarly literature. Secondly, the authors explain that Tesauro's previous experience as a specialised attorney in EU law laid the foundation for his concern regarding ensuring the effectiveness of EU law, as well as of the Court's actions, particularly within the framework of preliminary ruling procedures. Finally, the chapter dwells on some of Tesauro's Opinions addressing institutional and constitutional elements of EU law and internal market law. This part is based on quantitative research of the case law and is enriched by qualitative personal stories that brilliantly exemplify Tesauro's commitment to refining content, scope, and extent of the core principle of effective judicial protection in EU law. In the authors' perspectives, this stance is inherently linked to the significance Tesauro attributed to the principles and values aimed at safeguarding individuals' rights since the *van Gend & Loos* ruling.

The chapter by Chiara Amalfitano and Filippo Croci investigates the figure of Antonio Mario La Pergola, judge in 1994 and from 1999 to 2006 and Advocate General between 1995 and 1999. Firstly, the authors briefly recall his legal education, academic career, and the various institutional roles he held in the years preceding his appointment to the CJEU. Secondly, the authors reflect on La Pergola's contribution to European law before his appointment to the Court (as they put it, 'from Rome'), which they show is clearly evident from his time at the Italian Constitutional Court, where he was the reporting judge in a number of cases related to issues pertaining to the then European Community law (including the landmark *Granital* judgment of 1984), and later from his time as the Italian Minister for European Affairs. Thirdly, the chapter analyses the most prominent cases in which La Pergola was involved as Advocate General or as reporting judge. During his term as an Advocate General, the authors highlight that the most important Opinions written by La Pergola revolved around Union citizenship, equal treatment, non-discrimination, and freedom of establishment in EU law. According to Amalfitano and Croci, during his tenure as a judge, rulings where La Pergola acted as a reporting judge often included more than one reference to the Advocate General's Opinion, highlighting the necessity for the Court to engage extensively with the work of Advocates General.

Finally, the chapter on Antonio Saggio, judge (1989–1995), then President of the Court of First Instance (1995–1998), and subsequently Advocate General at the Court of Justice (1998–2000), is written by Celestina Iannone and Antonio Aresu. This chapter examines Saggio's career trajectory, which led him to Luxembourg, through qualitative interviews of those who shared a close relationship with him, such as family members, *référendaires*, and colleagues. The authors highlight Saggio's key role as an institutional player, especially in the establishment of the Court of First Instance. Rather than a professor, Saggio was a judge who came to Luxembourg from the Supreme Court of Cassation in Rome, where he resumed his judicial career after the end of his mandate. The chapter delves into Saggio's numerous contributions to CJEU case law, both as a judge and as an Advocate General. Finally, the authors highlight Saggio's commitment to the development of the Association of European Jurists (AIGE) – aimed at contributing to enhancing the 'European legal culture' in Italy – and to his writings before, during, and after his terms in Luxembourg. The authors show how Saggio's legacy can be found both in his legal approach to individual rights and social protections, and in his political vision of a borderless Europe.

The concluding remarks of Part I by Antonio Tizzano offer – as the title suggests – an 'insider's view' on Italian jurists at the CJEU. This chapter serves as a sort of '*intermezzo*', and emphasises the bidirectional character of the influence of national laws on Union law. On the one hand, it comes as no surprise that the natural reference for the reconstruction and definition of legal concepts used by the Treaties and the jurists at the Court has been primarily found in the Member States' domestic legal systems, especially in the early days of European integration. On the other hand, the extraordinary impact of Union law on the legal systems of Member States, facilitated by core principles such as primacy and direct effect, should not be underestimated. In this context, the process of 'Europeanisation' of national legal systems has evolved not only through the direct influence of Union legislation but also, and perhaps primarily, through less formal and institutionalised avenues. These avenues, prompted by doctrinal reflection and the working practices of jurists, including those central to this volume, are no less pervasive.

Part II: Methodological Reflections on the Collective Biographies

The seven chapters that comprise Part II provide comparative law, sociological, institutional, and methodological investigations into the 'Italian influence' on European law. They delve into research conducted on the biographies of judges and Advocates General, as well as into the overall research contribution of this volume, both to the literature focusing on judicial biographies and beyond.

Lucia Serena Rossi, appointed in 2018, recounts that she is the first Italian woman appointed to the CJEU. Rossi infers from her experience that judges and

Advocates General should possess deep knowledge, not only of the procedural technicalities before the Court, but primarily of the general principles of EU law. Indeed, as a judge at the Court, one must contend constantly with a multitude of substantive law aspects of EU law, perhaps akin to the responsibilities faced by judges of the Constitutional Courts of the Member States. In this respect, Rossi reflects on the composition of the Court and the background of judges and Advocates General, be it mainly the academia or the judiciary, and she notes the benefits that stem from such a diversity of career paths. Rossi also stresses the importance, for the CJEU's members, of keeping links with the protagonists of the judiciary in national Member States, especially through engagement with domestic training programs for national judges in lower, higher, administrative, criminal, and civil courts. In dealing with the differences between the work of judges and that of Advocates General, Rossi challenges the misconception that Advocates General are the ones responsible for drafting the first accurate study and conceptually framing of the legal questions in a case. She recalls instead that such legal framing is always done by the reporting judge, well before the hearing where the Advocate General is involved. Moreover, Rossi writes that multilingualism within the CJEU remains a crucial aspect of the EU today. However, French is the preferred working language at the Court and will continue to be in the years to come, despite the strong lobby advocating for a switch to either English or German.

Laure Clément-Wilz identifies three methodological challenges that scholars face when measuring the influence on EU law of a specific group of individual judges or Advocates General: the secrecy of deliberation, the 'euro-enthusiasm' of EU lawyers, and the opacity of the nomination process. She suggests that the biographical approach used by the editors of the volume offers a means to tackle these three challenges. The edited volume, she notes, delves into the legal fabric of the Court of Justice, akin to existing literature examining the Court from an 'institutional' perspective that 'entails a deeper focus on procedural and organisational choices of a legal institution and their connections to legal substance'. The book reveals the 'Italian essence of the legal fabric of the Court' (or the 'Italian-ness of the organisation of the Court'), notably in the design of both the preliminary ruling procedure and the General Court, and offers an important departure from the traditional viewpoint of French legal culture that dominates the CJEU, particularly with the use of French as the language of deliberation. Clément-Wilz interestingly notes that the volume not only explores the Court as an institutional actor but also delves into the substantive aspects of EU law and its evolving legal doctrines. In analysing the concrete outcomes of the CJEU rulings and Advocates General's Opinions, she observes that 'Italian Advocates General, much like their counterparts, demonstrate varying degrees of integration, occasionally surpassing the stance of the Court or lagging behind'. Despite this variability, what emerges from the biographies is that most of the Italian judges and Advocates General fully embraced the *Esprit de corps* of the Court of Justice once in Luxembourg, while some of them already endorsed such *Esprit* during their past experiences as *référendaires*.

Antoine Vauchez situates the volume within the realm of studies that address the influence of national legal traditions on EU law. He highlights, for instance, how the dominant position of French as the *langue du délibéré* at the CJEU has played a significant role in shaping the EU legal order and CJEU case law, often to a greater extent than non-French legal traditions. Vauchez also connects the matter of national legal traditions with that of national identity in the frame of the, more or less, confrontational dialogues between the Court of Luxembourg and the Supreme or Constitutional Courts of the Member States. The chapter illustrates the importance of a volume aimed not only at attributing recognition to legal figures, some of whom may have been forgotten, but also at unearthing the diverse legal and political stakes and contexts within which key judicial decisions were framed and interpreted. Vauchez notes that this approach mirrors the methodology employed in literature that researches landmark cases. If cases are not just the simple result of deliberation, in the same way biographies of European judges and Advocates General cannot be limited 'to their time at the Court but must be situated in their life-long professional trajectories'. As to the 'Italian-ness of EU law', the author clearly infers from the biographical chapters of in Part I the relevance of Italian judges and Advocates General in the creation of core EU legal doctrines and principles as well as in shaping the institution of the Court and its processes. He also identifies two main continuities in the Italian biographies. The first is the central role of legal academia and the under-representation of other groups or institutions, such as the members of the highest Italian courts and the Italian legal profession. The second identified continuity is the brokering role of the Italian jurists in the defence of European legal integration. Finally, Vauchez's chapter ends with the identification of a typology of three distinctive figures of Italian jurists at the Court: the legal diplomats embedded in the Ministry of Foreign Affairs; the statesmen politicians who lacked the specialisation in international or European law; and the specialists, most of them law professors in European Law, who were appointed at the Court in light of their legal expertise in the field.

Eleanor Sharpston deals with ('overt and covert') comparative legal reasoning in the work of the Advocates General. To do so, she first begins by noting that the duty of the Advocate General is to make the Court carefully think about the legal complexities of the case. This also means that, where the Court decides not to follow the Advocate General's Opinion, it would be strongly preferable if 'it explained clearly in the judgment why it has made that choice'. This is regrettably not the case according to Sharpston. Sharpston then questions the idea that there is an Italian way of being an Advocate General. As a matter of fact, in her opinion, what defines the work of Advocate General is one thing: to be always yourself in the writing of the Opinion, ie, to have full freedom, with not need, as is the case for the judges, to agree with the other members of the Court on a text accepted by the chamber (or at least the majority of it) in charge of the case. With respect to comparative reasoning, she highlights that sometimes a comparative law reasoning comes into play because it is what the case requires and this might be problematic due to the natural constraints that could arise, notably in terms of languages, notwithstanding the involvement of the research and documentation division at the CJEU. Other times, the input for a comparative law analysis comes from the Advocate General's own legal tradition and his/her own legal and professional background, and, in this sense, comparison must serve to generate an Opinion that is intellectually respectable and operationally sound.

Siniša Rodin dwells on the genesis of a legal tradition and on the role of courts in its creation. He begins his chapter by observing that 'it is nearly self-evident that the activities of the CJEU amalgamate the legal traditions of its Member States'. Rodin first identifies who the agents of a tradition are and then shows how a tradition develops through repetitive practice both at the national and European level. By looking into the EU legal order, he suggests that agents of the European legal tradition include judges, Advocates General, law clerks, legal academics, jurist linguists and experts, parties before the CJEU, and even national courts and other actors when applying EU law. Some of these agents influence the formation of the European legal tradition directly 'as participants and some of them indirectly as observers'. The interaction between national legal traditions and the EU law tradition is not one way street. On the one hand, the CJEU provides the framework for national judges on how to apply EU law and, on the other hand, national courts offer feedback on their national legal traditions as shown by the practice of the Italian Constitutional Court, illustrated by the *Taricco* saga. In this context, Rodin shows that there is also a covert dimension of tradition that is formed through four trends of change: increased reference to national law in the EU case law; legal detailing, in which 'justifications are increasingly sought in legal authority, both black letter and praetorian, and less in the legal context and purpose that inform legal interpretation'; increased interpretation of EU law '*à la lumière*' of the Charter of Fundamental Rights of the EU; and the increased role of the Grand Chamber as a dominant institutional agent of 'amalgamation' of domestic and EU legal traditions.

Michal Bobek's chapter is quite skeptical about the very possibility of measuring the Italian influence on EU law. First, Bobek remarks that the study of judicial biographies originated in US legal scholarship, with the ultimate goal of drawing connections between individual personalities and decision-making on the bench. In this respect, he puts forward a distinction between common law and civil law high courts, insofar as while in the former 'internal (dis)agreement and voting patterns are fully disclosed, and the reasons for them are made explicitly', in the latter, decisions are 'by default collegiate with (except for constitutional courts) no possibility for dissenting opinions'.

On this divergence rests, according to Bobek, a hostile environment in Europe to the infiltration of the study of judicial biographies, that is, establishing a credible connection between the individual judge and the judicial decision. Bobek clarifies that despite these challenges, a cohort of social scientists and jurists has emerged in recent years, endeavoring to comprehend the influence of judges' legal and professional backgrounds in the deliberation of the courts in which they serve. Finally, Bobek adds that judicial biographies, 'even if they initially proclaim to merely be setting out the social context, environment, or just the individual story of a judicial life, rarely stop there'. Hence, he concludes that the contention that a specific judicial influence wielded by an individual judge on the court, and consequently on the resultant collegial deliberations, can be discerned is likely to provoke criticisms and concerns.

4. CONCLUSION

In our conclusion, we draw upon key findings from the volume, employing the metaphor of art historians who elucidate the pivotal role of architects in making nuanced choices in designing their buildings. Much like art historians tracing the evolution of styles, we examine the Italian style as emblematic of the enduring attitudes towards the law among a cohort of Italian jurists, which permeated European case-law and institutional practices at the Court for half a century. Exploring both the procedural and substantive architecture of the CJEU, we illuminate the distinctive Italian traits within its architectural style and their evolutionary trajectory through history. By means of contextual, sociological, and comparative insights, the volume delineates the genesis of each architectural element, elucidating the pivotal role of Italian jurists in preserving or blending the Italian style or legal perspective within the broader European legal landscape at the Court.

Building on the comprehensive data extracted from the biographies of Italian jurists in Part I, alongside the varied methodological perspectives unveiled in Part II, our conclusion undertakes an examination of the concept of Italian influence on European law. Employing historical, sociological, and comparative law analyses, we identify four distinctive characteristics or traits that embody the Italian legal tradition, Italian *way*[22] or *Italian-ess*[23] and its impact on European jurisprudence, as elucidated through the narratives within the judicial biographies.

[22] See A Vauchez, 'Italian Ways of EU Law: Rooting Italy in European Legal Integration', in D Gallo, R Mastroianni, FG Nicola, and L Cecchetti (eds), *The Italian Influence on European Law: Judges and Advocates General (1952–2000)* (Oxford, Hart Publishing, 2024).

[23] See L Clément-Wilz, 'An Institutional View on the Influence of Italians Judges and Advocates General', in D Gallo, R Mastroianni, FG Nicola, and L Cecchetti (eds), *The Italian Influence on European Law: Judges and Advocates General (1952–2000)* (Oxford, Hart Publishing, 2024).

The first trait, viewed through a comparative law lens, discerns the Italian style[24] within European law. Despite the overshadowing presence of French and German jurists in Luxembourg, the Italian legal tradition offers significant contributions to the shaping of European law at the Court.[25] These include its adeptness in navigating diverse continental legal traditions, notably through the incorporation of Roman law principles. Moreover, the Italian legal style is marked by a reliance on scholarly writings to address legal lacunae and a strategic deployment of legal reasoning, which remains detached from social and political influences, often articulated through elegant legal formulas and forms.

A second trait has a focus on the *habitus* of the Italian jurists,[26] which we have named their 'profile', namely their legal culture marked by their educational, geographical, linguistic and professional backgrounds, and how this shapes their professional conduct in Luxembourg and back in Italy. Such a focus allows us to explain the different positions of the Italian jurists by showcasing their legal careers, expertise and the type of proximity they maintained to the political power that ultimately propelled their nomination at the Court.

The third trait uses sociological and comparative law insights to shows how the Italian jurists played a crucial role in the reception and transfer of European legal thought into the fabric of Italian law. In fact, the resilient network of Italian jurists at the Court successfully networked back home where legal professionals especially judges, lawyers, and academics in Italy, were eager to learn about the legal innovations taking place in Luxembourg. This network becomes a powerful transmission belt to reintegrate European law and its principles into the judicial and academic fabric of Italian law.

A final trait emerges in the doctrinal trend promoted and expanded by almost the majority of Italian jurists in advancing the protection of individual rights through doctrines of direct effect and effectiveness of EU law in the domestic legal context emerging from the case law of the CJEU. These four traits that appear from the biographical data collection in this volume constitute the core of the Italian influence on EU law. These traits are traced through the lives of individuals who acted as a lengthy and solid bridge between Luxembourg and the Italian legal context.

Our conclusive chapter is followed by an *Epilogue* by Professor J.H.H. Weiler, whose profound knowledge of both the European and Italian legal world is well known, reflecting on the goals of the entire edited volume.

[24] See JH Merryman, 'The Italian Style I: Doctrine' (1965) 18(2) *Stanford Law Review* 39.

[25] In this worth noting, in this respect, that the Italian contribution to the work of the Court counts also a high number of *référendaires*, not only those attached to the Italian members. A significant number of them are chosen for their cabinets by non-Italian judges and Advocates General.

[26] See P Bourdieu, *Outline of a Theory of Practice* (Cambridge, Cambridge University Press, 2013).

Part I

The Biographies of Italian Judges and Advocates General

A) First Generation (1952–60s)

2

Building the Foundations of the European Court of Justice: Massimo Pilotti (1879–1962)

VERA FRITZ

1. INTRODUCTION

MASSIMO PILOTTI (1879–1962) was the first president of the Court of Justice of the European Coal and Steel Community (ECSC), the ancestor of what is now the Court of Justice of the European Union.[1] He held the presidency of the Court from its inception in 1952 until 1958, when the Treaties of Rome transformed the ECSC jurisdiction into the Court of Justice of the European Communities. He thus counts among the select group of pioneers who not only steered the burgeoning institutions, but also played a fundamental role in constructing their foundations.

As with most other Italian judges from the European Court of Justice, Pilotti's trajectory remains until today mostly unknown to the public.[2] This chapter delves into his life and work prior to being appointed as a European judge, from his career in the Italian judiciary to his many activities on the international level. In fact, Pilotti was first a legal counsellor to the Italian Foreign Ministry, and later a Deputy Secretary General of the League of Nations and member of the Permanent Court of Arbitration in The Hague. Aligned with the book's objective to study Italy's nuanced and enduring impact on the European legal development, the chapter studies the formative role that Pilotti

[1] The research for this chapter was funded by Luxembourg's *Fonds National de la Recherche* (FNR). I would like to kindly thank Professor Francesco Bestagno, as well as the editors of this book, particularly Professor Fernanda Nicola, for precious comments on drafts of this chapter.

[2] For recent research highlighting his professional trajectory, see generally E Tollardo, *Fascist Italy and the League of Nations, 1922–1935* (London, Palgrave MacMillan, 2016); V Fritz, *Juges et avocats généraux de la Cour de Justice de l'Union européenne (1952–1972). Une approche biographique de l'histoire d'une révolution juridique* (Frankfurt, Klostermann, 2018); V Fritz, 'Massimo Pilotti (1879–1962): The Interwar Origins of Postwar Legal Integration' in S Vogenauer and P Bajon (ed), *Key Biographies in the Legal History of the European Union, 1952–1993* (Oxford, Oxford University Press, forthcoming).

played in defining the Court's identity and function. It also focuses on the legal activity of the Court and landmark judgments that shaped European legal history under his presidency. Through the lens of Pilotti's biography and work, the chapter hence embarks on a captivating exploration of the formative years of European integration.

2. PILOTTI'S EARLY CAREER AS A JUDGE AND A LEGAL ADVISER

Massimo Pilotti was born in 1879 in Rome. We do not know much about the early years of his life, such as his social background or his education. After obtaining a doctorate in law, he entered the Italian judiciary in 1901. In 1909, he became a judge at a district court in Rome. Four years later, he reached the capital's court of appeal. After the end of World War I, Pilotti combined his judicial career with the activity of legal adviser for the Italian Foreign Ministry. In 1919 and 1920, he spent much time in Paris, where the victors drafted peace treaties to be imposed on Germany, Austria-Hungary, Bulgaria and the Ottoman Empire. In July 1920, Pilotti attended the Spa conference, in which experts discussed the application of the reparations to be paid by Germany according to the Treaty of Versailles. Later that year, he was recruited to be Italy's deputy delegate at a major international financial conference held in Brussels. In 1924, Pilotti provided his legal expertise at the conference which led to the adoption of the Dawes Plan, which finally settled the reparation payments that Germany ought to make after the Great war.

This extensive experience as a legal counselor, along with his in-depth knowledge of ongoing challenges of international diplomacy, made Pilotti an ideal candidate to become involved in the activities of the League of Nations (hereinafter the League). This was the most important international organisation of the interwar period, which was meant to secure peace among the former belligerent nations. As one of the four permanent members of the Council of the League, Italy was endowed with heavy responsibilities in helping the organisation pursue its objective. However, after the accession to power of Benito Mussolini (1922–1943), this peacekeeping role became increasingly complicated because it clashed with Italy's national political interests, especially its colonial ambitions. This would quickly place Massimo Pilotti and other Italian staff of the League in a delicate position.[3]

3. MASSIMO PILOTTI AT THE LEAGUE OF NATIONS

Massimo Pilotti became involved in the work of the League in 1924, when he was appointed as a member of the Italian delegation in the organisation's Assembly

[3] A Berio, 'L'"Affare„ Etiopico' (1958) 25 *Rivista di Studi Politici Internazionali* 181.

and became the assistant of Italy's delegate Vittorio Scialoja, a former Minister of Justice and Foreign Affairs who was a prominent Roman law professor. He would continue to support the Italian delegation over the next few years, while still working in the Italian national judiciary, within which he was appointed President of the Trieste court of appeal in 1930. At the end of 1932, his years of activity as a legal adviser in crucial international conferences and in the League Assembly were rewarded, and he was appointed Deputy Secretary General of the League, next to the Spanish Pablo de Azcaraté. He dedicated his energy to the coordination of the Member States' intellectual cooperation on scientific and cultural issues.

In the early 1930s, Italy's position with regard to the League became increasingly critical as Mussolini expressed more interest in the construction of a colonial empire than in keeping up his country's leading role as a permanent member of the world peace organisation.[4] *Il Duce* was convinced that Italy had been treated unfairly with regard to the territorial policies of the Peace Treaties of 1919–1920 and was determined to rival the British and French colonial empires. He soon laid eyes on Abyssinia, one of the few uncolonised territories in Africa, bordered by Eritrea and Somaliland, where Italy already had a military presence. On 14 December 1934, the Ethiopian Emperor Haile Selassie alerted the Council of the League to the aggression that Italy's fascist government was carrying out against his country. However, the French Secretary General of the League, Joseph Avenol, was reluctant to involve the organisation in resolving the Italo-Abyssinian conflict. The League had already suffered a blow to its authority due to its failure to prevent Japan's invasion of Manchuria in 1931. His stance was bolstered by the desires of Britain and France to avoid war, preferring traditional diplomacy. Massimo Pilotti himself also worked tirelessly to prevent the League from condemning Italy, advising Avenol against League involvement but also providing counsel to Italy's fascist leaders on avoiding sanctions for their aggression.[5]

In October 1935, as Mussolini's forces invaded Abyssinia, the League could no longer remain passive. Italy was declared an aggressor and economic sanctions were imposed, though they were insufficient to halt Mussolini's conquest. In May 1936, Addis Ababa fell, ending the war. Two months after imposing

[4] For a detailed investigation of Mussolini's policies towards the League see especially Tollardo, *Fascist Italy* (n 2); EC Bona, *L'Italia e la sicurezza collettiva. Dalla Società delle nazioni alle Nazioni unite* (Perugia, Morlacchi, 2007). See also GW Baer, *The coming of the Italian-Ethiopian war* (Cambridge, Harvard University Press, 1967); A Rovine, *The first fifty years. The Secretary-General in World Politics 1920–1970* (Amsterdam, Sijthoff, 1970).

[5] Evidence for a vast correspondence between Pilotti and the Italian leaders, or the Italian representation in Geneva, can be found in Italy's *documenti diplomatici italiani*, published by the Foreign Ministry. See Ministero degli Affari Esteri, *I Documenti Diplomatici Italiani, Settime Serie 1922–1935 vol. XVI* (Instituto Poligrafico e Zecca dello Stato); Ministero degli Affari Esteri, *I Documenti Diplomatici Italiani, Ottava Serie 1935–1939 vol I* (Instituto Poligrafico e Zecca dello Stato); For a detailed analysis of Pilotti's role in the Abyssinian conflict, based on these sources, see also Fritz, *Massimo Pilotti* (n 2).

economic sanctions, the League lifted them, but the crisis persisted. In December 1937, Mussolini announced Italy's withdrawal from the League, leading Italian officials in Geneva to resign. Pilotti left his office as Deputy Secretary General and returned to Italy, where he resumed his career in the judiciary as the president of the Trieste court of appeal. A few years later, during World War II, this position would lead him to preside over the Supreme Court of the Province Ljubljana, the central region of Slovenia under Italian occupation. Not much is known about this episode of Pilotti's career and his war trajectory, except for the fact that he kept up this position in Ljubljana for two years.

4. FROM THE *CORTE DI CASSAZIONE* TO THE PRESIDENCY OF THE SUPERIOR COURT OF PUBLIC WATERS

We can again trace Pilotti's career in 1944, when he assumed the significant position of *Procuratore Generale* at the Italian *Corte di Cassazione*. This appointment marked a pivotal juncture in his career, coinciding with a tumultuous period in Italy's history that was characterised by the end of the war and the subsequent creation of the Italian Republic. The context of this time is crucial to understanding Pilotti's actions. Italy had been under fascist rule, led by Benito Mussolini since the 1920s, with the regime's alliances and conflicts drawing the nation into World War II. As the armed conflict came to an end in 1945, Italy found itself in a state of political transition. The fall of Mussolini's regime had led to the establishment of a provisional government, which paved the way for the formation of an Italian Republic via a referendum. Pilotti's stance during this period was marked by his hostility toward the abolishment of the monarchy.[6]

In June 1946, Italian citizens voted to decide between retaining the monarchy or embracing a republic. The *Corte di Cassazione*, responsible for announcing results and handling legal appeals, declared a provisional victory for the pro-republicans on 10 June. However, over 20,000 appeals flooded the court, mainly from pro-monarchist groups. In a context of growing civil unrest, Prime Minister Alcide de Gasperi officially confirmed the Republic's victory on 12 June, 1946. The next day, Enzo Selvaggi, a staunch monarchist, submitted a late appeal that contested the referendum's legality. Massimo Pilotti decided to accept the appeal despite the fact that its late introduction made it legally inadmissible. He also made a strong case in favour of the appeal, a position that was heavily criticised by contemporaries and has been described as an illegal complicity to

[6] A Mola, *Declino e Crollo Della Monarchia in Italia: I Savoia dall'Unita Al Referendum Del 2 Giugno 1946* (Milan, Mondadori, 2006); M Fiorillo, *La nascita della Repubblica Italiana e i problemi giuridici della continuità* (Milan, A. Giuffrè, 2000); MCI Montanelli, *L'Italia della Repubblica, 2 giugno 1946–18 aprile 1948* (Milan, Corriere Della Sera, 1988); BD Luigi, 'Il caso Pilotti' (1947) 11–12 *Il Ponte* 1108–1115.

obtain the cancellation of the vote.[7] Pilotti's actions however did not change the outcome of the referendum, as the *Corte di Cassazione* upeld the result in favour of the republic on June 18, 1946.

A few months later, Pilotti once again exhibited his antipathy toward the republic. In January 1947, during his customary general address at the inauguration of the new judicial year, he omitted any reference to Italy's newly established republican regime and refrained from acknowledging its provisional leader, Enrico de Nicola, who attended the ceremony. This conduct sparked a scandal, prompting a response from the Ministry of Justice. The following year, Pilotti was relocated from the *Corte di Cassazione* to the presidency of the superior court of public waters in Rome.

5. PILOTTI'S APPOINTMENT AS PRESIDENT OF THE COURT OF JUSTICE OF THE ECSC COMMUNITY

After the League of Nations' inability to prevent the cataclysmic World War II, international diplomacy found itself at a crossroads, yearning for new initiatives that would foster peace and drive economic prosperity in the tumultuous post-war era. Among these initiatives, one that stood out as a beacon of hope was the Schuman Plan, which led to the creation of the European Coal and Steel Community. Spearheaded by the French Foreign Minister Robert Schuman, the plan aimed to promote not only peace but also economic interdependence among European countries, particularly in France and West Germany. The signing of the Treaty of Paris on 18 April 1951 by these two states, as well as Italy and the Benelux countries, marked the birth of a community that was endowed with a unique structure, comprising a Special Council of Ministers, a Parliamentary assembly, and two supranational institutions – a High Authority responsible for steering the project in the common interest and a Court of Justice that provided a mechanism for legal recourse against High Authority decisions.

Although this first European Community was of a new kind, it was built on the experience of past international cooperation, and it was only logical that the six founding member states would, in their recruitment of the first high officials of the Community, select candidates who had prior experience in international organisations. Following article 32 of the ECSC Treaty, the members of the court should be appointed "by common accord of the governments of the Member States" for a six-year term. However, while the appointment process was collective, the selection of candidates was conducted independently, with each state nominating its own candidates.

[7] Historian Frédéric Attal stresses that it was striking that such a high-ranking jurist could present these arguments for the sole purpose of cancelling the referendum, the result of which did not suit his personal views. F Attal, 'La naissance de la République italienne (2–18 juin 1946)' (2007) 7 *Parlement[s], Revue d'histoire politique* 141, 150.

In the summer of 1952, when the allocation of positions among Member States was yet to be determined, Italy presented three candidates for Court positions to its ECSC partners.[8] Giovanni Colli, a prosecutor at the Italian *Corte di Cassazione*, was a prospective judge. For one of the two Advocate General positions that were going to be created, Italy initially considered a jurist who would ultimately become a judge in 1964, Riccardo Monaco.[9] Only in the event that Italy secured the presidency did Italy's authorities propose the name of Massimo Pilotti, who was referred to as '*premier magistrat d'Italie*' or Italy's most distinguished magistrate.[10] While Pilotti was not technically the highest-ranking magistrate in Italy at the time, as he had been reassigned to the court of public waters in 1948, his extensive international experience, including his appointment as a judge at the Permanent Court of Arbitration in The Hague in 1948, made him Italy's most internationally recognised magistrate. Since 1947, he had also been the president of the International Institute for the Unification of Private Law (Unidroit).[11]

Pilotti found himself in a fortunate position. As the ECSC project's initiator, France secured the Presidency of the High Authority for Jean Monnet, another former high-ranking League of Nations official. Simultaneously, the Federal Republic of Germany was granted the inaugural Presidency of the Special Council of Ministers, and Paul-Henri Spaak of Belgium assumed the role of President of the Parliamentary Assembly. This allowed Italy the opportunity to nominate the President of the Court of Justice. Along with six other judges and one Advocate General,[12] Pilotti was sworn into office as president of the new ECSC Court in December 1952.

6. PILOTTI'S VIEWS ON THE ECSC COURT OF JUSTICE

How did Massimo Pilotti approach his new role, and what was his vision for the Court of Justice of the European Coal and Steel Community? It is important to acknowledge from the outset that obtaining concrete answers to these questions is a challenging endeavour as a result of the limited availability of source material. Unlike some of his colleagues on the Court, Pilotti did not actively engage in academic publications, which typically serve as valuable insights into the perspectives of individuals who shaped the European Communities. This scarcity of public expression makes it difficult to ascertain his comprehensive vision and goals within the context of the ECSC.

[8] For a detailed analysis of the appointments of the first judges and Advocates General of the Court see Fritz, *Juges et avocats généraux* (n 2) 81–82.

[9] See E Greppi, 'Riccardo Monaco and the Doctrine of Supranationality in International Institutional Law', in this volume.

[10] National archives of Luxembourg, AE 11374, Note à Monsieur le Ministre des Affaires étrangères, 27 juin 1952 (document produced by Luxembourg based on information provided by the Italian government).

[11] Pilotti remained president of Unidroit until 1951.

[12] The appointment of the second Advocate General, Karl Roemer, occurred only in January 1953.

A notable source that provides a glimpse into Pilotti's initial aspirations and outlook for the Court is his solemn address delivered during the inaugural ceremony of the institution.[13] He commenced his speech by invoking the renowned Italian poet Dante, whom he described as a "universal genius who, in a sorely troubled period, dreamt of recreating in Europe a supranational entity". Pilotti then quoted from Dante's work "*La Monarchia*": "*Ubicunque potest esse litigium ibi debet esse iudicium*" – which translates to "Wherever there may be a dispute, there must be a judgment". This maxim was relevant to Pilotti on the national level, but it was magnified in the context of interstate relations.

Regarding the specific role of the Court, Pilotti's conception was at first quite restricted, as he stated that its task was to guarantee to all the parties involved in the creation of the Community respect for the limits within which the Communities' bodies must be contained.[14] This viewpoint aligned closely with the role that most Member States had in mind during the negotiations of the Schuman plan, as the Court was designed principally as a protection for national sovereignty and a guarantee that the ECSC High Authority would not exceed its powers. It thus stood in contrast to the more ambitious visions put forth by figures such as Walter Hallstein or Michel Gaudet, who recognised early on that the Court had the potential to be the nucleus of a future European constitutional court and held the promise of becoming a pivotal institution in the development of a federal European legal framework.[15] Even Jean Monnet, who initially had strong reservations with regard to the creation of a court in the framework of the ECSC Community, referred to it during the ceremony with more ambitious terms than Pilotti, qualifying it as a 'perspective for a federal European supreme court'.[16]

In contrast with others who described the ECSC Court as *sui generis*, Pilotti also did not highlight that the ECSC Court was of a new kind, different from previous international tribunals. Rather, he portrayed it as a continuity of interwar arbitration models, referring to the fact that since the Treaty of Locarno and the General Act of Arbitration, it had become an ideal to include the creation of a court with the power to make legally binding decisions in treaties that regulate relations between states.

However, while Pilotti did not stress the Court's novelty, his inaugural address does give away elements that indicate that he was open to the perspective of the

[13] Address given by President Massimo Pilotti (Luxembourg, 10 December 1952). Available at: www.cvce.eu/en/obj/address_given_by_massimo_pilotti_luxembourg_10_december_1952-en-38ef26e1-6c57-41d8-9215-c15ef1173c71.html.

[14] ibid.

[15] A Boerger and M Rasmussen, 'Transforming European Law: The Establishment of the Constitutional Discourse from 1950 to 1993' (2014) 10 *ECLR* 199.

[16] Address by Jean Monnet (Luxembourg, 10 December 1952). Available at: www.cvce.eu/en/obj/address_by_jean_monnet_luxembourg_10_december_1952-en-4274f797-40f7-43e2-86d3-09a9be6cd631.html.

institution taking on a role that trespassed its basic function as an international court as they had existed up to 1952. For example, he stated that the ECSC Treaty "open[ed] the legal process to disputes in the international field just as much as to the wide range of disputes concerning the internal organisation of the Plan and its workings, *whether they regard constitutional, administrative or purely civil law*".[17] He also referred to a 'supranational discipline', which the Member States had submitted themselves to. These statements mark a departure from traditional interpretations of the role of international courts and international law. It therefore seems that, while Pilotti aimed at aligning the Court's purpose with objectives set by the Member States, he remained open to innovations in its work.

It is not surprising that Pilotti held a more nuanced perspective on the Court's purpose compared with jurists such as Hallstein and Gaudet, given his professional background. His prior diplomatic experience provided him with substantial training in international law, particularly as it was practiced during the interwar period. Consequently, he imbued the Court with a wealth of concepts, practices, and insights acquired from his previous roles as a legal expert and high-ranking international official.[18] This influence is also evident in his involvement in the drafting of the Court's *règlement de procédure* in early 1953. Here, Pilotti drew heavily from the procedural rules of the International Court of Justice, and referenced experiences from this Court and its predecessor, the Permanent Court of International Justice.[19]

7. THE JUDICIAL ACTIVITY OF THE COURT UNDER PILOTTI'S PRESIDENCY

After the drafting of the court's procedural rules, the activity of its judges was notably limited. It wasn't until December 1953 that the first case was finally introduced, marked by the uncorking of a bottle of champagne.[20] The court's inaugural judgment was rendered on December 21st, 1954. Over the course of Pilotti's presidency, and up until the creation of the Court of Justice of the European Communities, the ECSC judges issued a total of twenty-seven judgments.

Surprisingly, in contrast to the initial motivations of the Member States in establishing the court, the majority of cases were not initiated by governments

[17] Above (n 13) with italics added.

[18] On such continuities, see Fritz, *Massimo Pilotti* (n 2).

[19] The *règlement de procédure* of the ECSC Court was a collaborative effort involving all the judges, not just the president. Nonetheless, Pilotti's draft served as a central point of reference for their discussions. See Historical Archives of the European Union, file CJUE 2396. The procedural rules that were ultimately adopted bear a striking resemblance to those of the International Court of Justice and reflect the significant influence of Pilotti's draft in shaping the final document.

[20] AV Houtte, Souvenirs de la Cour de justice 1953–1982, Cour de justice des Communautés européennes. XXXV ANNI 1952–1987 (Office des publications des Communautés européennes1987).

but rather by individual parties.[21] One distinctive feature that set the ECSC Court apart from the International Court of Justice was the provision that allowed companies and associations to initiate proceedings. In fact, not only Member States, but under Article 33, paragraph 2, also enterprises or associations could file appeals against decisions and recommendations that directly concerned them, or against general decisions that represented an abuse of power affecting their interests. Early on, the Court encouraged private parties to challenge decisions of the High Authority by ruling that for an application by an association or company to be admissible, it was enough for the applicant to formally *allege* that the High Authority had committed a misuse of powers, which affected them. Proof of this misuse would only be considered at a later stage, when the substance of the case was being considered by the Court. This legal stance bolstered the supranational nature of the ECSC Community, as private individuals typically lacked the right to litigate in traditional international courts created by public international treaties.[22] In a well-known case brought by the Belgian coal association *Fédération charbonnière*, the Court also developed, without explicitly naming it that way, for the first time an '*effet utile*' logic, by reasoning that

> [R]ules laid down by an international treaty or a law presuppose the rules without which that treaty or law would have no meaning or could not be reasonably and usefully applied, aiming to give the provisions of the treaty full effect.[23]

Let us also draw attention to the *Meroni* case, initiated by two Italian steel companies, which left a lasting impact on the EU's institutional framework.[24] Both companies challenged two specific decisions made by the High Authority, which mandated payments to a ferrous-scrap equalisation system managed by private legal entities in Brussels. Meroni argued that the High Authority had violated procedural rules, lacked sufficient justification for its decisions, and that the contribution rates were discriminatory. The Court invalidated the disputed decisions, asserting that the delegation of authority to the Brussels agencies violated the Treaties, as the High Authority couldn't grant these agencies powers different from those it received under the Treaties. Moreover, it stipulated that

[21] For detailed overviews of the ECSC Court's activity, see AK Mangold, *Gemeinschaftsrecht und deutsches Recht: die Europäisierung der deutschen Rechtsordnung in historisch-empirischer Sicht* (Tubingen, Mohr Siebeck, 2011) 97–107.; A Arnull, 'The many ages of the Court of Justice of the European Union', Working Paper, EUI AEL, 2020/02, https://hdl.handle.net/1814/67273. An older but still useful reference is D.G. Valentine, The First Judgments of the Court of Justice of the European Coal and Steel Community (1957) 20 *The Modern Law Review*, 596–619.

[22] Mangold, *Gemeinschaftsrecht und deutsches Recht* (n 21).

[23] *Fédération Charbonnière de Belgique v High Authority of the European Coal and Steel Community* Case 8/55 ECLI:EU:C:1956:7 [1956].

[24] *Meroni & Co., Industrie Metallurgiche, S.p.A. v High Authority of the European Coal and Steel Community* Case 9/56 ECLI:EU:C:1958:7 [1958]. For literature on this case, see especially M Patrin, 'Meroni Behind the Scenes: Uncovering the actors and context of a landmark judgment' (2021) 6 *European Papers – A journal on Law and Integration*, 539–551.

such a delegation was only permissible if it was confined to 'clearly defined executive powers' subject to rigorous scrutiny based on objective criteria. The Court grounded its reasoning in the 'balance of powers' principle, a vital safeguard for entities established by the Treaties, which would be undermined by the delegation of discretionary authority. *Meroni* remains a most contentious case in EU jurisprudence, with profound implications for the evolution of the EU's legal and institutional framework, particularly in the context of increasing agencification from the 1990s onwards.[25]

The first two state cases were brought to the Court by the governments of France and Italy, which both argued that the High Authority had infringed the Treaty by misusing its powers in a set of decisions, which had relaxed certain rules for the steel market relating to the publication of price-lists and conditions of sale. The court, working under Pilotti's presidency, sided with the High Authority and used this occasion to establish a fundamental principle that would soon became one of the foundations of European Community law, namely that it was the High Authority's role and even its duty to take into account the fundamental aims of the treaty when making its decisions.[26] From the outset, the Court thus established a first step towards 'teleological' interpretations of the Treaties.

It was also under the Pilotti presidency that the Court came to lay down for the first time the principle of direct applicability, which would almost a decade later be crucially extended in the famous ruling *Van Gend en Loos* and soon followed by the correlated principle for the primacy of European law established by *Costa v. ENEL*.[27] In two joined cases, introduced by the *groupement des industries sidérugiques luxembourgeoises*, the Court declared that the provisions of Article 4, which listed practices prohibited within the coal and steel community, 'were sufficient of themselves and directly applicable when they were not restated in any part of the Treaty'.[28]

8. THE DELICATE RENEWAL OF PILOTTI'S PRESIDENCY IN 1955 AND HIS RETIREMENT IN 1958

While the judges were appointed for a six-year term, the president's tenure was only secured for three years. After being appointed as president by the governments in 1952, in 1955 it was up to his fellow judges to determine whether Pilotti should continue to preside over the institution or be replaced. Archival

[25] ibid., 542.

[26] See *French Republic v. High Authority of the European Coal and Steel Community* Case 1/54 ECLI:EU:C:1954:7 [1954]; see also *Italian Republic v High Authority of the European Coal and Steel Community* Case 2/54 ECLI:EU:C:1954:8 [1954].

[27] See E Perillo, 'Alberto Trabucchi: the Defender of the European citizens' rights and the *Van Gend & Loos* ruling of the Court of Justice' in this volume.

[28] *Groupement des Industries Sidérurgiques Luxembourgeoises v. High Authority* Joined Cases 7/54 and 9/54 ECLI:EU:C:1956:2 [1956].

records reveal that he was, despite his reputation as an established international lawyer, considered to be a contentious president. Multiple German sources report that his fragile physical condition and regular absenteeism hindered his ability to fulfill his duties in Luxembourg.[29]

The Italian government was aware of the situation and saw a potentially beneficial solution. In the autumn of 1954, the Italian ambassador in Bonn proposed an agreement to the government of the Federal Republic of Germany. If the latter agreed to support the candidacy of the Italian Giuseppe Pella for the presidency of the Common Assembly the Italian government would be willing to approach Pilotti and persuade him to resign from the Court. This would pave the way for the German judge Otto Riese to become president.[30] Convinced that Giuseppe Pella would be elected regardless, the Federal Republic of Germany accepted the proposal and instructed its delegates to vote for Pella, who subsequently became president in 1954. Italy now held the presidencies of two of the four institutions of the ECSC. The following year, it was Italy's turn to fulfill its part of the informal agreement with Germany. However, the Italian government did not follow through with its commitment. Instead, it supported a second term for Pilotti as head of the Court. In December 1955, three years after the institution's inauguration, Pilotti presented himself as a candidate for re-election as president and was confirmed in his position by his peers.[31]

The establishment of the Court of Justice of the European Communities in October 1958 brought about significant changes. President Pilotti left his position, and the terms of the two Dutch judges, Adrianus Van Kleffens and Petrus Serrarens, came to an end. Pilotti was succeeded by a new president from the Netherlands, Andreas Donner, while two Italian judges, Rino Rossi and Nicola Catalano, took the place of the Dutch judges. This episode has been interpreted as an amicable trade-off between Italy and the Netherlands, in which the presidency of the Court was exchanged for the second judge's position. However, this perception is erroneous, because judge Serrarens' position had never been assigned to the Dutch government, but to the Confederation of Christian Trade Unions (CISC), of which Serrarens had been the Secretary General for several decades. His presence in the Court was meant to ensure that workers' interests were going to be taken into account in the legal developments of the ECSC Community. It was therefore not within the purview of the Netherlands' government to decide on the renewal of Serrarens' mandate in 1958.

[29] Archives of the German Foreign Ministry, B20-200, Bd. 53, Abteilung II B, 24 March 1953, Betrf. Personalfragen beim Montangerichtshof; Aufzeichnung, 30 September 1955, 213-221-09/1266/55-400 and Aufzeichnung 213-221-09/1262/54, 8 October 1954, Betr.: Präsidenten der Gemeinsamen Versammlung und des Gerichtshofs der Montangemeinschaft.

[30] Fritz (n 2) 100–101.

[31] ibid., citing Archives of the German Foreign Ministry, B20-200, Bd. 53, Gesandtschaft der Bundesrepublik Deutschland, Luxemburg, 213-221-09/71/55-401, 14 December 1955, Betr.: Wahl des Präsidenten der EGKS.

Behind the new allocation of positions on the bench in 1958 were rather long-held Italian claims for a more equitable distribution of Court positions among the Member States. Since 1952, the Italian government had felt that it was being treated unfairly in comparison to France and Germany, which on top of selecting a judge both had the privilege of nominating an Advocate General at the Court.[32] Italy first sought to establish a third Advocate General position, but article 166 EEC stipulated that the number of Advocates General could only be increased upon the express request of the Court itself. Moreover, the fact that Italy had held the presidency of the Court had somewhat compensated for the fact that it could not appoint an Advocate General like France and Germany.

With Massimo Pilotti's six-year term coming to an end in 1958, the Italian government saw an opportunity to pursue its objective from a new angle. When discussions regarding the presidencies of the new Communities arose at the end of 1957, Italian representatives remained reserved regarding the Court of Justice. As Germany and France preferred to focus on the executive bodies, the Netherlands secured the presidency of the Court. Shortly afterwards, the Italian government initiated a diplomatic campaign to secure a more substantial presence in the judicial body of the Communities. Since the proposal for a third Advocate General position had proven unsuccessful, the Italian representatives now targeted the presence of a judge who represented workers in Luxembourg and suggested that the judge nominated by the CISC should leave the Court to be replaced by an Italian judge.[33] In June 1958, Italy openly raised the issue by sending an aide-mémoire to other governments, which aimed at Serrarens' removal from the Court. During the Council of Ministers meeting on July 1, 1958, the Italian government obtained its desired outcome. Without providing an explanation or justification, the subsequent press release announced that the Court of Justice would now include two judges of Italian nationality.[34] After the retirement of Massimo Pilotti as president in 1958, Italy thus proposed two jurists to sit on the European bench of judges, Nicola Catalano and Rino Rossi.[35]

9. CONCLUSION

The presidency of Massimo Pilotti at the Court of Justice of the European Coal and Steel Community holds a unique place in the annals of European

[32] Fritz, *Juges et avocats généraux* (n 2) 102.

[33] ibid., 105–106.

[34] See in National Archives of the Netherlands, Inventory 2.03.01, File nr. 2820.

[35] See A Arena, ''Notre Nestor, Monsieur le Juge Rossi' (1889–1974): An Internationalist's Contribution to the Making of a Supranational Legal Order' in this volume; see also T Pavone, 'Making the European Court Work: Nicola Catalano and the Origins of European Legal Integration' in this volume.

legal history. As the first president of what is now the Court of Justice of the European Union, he contributed to shaping the foundations of the nascent European integration project. His early career as a judge in Italy, combined with his diplomatic experience and participation in the Permanent Court of Arbitration, positioned him as a valuable figure in shaping the Court's identity and function. The fact that he had previously served as a Deputy Secretary General at the League of Nations added credibility to the Court of Justice and bolstered the image of the ECSC as a symbol of peacekeeping and international cooperation. His controversial activities at the League of Nations during the Ethiopian crisis, serving fascist interests, were not known at the time of his appointment. His anti-republican standpoint, however, was certainly known by his contemporaries. Sending him to Luxembourg consequently not only served European interests, but also Italian ones, as it removed him from the national judiciary. His trajectory thus underscores the intricate interplay of national and European goals, as well as the multifaceted nature of European integration, in which individuals can simultaneously embody progress and conflict, continuities and discontinuities.

Once in Luxembourg, Pilotti played an important role in the setup of the Court and in the drafting of procedural rules that were very much in line with the Statute of the International Court of Justice at the Hague. Here, he balanced his traditional international law perspective with an awareness of the unique challenges and aspirations of the ECSC as a pioneer in the integration process. Archival records show that his fragile health kept him from taking on a strong leadership role in the years that followed the creation of the Court. This, however, did not keep the Court from issuing important cases, which had a lasting impact on the legal developments of the Communities.

At the age of 79 when he retired, Pilotti would no longer engage in any professional activities upon his return to Italy. He passed away on April 29, 1962, in Rome.

3

Making the European Court Work: Nicola Catalano and the Origins of European Legal Integration

TOMMASO PAVONE

1. INTRODUCTION: TWO PHOTOGRAPHS AND THE DEVELOPMENT OF EUROPEAN LAW

Buried deep within the Historical Archives of the European Union (HAEU) at the European University Institute in Florence lies dossier 'HAEU CJUE-2557.' It is the sole file in the archive dedicated to a man that is seldom included among the pantheon of Europe's founders: Nicola Catalano. Usually cited for his relatively uneventful stint as Italian judge at the European Court of Justice (ECJ) from 1958 to 1961, it was during his time 'tucked away in the fairyland Duchy of Luxembourg'[1] that someone snapped some of his few available photographs. In turn, those photos made their way to the back of dossier HAEU CJUE-2557, which was made available to researchers in 2015 – three decades after Catalano's death.[2]

Two photos of Catalano are particularly striking, because they appear to capture two very different men (see Figure 1). The photo on the left – 'MU 811' – is the portrait of a jovial, collegial, and relaxed man. It captures a smiling jurist subtly avoiding the camera's gaze, the portrait of someone who gets along without rocking the boat. Conversely, the subject of the photo on the right – 'MU 809' – confronts the camera head-on, staring straight into its lens. It is the portrait of an obstinate jurist, perhaps haunted by an air of frustration but clearly steadfast in his mission. Which of the two photos is closer to the mark?

[1] E Stein, 'Lawyers, Judges, and the Making of a Transnational Constitution' (1981) 75 *American Journal of International Law* 1, 1.

[2] On the opening of the archives and their significance, see: F Nicola and B Davis (eds), *EU Law Stories: Contextual and Critical Histories of European Jurisprudence* (New York, Cambridge University Press, 2017) 1; F Nicola, 'Waiting for the Barbarians: Inside the Archive of the European Court of Justice' in C Kilpatrick and J Scott (eds), *New Legal Approaches to Studying the Court of Justice* (New York, Oxford University Press, 2019).

To answer this question, we need only search the dossier for adjectives used to describe Catalano by those who knew him. A 'militant federalist,'[3] according to a co-author; a 'missionary' and a 'tenacious' 'burning flame,' according to two fellow judges; a man 'devoted to the cause of Europe,' according to one of his daughters.[4] In line with these witness accounts, this chapter channels the man in the fiercer of the two photos, depicting a determined agent of change on a quest to shape the origins of the European Community. Yet this chapter also channels the contrast between the two photos, illuminating a mutable man whose influence stemmed precisely from his capacity to transform himself and adjust to setbacks. To borrow from a popular Italian chansonnier: 'ideas can change the world, but the world doesn't often change. So your first revolution must be to change yourself.'[5]

Figure 1 *Two contrasting photographs of Nicola Catalano during his time as judge at the ECJ*

Source: HAEU CJUE-2557, 88.

This chapter uses the remarkably mutable professional life of Nicola Catalano as a springboard to exhume and examine the agents and struggles that lay beneath the uncertain founding of the European Community and its judicial order. I argue that Catalano made fundamental contributions to shaping European law, but I emphasise that these contributions occurred before and

[3] Letter from Riccardo Scarpa (18 September 1984). Historical Archives of the European Union (HAEU), CJUE-2257, "CATALANO Nicola," 18.

[4] HAEU CJUE-2557, 18, 29, 32, 9.

[5] This is an excerpt of the lyrics of the song "Vivere la Vita," written by Roman musician Alessandro Mannarino.

after his tenure as an ECJ judge. Catalano's brief stint at the ECJ occurred as the fledgling Court was starved of cases, ignored by Member States, and staffed with judges that were hostile to Catalano's Eurofederalist compulsions. Catalano played a critical role in transforming this idle state of affairs, but he could only do so once he was (unceremoniously) pushed out of the Court and could transform himself into an activist lawyer. Through strategic litigation and public advocacy, Catalano was the first practitioner in Italy to repeatedly push clients and national judges to activate Article 177 of the Treaty of Rome (the preliminary reference procedure), which Catalano perceived as a transmission belt to link local civil society, national judiciaries, and the ECJ to advance European integration. In so doing, Catalano shaped the destiny of an institutional mechanism that he designed himself as part of the *groupe de redaction* summoned by Paul-Henri Spaak to draft the Treaty of Rome in 1956. While today the preliminary reference procedure is widely acknowledged as the motor of European legal integration – the fuel that makes the European Court work – this paper traces how this institutional development was highly uncertain and contingent on the chameleonic agency of jurists such as Catalano, who blurred the boundaries between his roles as legal architect, judge, commentator, and attorney to become one of Italy's first 'Euro-lawyers.'[6] Triangulating between archival, interview, and secondary evidence, this chapter ties Catalano to the origins of a process of legal mobilisation that hinged less on the supranational genius of judges in Luxembourg or an innate functionalist demand for European rules and more on the tireless labour and entrepreneurship of attorneys, who were determined to erode diffuse resistances to European law within Member States.

This analysis proceeds in five parts. In Section 2, I unpack the origins of Catalano's Eurofederalist convictions and trace his impact as an innovative legal architect. While Catalano's influence as an agent of change culminated during the drafting of the Treaty of Rome, his ideas were forged years prior when he contributed to purging the Italian state of fascism and served as legal adviser in the Tangier International Zone and the European Coal and Steel Community (ECSC). In Section 3, I reconstruct Catalano's work as a judge once he was nominated to serve on the ECJ, uncovering novel evidence that what may appear like the climax of his career arguably proved to be its nadir instead. It was during his frustrating time in Luxembourg that Catalano shed his functionalist faith that the ECJ would 'work' on its own and began to identify the obstacles that prevented the Court from serving as a motor of European integration. Section 4 recounts Catalano's tireless labour as legal scholar and commentator after he

[6] On the concept of 'Euro-lawyers,' see: A Vauchez, *Brokering Europe: Euro-lawyers and the Making of a Transnational Polity* (New York, Cambridge University Press, 2015); T Pavone, *The Ghostwriters: Lawyers and the Politics Behind the Judicial Construction of Europe* (New York, Cambridge University Press, 2022).

was pushed out of the ECJ by the Italian government and returned to Rome. It highlights Catalano's efforts to draft legal commentaries that promoted the ECJ's rulings and excoriated recalcitrant national governments and courts, while also noting that his public advocacy proved limited in its impact. Section 5 traces Catalano's resurgent influence in the final mutation of his professional life as an entrepreneurial Euro-lawyer. It situates Catalano within a rag-tag group of trailblazing practitioners who mobilised European law before national courts to Europeanise domestic legal orders and to propel preliminary references to the ECJ to advance European integration – the 'ghostwriters'[7] that ultimately made the ECJ work. Finally, Section 6 concludes with an examination of what Nicola Catalano's example can teach us about the uncertain origins of European legal integration and the agents undergirding political development through law. I suggest that processes of institutional change depend on agents like Catalano, who are capable of integrating insider expertise with outside mobilisation and who balance strong ideational commitments with tactical pragmatism.

2. IF YOU BUILD IT ...: CATALANO AS LEGAL ARCHITECT

In a 1984 ceremony, which honoured Catalano following his death, ECJ President Alexander Mackenzie Stuart highlighted Catalano's 'co-authorship of the Treaties of Rome' and his personal invention of perhaps the most 'spectacular' institutional provision underlying the European judicial order:

> It's to M. Catalano that we owe the idea behind one of the most spectacular innovations of the Treaties of Rome ... the preliminary reference procedure ... Was he able, at the time, to predict the exceptional judicial developments that could be realised upon this cornerstone? ... without this procedure, the most important judgments of our Court wouldn't have seen the light of day.[8]

Indeed, both contemporary accounts and novel historical evidence decisively confirm that Article 177 of the Rome Treaty was the brainchild of Catalano, who proposed the procedure as part of the *groupe de rédaction* charged with drafting the Treaty text in late 1956 and early 1957. Yet even within the *groupe*, Article 177 was debated and drafted 'without awareness of this innovation's importance.'[9] How did Catalano develop this idea? How did he find himself at the right place at the right time to make this decisive contribution?

Catalano modelled the preliminary reference procedure on the constitutional blueprint of the Italian legal order. He was 'inspired by the new Italian system of judicial review' created by Law No. 87 in March of 1953, which enabled

[7] Here, I draw heavily on my new book; see ibid.

[8] ECJ President Alexander Mackenzie Stuart at the audience solennelle in honour of Nicola Catalano (18 October 1984). HAEU CJUE-2557, 27.

[9] P Pescatore, 'Les Travaux du 'Groupe de redaction' dans la Negociation des Traités de Rome' (1981) 34 *Studia Diplomatica* 159, 173.

any judge who doubted the constitutionality of legislation to stay the proceedings and refer the case to the Italian Constitutional Court.[10] In transplanting the outlines of this referral system to the European level, Catalano mobilised two distinctive ideas: that European law serves as a 'higher' law that is constitutional or federal in nature; and that courts should exercise judicial review powers and disapply national laws conflicting with European law – particularly state rules obstructing trade, free movement, and the liberalisation of state monopolies. These ideas, it turns out, grew out of three professional experiences that defined Catalano as a jurist years before the Treaty of Rome's drafting: his role in the dismantling of the fascist state in Italy; his role as legal adviser in the Tangier International Zone, in which he set out to protect foreign investors from state encroachment; and his involvement in the European Coal and Steel Community (ECSC).

Catalano witnessed first-hand how state power can be abused when he joined the state legal service created by the Italian fascist regime – the *Avvocatura dello Stato* – as a 29-year-old in 1939, at the height of Mussolini's rule and the outbreak of the Second World War. We know little about Catalano's activities during this period but there is evidence that – despite his deep involvement within the core of the fascist state – he did not develop a reputation as a fascist sympathiser (Catalano would later cite the 'horrors' committed by the Axis powers during World War II as the prime motive behind his philosophy of Eurofederalism).[11] We know this because with the fall of fascism, Catalano was selected to play a central role in the so-called 'purges' of the Italian state and Italian professions. One month after the liberation of Rome and under pressure from the United States and the Allies to 'liquidate' fascism,[12] in July 1944, the caretaker Bonomi government created a commission headed by anti-fascist diplomat Carlo Sforza to sanction and remove fascists from both the state bureaucracy and the liberal professions, with a special focus on journalists. Catalano was recruited by Sforza to supervise the 'de-fascistisation' of *Il Giornale d'Italia*, which had served as a notorious megaphone of fascist propaganda during the war. He undertook this task for two years while on leave from the state legal service. Had he harboured sympathies for the fascist state, it is unlikely that he would have been selected for this role instead of being purged himself.[13] Indeed, the Italian government soon tapped him again to serve as its agent in the conciliation commissions created by the 1947 peace

[10] A Boerger and M Rasmussen, *The Dual Nature of the European Community: The Making of the Institutional and Legal Dimensions of European Integration, 1950 to 1967*, 17. Draft book manuscript on file with author.

[11] N Catalano, *La Comunità Economica Europea e l'Euratom* (Milano, Giuffré, 1959) 1.

[12] M Giannetto, 'Defascistizzazione: legislazione e prassi della liquidazione del Sistema fascista e dei suoi responsabili (1943-1945)' 2 *Ventunesimo Secolo* 53.

[13] For more on this period in Catalano's life, see: V Fritz, *Juges et avocats généraux de la Cour de Justice de l'Union européenne (1952–1972): Une approche biographique de l'histoire d'une révolution juridique* (Frankfurt, Vittorio Klostermann, 2018) 197.

treaty with the Allies. These commissions were tasked with managing the return of goods and property stolen from citizens and states by the Axis powers, with the goal of fully integrating Italy within the new United Nations system.[14] From 1948 to 1950, these peace commissions provided Catalano with his first experience in applying a new body of international law that was capable of regulating the actions of national states.

Second, in the 1950s, Catalano gained first-hand experience within two supranational institutions in which he cultivated his federalist and liberalising conception of international law and courts. In 1951, he left the Italian state's legal service to serve as chief legal adviser to the Tangier International Zone.[15] The Zone was a complex institutional system created by the Sultan of Morocco (a French protectorate), several European colonial states, and the United States to establish a neutral free-trade zone and international tax haven.[16] Paul Reuter, one of the primary legal architects of the ECSC, cited the Tangier Zone as the first 'form of federal integration' at the international level, and for good reason.[17] The Zone established an international court – the Mixed Tribunal, which was comprised of five foreign judges from Italy, France, Spain, Belgium, and Britain – that was charged with safeguarding the commercial and property rights of foreign nationals against encroachment by the Sultanate.[18] The Mixed Tribunal was both active and innovative: not only did it hand down thousands of yearly rulings, but it also proclaimed that it could exercise supranational judicial review. The Tribunal interpreted the international laws that created the Tangier Zone as 'constitutional treaties' and regularly disapplied legislation of the Sultanate when 'it deemed it contrary to the economic freedoms guaranteed' by the treaties.[19] Michel Eperlding has recently uncovered how, in 1951, Catalano was asked to draft a memo expressing his opinion on the Tribunal's constitutional authority, in his role as legal adviser to the Zone. Although Catalano expressed scepticism that the Tribunal was a full-fledged 'constitutional judge,' he endorsed and approved the Tribunal's authority to disapply legislation when it infringed upon the treaties and foreign investor protections that constituted the Tangier Zone.[20]

In 1953, Catalano left Tangier for Brussels to join the Legal Service of the first supranational institution in continental Europe: the High Authority of

[14] A Arena and A Rosanò, 'Nicola Catalano (1910–1984): Eurolawyer Extraordinaire' (HEC Working Paper 2022/05, Alcide de Gasperi Centre for Research at the EUI) 1, 8, 9; Fritz (n 13) 198.

[15] On Catalano's nomination by the Italian government to serve as legal adviser to the Tangier International Zone, see: Fritz (n 13) 198.

[16] JP Bebats, 'Tanger, son statut, sa zone (1923–1956)' (1996) 31/32 *Horizons Maghrébins* 17.

[17] M Eperlding, 'Juristes internationalistes, juristes mixtes, Euro-Lawyers: l'apport de l'expérience semi-coloniale à l'émergence d'un droit supranational' (2022) 22 *Clio@Themis. Revue électronique d'histoire du droit* 1, 8.

[18] KHN, 'Twenty-Five Years of Mixed Court of Tangier' (1952) 1 *American Journal of Comparative Law* 115.

[19] Eperlding (n 17) 9.

[20] ibid 10.

the ECSC. It was in this third international stint that Catalano was able to truly put his federalist convictions into action. As Anne Boerger and Morten Rasmussen have meticulously traced in their archival research, 'we know that the Legal Service of the High Authority already championed a constitutional approach to the interpretation of European Law' during Catalano's tenure in the mid-1950s.[21] In defending the High Authority before the Court of Justice, Catalano and fellow members of the Legal Service promoted the teleological and federalist approach to European law (albeit with only partial success at the time) that would eventually become the defining feature of the ECJ's 'law of integration'.[22] On several occasions, Catalano even chose to defend the High Authority against the Italian government in litigation before the Court of Justice.[23] Reflecting on these years, future ECJ judge Riccardo Monaco recalled his 'friendly legal jousting [with Catalano] before the Court of Justice … me as jurisconsult for the Italian government and he as counsel of the European Communities.'[24] Catalano's Eurofederalist zeal was becoming increasingly evident.

These were the experiences that Catalano brought with him when in November 1956 he was summoned by Paul-Henri Spaak to serve in the *groupe de redaction* to draft the Treaty of Rome. Instantly, the group 'split between a federalist faction and a more conservative group,' and unsurprisingly, Catalano became leader of the federalist contingent alongside Michel Gaudet of France and Pierre Pescatore of Luxembourg.[25] Catalano and Gaudet – who were friends from their days serving together in the High Authority's Legal Service[26] – were in charge of designing the institutional features of the new European Community. While the jurists were constrained by clear directions from government heads of delegation concerning the design of the Treaty's political institutions – the Commission and the Council – Member States were far less interested in the 'subtle constitutional elements' and design of the European Court of Justice. This provided Catalano and his allies with sufficient room of manoeuvre to 'smuggle in solutions' and to ghost-write the 'breakthrough' of Article 177: the preliminary reference procedure and its system of judicial review.[27]

[21] A Boerger and M Rasmussen, 'Transforming European Law: The Establishment of the Constitutional Discourse from 1950 to 1993' (2014) 10 *European Constitutional Law Review* 199, 203.

[22] ibid 204; JB Cruz, *What's Left of the Law of Integration?* (New York, Oxford University Press, 2018).

[23] Fritz (n 13) 199.

[24] Vauchez (n 6) 110.

[25] Boerger and Rasmussen (n 21) 54.

[26] Gaudet had served as head of the High Authority's Legal Service during Catalano's tenure. See: J Bailleux, 'Michel Gaudet a law entrepreneur: the role of the legal service of the European executives in the invention of EC Law and of the Common Market' (2013) 50 *Common Market Law Review* 359.

[27] Boerger and Rasmussen (21) 54.

Catalano did not waste time mobilising to set the agenda behind the scenes. He proposed his 'daring' innovation just two days after the first meeting of the *groupe juridique*, stunning his colleagues with a full-fledged design for the preliminary reference procedure. According to novel archival evidence unearthed by Boerger and Rasmussen, Catalano's proposal was controversial because it 'completely sidestepped the national governments that were at the centre of the infringement procedure' and signified 'an important step towards turning the ECJ into a European constitutional court.'[28] Even Catalano's Eurofederalist ally – Pierre Pescatore – doubted that this controversial innovation was as 'crucial' as Catalano made it out to be.[29] Catalano retorted by framing the procedure as an institutional failsafe, given the likelihood that intergovernmental pressures on the fledgling European executive – the Commission – would sometimes block it from availing itself of the infringement procedure to enforce the law.[30] To then obtain the support of the more conservative faction of the group, Catalano agreed to drop some of the more ambitious yet controversial elements of his proposal. For instance, instead of the ECJ possessing the exclusive authority to interpret European law, that authority would be shared with national courts, and a sentence in Catalano's proposal that stated that national courts had the 'obligation' to apply ECJ judgments was dropped.[31]

Upon reaching consensus, the group of jurists submitted the proposed text for Article 177 to the heads of delegation of member governments. With their sights set squarely on the design of the EC's political institutions, government representatives approved the proposal in January 1957 'without much discussion and endorsed what would become one of the most famous articles in the EEC treaty.'[32] As its prime architect, this result was a major triumph for Catalano who, as we will see, initially held onto a functionalist faith that citizens and national courts would soon flock to the ECJ via Article 177. And when it rains good news, it pours: a few months later, in early 1958, Catalano received notice from the Italian government that he would be nominated as the new Italian judge on the ECJ. Novel archival evidence even indicates that Catalano was being seriously considered to serve as President of the Court.[33] These months arguably represented the apex of Catalano's Eurofederalist triumph. Little did Catalano know that a series of setbacks and frustrations were waiting for him in the years to come, which would also threaten the European judicial order that he helped to build.

[28] ibid 17.

[29] P Pescatore, 'Les aspects fonctionnels de la Communauté Économique Européenne, notamment les sources du droit' in, *Les aspects juridiques de la Communauté Économique Européenne* (Liège, Faculté de droit de Liège, 1958) 60.

[30] On how this intuition proved extraordinarily prescient, see: R.D. Kelemen and T Pavone, 'Where Have the Guardians Gone? Law Enforcement and the Politics of Supernational Forbearance in the European Union' (2023) 75 *World Politics* 779.

[31] Boerger and Rasmussen (n 21) 19.

[32] ibid 21.

[33] Fritz (n 13) 200.

3. … THEY WON'T COME: CATALANO AS ECJ JUDGE

As one of the ECJ's institutional architects, being nominated by the Italian government to serve on the Luxembourg court in 1958 was a crowning achievement for Catalano. Yet we must be wary of reading history backwards. For the ECJ that Catalano joined was not yet the active, renowned, and prestigious Court that we know today. The ECJ was 'tucked away' in Luxembourg with 'benign neglect,' in a humble mansion on a temporary lease.[34] Its early members were 'very disappointed' that the Court remained largely unknown in national jurisdictions, a state of affairs that was 'not particularly satisfactory'.[35] Furthermore, Catalano's pugnacious personality gained him few allies in the Court and enabled his ideological rival – the jurist selected as the Court's President, André Donner – to forge a conservative majority to sideline Catalano's 'militant federali[sm].'[36]

The honeymoon period in Luxembourg thus proved short for Catalano, who had numerous reasons to grow disillusioned as an ECJ judge. First, as the creator of the preliminary reference procedure, he had to wait until his final year at the ECJ (1961) before a national court – the Court of Appeal in the Hague – finally referred a case to Luxembourg.[37] While that referral was reason enough to open a bottle of champagne,[38] this was a rather sorry state of affairs, compounded by the fact that Catalano would never witness a solicitation by an Italian judge during his tenure in Luxembourg. 'If you build it, they will come,' the functionalist ethos goes: institutions should create their own social demand.[39] To Catalano it must have been painfully evident that even though the ECJ was built, few lawsuits were coming.

Catalano's disenchantment with a functionalist faith in Article 177 generating its own demand for European justice caused him to have a change of heart. When, in November 1956, Catalano had proposed the preliminary reference procedure as part of the Treaty of Rome's *groupe de rédaction*, he drew inspiration from the Italian system of constitutional referrals and thus deemed it 'preferable' that 'only courts of last instance be prescribed to stay the proceedings and solicit a preliminary ruling from the Court of Justice'. The reason is that he worried that the ECJ would be plagued by the same 'excessive multiplication'

[34] Stein, 'Lawyers, Judges, and the Making', 1.

[35] M Lagrange, 'The Court of Justice as a Factor in European Integration' (1967) 15 *American Journal of International Law* 709, 717; M Rasmussen, 'The Origins of a Legal Revolution' (2008) 14 *Journal of European Integration History* 77, 92.

[36] Letter from Riccardo Scarpa (18 September 1984). HAEU CJUE-2257, 1.

[37] *De Geus en Uitenbogerd v Bosch and Others* Case 13/61 ECLI:EU:C:1962:11 [1962] ECR 47.

[38] D Kochenov, 'Book Review: Preliminary References to the European Court of Justice, by Morten Broberg and Niels Fenger' (2010) 37 *Legal Issues of Economic Integration* 375.

[39] The idea that institutions drive social demand for formal rules in an expansive feedback loop is captured by the notion of 'spillover' in neofunctionalist theories of European integration drawing on Ernst Haas' work: E Haas, *The Uniting of Europe: Political, Social, and Economic Forces, 1959–1957* (Stanford, Stanford University Press, 1958).

of referrals as had beset the Italian Constitutional Court, since he assumed that national 'lower courts [would] not hesitate' to solicit the ECJ.[40] But whereas the Italian Constitutional Court had been 'flooded' with 16 referrals in its first year alone, the ECJ had not received any. So, by the close of his second uneventful year at the ECJ, Catalano 'changed his views:' All national judges needed to be encouraged to solicit the ECJ as much as possible.[41]

Catalano's pragmatic change of heart led to public skirmishes with his colleagues. In a 1959 ECJ visit to the Netherlands, he 'openly disagreed' with fellow judges in front of Dutch officials over how frequently national courts should turn to Luxembourg. When Advocate General Lagrange recommended that 'national courts avoi[d] using the [Article 177] system too much,'[42] Catalano interjected, rebutting 'to Dutch Ministry of Justice's officials that national courts should avail themselves generously of the preliminary reference procedure and send as many questions to Luxembourg as possible'.[43] As we will see, this skirmish presaged how Catalano's willingness to defend his views would spark clashes with fellow judges and erode his influence at the Court.

What must have also become evident to Catalano was that national governments were as neglectful of the ECJ as national courts were. Government officials accorded little deference to the Court in its early years and initially appeared uninterested in the Article 177 procedure. When, in 1961, the ECJ served the Member States a special 'notice to attend' arguments in the first preliminary reference case, it was met with radio silence. State representatives 'did not appear at the hearing', the Court bitterly pointed out in its judgment.[44] Even worse, Catalano's home state appeared to treat the Luxembourg Court more as a site for political patronage than as an independent judicial authority, and this was signalled to Catalano in the brusquest of ways.

When, in October 1961, Catalano was reappointed for a full six-year term, he did not know that the Italian government had decided several months prior that it would cut Catalano's term short. This forced ousting of a sitting ECJ judge would make way for Alberto Trabucchi, the younger brother of Italian Minister of Finance Giuseppe Trabucchi who was also close to Foreign Minister Antonio Segni, to be appointed to the Court.[45] Unlike Catalano, the younger Trabucchi had not been directly involved in negotiating the Treaty of Rome and his experience beyond academia and private practice was more limited – though

[40] Catalano (n 11) 35.

[41] Boerger and Rasmussen (n 21) 18.

[42] M Rasmussen, 'Revolutionizing European Law: A History of the Van Gend en Loos Judgement' (2014) 12 *International Journal of Constitutional Law* 136, 146.

[43] Boerger and Rasmussen (n 21) 18.

[44] ibid 49.

[45] Vera Fritz documents this event – and the apparent reasons for replacing Catalano with Trabucchi – by triangulating between primary source evidence from the archives of German Embassy detailing Catalano's departure and Trabucchi's nomination, an interview she conducted with Trabucchi's son, and via an interview and the writings of Paolo Gori, Catalano's *référendaire* (and of subsequent Italian judges at the Court): See: Fritz (n 13) 112–114.

he did compile a compendium of EU law and occasionally served as legal advisor to the ECSC High Authority.[46] President André Donner perceived that Trabucchi was more a specialist in Italian private and comparative law than in European or public law. So in December 1961, Donner penned a worried letter to the Council of Ministers urging Member States to reconsider and not to 'weaken the efficacy of the Court' in the field of public law.[47] The Italian Government ignored Donner's request, pushing Catalano to resign to make way for Trabucchi barely a month into his second term.[48] In his resignation letter, Catalano attributed his 'most regretful' departure to 'personal and family reasons'[49] – which, based on the archival research of historian Vera Fritz, was a facetious euphemism, given Catalano's personal commitment to the Court and to serving the European Community.[50]

Catalano had one last reason to regret his departure from the ECJ. As he was reminded on the day he left the Court, Catalano's difficult personality had worn on his colleagues and had effectively clipped his wings in Luxembourg. Catalano made it a habit to wear his militant Europeanism on his sleeve, pedantically reminding fellow judges of his participation in the Treaty of Rome's *groupe de rédaction* and how he felt 'responsible for the institutional system of the Rome Treaty'.[51] So during his farewell speech to Catalano, President Donner could not resist a not-so-subtle jab at how his colleague's scorched-earth Europeanism had come back to bite him:

> A flame consumes, one could even get burned and those who get too close to the fire can sometimes get scorched. '*Terar dum prosim*,' I am consumed by the cause that I defend, that could be your motto. That is to say that your ardent conviction didn't contribute to making life easy on yourself and those with a different point of view. But even if you weren't always the most accommodating colleague, we gladly accepted it, precisely because we know that your obstinacy and your tenacity stem from your total devotion to the European idea …
>
> We were forced to recognise that you always strove to logically lay out your opinions … which often placed those who didn't share your ideas in a difficult

[46] See, for instance, Trabucchi's role in the 1962 *Meroni* case: M Patrin, 'Meroni Behind the Scenes: Uncovering the Actors and Context of a Landmark Judgment' (2021) 6 *European Papers* 539.

[47] Letter of ECJ President André Donner to the President of the Council of Ministers of the European Community (15 December, 1961). HAEU CJUE-2557, 44.

[48] Some scholars have highlighted the early departure of British Advocate General Eleanor Sharpston after Brexit as an example of Member States meddling with the Court and a threat to judicial independence. Catalano's forced departure from the ECJ suggests that such meddling is hardly new, though crucially, Sharpston's departure was certainly not orchestrated by her home government – the United Kingdom – as in the case of Catalano. See: D Kochenov and G Butler, 'Independence of the Court of Justice of the European Union: unchecked Member States power after the Sharpston affair' (2021) 27 *European Law Journal* 262.

[49] Letter of resignation of ECJ Judge Nicola Catalano to ECJ President André Donner (30 November 1961). HAEU CJUE-2557, 57.

[50] Fritz (n 13) 112–114.

[51] N Catalano, *Zehn Jahre Rechtsprechung des Gerichtshofs der Europaischen Gemeinschaften* (Cologne, Institut für das Recht europaischen Gemeinschaften, 1965) 42.

> situation … I wouldn't dare say we come from the same school of thought, but that's of little importance …[52]

Responding to Donner, Catalano defiantly made his colleagues' criticisms his own:

> [ECJ Judge Charles Leon] Hammes, to tease me, once told me that I had the spirit of a missionary. I accepted this characterisation. I think it matches what I firmly believe, the mission of Europe, the construction of Europe which is in the process of being built, and thus the mission of our Court.[53]

Such rebuttals aside, Donner's jab stung because it betrayed how Catalano had been marginalised as a European judge. Donner really did come from a different school of thought than Catalano: he resisted both a Eurofederalist and a constitutionalist interpretation of the Treaties,[54] and he exercised his authority as President to sideline Catalano's views. For instance, throughout Catalano's tenure, Donner had the sole prerogative of assigning judge rapporteurs to the cases brought to Luxembourg. Rapporteurs play a significant role because they draft a preliminary report on the case for their colleagues, suggest the chamber allocation, and prepare a draft judgment. In so doing, rapporteurs have particular agenda-setting influence over the outcome of a case,[55] and there is compelling empirical evidence that ECJ Presidents select rapporteurs based on whether they deem them trustworthy, competent, and sufficiently influential to broker consensus.[56] By this metric, Donner did not hold Catalano in high esteem. Of the seven judges that served from 1958 to 1961, Catalano was the least likely to be selected as rapporteur (see Figure 2 and Table 1), despite being most familiar with the Treaty of Rome and its drafting history. Specifically, Catalano was rapporteur in only six cases – an average of only 1.5 cases per year. By contrast, Donner's favoured judge – Louis Delvaux of Belgium, a more moderate personality than Catalano – served as rapporteur in fourteen cases during the same time period – an average of 3.5 cases per year.[57] Catalano had so little to do at the ECJ that he regularly petitioned his colleagues to depart from Luxembourg to attend slews of academic and professional conferences, including more than a dozen conferences in 1960 alone.[58]

[52] Speech by ECJ President André Donner on the occasion of Nicola Catalano's departure from the Court (8 March 1962). HAEU CJUE-2557, 32.

[53] Speech by departing ECJ Judge Nicola Catalano (8 March 1962). HAEU CJUE-2557, 29.

[54] JH Reestman and M Claes, 'For History's Sake: On Costa v. ENEL, André Donner and the Eternal Secret of the Court of Justice's Deliberations' (2014) 10 *European Constitutional Law Review* 191.

[55] M Jacobs, M Munder, and B Richter, 'Subject Matter Specialization of European Union Jurisdiction in the Preliminary Rulings Procedure' (2019) 20 *German law Journal* 1214.

[56] S Hermansen, 'Building Legitimacy: Strategic case allocations in the Court of Justice of the European Union' (2020) 27 *Journal of European Public Policy* 1215; S Hermansen and D Naurin, 'Holding Judges to Account: Policy, Performance, and Impartiality' (2021). Working paper on file with author.

[57] One indicator that Delvaux was more conservative than Catalano is the fact that he was one of only three out of seven ECJ judges who did not publicly promote the 1963 *Van Gend en Loos*: A Vauchez, 'Integration-through-Law: Contribution to a Socio-History of EU Political Commonsense' (2008) *EUI Working Papers RSCAS 2008/10* 1, 14.

[58] HAEU CJUE-2557, 75.

Table 1 *ECJ judges ranked by number of cases for which they were selected as judge rapporteur, 1958–1961*

ECJ Judge	# cases as rapporteur 1958–1961	avg # yearly cases as rapporteur 1958–1961	total # cases as rapporteur	years as ECJ judge
Louis Delvaux	14	3.5	42	1952–1967
Charles Léon Hammes	10	2.5	35	1952–1967
Andreas Donner	9	2.25	172	1958–1979
Rino Rossi	7	1.75	12	1958–1964
Jacques Rueff	7	1.75	10	1952–1962
Otto Riese	7	1.75	22	1952–1963
Nicola Catalano	6	1.5	6	1958–1961

Figure 2 *ECJ judges by number of cases for which they served as judge rapporteur, 1958–1961*

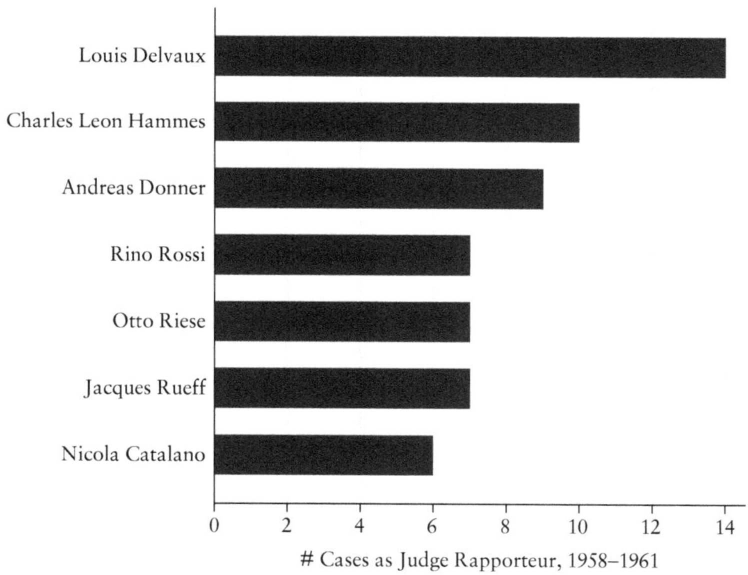

Where these statistics suggest Catalano's marginalisation at the Court, the historical record confirms it. First, the six cases in which Catalano served as rapporteur were of limited importance and scarcely contributed to the development of European law.[59] They included rejections of a couple of nitty-gritty applications for annulment of ECSC High Authority decisions,[60] declarations

[59] Arena and Rosanò (n 14) 1.

[60] See *Société metallurgique de Knutange v High Authority* Joined Cases 15/59 and 29/59 ECLI:EU:C:1959:13 [1960] ECR 2; *Niederrheinische Bergwerks AG v High Authority* Joined Cases

of inadmissibility of another couple of applications,[61] and resolving a dispute concerning ECJ procedural rules governing documentary languages.[62] Catalano's only judgment of note was in an internal ECJ staff case spotlighting his willingness to challenge Donner: in Case 15/60, Catalano annulled a decision by the ECJ President that had revoked a separation allowance due to a typist formerly employed by the Court.[63] By contrast, the very few ECJ decisions that advanced European law delivered during Catalano's tenure were drafted by other judge rapporteurs – most prominently Otto Riese in *Humblet*, in which the Court first claimed it had the authority to adjudicate whether 'a legislative or administrative measure adopted by the authorities of a Member State is contrary to Community law'.[64]

Second, recent legal histories have traced how Donner initially succeeded in steering the Court away from Catalano's Eurofederalism and towards a more moderate stance. Allying himself with the more traditionalist Riese and Jacques Rueff, Donner sought 'not to break with the elements of international law and [to] instead emphasise the contractual nature of the EEC Treaty'.[65] Representative in this regard is the 1959 *Stork* ruling (also drafted by Riese as rapporteur), in which the ECJ refused to recognise that Community law protected citizens' fundamental rights common to the constitutional traditions of the Member States.[66] Ironically, it was Catalano's departure from the Court that helped constitute the more Eurofederalist majority that had eluded him. Catalano's replacement, Alberto Trabucchi, quickly won over his colleagues with his sharp wit and a persuasive collegiality that Catalano lacked. Fellow Italian judge Rino Rossi, for instance, was so 'mutually hostile' with Catalano that he would 'most probably have voted the opposite of Catalano' in any case concerning direct effect and supremacy out of sheer spite.[67] The more affable Trabucchi, on the other hand, drew on his private law expertise to persuade colleagues such as Rossi and Delvaux that European law must be endowed with

2/60 and 3/60 ECLI:EU:C:1961:15 [1961] ECR 134. Catalano as rapporteur dismissed these mundane applications for annulment lodged by an operator of a blast furnace who was challenging an additional contribution for excess scrap metal purchased that was imposed by the ECSC High Authority.

[61] *Vloeberghs v High Authority* Joined Cases 9/60 and 12/60 ECLI:EU:C:1961:18 [1961] ECR 199; *Wilhelmus Severinus Antonie Nannes Gorter v Councils of the European Economic Community and of the European Atomic Energy Community* Case 12/61 ECLI:EU:C:1961:29 [1961] ECR 271.

[62] *Acciaieria Ferriera di Roma v High Authority* Case 1/60 ECLI:EU:C:1960:22 [1960] ECR 165.

[63] *Simon v Court of Justice* Case 15/60 ECLI:EU:C:1961:11 [1961] ECR 116.

[64] *Jean Humblet v Kingdom of Belgium* Case 6/60 ECLI:EU:C:1960:48 [1960] ECR 560, 569.

[65] Rasmussen, 'The Origins of a Legal Revolution' 94; M Rasmussen, 'Establishing a Constitutional Practice of European Law: The History of the Legal Service of the European Executive, 1952–65' (2012) 21 *Contemporary European History* 380.

[66] *Friedrich Stork & Cie v High Authority of the European Coal and Steel Community* Case 1/58 ECLI:EU:C:1959:4 [1959] ECR 19. Of course, the ECJ would later reverse this decision in the *Stauder* (1969), *Internationale Handesgesellschaft* (1970) and *Nold* cases (1974). See: F Schimmelfennig, 'Competition and community: constitutional courts, rhetorical action, and the institutionalization of human rights in the European Union' (2006) 13 *Journal of European Public Policy* 1247, 1252; Arena and Rosanò (n 14) 11.

[67] Rasmussen, 'Establishing a Constitutional Practice', 375, 389.

the capacity to advance individual rights – a view that contrasted with Donner's, yet proved decisive in *Van Gend*. When French judge Rueff was replaced with future ECJ President Robert Lecourt in 1962 – another ambitious judge marked by his capacity to persuade – Trabucchi gained a Eurofederalist ally to spearhead the 'legal revolutions' of 1963–1964 and overcome the dissents of Donner, Riese, and Hammes.[68]

4. A VOICE CRYING IN THE WILDERNESS: CATALANO AS A LEGAL COMMENTATOR

By the time that *Van Gend* was decided, Catalano had returned to Rome as a law professor. He immediately got to work celebrating the 'rightful' *Van Gend* decision in *Il Foro Padano* and promoting the doctrine of direct effect by drafting a report on the subject for the Federation Internationale Pour le Droit Européen (FIDE). Catalano also publicly urged the Court to take the 'next step' of establishing the primacy of European law in *Costa*.[69] Yet these judicial victories were also bittersweet. For with his feet squarely back in Rome, Catalano was growing concerned that the ECJ's legal revolution was meeting far more resistance within the political and judicial confines of the Member States than his ex-colleagues may have realised.

Indeed, by the mid-1960s, the gap between the ECJ's ambitions in *Van Gend* and *Costa* and the 'Eurosclerosis' gripping Member States had become all-to-evident to Catalano, who repeatedly took to law reviews to channel his frustrations and call for Europeanising change. Yet in such a turbulent political context, Catalano's Eurofederalist laments sometimes rang like the proverbial voice crying in the wilderness.

To wit, this period marked the beginning of the era of political Eurosclerosis unleashed by the 'empty chair crisis' of 1965, wherein Europe's most powerful anti-federalist politician – French President, Charles de Gaulle – paralysed the Council of Ministers for seven months by recalling France's permanent representative.[70] The 'Luxembourg compromise' that resulted in January 1966 enabled any Member State government to veto new European legislation by declaring that an important national interest was at stake, thereby threatening to paralyse intergovernmental decision-making for years to come.[71] Catalano

[68] ibid; Reestman and Claes, 'For History's Sake', 193; W Phelan, 'The revolutionary doctrines of European law and the legal philosophy of Robert Lecourt' (2017) 28 *European Journal of International Law* 935, 943; W Phelan, 'Robert Lecourt: The ECJ Judge as Journalist and Political Organiser' (2020) *TRiSS Working Paper Series* 1, 7.

[69] Vauchez (n 6) 125, 128.

[70] NP Ludlow, 'Challenging French leadership in Europe: Germany, Italy, the Netherlands and the outbreak of the empty chair crisis of 1965–1966' (1999) 8 *Contemporary European History* 231.

[71] On the public and press perception of the empty chair crisis and Luxembourg compromise as threatening the entire project of European integration, see: H Wallace and P Winand, 'the Empty Chair Crisis and Luxembourg Compromise Revisited' in J-M Palayret, H Wallace, and P Winand

lamented these political developments in his commentaries, noting how they made the promise of European federalism 'unworkable':

> The construction of Europe is passing through a moment of crisis, characterised especially by the strenuous resistance of state powers to Community action. Despite the repeated and overt affirmations of Europeanism, States still do not fully submit to the necessary supremacy of Community action, without which the very structure of European economic integration, which is a federal-type structure, would be unworkable.[72]

But the 1960s also opened an era of judicial Eurosclerosis, as national high courts signalled their resistance to the full reach of the ECJ's direct effect and supremacy doctrines.[73] None was clearer on the matter than the Italian Constitutional Court, which became a target of fierce criticism by Catalano. In 1964, the Constitutional Court refused to acknowledge the direct effect and supremacy of European law,[74] affirming instead a dualist theory whereby Italian legislation could trump preceding Community laws (the principle that *lex posterior derogat legi priori*). In its judgment, the Constitutional Court channelled the 'predominant opinion of Italian international law scholars', including the early writings of Catalano himself.[75] By 1964, however, Catalano had read the tea leaves and renounced his earlier views: national judges' continuing devotion to dualism and the *lex posterior* principle was as threatening to the future of European integration as the obstinacy of Charles de Gaulle.

So, Catalano took to the newly minted *Common Market Law Review* and to *Il Foro Italiano* to convey 'respectful but definitive disapproval'. European integration was 'a real and fundamental turning point in the history of our times … whether one wishes it or not', giving rise to a polity with 'all the aspects of a structure of a federal nature'. Catalano then addressed the Constitutional Court's judges directly:

> It is time to conclude. The conclusions are rather bitter ones. It suffices to [note] the impressive brevity of the [Constitutional Court] judgment under discussion … to

(eds), *Visions, Votes, and Vetoes: The Empty Chair Crisis and the Luxembourg Compromise Forty Years On* (Brussels, Peter Lang, 2006). For more sanguine empirical evidence that, behind the scenes, the Luxembourg compromise may not have had as paralysing effect as was publicly perceived (at least in the 1970s and 1980s), see: J Golub, 'In the Shadow of the Vote? Decision Making in the European Community' (2003) 53 *International Organization* 733.

[72] N Catalano, 'Sentenza 1 marzo 1966 (in causa 48/65)' (1966) 89 *Il Foro Italiano* 81, 94. For a broader discussion of the contemporary relevance of this commentary and Catalano's views: Arena and Rosanò (n 14).

[73] For broader historical overviews of national supreme court resistance to the ECJ, see: L Goldstein, 'State resistance to authority in federal unions: the early United States (1790–1860) and the European Community (1958–94)' (1997) 11 *Studies in American Political Development* 149; K Alter, *Establishing the Supremacy of European Law* (New York, Cambridge University Press, 2001); B Davis, *Resisting the European Court of Justice* (New York, Cambridge University Press, 2013); Pavone (n 6).

[74] Judgment No. 14/1964 *Costa* v. *Ente Nazionale per l'Energia Elettrica* (Italian Constitutional Court).

[75] See, for instance: Catalano (n 11) 145. For an analysis of Catalano's u-turn on dualism and the *lex posterior* principle: A Arena, 'From an Unpaid Electricity Bill to the Primacy of EU Law' (2019) 30 *The European Journal of International Law* 1017, 1025.

realise, once again, how much a limited knowledge of the relevant texts, and a lack of interest in them, risks transforming our widely proclaimed but vague enthusiasm for Europe into a mere verbal demonstration ... Could the Constitutional Court change its attitude? This would be particularly desirable.[76]

In all, Catalano authored 50 publications in the years following his departure from Luxembourg. This corpus of writings was decidedly Janus-faced, at once 'plead[ing] the cause for Europe to which he dedicated his entire life'[77] while also criticising recalcitrant national governments and courts. Yet despite his many forceful calls for change, there is little evidence that Catalano's pen was persuading many Italian judges – or Italian legal scholars – to alter their views. With the exception of the occasional law professor who sympathised with Catalano, 'his voice remained relatively isolated in the Italian debate',[78] which continued to follow in the dualist wake of the Italian Constitutional Court. As Catalano's former ECJ colleague Maurice Lagrange bitterly wrote in 1969, in Italy the promise of European integration had become the 'victim of its professors', who conservatively looked to Rome with far more interest than they looked to Luxembourg.[79]

By the late 1960s, then, the traditional avenues for Catalano to participate in advancing European integration were closing. As a judge he had been unceremoniously pushed out of the ECJ by his own nominating state, and as law professor his legal commentaries were having limited impact. The only unexplored pathway left was to take matters into his own hands as an entrepreneurial lawyer.

5. BREAKTHROUGH: CATALANO AS A PRACTISING EURO-LAWYER

Catalano foretold his turn to Euro-lawyering and litigation in his writings. In 1966, he argued that private litigation and the construction of preliminary references to the ECJ may be the only means to combat Eurosclerosis and compensate for the absence of political will:

[In this] moment of crisis for the Community ... It is only the Court that, through a lucid but courageous interpretation of Community law, can incite Member States and Community institutions to scrupulously respect the obligations sanctioned by the Treaties founding the European Communities. But for this to be possible, it is necessary to ensure any means for action to those willing to act ... litigation proposed by private [citizens] ... constitutes at once a driver and a defense against political pressures that would otherwise be insurmountable.[80]

[76] N Catalano, 'Annotation by M. Nicola Catalano' (1964) *Common Market Law Review* 225, 225, 228, 234.

[77] ECJ President Alexander Mackenzie Stuart at the audience solennelle in honour of Nicola Catalano (18 October 1984). HAEU CJUE-2557, 27.

[78] Boerger and Rasmussen (n 21) 208.

[79] M Lagrange, 'Les obstacles constitutionnels à l'intégration européenne' (1969) 5 *European Constitutional Law Review* 240, 242.

[80] Catalano (n 72) 94.

Strikingly, even Catalano's closest collaborators ignored or understated their colleague's pioneering role as a lawyer. Upon being contacted by the ECJ on the occasion of Catalano's death, Riccardo Scarpa – with whom Catalano co-authored *Principi di Diritto Comunitario* – replied that there was 'little to say' about Catalano's professional activities.[81] In this dismissive view, Scarpa channelled the initial consensus amongst Member States themselves. When the president of the French bar association contacted his government in 1958 to request that lawyers have a seat at the policymaking table in the new European community, the government replied in a terse letter that 'the [European] common market can have nothing to do with lawyers'.[82] Yet Catalano was one of the first lawyers to prove that consensus wrong by seizing an opportunity for strategic litigation. Catalano and a few fellow pioneers exploited the growing chasm between the ECJ's Eurofederalist jurisprudence and the foot-dragging and diffuse resistances to European law that pervaded states and national courts. Through this process of legal mobilisation, Catalano resurrected his capacity to impact European integration, becoming part of a cohort of lawyers who aspired to serve as a 'private army of the [European] Communities'[83] by catalysing preliminary references to the ECJ.

In my book, *The Ghostwriters: Lawyers and the Politics behind the Judicial Construction of Europe*, I identify Catalano as part of a rag-tag group of first-generation Euro-lawyers who mobilised European law before national courts to promote policy changes and propel referrals to the ECJ (see Table 2). Catalano and these legal practitioners shared four traits that distinguish them from the rest of the bar.

First, all of the first Euro-lawyers were old enough to remember surviving the destruction of the Second World War and were deeply suspicious about abuses of state power (born in 1910, Catalano was just old enough to also remember surviving the First World War). These Euro-lawyers were proto-typical agents of political liberalism[84] – ideationally committed to European integration as an opportunity to unite states and to moderate their power via peaceful, legalistic means. Catalano opened his first book – *La Comunità Economica Europea e l'Euratom*, published as the ink was still drying on the text of the Treaty of Rome – by appealing to the 'idealistic impulses' of his readers, reminding them of the 'horrors, devastations, and miseries' of the Second World War and the need to overcome the 'increasingly anachronistic' state 'barriers' to the creation of a 'United States of Europe'.[85]

[81] Letter from Riccardo Scarpa (18 September 1984). HAEU CJUE-2557, 18.

[82] SP Laguette, *Lawyers in the European Community* (Luxembourg, Office for Official Publications of the European Communities, 1987) 269.

[83] Vauchez (n 6) 88.

[84] On lawyers as (contingent) agents of political liberalism, see: T Halliday and L Karpik, *Lawyers and the Rise of Western Political Liberalism* (New York, Oxford University Press, 1997); T Halliday, L Karpik, and M Feeley, *Fighting for Political Freedom* (New York, Bloomsbury, 2007).

[85] Catalano (n 11) 1.

Table 2 *Catalano and other leading first-generation Euro-lawyers in Italy, France, and Germany*

Country	Euro-lawyers	Born before WWII?	Worked at European Institution	Member of European lawyers' association?	# Refs. to ECJ (Total)	# Refs. Pre-1980	# Cases argued before ECJ	Time span
Italy	Fausto Capelli and Giovanni Maria Ubertazzi (Milan)	Yes(both)	No	Yes (AIGE)	78	42	97	1970–2018
	Emilio Cappelli and Paolo De Caterini (Rome)	Yes(both)	Yes (Commission)	Yes (FIDE, AIGE)	25	9	35	1971–2014
	Wilma Viscardini (Padova)	Yes	Yes (Commission)	Yes(UAE)	19	3	35	1975–2015
	Nicola Catalano (Rome)	Yes	Yes(ECSC,ECJ)	Yes (FIDE, AIGE)	16	15	27	1968–1982
France	Lise and Roland Funck-Brentano (Paris)	Yes(both)	No	Yes (AJE, UAE)	15	4	26	1977–1997
	Martel Véroone (Lille)	Yes	No	Yes(CCBE)	9	6	16	1974–1988
	Paul François Ryziger (Paris)	Yes	Yes(ESCS)	Yes (FIDE)	6	1	12	1962–1992
	Robert Collin (Paris)	Yes	No	Yes (AJE)	8	5	11	1964–1993
Germany	Fritz Modest, Jürger Gündisch, Klaus Landry, Barbara Festge, Gabriele Rauschning (Hamburg)	Yes (all)	No	Yes (FIDE, UAE, DNRV)	140	65	163	1967–2014
	Dietrich Ehle (Cologne)	Yes	No	?	90	36	143	1962–2019
	Peter Wendt (Hamburg)	Yes	No	?	22	18	26	1965–1985
	Gert Meier (Cologne)	Yes	No	Yes (FIDE)	17	6	21	1973–2001

Source: Table is reprinted from Pavone, *The Ghostwriters*, 143.

Notes: Beyond FIDE, association names are: AJE, Association des Juristes Européens; AIGE, Associazione Italiana Giuristi Europei; DNRV, Deutsch-Niederländische Rechtsanwaltsvereinigung; UAE, Union des Avocats Européens; CCBE, Conseil des Barreaux Européens.

Second, most of the first-generation Euro-lawyers participated in the founding and leadership of the first European law associations – such as FIDE founded in 1961 – and their national branches – such as the Associazione Italiana Giuristi Europei (AIGE) in Italy, established in 1958. Catalano became President of AIGE and was active in FIDE (whose very founding he brainstormed in correspondence with Michel Gaudet), the governing council of the Italian branch of the European Federalist Movement, and the federalist wing of the Italian Liberal Party.[86] Although these associations mostly remained a 'miscellaneous network'[87] rather than a full-fledged 'jurist advocacy movement' or 'litigation support structure',[88] their pedagogical and advocacy activities were still important because in the 1960s and 1970s most national law schools neglected any coursework in European law.[89]

Third, the first Euro-lawyers derived pleasure from exercising their agency. Like the independent-minded and irascible Catalano, they tended to have difficult, mischievous personalities,[90] and they saw their lawyering as a politics via other means: a tool to contribute to what Catalano described as the 'mission of Europe … and thus the mission of our Court' from the ground-up.[91] Paolo de Caterini, a first-generation Euro-lawyer and law professor who knew Catalano and other pioneers of Euro-lawyering personally, recalls how

> we just happened to be the only actors on the stage! … [We] set the fuse, and it exploded, with big booms well into the 1980s! There was a sense that we could do the unthinkable! … That by [constructing test cases], we could sometimes bring down the whole closet! It wasn't about omnipotence, but about participating.[92]

Finally, although the first Euro-lawyers were a relatively uncoordinated group, they encountered the same obstacles to mobilising European law before national courts and thus converged upon a shared repertoire of strategic litigation. Facing overworked judges who ubiquitously lacked training

[86] Fritz (n 13) 201; Letter from Riccardo Scarpa (18 September 1984). HAEU CJUE-2557, 18.

[87] R Byberg, 'A Miscellaneous Network: The History of FIDE 1961–94' (2017) 57 *American Journal of Legal History* 142; A Bernier, 'Constructing and Legitimating: Transnational Jurist Networks and the Making of a Constitutional Practice of European Law, 1950–70' (2012) 21 *Contemporary European History* 399.

[88] On jurist advocacy movements and litigation support structures, see: K Alter, 'Jurist Advocacy Movements in Europe and the Andes' (2016) 65 *iCourts Working Paper Series* 1; C Epp, *The Rights Revolution: Lawyers, Activists, and Supreme Courts in Comparative Perspective* (Chicago, University of Chicago Press, 1998).

[89] Vauchez (n 6) 77; J Bailleux, 'Penser l'Europe par le droit' (PhD thesis, Université Paris 1 Panthéon-Sorbonne 2012), 422.

[90] Besides Catalano, other difficult personalities included Peter Wendt in Germany and Emilio Cappelli in Italy. See: Pavone (n 6) 152.

[91] Speech by departing ECJ Judge Nicola Catalano (8 March 1962). HAEU CJUE-2557, 29.

[92] Pavone (n 6) 131, 151.

and knowledge of European law,[93] these trailblazing lawyers sought clients willing to lodge test cases illuminating non-compliance with European law; they educated national judges about the duty and benefits of applying European rules; and they literally ghost-wrote the preliminary references to the ECJ that judges lacked the time, knowledge, and inclination to write themselves.

Novel qualitative and archival evidence illuminates how from 1968 until his death in 1984, Catalano mobilised the foregoing repertoire of strategic litigation to catalyse 16 preliminary references to the ECJ – most from Italian lower courts, but also one from a French court (the Tribunal administratif de Paris; see Table 3 and Figure 3). Three courts – the Court of Appeal of Rome, the Court of Appeal of Turin, and the Pretura of Bari – solicited the European Court for the very first time when Catalano showed up. And the geographic scope of Catalano's solicitation of referrals was impressive, spanning seven courts from Paris to Bari. In soliciting these referrals, Catalano supplied the ECJ with opportunities to develop European law and hold states accountable to their treaty obligations. Perhaps even more importantly, Catalano sought to teach the bench how to think and write like a European court of first instance. Catalano acknowledged as much in an article he wrote in *Il Foro Italiano*, wherein he called on national courts to mimic the reasoning and 'style' of ECJ judgments.[94] He also sought to directly impact the fate of the preliminary reference procedure, for which he unsurprisingly felt so personally 'responsible'.[95]

Table 3 *Preliminary references solicited by Catalano as a practising Euro-lawyer*

Case	Case Name	Referring Court
C-13/68	Salgoil v Ministero del commercio con l'estero	Corte d'appello di Roma
C-82/71	S.A.I.L.	Pretura di Bari
C-113/75	Frecassetti v Amministrazione delle finanze dello Stato	Tribunale civile e penale di Genova
C-27/77	Cargill v ONIC	Corte suprema di Cassazione
C-36/77	AIMA v Greco	Tribunal administratif de Paris
C-811/79	Amministrazione delle finanze dello Stato v Ariete	Corte d'appello di Torino

(continued)

[93] ibid 52; T Pavone, 'Revisiting Judicial Empowerment in the European Union: Limits of Empowerment, Logics of Resistance' (2018) 6 *Journal of Law & Courts* 303.

[94] N Catalano, 'Lo stile delle sentenze della Corte di giustizia delle Comunità europee' (1965) 92 *Il Foro Italiano* 141.

[95] Catalano (n 51) 42.

Table 3 *(Continued)*

Case	Case Name	Referring Court
C-826/79	Amministrazione delle finanze dello Stato v MIRECO	Corte suprema di Cassazione
C-66/80	International Chemical Corporation v Amministrazione delle fianze dello Stato	Tribunale civile e penale di Roma
C-206/80	Orlandi	Tribunale civile e penale di Roma
C-207/80	Carapelli	Tribunale civile e penale di Roma
C-209/80	Saquella	Tribunale civile e penale di Roma
C-210/80	De Franceschi	Tribunale civile e penale di Roma
C-212/80	Meridionale Industria Salumi and Others	Corte suprema di Cassazione
C-215/80	Orlandi	Corte suprema di Cassazione
C-216/80	Molino	Corte suprema di Cassazione
C-199/82	San Giorgio	Tribunale di Trento

But how, precisely, did Catalano influence national judges? To unpack Catalano's pugnacious strategy for Euro-lawyering, it is helpful to focus on novel archival evidence concerning an exemplary preliminary reference: The *SAIL* case (C-82/71), or the first ever referral to the ECJ by a southern Italian court (the Pretura of Bari, near Catalano's hometown of Castellaneta in the Apulia region) and a 'veritable masterclass in judicial ghostwriting'.[96] This case spurred the ECJ to strike down two Fascist-era national regulations (promulgated in 1929 and 1938) that had established state 'milk centres', which held a monopoly on local milk production and distribution. For instance, in Bari, milk could only be imported into the city when local demand exceeded supply, and state prefects held exclusive authority to determine the territorial boundaries of the centres' monopoly. Given his commitment to economic liberalisation via Europeanisation, Catalano detested state-owned monopolies and price controls exemplified by the Italian milk centres[97] – so he lodged a lawsuit designed to dismantle them.

[96] Pavone (n 6) 184.

[97] On Catalano's views on the matter, see his editorial: N Catalano, 'Quel Pasticciaccio Agricolo Comunitario' (1984) *Mondo Economico* 28. Many thanks to Daniela Caruso for bringing this editorial to my attention.

Figure 3 *Locations where Catalano solicited national court referrals to the ECJ and distribution of referrals from Italian and French courts, 1961–1984*

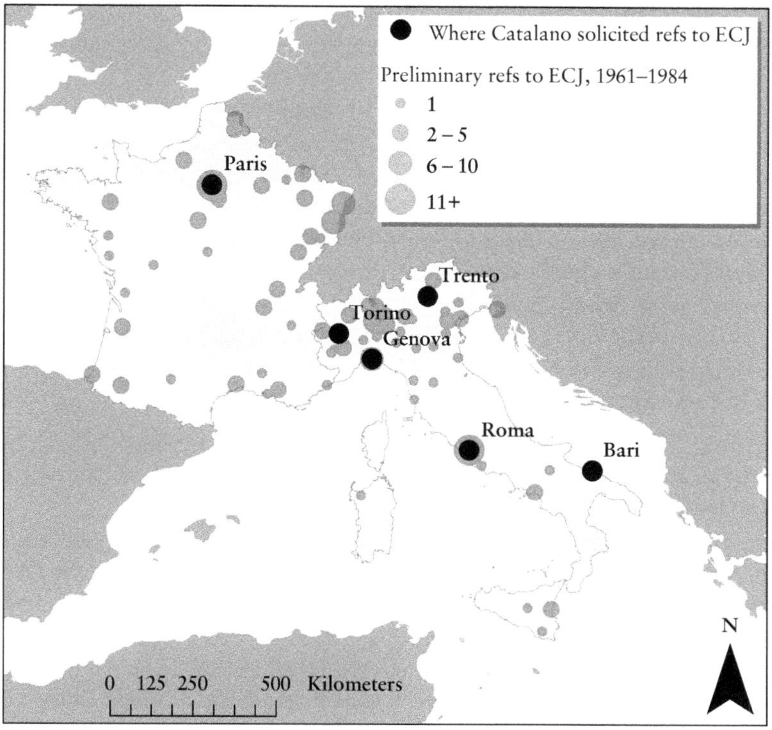

The public facts of this dispute are as follows. A farmer from a hillside town imported some cases of milk 'within the boundary of the 'prohibited' urban area of Bari' wherein a state milk centre operated. Two city officials reported the farmer and criminal proceedings were lodged. Before the Pretura, a surprisingly vigilant judge doubted that the milk centres complied with Article 37 of the Treaty of Rome, which forbids 'State monopolies of a commercial character' from serving as de-facto quantitative restrictions on trade. So, the judge referred the case to Luxembourg.[98]

The foregoing narrative constitutes the 'public transcript' of the *SAIL* case. But there is a 'hidden transcript' to this case:[99] newly obtained documents from the ECJ's Historical Archives reveal that Catalano was the referral's central choreographer, as he returned to Puglia, where he was born in 1910, and persuaded a humble local judge to take the unprecedented step of soliciting a

[98] Consolidated version of the Treaty establishing the European Community [2002] OJ C 325, 24/12/2002 P. 0047–0048.

[99] On 'public' versus 'hidden' transcripts, see: JC Scott, *Domination and the Arts of Resistance: Hidden Transcripts* (New Haven, Yale University Press, 1990).

faraway European Court. The original dossier for the *SAIL* case demonstrates that Catalano drafted a 28-page memo providing his judicial interlocutor with a (strategic) crash course in European law, an excoriation of national law, an elaboration of the imperative of soliciting the European Court quickly, and a full-fledged preliminary reference ready for copy-and-paste.

First, Catalano opened his memo by implicitly drawing on his inside expertise as ex-ECJ judge: he discussed the 'rationale' of 'The authors of the Treaty,' used adjectives like 'certain' and 'definitive' to quell all interpretive doubts regarding European law, and supplemented these affirmations with cogent language and underlining to make the memo easy to skim. Notice also how Catalano clearly learned his lesson from his time as a Luxembourg judge: instead of debating or patronising his judicial counterpart – the kind of pedantic obstinacy that had turned off his ECJ colleagues a decade prior – he collaboratively cajoled his 'illustrious' interlocutor to pivot his attention from Rome to Luxembourg:

> We could ask the Illustrious Pretore to refer to the Constitutional Court ... but we prefer to base our defense upon the much more certain grounds of the monopoly's incompatibility ... with the Treaty of Rome ...
>
> The European Economic Community, is first of all based upon a customs union implying the definitive and total suppression – within a transition period happily expired on 31.12.1969 – of customs duties and quantitative restrictions ... and all "measures having equivalent effect" to a quantitative restriction.
>
> In this vein art. 37 of the treaty "progressively adjusts any State monopolies of a commercial character in such a manner as will ensure the exclusion, at the date of the expiry of the transitional period, of all discrimination between the nationals of Member States in regard to conditions of supply or marketing of goods."
>
> The rationale of the foregoing provision is evident. The authors of the Treaty realised that the abolition of quantitative restrictions would be insufficient to eliminate discriminations brought by state monopolies of a commercial character ... Any monopoly, especially a local one, is certainly incompatible if its sole objective and effect is to prevent market exchange ...[100]

Catalano proceeded to make a forceful, Janus-faced appeal, casting national law in the poorest possible light (an 'absurd' means for legalised corruption, an outdated fascist legacy, and a 'suicidal' policy) while outlining the judge's 'imperative' and 'binding' obligation to recognise the primacy of European law:

> ... this anachronistic monopoly of the milk centres ... this absurd monopoly ... the corporative origins of this system during the full- fledged fascist regime ... represent local centres of power with notable bearing for politics- or, more precisely, for local sub-politics ...

[100] HAEU CJUE-1277, affaire 82/71, Società Agricola Industria Latte SAIL, 23–24. Historical Archives of the European Union (HAEU).

> The vigorous opposition to the milk centres' monopoly by all agricultural associations proves that ... applying criminal sanctions to protect these very monopolies is in truth a suicidal violation, in that it conflicts with the agricultural, economic, and even public health interests of this Country ...
>
> We must now demonstrate the reach and imperative of Art. 37 EEC, even within the national legal order and particularly before national courts.
>
> It must first be recalled that, unlike traditional international law, the EEC Treaty not only contains obligations binding upon Member States and laws that are directly applicable and operable without implementing legislation, but it forbids (art. 5, section 2) Member States from adopting any laws which compromise the realisation of the Treaty's objectives ...
>
> This structure – which is a federal-type structure – is indeed characterised by the transfer of sovereignty and new powers to the Community ... the Court of Justice ... affirmed that contraventions of the foregoing provisions constitute violations of the rights of citizens, rights which national courts are required to protect ... the national judge is required to disapply national law if it contrasts with the Community rule that must prevail.[101]

What is striking here is that even as Catalano worked to educate the judge about European law, he did so strategically, focusing his interlocutor's gaze on some favourable aspects to his case while omitting others. For instance, Catalano did not mention that as he was pushing forth the *SAIL* case (in June and July of 1971), the EEC's Council of Ministers was drafting Regulation No. 1411/71,[102] which authorised the Italian state to maintain its milk centre regime until March 1973 – an inconvenient fact that would have problematised his mobilisation of European law.[103]

Finally, Catalano cajoled the judge to solicit the ECJ by subsidising the labour costs of motivating the preliminary reference and drafting the questions to be submitted to Luxembourg. In so doing, Catalano was careful not to impugn the judge's authority or to appear like a snake oil salesman: while acknowledging the judge's 'abilities', Catalano nonetheless underscored the pragmatic reasons to solicit the ECJ immediately and the risks of interpreting European law directly. One cannot help but suspect that Catalano's sense of urgency – his appeal to solicit the ECJ 'right now' – may have been strategic too. By obtaining a speedy referral, Catalano ensured that the case file would be on its way to Luxembourg

[101] ibid 23, 32.

[102] See: Council Regulation (EEC) 1411/71 of 29 June 1971 laying down additional rules on the common organisation of the market in milk and milk products for products falling within tariff heading No 04.01 [1971] *OJ* L 148/4, 414–415.

[103] I thank Daniela Caruso for highlighting this point. Before the ECJ, the Commission sided with Catalano, arguing that the entry into force of Regulation No. 1411/71 is 'irrelevant' and 'the fresh authorisation cannot, in accordance with the principle which must be fundamental in Community law, adversely affect rights acquired by individuals on the basis of a provision which at that moment produces direct effects in the legal system of the Member States.' See: HAEU CJUE-1277, 236.

before the publication of Regulation No. 1411/71 in the *Official Journal* could attract the judge's attention:[104]

> The Pretore charged [with the dispute] would certainly have the discretion to decide the question. However, in good conscience and while being fully convinced of his abilities – we believe that due to the delicate nature and the novelty of this very question, a judgment that eschews the light of the only specialised court in this domain could be deemed unwise ... Reasons of opportunity, prudence, and procedural economy advise soliciting the Court of Justice right now ...
>
> With this premise ... we will permit ourselves to suggest the questions of interpretation to submit to the Court of Justice ...[105]

The Pretore was clearly persuaded. One month later, the judge copied Catalano's proposed reference largely verbatim and submitted it to Luxembourg (see Figure 4). Once back before the ECJ, Catalano restated his position and achieved his desired outcome. Although the Italian state's legal service asked the ECJ to dismiss the case since 'the answers ... would influence the application of the criminal law of a Member State,' the Court sided with Catalano, declaring 'inapplicable' 'all provisions of national legislation' establishing the milk centres' monopoly and imposing criminal penalties (and holding that Regulation No. 1411/71 was also 'inapplicable to [the] events' in the case because they occurred before the regulation entered into force). For good measure, the Court took the liberty to remind the Italian government that the 'effectiveness of Community law cannot vary according to the various branches of national law which it may affect'.[106]

Catalano's litigation strategy in *SAIL* fits a broader pattern. Like other first-generation Euro-lawyers listed in Table 2, Catalano wielded preliminary references primarily to seek the interpretation of European law and to reform national law rather than to challenge the validity of European rules.[107] Indeed, the last preliminary reference that Catalano solicited before his death – *San Giorgio* (C-199/82)– testifies to how he never lost his 'creative passion' for advancing European law.[108] In brokering that referral from the Tribunal of Trento, Catalano empowered the ECJ to 'modify [its caselaw] in a substantive manner' by prohibiting Member States from placing conditions upon the repayment of domestic charges when those charges violate individuals' free movement rights.[109] Legal commentators hailed how the Court took a 'step forward ... towards a more effective and useful protection of the individual's rights' and 'strengthen[ed] ... the remedies against a violation of the rule of law'.[110]

[104] ibid 160.

[105] ibid 41.

[106] *SAIL* Case 82/71 ECLI:EU:C:1972:20 [1972] ECR 120, 135, 139.

[107] 80% of preliminary references solicited by first-generation Euro-lawyers sought the interpretation and application of European law, whereas only 20% challenged its validity. See: Pavone (n 6) 154.

[108] ECJ President Alexander Mackenzie Stuart at the audience solennelle in honour of Nicola Catalano (18 October 1984). HAEU CJUE-2557, 27.

[109] F Hubeau, 'Annotation of Case C-199/82, *Amministrazione delle Finanze dello Stato v. San Giorgio S.p.A.* [1983], ECR 3595' (1984) 22 *Common Market Law Review* 96, 99.

[110] ibid 100, 108.

Figure 4 *Catalano's draft preliminary reference and the Pretore of Bari's nearly identical referral in the SAIL case*

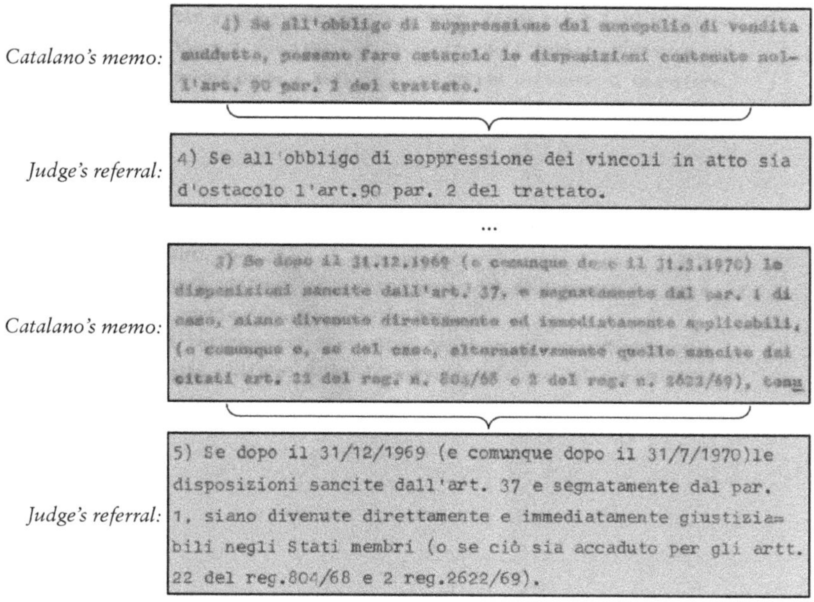
Catalano's memo:

4) Se all'obbligo di soppressione del monopolio di vendita suddetto, possano fare ostacolo le disposizioni contenute nell'art. 90 par. 2 del trattato.

Judge's referral:

4) Se all'obbligo di soppressione dei vincoli in atto sia d'ostacolo l'art.90 par. 2 del trattato.

...

Catalano's memo:

3) Se dopo il 31.12.1969 (o comunque dopo il 31.3.1970) le disposizioni sancite dall'art. 37, e segnatamente dal par. 1 di esso, siano divenute direttamente ed immediatamente applicabili, (o comunque e, se del caso, alternativamente quelle sancite dai citati art. 22 del reg. n. 804/68 e 2 del reg. n. 2622/69), [illegible]

Judge's referral:

5) Se dopo il 31/12/1969 (e comunque dopo il 31/7/1970)le disposizioni sancite dall'art. 37 e segnatamente dal par. 1, siano divenute direttamente e immediatamente giustiziabili negli Stati membri (o se ciò sia accaduto per gli artt. 22 del reg.804/68 e 2 reg.2622/69).

Source: CJUE-1277, 12, 44.
Notes: Adapted from Pavone, *The Ghostwriters*, 188.

The *SAIL*, *San Giorgio*, and 14 other preliminary references solicited by Catalano testify to his resilience and creative capacity to reinvent himself as a Euro-lawyer. Ironically, Catalano's renewed impact as a litigator also served to prove one of his former rivals right. In a speech delivered on Catalano's last day at the ECJ, President André Donner predicted that one way or another, his Eurofederalist counterpart would find his way back to Luxembourg:

> We are certain that in the future we will encounter you once again involved in European affairs, either as theorist in your publications, or as a practitioner in your other activities ... one cannot easily neglect the opinion of Mister Catalano.[111]

6. CONCLUSION: LEOPARDS, CHAMELEONS, AND EUROPEAN LEGAL INTEGRATION

In a recent editorial, Joseph Weiler – who did more to advance the study of the judicial construction of Europe than any scholar of his generation – emphasised

[111] Speech by ECJ President André Donner on the occasion of Nicola Catalano's departure from the Court (8 March 1962). HAEU CJUE-2557, 32.

the dangers of a 'Court-centric' view of the development of the EU legal order in light of recent scholarship:

> My generation of European Law lawyers are hopelessly Court-centric. That's what we know (or think we know). That is what interests us. European Law is about the Court of Justice of the European Union … But there is another blind spot (more a black hole than a spot) in the Court-centric view of European law: the role of lawyers – in bringing cases, in arguing cases, in strategising litigation, in virtually putting words in the mouth of the judges.[112]

Nicola Catalano's tortuous yet steadfast quest to promote the development of European law exemplifies how Weiler's conclusion is not only fertile theoretically, but also imperative practically. Taking the role of Euro-lawyers seriously and broadening our lens beyond the ECJ's *Palais de justice* not only helps us better understand the patchworked development of the EU and its legal order; it also helps us appreciate what actions were necessary to make the European Court work in the first place. Like any judicial institution ensconced in an uncertain process of political development, the fledgling ECJ risked being starved of cases, being ignored by citizens and by civil society, and having its rulings infringed by the inertia or intransigence of national governments. Convinced Eurofederalists like Catalano could not sit idly by in Luxembourg and will a supranational legal order into being. Constrained as institutional insiders, they could not passively presume to 'have history on their side'.[113] Instead, they had to *make* history by rolling up their sleeves and engaging in various forms of legal mobilisation beyond and outside the ECJ.

Entrepreneurs like Catalano first had to invent an institutional infrastructure – the preliminary reference procedure – that could interlink the ECJ with domestic 'compliance constituencies'[114] – such as citizens, interest groups, legal professionals, and national courts. Once they embedded this infrastructure within the Treaty of Rome, Euro-lawyers soon realised that they could not rely on a functionalist faith that 'if you build it, they will come'. Instead, they had to blur the boundaries between their institutional role as judges and their social role as members of civil society to catalyse demand for European justice. They crafted favourable legal commentaries, founded and participated in Euro-lawyers' associations, and constructed the necessary test cases that could gradually embed national courts into a federated network of European courts.[115] They had to

[112] J Weiler, '10 Good Reads 2022' (*EJIL:Talk*, 2 December 2022) www.ejiltalk.org/10-good-reads-2022/.

[113] As Albert Hirschman has written, 'people enjoy and feel empowered by the confidence, however vague, that they '*have history on their side*':' A Hirschman, *The Rhetoric of Reaction* (Cambridge, Harvard University Press, 1991) 158.

[114] K Alter, *The New Terrain of International Law: Courts, Politics, Rights* (Princeton, Princeton University Press, 2014) 19.

[115] On the role of lawyers as 'boundary-blurrers' and architects of transnational legal change, see: S Liu, 'Globalization as Boundary-Blurring: International and Local Law Firms in China's Corporate Law Market' (2008) 42 *Law & Society Review* 771.

forge the lifeblood of the European legal order and imprint its skeletal infrastructure with a human face.

None of these efforts were preordained to succeed in the long-run, and even in the short-run Euro-lawyers hit their fair share of setbacks. What distinguished the more impactful legal entrepreneurs like Nicola Catalano was the missionary zeal that propelled them to learn from their frustrations and to reinvent themselves for the cause of European legal integration. Ideationally, these pioneers behaved as *leopards*, never changing their spots when it came to their drive to unite European states through law. This was the *fil rouge* that kept individuals like Catalano going in the face of failure. Yet, in practice these jurists behaved as *chameleons*, pragmatically modifying their actions, developing new strategies, and switching roles in pursuit of their commitments. This was the mutability that enabled Nicola Catalano to overcome his own shortcomings and to leave a definitive mark on the development of a European community based on the rule of law.

4

"Notre Nestor, Monsieur le Juge Rossi" (1889–1974): An Internationalist's Contribution to the Making of a Supranational Legal Order

AMEDEO ARENA

On 8 October 1964, a packed courtroom of the European Court of Justice ('ECJ') bid farewell to Judge Rino Rossi. In his speech, the President of the ECJ, Charles Léon Hammes, addressed his outgoing colleague as 'notre Nestor',[1] the wise veteran from Greek mythology, conveying the esteem and respect that Rossi had come to command during his six-year tenure in Luxembourg.[2]

Exiting the stage at the venerable age of 75, Rossi had been the oldest member of the ECJ from 1958 to 1964. His 'internationalist' vision of the European Communities set him apart from some of his 'supranationalist' colleagues:[3] he perceived the three Communities no differently than other Post-war international organisations. And yet, as it will become apparent, the ECJ's oldest member and his internationalist views played a key role in the emergence of Community law as a 'new legal order' distinct from international law.

1. INTRODUCTION: FROM THE ALPINE VALLEYS TO LUXEMBOURG

Rossi's journey began in the alpine town of Chiavenna, in Northern Italy, on 14 August 1889. The eldest brother in a large, struggling family, Rossi's life was

[1] Speech by Hammes at the ECJ Solemn Hearing of 8 October 1964, Historical Archives of the European Union (HAEU), CJUE-2558, 31.

[2] See, *eg*, Homer, Iliad, 1.245; Homer, Odyssey, 1.280; Plato, Laws, 4.711e-4.7112a ('whenever the greatest power combines in a person with wisdom and moderation, then the seed of the best polity is planted').

[3] For the distinction between 'internationalists' and 'supranationalists', see J. Bailleux, 'Comment l'Europe vint au droit' (2010) 60 *Revue française de science politique* 295–318.

marked by early responsibility. After the untimely death of his parents, town clerk Luigi Rossi and his wife Edvige Beretta,[4] Rossi took on the mantle of caregiver to his siblings.[5] These early experiences honed his determination, leading him to earn a law degree from the University of Bologna in 1914[6] and to start practising as a lawyer.

Rossi was a blend of charisma and old-world elegance. He was a man who appreciated the finer things in life – the sophistication of formal attire, even in the comfort of his own home, the soothing harmonies of classical music, and the thrill of hunting. Yet, he was a man of restraint, eschewing the temptation of alcohol,[7] even in regional delights like *risotto al barolo*.[8]

In 1922, he married Flaminia Luigia Arnaud, a 19-year-old woman of French descent from Caraglio, a small Piedmontese town. The couple's only child, Carlo Maria Rossi Arnaud, was brought up in a disciplined and traditional environment, a reflection of Rossi's own upbringing. Like his father, Carlo made his mark in the world, serving as Italy's Ambassador in Dakar and Sofia.[9]

Rossi was not a man to shy away from challenges. An unyielding mountaineer, he was undaunted by the loftiest peaks, as his record with the Valtellina Chapter of the Club Alpino Italiano attests.[10] He was a pioneer of *alpinismo senza guide* – venturing into the wild, untamed cliffs of the Alps without the aid of a local guide.[11]

As the drums of World War I began to beat, Rossi enlisted as an *alpino*, a member of Italy's mountain infantry. His courage became legendary on 16 January 1916: at over 3000 meters, he ventured behind enemy lines with a handful of other skiers to obliterate two blockhouses. His heroism was immortalised with a back-cover illustration in *La domenica del corriere*[12] and a commendation in the War Bulletin by Luigi Cadorna, then Chief of Staff of the Italian Army.[13]

At the end of World War I, Rossi represented Italy on the Armistice Committee. He then embarked on a remarkable career in the Italian judiciary,

[4] The Author is grateful to Tiziana Marino of the Archives of Sondrio for these details.

[5] Detail provided by Elena Rossi Arnaud, Rossi's granddaughter.

[6] University of Bologna, Student file no. 6465.

[7] Speech by Hammes at the Solemn Hearing of 8 October 1964, HAE, CJUE-2558, 32. Detail confirmed by Elena Rossi Arnaud.

[8] Detail provided by Elena Rossi Arnaud.

[9] *See* Stefano Baldi, Ambasciatori d'Italia a Sofia (2020) 69, available at: http://baldi.diplomacy.edu/italy/Baldi_Ambasciatori_d_Italia_a_Sofia_2020.pdf.

[10] Rossi was Board member of the Valtellina Chapter of that Club in 1908, 1913, 1914, 1916, and 1917. The Author is grateful to two members of that Chapter, Enrica Andreola and Giorgio Boccalari, for the details on Rossi's mountaineering accomplishments.

[11] According to the monthly review of the *Club alpino italiano*, Rossi made several ascents without a guide. He was also a member of the *Gruppo lombardo alpinisti senza guide* (Lombard Group of Alpinists Without Guides).

[12] A Beltrami, 'La Guerra a tremila metri: nuclei di nostri skiatori distruggono due blockhouse per mezzo di mine' (19169 18(5) *La domenica del corriere*.

[13] Italian War Bulletin of 20 January 1916.

with notable international assignments.[14] He served as Justice of Peace, first in the tranquillity of Caraglio (1920), then in the bustling heart of Turin (1924). His career thus took him to Rhodes, then under Italian sovereignty along with the other Aegean islands, where he served as President of the Tribunal (1928).[15] After a short tenure at the Court of Rome, he was selected as Judge-Consul in Cairo (1936).

In 1941 he was posted in Rhodes for a second time to serve as President of the Court of Appeal and Director of Justice Affairs of the Italian government in Rhodes. Following the end of World War II, in 1945 Rossi took up the role of judge at the L'Aquila Court of Appeal, in Central Italy. He had to undergo a series of epuration proceedings for his involvement in the Nazi-Fascist administration of the island after 8 September 1943,[16] but the Disciplinary Court of the Ministry of Justice definitively acquitted him in 1947.[17]

Rossi's career in the Italian judiciary then took him to the Eternal City: in 1948 he was appointed as a Judge at the Rome Court of Appeals, and in 1951 he started working as Deputy Attorney General of the Supreme Court of Cassation in Rome. In March 1958, the High Council of the Judiciary gave its favourable opinion to Rossi's promotion as President of the Chambers of the Supreme Court of Cassation, but before he could take up that office, he was appointed as a Judge of the ECJ on 7 October 1958.

2. ROSSI'S APPOINTMENT TO THE 'SINGLE COURT OF JUSTICE'

Rossi's appointment to the ECJ occurred at a crucial moment in the life of the Institution. Following the entry into force of the Treaties of Rome, the Court established by the ECSC Treaty was replaced by a 'Single Court of Justice' for the three European Communities,[18] which would be known as 'Court of Justice of the European Communities'.[19] That event ushered in significant changes in the ECJ's membership:[20] the Dutch Judges Adrianus Van Kleffens and Petrus Serrarens, along with the Italian President Massimo Pilotti, left the ECJ on

[14] See Rossi's resume in his ECJ personal file, HAEU, CJUE-2558, 49.

[15] See L Castiglioni, 'Il mosaico Egeo: incontri, scontri e continuità nel Dodecaneso (1912–1945)' in *Grecia e Italia 1821–2021: due secoli di storie condivise* (Athens, ATP Books, 2023) 525–548.

[16] See L Pignataro, 'Le isole italiane dell'Egeo dall'8 settembre 1943 al termine della II guerra mondiale' (2001) 37(3) *Clio Rivista Trimestrale di Studi Storici* 465–552; M Clementi, 'The End of the Rhodes Jewish Community', in G Orsina and A Ungari (a cura di), *The "Jewish question" in the territories occupied by Italians, 1939–1943* (Rome, Viella, 2019) 215–232.

[17] Supreme Disciplinary Court for the Judiciary, Judgment of 19 July 1947, Italian State Archive, Ministry of Justice, Supreme Disciplinary Court for the Judiciary, folder no. 53, file no. 624.

[18] See Article 3 of the Convention on certain institutions common to the European Communities, attached to the Treaties of Rome, 25 March 1957.

[19] *Cf.* Minutes of the Conference of the representatives of the Member States concerning the establishment of the Court of Justice of the European Communities, Brussels, 7 October 1958, HAEU, CJUE-2632, 176.

[20] See V Fritz, *Juges et Avocats Généraux de la Cour de Justice de L'Union Européenne (1952–1972)* (Frankfurt, Klostermann, 2018) 102–109.

6 October 1958; on the following day, the Dutch President Andreas Donner and the Italian Judges Nicola Catalano and Rossi were sworn in.[21]

When, in the Spring of 1958, Rossi was considered for one of the positions at the ECJ,[22] he had 38 years of experience in the Italian judiciary. Unlike many Italian judges, he had served on overseas courts, he spoke English, French and German,[23] and had taken part in the drafting of the rules of procedure of the ECSC Court of Justice.[24] Having authored many publications on foreign and comparative law,[25] he was ready to plunge into an entirely new subject, ie Community law.[26]

Moreover, Rossi's name was already a familiar one in the Italian Ministry of Foreign Affairs, where he had served in 1940 prior to his transfer to Rhodes. In 1950, Rossi had been one of the Italian candidates for the position of legal adviser to the Tangiers Zone, a position that was eventually assigned to his future colleague at the ECJ, Catalano.[27] Moreover, Rossi was well acquainted with the eminent international law professor Riccardo Monaco, then Secretary General of the Diplomatic Disputes Service of the Ministry of Foreign Affairs.[28] A recently declassified letter revealed that Monaco himself was slated for the ECJ in 1958, but as he did not want to leave Rome at that time, he made every effort so that Rossi could be appointed judge in his place,[29] a detail confirmed in Monaco's autobiography.[30]

3. ROSSI'S EXTRA-CURIAL STATEMENTS ON COMMUNITY LAW AND THE ECJ

Throughout his tenure at the ECJ, Rossi held firm to the old Italian adage stating that 'judges should speak only through their judgments'. His opinions,

[21] On Nicola Catalano, see the chapter by T Pavone in this volume. *See also* A Arena and A Rosanò, 'Nicola Catalano (1910–1984): concepteur du renvoi préjudiciel en interprétation et apôtre de la primauté du droit Communautaire', in N Catalano, *Manuel de droit des communautés européennes* (2nd ed, Bruylant, Brussels, 2023), XIX–XXXIX.

[22] *See* National Archives of the Netherlands (AN/PB), 2.05.118 – 20025, 76 (noting that the Representatives of the Governments of the Member States nominated the candidates at the Conference held on 1 July 1958). The Author is grateful to Vera Fritz for showing him the Dutch and German diplomatic documents referred to in this chapter.

[23] *See* Rossi's Biography in the German Foreign Office Archives (PAAA) B-20-200, Band 420, 22.

[24] Fritz (n 20) 62, fn 104 (citing Telegram of 18 August 1958 in PAAA, B20-200, Bd. 272, 51).

[25] *See, eg*, R Rossi, 'La legge penale americana vista con occhi russi' (1951) I *Giustizia Penale* 28; R Rossi, 'Pregi e difetti dell'amministrazione della giustizia in Canadà' (1951) I *Giustizia Penale* 275; R Rossi, 'Le recenti riforme del diritto di famiglia in Inghilterra' (1953) Rivista di diritto matrimoniale 44–53; R.Rossi, 'Il nuovo codice penale della Corea' (1953) III *Giustizia Penale* 275.

[26] See Speech by Hammes at the Solemn Hearing of 8 October 1964, 5, HAEU, CJUE-2558, 31 ('Dès le début vous vous êtes plongé dans la matière entièrement nouvelle avec laquelle nos fonctions vous confrontaient)'.

[27] Fritz (n 20) 198–199. See also Michel Erpelding, 'Juristes internationalistes, juristes mixtes, Euro-Lawyers : l'apport de l'expérience semi-coloniale à l'émergence d'un droit supranational' (2022) *Clio@Themis* 22, at http://journals.openedition.org/cliothemis/2023.

[28] See the chapter by Edoardo Greppi on Riccardo Monaco in this volume.

[29] Confidential letter of 13 July 1964 by Rossi to the other ECJ Members, HAEU, CJUE-2635, 42–43.

[30] R Monaco, *Memorie di una vita. Memorie per l'Europa* (Rome, Ledip, 1996) 184.

therefore, were less discernible compared to those of other judges like Catalano, who published extensively on Community law before, during, and after his term at the ECJ.[31] Given Rossi's reticence, the scant extra-curial sources available provide some invaluable glimpses into his viewpoints on Community law.

On 9 February 1962, Rossi gave a talk on the ECJ at the University of Bologna.[32] He opened his speech by presenting the three Community Treaties, which in his opinion had a twofold nature. They were '*international agreements* between the Member States setting out common rules for the internal market' and they constituted 'the internal legal orders of *international unions* endowed with legal personality distinct from that of their Member States'.[33] The Treaty of Paris sought to establish a 'customs union' in the coal and steel sector, but had achieved only a 'limited' and 'incomplete' economic integration.[34] The Treaties of Rome sought to extend integration into additional sectors, but their broader objectives called for an expansion of the powers of the Member States at the expense of those of the European Executives.[35]

Rossi then turned to the ECJ, which had a twofold nature too: it was an '*international* court', set up to resolve disputes between the Member States on the application of the Community Treaties, and a 'Community court', ie, the judicial organ of the 'internal legal order' established by those treaties.[36] The ECJ's main tasks as a Community court were – except for some exceptional 'constitutional' prerogatives – akin to that of a 'domestic administrative court', ie, reviewing the legality of the acts of the Community Institutions.[37]

On the issue of standing before the ECJ, Rossi noted that the standing of Member States was broader than that of individual applicants, as the former could challenge both general and individual Community acts, whilst the latter could only challenge acts encroaching upon their individual legal sphere.[38]

Concluding his speech, he remarked that certain ECJ rulings had straddled the fine line between 'interpreting [Community] law' and 'supplementing' it, inciting 'perplexities within parts of the Court'. Those perplexities, he warned, would 'persist as long as the administration of justice is entrusted to thinking beings'.[39]

These statements reveal Rossi's *internationalist* conception of the European Communities,[40] as State-centric 'international unions' that were similar to other

[31] For a comprehensive biography of Catalano's works, see the one included in Catalano (n 21).

[32] R Rossi, *La Corte di Giustizia delle Comunità Europee* (1962) *Organizzazione scientifica e tecnica amministrativa* 130–153.

[33] ibid., 144–145 (Author's translation, emphasis added).

[34] ibid., 130 (Author's translation).

[35] ibid., 131.

[36] ibid., 144 (Author's translation).

[37] ibid., 146 (Author's translation).

[38] ibid., 150.

[39] Rossi (n 32) 153.

[40] For the distinction between 'internationalists' and 'supranationalists' in the wake of the Stresa Conference, see J Bailleux, 'Comment l'Europe vint au droit' (2010) 60 *Revue française de science politique* 295–318.

Post-war intergovernmental organisations. Rossi's restrictive stance on individual standing before the ECJ aligns with this conception, given that individual access to courts established by treaties was an exception rather than the norm in the international law of that era. Although Rossi's conception of the European Communities was not as extreme as the 'contractualist' perspective held by Gaetano Arangio-Ruiz (who conceived international law as a system of 'private-law like' rules that could not give rise to international organisations with separate legal orders),[41] it did not go much further than the 'institutional' approach to international organisations shared by many Italian international law scholars of the time.[42] For instance, Rossi's 'perplexities' about the ECJ judgments that had 'supplemented' the text of the Community Treaties is in line with the traditional approach to treaty interpretation, according to which 'restrictions upon the independence' of the signatory states 'cannot [...] be presumed',[43] let alone limitations of their 'sovereign rights'[44] – contrary to what the ECJ would rule the following year in *Van Gend en Loos*.[45]

Unlike other international law scholars such as Monaco, who immediately recognised the *sui generis* nature of the European Communities relative to other international organisations,[46] Rossi's account somewhat downplayed their *supranational traits*, especially in the case of the EEC and Euratom.[47] By focusing exclusively on the economic goals of the Community Treaties and neglecting their *federal aspirations*, Rossi's views radically diverged from those of Catalano, who regarded the three Communities as 'partial federations'.[48]

Drawing upon his long experience in the judiciary, Rossi advocated a 'pragmatic' approach to Community law that eschewed theoretical categorisations. In his 1962 book review of Catalano's *Manuale di diritto delle Comunità Europee*,[49] Rossi noted that 'rivers of ink' had been spilled on the notion of 'supranationalism' and other 'intelligent and ambitious theoretical frameworks' that proved 'meaningless in practice', whereas the 'practical assessment' of Community law was the 'most meaningful way to really understand the *raison d'être* of the Communities and the concrete goals they pursue'.[50]

[41] See G Arangio-Ruiz, 'Rapporti contrattuali fra Stati ed organizzazione internazionale. Per una teoria dualista delle unioni di Stati' (1950) 82 *Archivio Giuridico Filippo Serafini* 6.

[42] For an overview of those scholars, see E Milano, 'The Main International Law Issues Arising in the Aftermath of World War II', in G Bartolini (ed), *A History of International Law in Italy* (Oxford, Oxford University Press), 2020) 418–425.

[43] Permanent Court of International Justice, *Lotus*, 1927, Series A, 18.

[44] See AP Sereni, *Diritto internazionale* (Vol. I, Milan, Giuffrè, 1956) 181.

[45] *NV Algemene Transport- en Expeditie Onderneming van Gend & Loos v Netherlands Inland Revenue Administration* Case 26/62 ECLI:EU:C:1963:1 [1963] 1963 ECR 1, 12.

[46] R Monaco, 'Caratteri istituzionali della Comunità economica europea' (1958) 41 *RDI* 9, 11. See the chapter by Edoardo Greppi on Riccardo Monaco in this volume.

[47] Rossi (n 32) 133 (noting that the 'new Communities' had 'deficiencies in terms of supranationality').

[48] N Catalano, *La Comunità economica europea e l'Euratom* (Milan, Giuffrè, 1957) 6.

[49] R Rossi, 'Recensione a 'Manuale di Diritto delle Comunità Europee' di Nicola Catalano' (1962) 29(4) *Rivista di Studi Politici Internazionali* 649–650.

[50] ibid.

Rossi reaffirmed his 'pragmatic' approach at his ECJ farewell speech in 1964. On that occasion, he wished that at least one third of the future members of the ECJ would have prior experience in the judiciary,[51] because he believed that former judges had really 'made a difference in the [ECJ] deliberations and in the jurisprudence as a whole'.[52]

In his six-year tenure at the ECJ, Rossi's only *attaché* – that is how *référendaires* were called until 1968 – was Sergio Neri.[53] Neri had academic ambitions[54] and had published extensively on Community law, both before and during his service at the ECJ, which continued for many years after the end of Rossi's mandate.[55] In 1958, Neri published a lengthy article on individual challenges against Community acts,[56] which largely anticipated Rossi's statements on the limited standing of individual applicants at his 1962 talk in Bologna. In 1960, Neri co-authored a collection of the preparatory work of the EEC Treaty,[57] which dovetails with Rossi's internationalist conviction that the ECJ should 'interpret' but not 'supplement' the Community treaties. Finally, Neri's 1964 article on the nature of the European Communities reveals that, even after the groundbreaking ruling in *Van Gend en Loos* of 1963, he still believed that the European Communities were 'international unions',[58] as Rossi had stated two years earlier in Bologna.

4. PROLOGUE TO ROSSI'S JUDICIAL ANTHOLOGY: INDIVIDUAL CHALLENGES AGAINST COMMUNITY ACTS IN THE EARLY JURISPRUDENCE OF THE ECJ

Throughout his six-year tenure at the ECJ, Rossi was a judge in the Second Chamber, which he chaired from 1 October 1959 to 30 September 1960 and from 18 May 1962 to 30 September 1963.[59] Rossi served as rapporteur in

[51] Speech by Rossi at the ECJ Solemn Hearing of 8 October 1964, HAEU, CJUE-2558, 25.

[52] ibid.

[53] See Excerpt of the minutes of the ECJ meeting of 29 May 1968, HAEU, CJUE-2540, 18 (establishing the designation '*référendaire*' in the various official languages of the European Communities).

[54] Neri was *Libero docente* of International Law at the University of Florence.

[55] After the end of Rossi's mandate, Neri served as *référendaire* for Riccardo Monaco and subsequently for Giacinto Bosco. Then he went on to become the Director of the ECJ's Research and Documentation Directorate.

[56] S Neri, 'Il ricorso di legittimità del privato nei trattati C.E.C.A. e C.E.E.' (1958) 25 *Rivista di Studi Politici Internazionali* 230 and 240.

[57] S Neri and H Sperl, *Traité instituant la Communauté Économique Européenne : travaux préparatoires ; déclarations interprétatives des six gouvernements; documents parlementaires* (Luxembourg: Cour de justice des Communautés européennes, 1960).

[58] S Neri, 'Sulla Natura Giuridica delle Comunità Europee' (1964) *Rivista di diritto internazionale* 264. *See also* the letter by Sergio Neri to Michael Waelbroeck of 27 October 1965, HAEU, MW-0021, 57 (noting that his correspondent shared his concerns about the use of 'quasi-federal' definitions in respect of the European Communities).

[59] See Memorandum on the ECJ Presidents of Chambers since 1953, HAEU, CJUE-2517, 8–9.

34 cases.[60] This anthology will focus on two of those cases, both concerning the standing of individual applicants wishing to challenge Community acts: *Plaumann*,[61] which provided an evergreen definition of 'individual concern' for actions for annulment under Article 173(2) EEC, and *Acciaierie Fonderie Ferriere di Modena*,[62] which applied a similar notion to actions for annulment under Article 33(2) ECSC. Before turning to those rulings, a brief overview of the standing of individual applicants under the ECSC and EEC Treaties is in order, because, as it will become apparent, 'past is prologue'.

Although the Schuman Declaration envisaged 'means of appeal against the decisions' of what would become the ECSC High Authority, Jean Monnet originally believed that only Member States should be given standing before the ECJ.[63] However, as the High Authority had the power to directly address recommendations and decisions to individual enterprises, it was deemed appropriate that these entities too should have standing before the ECJ.[64] Thus, the final version of Article 33(2) ECSC enabled coal and steel undertakings and their associations to challenge: i) 'individual decisions and recommendations concerning them' and ii) 'general decisions and recommendations which they deem to involve an abuse of power affecting them'.

A restrictive approach to individual standing emerged from the negotiations.[65] In particular, the member of the French delegation Maurice Lagrange revealed that, in drafting second part of Article 33(2) ECSC, the 'intentions of the authors of the [ECSC] Treaty' were not really to allow individual applicants to challenge genuine general acts, but only to contest 'a decision which, while in fact individually affecting an undertaking, is 'disguised' […] as, to all appearances, a general decision and is, in consequence, clearly invalidated as a misuse of powers' (hereafter, the 'disguised act of individual concern' theory).[66]

Catalano, on behalf of the High Authority, presented the disguised act of individual concern theory to the ECJ in *ASSIDER*, the very first case involving individual applicants.[67] The ECJ impliedly dismissed that argument, holding

[60] Joined cases were counted as the sum of their constituent cases. 26 cases concerned the ECSC Treaty; 7 cases concerned the EEC Treaty; 1 case concerned both the EEC and Euratom Treaties.

[61] *Plaumann & Co. v EEC Commission* Case 25/62 ECLI:EU:C:1963:17 [1963].

[62] *Acciaierie Fonderie Ferriere di Modena and others v High Authority* Joined Cases 55/63 to 59/63 and 61/63 to 63/63 ECLI:EU:C:1964:37 [1964].

[63] See Note on the interview of J Monnet with PA Blaisse of 18 September 1950, Fondation Jean Monnet, AMG 6/5/7. See also A Boerger-De Smedt, 'La Cour de Justice dans les négociations du traité de Paris instituant la CECA' (2008) 14 *Journal of European Integration History* 28.

[64] ibid.

[65] A Boerger-De Smedt, 'Negotiating the Foundations of European Law, 1950–57: The Legal History of the Treaties of Paris and Rome' (2012) 21 *Contemporary European History* 344–347.

[66] See *ASSIDER v High Authority and ISA v High Authority* Cases 3 and 4/54 ECLI:EU:C:1954:6, 1954–1954 ECR 87 [1954], Joined Opinion of AG Lagrange (citing the Luxembourg ratification law of the ECSC Treaty as evidence of the drafters' intent). See also *Fédéchar v. High Authority* Cases 8/55 and 9/55 ECLI:EU:C:1956:6, 1954–1956 ECR 245, 272 [1956], Joined Opinion of AG Lagrange of 12 June 1956 (arguing that the Luxembourg ratification law 'clearly reflect[ed] the firm intention of the authors of the [ECSC] Treaty').

[67] *ASSIDER v High Authority* Case 3/54, Reply on behalf of the High Authority of 19 March 1954, HAEU, CJUE-0523, 42–43.

that, for the admissibility of individual actions against a general decision, it was 'enough for the applicant formally to allege that there has been a misuse of powers affecting it' and that, in the case of associations of undertakings, it was sufficient to claim 'a misuse of powers affecting one or more' of its members'.[68] The ECJ hammered the final nail into the coffin of the disguised individual act theory in *Fédéchar*, in which it squarely held that individual applicants could challenge 'not only individual decisions but also general decisions in the true sense of the term', as long as they alleged to be 'the subject or at any rate the victim of the misuse of powers'.[69]

The ECJ also adopted a liberal interpretation of the wording 'concerning them' in the first part of Article 33(2) ECSC, enabling undertakings and their associations to challenge individual decisions that, whilst apparently addressed to others, were of individual concern to the applicants. In *Groupement des Industries Sidérurgiques Luxembourgeoises*, the ECJ ruled that it was 'not necessary for the [impugned] decision to manifest [its individual] character in relation to the applicant',[70] as long as the latter could claim 'that the decision concerns it' and supported its claim 'by an appropriate statement explaining the interest which it has in having the decision declared void'.[71] The ECJ construed that notion of 'interest' broadly, enabling individual applicants to challenge, for instance, an individual decision addressed to a Member State upholding a tariff that benefitted the competitors of the applicant companies.[72]

The ECJ's endeavours 'to force the door open, if not wide, at least wider'[73] did not go unnoticed by the Member States' governments. That became apparent during the negotiations of the Treaties of Rome, when the jurists of the Drafting Committee[74] introduced some carefully worded requirements to the admissibility of individual actions, while simultaneously extending the pool of individual applicants.[75] Article 173(2) EEC, thus enabled natural and legal persons

[68] *ASSIDER v High Authority* Case 3/54 ECLI:EU:C:1955:2 [1955] 1954–1956 ECR 63, 69.

[69] *Fédération Charbonnière de Belgique (Fédéchar) v High Authority* Case 8/55 ECLI:EU:C:1956:7 [1956] 1954–1965 ECR 245, 257–258.

[70] *Groupement des Industries Sidérurgiques Luxembourgeoises v High Authority* Joined cases 7/54 and 9/54 ECLI:EU:C:1956:2 [1956] 1954–1956 ECR 175, 192.

[71] *De Gezamenlijke Steenkolenmijnen in Limburg v High Authority* Case 30/59 ECLI:EU:C:1961:2 [1961] 1961 ECR 1, 16.

[72] *Chambre syndicale de la sidérurgie de l'est de la France and others v High Authority* Joined cases 24/58 and 34/58 ECLI:EU:C:1960:32 [1960] 1960 ECR 281, 292.

[73] See *ASSIDER v High Authority and ISA v High Authority*, Joined Opinion of AG Lagrange (n 66) 89 (advising the ECJ against forcing the meaning of the ECSC Treaty to give individuals a broader standing), but see Joined Opinion of AG Lagrange in *Fédéchar v High Authority* (n 66) 276 (noting that a 'perfectly legitimate effort to open access to our Court to the largest number of those who are subject to its jurisdiction' was underway).

[74] On the work of the Drafting Committee, see the comprehensive account of M Rasmussen, *Between Constraints and Innovation: The Role of the Groupe de Rédaction and the Legal Shape of the EEC Treaty*, Jean Monnet Working Paper no. 1/23.

[75] The wording of what would become Article 173(2) EEC was adopted by the Drafting Committee in its meeting of 13 December 1956 (Art. 26), HAEU, CM3-NEGO 258 and left unchanged in subsequent meetings, except for the denomination of the impugned acts, which originally referred to 'individual decisions' and 'general decisions' but was subsequently harmonised with the nomenclature of EEC acts introduced in January 1957.

to challenge i) 'a decision addressed to that person' as well as ii) 'a decision which, although in the form of a regulation or a decision addressed to another person, is of direct and individual concern to the former'.

By many accounts, the *ethos* of the new wording was to set stricter limits on the standing of individuals relative to Article 33(2) ECSC as interpreted by the ECJ.[76] Catalano, a member of the Drafting Committee, revealed that the purpose of the second part of Article 173(2) EEC, as apparent from its French version,[77] was to reframe, in clearer terms, the disguised act of individual concern theory underlying the second part of Article 33(2) ECSC.[78] Would the ECJ follow or defy the intent of the drafters this time?

The ECJ first applied the new regime for individual challenges against EEC regulations in the *Agricultural Associations* judgment of 14 December 1962.[79] Several associations of agricultural producers and traders had challenged certain provisions of EEC regulations that harmed the economic interests of their associates. The ECJ declared the actions inadmissible, finding that the applicants were not individually concerned because, although the impugned provision affected 'the interests [of the applicants] and of the members of the applicant associations … those members [were] concerned by the said provision *in the same way as all other agricultural producers* of the Community.'[80]

The ECJ added that it could not 'accept the principle that an association, in its capacity as the representative of a category of businessmen, could be individually concerned by a measure affecting the general interests of that category', as this would 'result in the grouping, under the heading of a single legal person, of the interests properly attributed to the members of a category, who have been affected as individuals by *genuine regulations*'.[81]

Not only that passage marked a clear U-turn in the ECJ's approach to the standing of associations of undertakings relative to its 1955 judgment in *ASSIDER*,[82] but it signalled that, this time, the ECJ was willing to align with the intent of the authors of the EEC Treaty in allowing only actions against disguised acts of individual concern, not 'genuine regulations'. Indeed, at the beginning of the *Agricultural Associations* judgment, the Community judges noted that the EEC Treaty had laid down 'more restrictive conditions

[76] See Boerger-De Smedt (n 65) 353; M Wolferen, 'The Limits to the CJEU's Interpretation of Locus Standi, a Theoretical Framework' (2016) 12 *Journal of Contemporary European Research* 923.

[77] '[D]ecisions […] prises *sous l'apparence* d'un règlement ou d'une décision adreseée à une autre personne' (emphasis added).

[78] N Catalano, 'La protezione giurisdizionale nel sistema del trattato C.E.E. nei confronti degli atti non normativi' (1965) 88 *Foro Italiano* 77.

[79] *Confédération nationale des producteurs de fruits et légumes and others v EEC Council* Joined Cases 16/62 and 17/62 ECLI:EU:C:1962:47 [1962] 1962 ECR 471. See also the substantially identical judgment in *Fédération nationale de la boucherie en gros et du commerce en gros des viandes and others v EEC Council* Joined cases 19/62 to 22/62 ECLI:EU:C:1962:48 [1962] 1962 ECR 491.

[80] *Confédération nationale des producteurs de fruits et légumes and others v EEC Council* (n 79) 472, 479 (emphasis added).

[81] ibid. (emphasis added).

[82] *ASSIDER v High Authority* (n 68) 63, 69.

than [...] the ECSC Treaty for the admissibility of applications for annulment by private individuals' and added that 'it would not be appropriate for the Court to pronounce on the merits of this system which appears clearly from the text under examination'.[83]

5. INDIVIDUAL CHALLENGES AGAINST EEC DECISIONS ADDRESSED TO OTHER PERSONS: *PLAUMANN*

The second part of Article 173(2) EEC also applied to challenges against acts of individual (and direct) concern to the applicant disguised as decisions addressed to other persons. Would the ECJ confirm its liberal approach to standing under the first part of Article 33(2) ECSC or align to the more restrictive trend heralded by *Agricultural Associations*? The Community judges provided an unequivocal answer in *Plaumann*,[84] the most renowned case in which Rossi served as rapporteur.

In June 1961, the German government had requested the EEC Commission permission to apply a custom duty of 10% to fresh clementines imported from third countries, in lieu of the 13% duty set out in the Common Customs Tariff.[85] By its decision addressed to Germany of 22 May 1962, the EEC Commission had declined the request, noting that a higher tariff would encourage intra-Community production of clementines and mandarins, especially in Southern Italy, by protecting it from imports from third countries.[86] Plaumann & Co, a Hamburg-based importer of clementines from outside the EEC, thus brought an action for annulment against the EEC Commission decision under Article 173(2) EEC.[87] The EEC Commission, unsurprisingly, argued that the action for annulment was inadmissible.[88]

In its judgment on 15 July 1963,[89] the ECJ rejected the EEC Commission's contention that a Member State could not be regarded as 'another person' within the meaning of Article 173(2) EEC, noting that the Treaty provisions on the right to bring an action 'must not be interpreted restrictively'.[90] The ECJ also rejected the EEC Commission's submission that the contested decision was 'a regulation in the form of an individual decision', noting that it was addressed to the German government and therefore it constituted a decision

[83] *Confédération nationale des producteurs de fruits et légumes and others v EEC Council* (n 79) 478.

[84] *Plaumann* (n 61). See the ECJ case file HAEU, CJUE-0739 and the Joint Legal Service case file HAEU, CECA_SEJC-358–363.

[85] Dossier de procédure of Case 25/62, *Plaumann & Co. v EEC Commission*, HAEU, CJUE-0739, 29–31.

[86] ibid.

[87] ibid., 57–66.

[88] ibid., 99.

[89] *Plaumann* (n 61) 96.

[90] ibid., 106–107.

'referring to a particular person and binding on that person alone'.[91] By rejecting those arguments, the ECJ essentially refused to give decisions addressed to Member States a broader protection against individual challenges than that afforded to regulations.[92]

On the issue of 'individual concern', the ECJ applied the same approach it had employed for individual challenges against regulations in *Agricultural Associations*. The Community judges noted that Plaumann had been affected by the impugned decision 'as an importer of clementines', ie, 'by reason of a commercial activity which may at any time be practised by any person' and was thus unable 'to distinguish the applicant in relation to the contested Decision as in the case of the addressee'.[93] The ECJ accordingly declared the action for annulment inadmissible and ordered the applicant to bear the costs of the proceedings.[94]

Plaumann became a *locus classicus* of Community law[95] because it provided, for the first time, a quotable definition of 'individual concern' under Article 173(2) EEC, the so-called '*Plaumann* formula', which the ECJ would be apply not only to individual challenges against decisions addressed to other persons, but also to individual challenges against regulations:

> Persons other than those to whom a decision is addressed may only claim to be individually concerned if that decision affects them by reason of certain attributes which are peculiar to them or by reason of circumstances in which they are differentiated from all other persons and by virtue of these factors distinguishes them individually just as in the case of the person addressed.[96]

As the ECJ does not issue separate opinions, it is impossible to determine to what extent the *Plaumann* formula came out of Rossi's pen, but it certainly aligned with his extra-curial writings. In his 1962 talk in Bologna, he had stated that individual applicants could challenge acts that, in spite of their formal appearance, 'substantially affected the legal sphere of the individual',[97] a wording remindful of the disguised act of individual concern theory that, according to his *attaché* Neri, underlay Article 173(2) EEC.[98]

The *Plaumann* formula embodied a 'certain idea of judicial protection' that was prevalent in several Member States at the time:[99] certain acts – notably, those

[91] ibid.
[92] See L Goffin, 'Annotation to Plaumann & Co v. EEC Commission' (1963) 1 *Common Market Law Review* 354.
[93] ibid., 107.
[94] ibid., 108–109.
[95] See A Vauchez, 'EU Law Classics in the Making: Methodological Noted on the *Grands arrêts* of the European Court of Justice', in FG Nicola and B Davies (eds), *EU Law Stories* (Cambridge, Cambridge University Press, 2017) 21 (expressly mentioning *Plaumann* at 26).
[96] *Plaumann* (n 61) 107.
[97] R Rossi (n 32) 150.
[98] Neri (n 56) 240.
[99] ibid. See also J Ziller, 'La dialectique du contentieux européen: le cas des recours contre les actes normatifs', in *Les droits individuels et le juge en Europe: mélanges en l'honneur de Michel Fromont* (Strasbourg, Presses universitaires de Strasbourg, 2001) 443–464.

having a 'quasi-legislative character', such as regulations[100] and State-addressed decisions[101] – should only be challenged *incidentally* by individual applicants, ie, through the preliminary ruling of validity or the objection of illegality set out in the Community Treaties.[102] The Community judges, albeit with some initial reluctance, espoused that idea, possibly comforted by the thought that setting a higher bar for the admissibility of individual challenges against EEC acts could be conducive to European integration, especially at a time where the EEC Institutions were struggling to implement Community policies.[103]

Since 1963, the *Plaumann* formula appeared in more than 300 ECJ rulings[104] and, despite decades of academic criticism for its adverse effects on the judicial protection of individuals[105] and on public interest litigation,[106] it continues to define the ECJ's interpretation of 'individual concern' for actions for annulment under Article 263(4) TFEU,[107] thus displaying a loyalty to the intentions of the authors of the EEC Treaty that stands in stark contrast with the pro-integration approach to treaty interpretation underlying many landmark rulings of the so-called foundational period.[108]

[100] *Confédération nationale des producteurs de fruits et légumes and others v EEC Council and Fédération nationale de la boucherie en gros et du commerce en gros des viandes and others v EEC Council* Joined Cases 16/62 and 17/62 and 19/62 to 22/62 ECLI:EU:C:1962:40 [1962] 1962 ECR 471, 486, Joined Opinion of AG Lagrange of 20 November 1962.

[101] *Plaumann & Co. v EEC Commission* Case 25/62 ECLI:EU:C:1963:7 [1963] 1963 ECR 95, 121, Opinion of AG Roemer of 28 May 1963.

[102] Opinion of AG Lagrange (n 100) 487.

[103] ibid. (noting that agricultural regulations were approved 'only after significant difficulty, and sometimes after a compromise reached in the Council, still wedded to the rule of unanimity').

[104] A search on the ECJ's case-law search engine conducted on 18 June 2023 for judgments and orders containing the phrase 'en raison de certaines qualités qui leur sont particulières' yielded 303 matches.

[105] See G Bebr, Judicial Control of the European Communities (London, Stevens, 1962); A Barav, 'Direct and Individual Concern: An Almost Insurmountable Barrier to the Admissibility of Individual Appeal to the EEC Court' (1974) 11 *Common Market Law Review* 191; H Rasmussen, 'Why Is Article 173 Interpreted against Private Plaintiffs?' (1980) 5 *European Law Review* 112; A Arnull, 'Private Applicants and The Action for Annulment Under Article 173 of the EC Treaty' (1995) 32 *Common Market Law Review* 7; A Albors-Llorens, 'The Standing of Private Parties to Challenge Community Measures: Has the European Court Missed the Boat?' (2003) 62 *Cambridge Law Journal* 77; L Gormley, 'Judicial Review – a New Dawn after Lisbon?', in H Koch and K Hagel-Sorensen (eds), *Europe. The New Legal Realism: Essays in Honour of Hjalte Rasmussen* (Copenhagen, Djøf Publishing, 2010).

[106] *See* M Pagano, 'Overcoming *Plaumann* in EU Environmental Litigation – An Analysis of ENGOs Legal Arguments in Actions for Annulment' (2019) *Diritto e Processo* 311–360; M van Wolferen, 'The Limits to the CJUE's Interpretation of Locus Standi, a Theoretical Framework' (2016) 12(4) *Journal of Contemporary European Research* 914–930; A Cygan, 'Protecting the Interests of Civil Society in Community Decision-Making: The Limits of Article 230 EC' (2003) 52(4) *The International and Comparative Law Quarterly* 995–1012.

[107] In particular, in *Unión de Pequeños Agricultores v Council* Case C-50/00 P ECLI:EU:2002:462 [2002], para 44, the ECJ ruled that the 'individual concern' requirement must be interpreted 'in the light of the principle of effective judicial protection', but that 'such an interpretation cannot have the effect of setting aside the condition in question, expressly laid down in the Treaty'.

[108] See R-M Chevallier, Methods and Reasoning of the European Court in its Interpretation of Community Law (1965) 2 *Common Market Law Review* 32–35 (noting that in 1962 the ECJ started 'to decide cases in the spirit of a national court and no longer of [an] international court'). *See also* the analysis of the ECJ interpretation approaches in D Gallo, *L'efficacia diretta del diritto dell'Unione Europea negli ordinamenti nazionali* (Milan, Giuffrè, 2018) 39–46.

6. INDIVIDUAL CHALLENGES AGAINST ECSC GENERAL DECISIONS: *ACCIAIERIE FONDERIE FERRIERE DI MODENA*

If the *Agricultural Associations* judgment of 1962 had brought the judicial interpretation of Article 173(2) EEC into line with the intentions of the drafters as regards individual challenges against EEC regulations, it had also brought to the fore a divergence *vis-à-vis* the ECJ's approach to individual challenges against ECSC general decisions under Article 33(2) ECSC. The opportunity to reconcile the interpretation of those two provisions materialised in another case in which Rossi served as rapporteur: *Acciaierie Fonderie Ferriere di Modena et al v. High Authority.*[109]

Eight Italian companies had brough actions for annulment against a decision of the High Authority setting out the elements for the calculation of the contribution that companies consuming ferrous scrap owed to the ECSC scrap equalisation fund.[110] To overcome the High Authority's plea of inadmissibility, the applicants had claimed that the impugned decision was either a bundle of individual decisions concerning them as per the first part of Article 33(2) ECSC, or a general decision involving an abuse of power affecting them as per the second part of that provision.

In its judgment of 9 June 1964,[111] the ECJ rejected both arguments. As to the contention that the impugned act was a bundle of individual decisions, the ECJ ruled that a decision could only be regarded as individual if 'its provisions are likely to affect directly and individually the situations of the persons to whom they apply'.[112] Insofar as the impugned decision set out 'general factors necessary for making a provisional calculation of the equalisation rate', rather than 'a definitive statement of account of the amounts payable by each undertaking', it did not 'individually and directly affect the legal position of undertakings using ferrous scrap' and thus could not be regarded as a bundle of individual decisions concerning the applicants.[113]

The ECJ then turned to the issue of whether the impugned act could be regarded as a general decision involving a misuse of powers affecting the applicants. It noted that, for an individual challenge against a general decision to be admissible, the applicant had to provide 'convincing reasons why the adoption of the contested decision is directly prejudicial to its interests'.[114] In this case, the ECJ found that the impugned decision affected 'all the applicants in

[109] *Acciaierie Fonderie Ferriere di Modena and others v High Authority* (n 62). See the ECJ case file HAEU, CJUE-739 and the Joint Legal Service case file HAEU, CECA_SEJC-399-413.

[110] All scrap-consuming companies established in the Community were required to contribute to that fund. See G Cottrau, 'Il meccanismo di perequazione del rottame nella giurisprudenza della Corte di giustizia delle Comunità Europee' (1961) *Il diritto negli scambi internazionali* 120.

[111] *Acciaierie Fonderie Ferriere di Modena and others v High Authority* (n 62) 211.

[112] ibid., 228.

[113] ibid.

[114] ibid.

the same degree', so it was 'impossible to maintain that it directly damage[d] the individual interests of each of them and that it was vitiated by a misuse of powers 'affecting them''.[115] Accordingly, the ECJ declared actions for annulment inadmissible.

Acciaierie Fonderie Ferriere di Modena marked a notable departure from the ECJ's liberal approach to individual standing, by aligning the interpretation of Article 33(2) ECSC with that of Article 173(2) EEC. In other words, the ECJ turned the low bar, set in 1956 in *Fédéchar*, that individual applicants allege being 'the subject or at any rate the victim' of a general decision,[116] into the high hoop that individual applicants provide 'convincing reasons' that the general decision 'directly damages the individual interests of each of them'. That test overlaps to a significant extent with the one set by the ECJ to prove that a general decision is in fact 'a bundle of individual decisions', ie, whether 'its provisions are likely to affect directly and individually the situations of the persons to whom they apply'.[117] Although those judge-made tests found little support in the text of the second part of Article 33(2) ECSC – which unlike Article 173(2) EEC does not contain the words 'direct and individual concern' – they appear entirely consistent with what Lagrange described as the 'intentions of the authors' of that provision, ie, the disguised act of individual concern theory.[118]

Once again, in the absence of separate opinions, it is impossible to know to what extent Rossi contributed to the outcome of *Acciaierie Fonderie Ferriere di Modena*, but the congruencies between that judgment and his 1962 talk in Bologna are undeniable. On that occasion, Rossi had argued that Article 173(2) EEC had expressed 'in simpler but technically superior form' the same judicial remedy laid down in Article 33(2) of the ECSC, ie, an individual challenge against ostensibly general acts that 'encroached upon the legal sphere of an individual', because 'adopting an act that is, in form, general act to affect, in substance, the legal sphere of an individual constitutes a typical case of abuse of power'.[119] Four years earlier, also Neri had argued that the disguised act of individual concern theory underlay both Article 173(2) EEC and Article 33(2) ECSC and had wished that the ECJ would interpret the two provisions consistently in spite of their textual differences,[120] which is precisely what the ECJ achieved in *Acciaierie Fonderie Ferriere di Modena*.

[115] ibid.
[116] *Fédération Charbonnière de Belgique (Fédéchar) v High Authority* (n 69) 257–258.
[117] See P Gori, 'Commento all'art. 33 CECA', in R Quadri, R Monaco and A Trabucchi (eds), *Commentario al Trattato CECA* (Giuffrè, Milan, 1970) 399–400.
[118] See *ASSIDER v High Authority and ISA v High Authority*, Joined Opinion of AG Lagrange (n 66) 87.
[119] Rossi (n 32) 150.
[120] Neri (n 56) 230 and 240.

7. ROSSI'S CONTRIBUTION TO THE *ESPRIT DE CORPS* AND HIS RELATIONSHIP WITH OTHER ECJ MEMBERS

During his farewell address at the ECJ, Rossi reflected on the curiosity he initially held regarding the functioning of the ECJ, given its composition of judges of different nationalities, in light of the tensions among judges of the same nationality he had experienced at the Italian Supreme Court.[121] However, he noted that 'after some small crises', the ECJ proved to work exceptionally well and that, unlike the Italian Supreme Court, its rulings were 'always the fruit of the collaboration of all the judges'.[122]

Determining precisely what Rossi intended by 'small crises' is difficult, but it might refer to some tensions he encountered with his colleague Catalano. In an open letter published on the 35th anniversary of the ECJ, President Donner referred to a 'constant incompatibility' between Rossi and Catalano and that 'their votes often cancelled each other out'.[123] In a more recent publication, Paolo Gori, who served as *attaché* for Catalano and for his successor Alberto Trabucchi,[124] added that Catalano's 'combative personality' was the cause of an 'incompatibility of character' with Rossi, who instead had developed a harmonious connection with Trabucchi, thanks to the latter's 'diplomatic skills' and his profound 'understanding of the human soul'.[125]

The amicable relationship between Rossi and Trabucchi may have been pivotal in *Van Gend en Loos*, a case that, according to some accounts, was decided by a very slim margin: four votes to three.[126] While the Community judges, in line with Advocate-General Roemer's Opinion, initially seemed unwilling to recognise the direct effect of Article 12 EEC, a memo circulated by Trabucchi (and supported by Rossi and Lecourt) swayed the majority in favour of direct effect.[127]

Morten Rasmussen speculated that if Catalano had still been on the panel, he would have supported direct effect, prompting Rossi to oppose it, due to

[121] Speech by Rossi at the ECJ Solemn Hearing of 8 October 1964, 1–2, HAEU, CJUE-2558, 24–25.

[122] ibid. (Author's translation).

[123] AM Donner, 'Letter from a former president to the present one', in *Court of Justice of the European Communities, XXXV Anni: 1952–1987* (Luxemburg, 1987) 20.

[124] See E Perillo, 'Alberto Trabucchi: the Defender of the European citizens' rights and the Van Gend & Loos ruling of the Court of Justice', in this volume.

[125] P Gori, *Quindici anni insieme ad Alberto Trabucchi alla Corte di giustizia della C.E.*, in *La formazione del diritto europeo: giornata di studio per Alberto Trabucchi nel centenario della nascita* (Padova, CEDAM, 2008) 77 (Author's translation).

[126] ibid., 71–83; M Rasmussen, 'Establishing a Constitutional Practice of European Law: The History of the Legal Service of the European Executive 1952–65' (2012) *Contemporary European History* 389, fn 84.

[127] ibid. noting that, according to the oral testimonies provided by Paolo Gori and Pierre Pescatore, the four votes in favour of direct effect were those of Trabucchi, Rossi, Lecourt, and Delvaux. But see the chapter by Perillo (n 124), which argues that, after Trabucchi's memo, Donner might have decided to support direct effect too.

their mutual hostility.[128] Yet, this theory should be approached with caution, considering that Rossi himself provided – prior to Trabucchi's memo – an argument in favour of direct effect, ie, that that each Member State had undertaken *vis-à-vis* the other Member States to recognise its own citizens as legal subjects.[129]

Moreover, regardless of any purported disagreements with Catalano, Rossi criticised the partial renewal of the ECJ judges and Advocates General that took place every three years, claiming that the 'complete immovability' of ECJ members was in practice ensured 'for a really short time', which was 'not conducive to their independence'.[130] Rossi probably hinted at the Italian government's hesitations in renewing Catalano's mandate in 1961,[131] thus suggesting that Rossi had developed an *esprit de corps* that took precedence over their alleged incompatibility.[132]

Sources also point to some tensions between Rossi and President Donner. When Donner was elected President of the ECJ in 1958, Rossi reportedly commented that it was 'regrettable' that Riese had withdrawn his candidacy and that it was 'absurd' that the presidency would be entrusted to the youngest member of the ECJ.[133]

Those tensions reached their peak towards the end of Rossi's mandate. On 13 July 1964, Rossi informed the other members of the ECJ that he had reached an 'understanding' with his successor Riccardo Monaco: Rossi would remain in office for a few additional months following the end of his tenure, so that Monaco could attend to the responsibilities of the 'very important position he currently occupies' in Rome.[134] This proposal, which found support in the text of the ECJ Statute,[135] enraged Donner, who considered it a 'nefarious scandal for the prestige and functioning of the ECJ'[136] and resolved to tender his resignation as President of the ECJ on 16 July 1964.[137]

Hammes called for an extraordinary plenary meeting on 1 August 1964 to discuss the issue,[138] but he subsequently called it off as a compromise was reached a few weeks later between Donner, on the one hand, and Hammes,

[128] Rasmussen (n 126) 389, fn 80.

[129] See A Trabucchi, *Note a mm. les juges*, in *La formazione del diritto europeo: giornata di studio per Alberto Trabucchi nel centenario della nascita* (Padua, Cedam, 2007) 173.

[130] Rossi (n 32)135–136.

[131] See Fritz (n 20) 112–114.

[132] See PAAA, B-20-200, Band 868, 49 ('Mr Rossi was very displeased with the behaviour of the Italian government in replacing Mr Catalano').

[133] Fritz (n 20) 112, fn. 125 (citing PAAA, B20- 200, Bd. 868, 30).

[134] Letter by Rossi to the other members of the ECJ of 13 July 1964, HAEU, CJUE-2635, 42 (Author's translation).

[135] Article 5 of the Protocol on the Statute of the EEC Court of Justice indeed provided: 'a Judge shall continue to hold office until his successor takes up his duties'.

[136] ibid.

[137] Letter by Donner to Hammes of 16 July 1964, HAEU, CJUE-2635, 40.

[138] Letter by Hammes to Donner of 18 July 1964, HAEU, CJUE-2635, 39.

Delvaux, Lecourt, Strauss, and Rossi, on the other: Donner would keep his position as President until the end of the term but would not seek re-election; in exchange, it would be established that the mandates of the judges end and begin as per the appointments made by the Governments of the Member States in accordance with the Treaties.[139] Rossi's *esprit de corps*, thus, ultimately took precedence over his friendship with Monaco, even though the latter had been instrumental in Rossi's appointment to the ECJ six years earlier.

8. EPILOGUE

Rossi left the ECJ on 7 October 1964, at the age of 75. He spent most of his final years in Rome and Cuneo, as well as at his summer house in Bernezzo,[140] but visited Luxembourg regularly, as remarked by Robert Lecourt in his eulogy.[141] He died in Rome on 6 February 1974,[142] at the age of 84, leaving a wife, a son, and four nephews.

The overall profile of Rossi emerging from this brief biography is consistent with the nickname 'Nestor' that Hammes gave him as he stepped down from the ECJ: that of elderly judge, who viewed the European Communities no differently than other Post-war international organisations. In his extra-curial statements, Rossi characterised the three Communities as '*international* unions'. He omitted any mention of their *federal* aspirations, understated their *supranational* and argued that the Community judges should 'interpret', but not 'supplement' the Community Treaties.[143]

For the first half of his mandate, Rossi was likely part of the *internationalist* majority of the ECJ, which did not want 'to break with the elements of international law and instead emphasise[d] the contractual nature of the EEC Treaty'.[144] However, the appointment of Trabucchi and Lecourt in 1962 changed the internal balance within the ECJ and paved the way for what has been called the 'European legal revolution'.[145]

Despite his *internationalist* views, Rossi embraced that *supranationalist* turn, by providing a legal argument (and likely one of the votes) in favour

[139] Letter by Donner to Hammes of 20 July 1964, HAEU, CJUE-2635, 23 (proposing the compromise) and Letter by Hammes to Donner of 21 July 1964, CJUE-2635, 22 (accepting the compromise).

[140] Detail provided by Elena Rossi Arnaud.

[141] Eulogy for Rossi by Lecourt, 12 February 1974, 4 HAEU, CJUE-2558, 9 (mentioning that, after leaving the ECJ, Rossi would return to Luxembourg several times each year).

[142] Municipality of Rome, Registry of the Death Certificates, 1974, I, 110.

[143] Rossi (n 32) 130–153.

[144] M Rasmussen, 'The Origins of a Legal Revolution' (2008) 14 *Journal of European Integration History* 77, 94.

[145] *See* M Rasmussen, 'From Costa v ENEL to the Treaties of Rome: A Brief History of a Legal Revolution', in M Poiares Maduro and L Azoulai (eds.), *The Past and Future of EU Law* (Oxford, Hart, 2010), 69–85.

of the direct effect of Community law in *Van Gend en Loos*,[146] and by joining the overwhelming majority in favour of primacy of Community law in *Costa v. ENEL*.[147] By emphasising the 'spirit' of the EEC Treaty, those judgments broke away from the traditional canons of treaty interpretation, ushering the rise of a 'new legal order' distinct from international law.[148]

Yet, in parallel with this 'legal revolution', Rossi also played a part in the 'counter-revolution' on the standing of individual applicants, which took place in *Agricultural Associations* (1962), in *Plaumann* (1963), and in *Acciaierie Fonderie Ferriere di Modena* (1964). Those judgments marked an *internationalist* U-turn relative to the ECJ's liberal approach to individual standing of its early judgments and brought the interpretation of Article 173(2) EEC and Article 33(2) ECSC back in line with the 'intentions of the authors' of the Community Treaties.[149]

Those two developments can be regarded, at least to some extent, as interdependent. Restricting the access of individuals to actions for annulment may have contributed to the success of the preliminary ruling procedure: the ECJ repeatedly referred to the latter as an alternative to the former to ensure the judicial protection of individuals.[150] Crucially, the ECJ's *internationalist* U-turn on individual standing may have facilitated the acceptance of the ECJ's *supranationalist* turn on the domestic effects of Community law, insofar as it showed the Member States' governments that they could still, as 'Masters of the Treaties', prompt the ECJ to reconsider the judgments they found unacceptable.[151]

[146] See Rasmussen (n 126) 389, fn 84; Trabucchi (n 129) 173.

[147] See P Gori, 'La "storia" della causa', in B Nascimbene (ed.), *Costa c ENEL: Corte costituzionale e Corte di giustizia a confronto, cinquant'anni dopo* (Milan, Giuffrè, 2015) 89 (noting that even the judges who had remained in the minority in *Van Gend en Loos* had come to terms with the implications of that ruling by the time of the *deliberé* of *Costa v. ENEL*, which was decided without heated discussions).

[148] *See* E Stein, 'Toward Supremacy of Treaty-Constitution by Judicial Fiat: On the Margin of the Costa Case' (1965) 63 *Michigan Law Review* 491, 513; *but see* B de Witte, 'EU Law: Is It International Law?' in C Barnard and S Peers (eds), European Union Law (Oxford, Oxford University Press, 2014) ch 7, 187.

[149] See, eg, G D'Agnone, *L'interpretazione soggettiva nella giurisprudenza della Corte di giustizia dell'Unione europea* (Turin, Giappichelli, 2020); S Lattanzi, *I "travaux préparatoires" del diritto dell'Unione Europea: tassonomia, ruolo e funzioni* (Padua, CEDAM, 2022).

[150] See, eg, Case 294/83, *Parti écologiste "Les Verts" v Parliament*, ECLI:EU:C:1986:166 [1986], para 23; Case C-50/00 P, *Unión de Pequeños Agricultores v Council*, ECLI:EU:C:2002:462 [2002], para 40; Case C-583/11 P, *Inuit Tapiriit Kanatami and Others v Parliament and Council*, ECLI:EU:C:2013:625 [2013], para 93. See also R Mastroianni and A Pezza, 'Striking the Right Balance: Limits on the Right to Bring an Action Under Article 263(4) of the Treaty on the Functioning of the European Union' (2015) 30(4) *American University International Law Review* 770–780.

[151] On the reasons underlying the national governments' acquiescence to the 'legal revolution', see K Alter, *Establishing Supremacy: The Making of an International Rule of Law in Europe* (Oxford, Oxford University Press, 2003) 182–208. On the legal implications of that acquiescence, see A Arena, 'The Twin Doctrines of Primacy and Pre-emption', in R Schütze and T Tridimas (eds), *Oxford Principles of European Union Law* (Oxford, Oxford University Press, 2018) 310–311.

In conclusion, Rossi's biography stands as a testament to the intriguing complexity of the European integration process, which eludes incremental or linear narratives[152] as well as simplistic dichotomies between *internationalists* and *supranationalists.*[153] Rather, that process is shaped by the practical solutions that ideological allies and adversaries alike have devised to its periodical crises.[154] The study of those solutions still remains, as Rossi put it in 1962, the best tool to understand the *raison d'être* of European integration.[155]

[152] See B Davies and FG Nicola, 'Introduction to EU Law Stories', in Nicola and Davies (n 95) 3.

[153] For instance, the 'legal revolution' on the domestic effects of Community law and the 'counter-revolution' on the standing of individual applicants were supported not only by Rossi, but also by his 'ideological rival' Catalano.

[154] See J Monnet, *Mémoires* (Paris, Fayard, 1976) 488.

[155] See Rossi (n 49) 650.

Part I

B) Second Generation (1960s–70s)

5

Alberto Trabucchi: The Defender of the European Citizens' Rights and the Van Gend & Loos *Ruling of the Court of Justice*

EZIO PERILLO

1. TRABUCCHI'S EDUCATIONAL AND PROFESSIONAL BACKGROUND

ALBERTO TRABUCCHI'S VERY long professional career, which spanned more than fifty years during the last century, has covered several scientific legal fields, including philosophy of law, Roman, civil, agricultural, comparative-private law and European law. He was born in Verona on 26 July 1907, from Marco Trabucchi a lawyer and Maria Zamboni, sister of the philosopher Giuseppe Zamboni. He died in Padua 18 April 1998. Trabucchi was married to Fernanda Sparavieri and they had five children who grew up in Illasi where Trabucchi was the mayor for over forty years.

In 1928 he presented his dissertation for his law degree in civil procedural law on the '*role of the parties in collective contracts*' under the supervision of Francesco Carnelutti, one of the most eminent Italian civil law professors of all time who collaborated to the drafting of the 1940 Italian Civil Procedure Code. At the age of twenty-two Trabucchi became lecturer in philosophy of law and was subsequently confirmed as assistant professor in civil law at twenty-eight.[1] From 1941 to 1982 he uninterruptedly held a full professorship in civil law, first at Ca' Foscari University in Venice (1941–1942) and then at the prestigious, historical Faculty of Law of Padua University. From 1945, he was Director of the Institute of Private Law of the same Faculty where, for some years, he also taught comparative private law. In 1954–55, the Ca' Foscari students had the advantage of attending his lectures on Roman and agricultural

[1] His studies in philosophy of law explain, in particular, his constant interest in the general principles of law and in its philosophical foundations, which also proved to be decisive in his judicial activity, starting specifically with the *Van Gend & Loos* judgment and its 'New European philosophy' (see below, section 2).

law. In 1955 he co-founded the well-known *Rivista di Diritto Civile*, which he directed until his death.

He published several books and hundreds of scientific articles in various fields of civil law, in particular on the general principles of law, contracts, civil liability and family law. In the field of Community law, before his appointment as judge, he published the *Code des Communautées Européennes* with Giulio Pasetti (Milan, Giuffrè, 1961), and then, while in office, *Il Commentario al Trattato CEE* (Milan, Giuffrè, 1965) and *Il Commentario al Trattato CECA* (Milan, Giuffrè, 1970), both edited together with Riccardo Monaco and Rolando Quadri. Among his articles on this subject, I will limit myself to mentioning the following ones, all available in the volume published in honour of Alberto Trabucchi (*Cinquant'anni nell'esperienza giuridica. Scritti di Alberto Trabucchi raccolti e ordinati da Giorgio Cian e Renato Pescara* (Padova, CEDAM, 1988): 'Un nuovo diritto' (originally published in 1963); 'Per una visione sistematica del Diritto Comunitario' (originally published in 1967); 'L'Europa e l'Unità del diritto' (originally published in 1975); 'Sviluppo della giurisprudenza e suo significato nella disciplina comunitaria della concorrenza' (originally published in 1975); and 'Significato e valore del principio di legalità nel moderno diritto civile' (originally published in 1975). During his more than forty years as law professor he also performed, without leaving his university chair for even a moment, a wide range of professional legal activities. He was attorney-at-law before the Italian Constitutional Court (ICC) and the *Suprema Corte di Cassazione*, as well as a renowned legal counsel in the whole peninsula. Last, but not least, Trabucchi served as judge (1962–1972) and Advocate General (1973–1976) at the Court of Justice of the European Communities (CJEC, now CJEU). In the history of this salient, European jurisdiction based in Luxembourg, he was the first member to exercise these two different functions, and was the first Italian jurist to be appointed as Advocate General.

This concise outline is by no means sufficient to describe professor Trabucchi's outstanding personality and all his impressive, professional achievements.[2] However, I dare to say that, in his eclectic professional life, there are two specific accomplishments he was particularly proud of: first of all, his *Istituzioni di diritto civile*, one of the most authoritative, Italian legal handbooks which, in 2021, broke a record, in the Italian legal manuals ranking, reaching fifty editions, nearly one edition per year and a half, since its first publication in 1943. Generations of Italian judges, lawyers and jurists have studied on this inimitable law-book, and today's students in law continue to do so. It is a volume that each of them, after the law-degree, proudly keeps at hand, on the shelves of their own personal library.

The second accomplishment was his pivotal role in the adoption of the *Van Gend & Loos* (1963) and *Costa/Enel* (1964) judgments during his tenure at the ECJ.

[2] For a broader historical description of his legal profile, see '*Alberto Trabucchi*' Treccani, *Dizionario Bibliografico Degli Italiani* Vol. 96 (2019) and AA.VV., *La formazione del diritto europeo: giornata di studio per Alberto Trabucchi nel centenario della nascita* (Padua, Cedam, 2007).

These two judgments are today famous worldwide because they constitute the pillars of the so-called *acquis communautaire*: the set of principles, rules and jurisprudence of Community law that, since the first European enlargement in 1972,[3] every Member State had to accept and respect in order to become a member of the Community. This is still the case for states wishing to attain membership in the European Union today (see section 5 below).

To gain better insight into professor Trabucchi's specific European portrait, this chapter will therefore be structured as follows: in section 2, I will sketch out the most important features of the *Van Gend & Loos* ruling (which celebrates its 60th anniversary at the time of writing). In section 3, I will outline the legal and political context of this judgment, whereas section 4 will be focused on judge Trabucchi's crucial internal note to his European Court fellows, a note that changed the destiny of this ruling. In the final sections 5, 6 and 7, I will illustrate Trabucchi's achievements at the Court of Justice in Luxembourg and in the years following his tenure as a judge and Advocate General.

2. THE 'NEW' EUROPEAN ECONOMIC COMMUNITY (EEC) LEGAL ORDER AND THE REAL IMPACT OF *VAN GEND & LOOS* ON EU PRIMARY LAW

Much has been written about *Van Gend & Loos* preliminary ruling case – or the *Tariefcommissie* case, as Trabucchi used to call it, quoting the name of the referring Dutch jurisdiction – by jurists, historians and political scientists from various cultures and schools. *Van Gend & Loos* has sparked interest not only among European scholars, but also on the other side of the Atlantic, starting with the first, academic pioneers in this field, Professors Eric Stein and, later on, Joseph H H Weiler, as well as several of their respective alumni.[4]

Some of them consider *Van Gend & Loos* (VGL) a political judgment; others call it 'revolutionary' because it established a 'constitutional autonomous' legal system, almost proto-federal.[5] There are still others who think that VGL has substantially been the European Commission's judicial spin-off, in the sense that the Court of Justice, in drafting the most important grounds of this ruling,

[3] The initial European Communities were composed of six Member States, Belgium, Netherlands, Luxembourg (Benelux), Germany, France and Italy. United Kingdom, Denmark and Ireland were the first European States to join the European Communities on January 1, 1973.

[4] E Stein, 'Lawyers, judges and the Making of a Transnational Constitution' (1981) 75 *Am. J. of Int'l L.* 1–27; JHH Weiler, 'The Transformation of Europe' (1991) 100 *The Yale L.J.* 2403; K Alter, *Establishing the Supremacy of European law: The Making of an International Rule of Law in Europe* (Oxford, Oxford University Press, 2001); D Halberstam, 'It's the autonomy stupid!' A Modest Defense of Opinion 2/13 on EU Accession to the ECHR, and the Way Forward' (2015) *University of Michigan Public Law and Legal Theory Research Paper Series*, Paper No. 432, February 2015.

[5] M Rasmussen, 'Revolutionizing European Law: A History of the Van Gend en Loos Judgment' (2014) 12 *Int'l J. of Const. L.* 136; F Bignami, 'Rethinking the Legal Foundation of the European Constitutional Order: The Lessons of the New Historical Research' (2013) 28 *Am. U. Int'l L. Rev. 1311*.

practically adopted all the arguments put forward by the Commission's Legal Service.[6]

According to Weiler, VGL essentially 'constituted' this new legal order, though without being 'the work of an Activist Court'.[7] Its reasoning was 'impeccable' he stated, its 'impact was profound and noble', but ultimately '*Van Gend & Loos* and its progeny also accentuate the enduring legitimacy crisis of the Union', that is, its democratic deficit.

More recently, Morten Rasmussen has considered that 'the new legal history of the EU tells a different story [from the one] promoted [since the 1960s,] by the European institutions and most European law scholars'. This new trend argues that 'an [EU] constitutional legal order with a powerful CJEU built on a claim of constitutional autonomy [...] has never been accepted nor codified by the Member States'.[8]

I think Judge Trabucchi would have been of a different opinion from Weiler and Rasmussen's statements. First of all, in his view, the Messina Conference (June 1955) and the subsequent Treaty of the European Economic Community (EEC, Rome, March 1957) clearly opted for a European legal perspective that was to be different from the 'federal or confederal' one described in the Treaty on the European Defense Community (EDC), the one that, unexpectedly, the French Parliament rejected in August 1954, only few months after its signature.[9]

The main objective of the post-Messina Conference was therefore limited to strengthening the potentialities of the current European Coal and Steel Community Treaty (ECSC), which had already produced very positive economic results, to move, through the adoption of a second Treaty, towards a kind of 'enhanced' European Community. A new system with a wider range of economic competences and composed not only of States and intergovernmental institutions but also of citizens (ie, intra-community workers or economic operators), with each having its own legal and autonomous prerogatives.

In institutional terms, this was to be a European Community in permanent progress, ie, without a 50-year deadline as in the case of the ECSC Treaty: the

[6] See J Bailleux, 'Michel Gaudet a law entrepreneur: the role of the legal service of the European executives in the invention of EC Law' (2013) 50(2) *Common Market Law Review* 359–367; A Boerger and M Rasmussen, 'The Making of European Law: Exploring the Life and Work of Michel Gaudet' (2017) 57(1) *The American Journal of Legal History* 51–82.

[7] See, JHH Weiler, 'Revisiting Van Gend & Loos: Subjectifying and Objectifying the Individual', in *The 50th Anniversary of the Judgement in Van Gend & Loos, Conference Proceedings* (Luxembourg, 2013), available at curia.europa.eu/jcms/upload/docs/application/pdf/2013-12/qd30136442ac_002.pdf. A thesis that is, I dare to say, slightly over the top. In my personal opinion, the VGL recognition of the citizens' direct effect prerogative (see section 3 below), rather than accentuating the 'democratic' deficit of the Communities, promptly prevented the onset of a 'judicial' deficit, ie, the lack of any direct legal action that single market-operators could claim in defence of their European rights. An even more worrying deficit – I must say – as it would have been contrary to the rule of law principle.

[8] M Rasmussen '*A More Complex Union*' (*Verfassungsblog*, 4 November 2021), available at https://verfassungsblog.de/a-more-complex-union/.

[9] In particular, according to Art. 38 of this Treaty, the EDC Parliamentary Assembly was to meet as a constituent assembly to draft a 'federal or confederal constitution [...] based on the principle of separation of powers and entailing, in particular, a bicameral representative system'.

first institutional, legal 'construction'[10] towards 'an ever-closer union among the peoples of Europe'.[11]

Consequently, according to Trabucchi, the EEC Treaty was to be interpreted with a view to the future, not only in the light of its new economic objectives but also in accordance with the fundamental principle of the rule of law, common to all the six Member States and governing the functioning of the new system as a whole.

Finally, the governments of the Member States gave no name or legal qualification to this future European construction precisely to avoid the risk of another political debacle at the national parliamentary level, like the one triggered by the EDC Treaty and its Art. 38.

So, in an attempt to interpret Trabucchi's thoughts, within the framework of this new Messina-Rome European philosophy, and to make a sharp distinction between these different, academic interpretations of VGL's state of reasoning, I would say that constitutionality – even accepting, for the sake of argument, this questionable addendum – is all about the relationships between Member States and the Community's institutional prerogatives, essentially: primacy or non-primacy of the Community law.

On the other hand, direct effect is only about citizens, their European rights prevailing over a contrary, domestic law provision, and the judicial protection they are entitled to receive at national level.

That is why the Court of Justice, relying only on this second, innovative perspective, clearly highlighted in VGL that 'the vigilance of individuals concerned to protect their rights amounts to an effective supervision [that is a direct, national legal protection] in addition to the supervision entrusted [at the Community level] by … the diligence of the Commission and of the Member States'.

These phrases, as better detailed in section 4 below, were most likely written by Judge Trabucchi himself.[12]

Fifteen years later, giving his farewell speech when leaving the Court of Justice, Trabucchi made a prudent but clear reference to the VGL ruling, saying the following: 'What are we to think? That this new Community law has been created, or has been found and discovered? I don't know, or I don't want to say it. It is certain that at this stage the contribution of the civil perspective was essential'.[13]

And here it comes, at last, the VGL 'civil' direct effect perspective! A perspective which was neither constitutional nor proto-federal and even less

[10] The first two paragraphs of the so-called Declaration of the Messina Conference were so worded: 'the moment has come to go a further step towards the construction of Europe [that is …] towards the setting up of a united Europe through the development of common institutions, the gradual merging of national economies, the creation of a common market, and the gradual harmonisation of some of their social policies'.

[11] See, Consolidated Version of the Treaty Establishing the European Community [1957], preamble. See also the first VGL substantial ground.

[12] For instance, 'the vigilance of individuals' was a typical expression frequently used by professor Trabucchi with his civil law students, an aphorism directly taken up from the Roman law doctrine, stating precisely that: '*vigilantibus non dormientibus jura succurrunt*' (law helps those who look after their rights and not those who sleep).

[13] Formal Hearings of the Court of Justice, 1976, 31.

anti-democratic. It was, instead, the acknowledgement of 'the new EEC legal order dimension', as expressly requested by the European leaders.

Finally, putting aside the *querelle* of whether VGL was a political, revolutionary or some other kind of ruling, let's delve into a more concrete question: what is the real impact that this judgment ultimately has had on the primary EC-EU law in force today?

If we jump straight from 1963 (VGL) to 2009, the year the Lisbon Treaty entered into force with all its *acquis communautaire* included (see section 4 below), I would venture to say that the VGL's phrases – just mentioned above – produced the most significant shift that a judgment of the Court of Justice has ever had, not only on European primary law but also on the legal orders of the Member States.

Through the new Article 19 TEU, which frames the competences of the Court of Justice in general terms, the masters of the Lisbon Treaty introduced a new fundamental obligation: 'Member States shall provide remedies sufficient to ensure effective legal protection in the fields covered by Union law'. Needless to say, the 'vigilance of individuals', ie, their VGL 'effective supervision' on the compatibility of internal, State rules versus their Community law rights, coupled with an 'effective legal protection' which the Member States must provide through Article 19 TEU, are the core scope of this specific European legal philosophy and the two main mechanisms for monitoring, at the national level, the proper functioning of the new construction.

But that's not all. From an institutional point of view, VGL also marks the very day on which the Court of Justice, a jurisdiction predominantly perceived, at that time, as an international, administrative law Court, finally assumed its true, legal identity as judge of the 'institutional balance' of the entire system, as is the case of any other national Supreme Court.[14]

Its task: to ensure that the different, legal prerogatives at stake in this new legal order, those of the institutions, of the Member States and, last but not least, of their citizens, be fully respected.

Nothing more, at this stage of the European process, and nothing less either.[15]

But, isn't this, again, a kind of 'constitutional' jurisdiction, someone could ask? Not really. Unfortunately, since the EDC Treaty French' collapse in August 1954 and even more so after the debacle of the European Constitution Treaty in 2005, we must acknowledge that this noble word has become a kind of 'forbidden', if not 'damned', legal term in connection to European integration.

In any case, after VGL the Court of Justice did not become, *motu proprio*, a constitutional jurisdiction. Nor has the Court remained nameless. The Lisbon Treaty has made it clear, for the first time in the history of the EU Treaties, that the Court of Justice is the Court 'of the European Union'.[16] That is, the only jurisdiction in this integrated legal order that has been entitled, by the

[14] See *Parliament v Council* Case C-70/88 ECLI:EU:C:1990: 217 [1990] para 23.

[15] See, G Tesauro, 'Commento all'articolo 19 TEU', in A Tizzano (eds), *Trattati dell'Unione Europea* (Milan, Giuffré, 2014) 204–210.

[16] Consolidated Version of the Treaty on European Union [2008] OJ C115/13, Art. 13.

Masters of the Treaties, to exercise, autonomously, its exclusive, jurisdictional prerogatives (particularly that which consists, as is the case for all national Constitutional Courts, in reviewing the legality of EU 'legislative acts': see the new Art. 263 TFEU) and having therefore, when necessary, the last word to say on these specific matters, more or less like the American Supreme Court.

Consequently, not a constitutional Court without a Constitution, but the EU institutional Court within an EU autonomous legal order.[17]

But how was it possible, for the Judges adjudicating the VGL case to discover this new European philosophy? This question will be examined in more detail below.

3. THE TWO CONCEPTS OF DIRECT EFFECT AND THE VOTE OF THE EUROPEAN JUDGES IN VGL

First of all, to better grasp the 'civil logic' of Trabucchi's VGL ruling, it could be useful to distinguish the notion of objective direct effect from that of subjective direct effect.

The objective direct effect refers to the characteristic of the particular Community rule by which a precise and unconditional obligation is established upon the Member States that they must therefore 'immediately' fulfill, *erga omnes*, without adopting any internal, implementing act whatsoever.

The subjective direct effect, on the other hand, indicates the specific Community prerogative enjoyed by every single European *justiciable*: the *contro-partita*, in Trabucchi's Italian version of VGL, ie, the return of the Member State's EC duty.

This is the right to bring, before a national judge, a legal action against any kind of internal, binding measure – legislative, judicial or administrative – that arbitrarily breaches a direct, objective European obligation. An obligation which is, per se, neither at the disposal of the Member States nor the EU institutions.

Indeed, 'in the fields covered by Union law',[18] the beginning of the Member State or EU institutions' *arbitrium* coincides with the end of the rule of law of the European Union that protects all persons and entities belonging to this system.[19]

Secondly, from the point of view of the judicial decision-making process inside the Court of Justice, VGL was a judgment adopted by a full-fledged panel of seven judges, initially split into two opposing fronts: three against

[17] On the autonomous character of this legal order, identified already at the time of VGL, see Judge Trabucchi *note en délibéré* (section 4 below) and VGL, according to which 'independently of the legislation of Member States, Community law [in the French version: '*le droit communautaire, indépendant* [ie, autonomous] *de la législation des États membres*], [...] imposes obligations in a clearly defined way upon individuals as well as upon the Member States and upon the institutions of the Community'.

[18] Art. 19 TUE.

[19] On the rule of law as EU fundamental principle, see, E Perillo, 'Les 70 ans de la Cour de justice au service des citoyens de l'Union' (2022) 47 *La Semaine Juridique* 2238; see, also, E Perillo 'Il rispetto dello 'Stato di diritto europeo' alla luce delle sentenze Ungheria e Polonia sulla clausola di condizionalità finanziaria. Quali prospettive?' (BlogDUE, 16 March 2022), available at www.aisdue.eu/en/ezio-perillo/.

(let me call them the 'senators' of the Chamber): André Donner, the President from The Netherlands; Leon Hammes, the Judge-Rapporteur from Luxembourg; and Otto Riese, the German Judge; and three in favour: Trabucchi and Lecourt, from France – who were the last entries at the Court – as well as Rino Rossi, the other Italian Judge.[20]

Now, when within a tiny supreme court, judges are confronted in a face-to-face debate between two alternative systemic solutions (Community law primacy or non-primacy), the term 'prudential' is the right watchword to avoid, as much as possible, any further, acrimonious internal ruptures.

It was the *note en délibéré* that Judge Trabucchi sent to his colleagues after the Court's first deliberating meeting (the first 'tentative vote', in the U.S. Supreme Court legal language) that finally changed the course of action of *Van Gend & Loos*. A draft of this note, written in Italian by Judge Trabucchi himself, was disclosed, many years later, by his *référendaire*, Professor Paolo Gori, who officially announced this discovery at the 50th VGL anniversary Conference organised by the Court of Justice.[21]

4. THE *NOTE EN DÉLIBÉRÉ* OF JUDGE TRABUCCHI

Here below is an English summary of this crucial note, the only document which, in the entire history of the Court of Justice, has indirectly overcome the secrecy of its deliberations:

> After our first meeting in the chamber, I kept thinking about the solution, I would say prudential, towards which the Court seems to be oriented, in the sense that [...] the main outcome would be to maintain the scope and the effects of the Treaties of Rome within the scheme of a common international treaty. [However, the question raised by the Dutch Court is] not whether Article 12 of the Treaty [imposing to the Members States the obligation of not increasing custom duties] is of immediate application, but if it gives rise to a right for citizens vis-à-vis their State and more precisely against the legislative activity of their own State. [Well,] if we do not want to base our solution on something new, [that is] on a new right of citizens [which these nationals can directly claim before their judges] even against their own legislating State, it appears difficult to me not to share the solution proposed by the Advocate General [and also proposed in large part by the Judge-Rapporteur]. It would be even more difficult, in my opinion, to argue, in a judgment, in favour

[20] Four in favour and three against is indeed the score usually retained by the historians (see especially, M Rasmussen, 'Revolutionizing European law: A history of Van Gend en Loos judgement' (2014) 12 *The International Journal of Constitutional Law* 136, 154). Personally, I wouldn't be so sure. It is, for example, hard to believe that President Donner did decide, at the end of the deliberations, to remain in the minority's corner knowing the importance of this verdict, both for 'his' Court of Justice and for the Community's citizens. Moreover, only a few months after the judgment, he published an important article, which emphasised '*the cardinal importance* [of this judgment] *for the entire operation of the EEC Treaty*' (A Donner, 'National law and the Case law of the Court of Justice of the European Communities' (1963) 1 *Common Market Law Review* 8, 13). As far as I know, President Donner was not the kind of judge who could change his mind so quickly.

[21] See footnote n 7 above.

> of accepting a new concept of common international law, no longer based on horizontal [intergovernmental or institutional] coordination, but covering principles that, in cases of self-executing treaties, individuals could also invoke against various manifestations of sovereignty of their own State. [Consequently,] for a direct application of the rule of the Treaty, it is necessary to find, in addition to the States subject to the obligation referred to in Article 12, the recipients of the corresponding right. [Now, as we know,] the subjects of law in the classical system [ie, the individuals] cannot be protected directly against legislative acts of their own State. [Ultimately,] only if an autonomous Community's law that goes beyond the traditional system of the uncontrolled autonomy of States vis-à-vis their citizens will be acknowledged, would the individual be able to receive direct protection against her/his own State, because her/his right, which corresponds to the duty of others [ie, of the Member States], will not find its only guarantees of recognition and protection in the State to which the individual belongs.[22]

Tactically speaking, this was a very calibrated message.

In fact, instead of continuing to hammer on the European Commission's implicit primacy principle perspective and its corollaries (a thesis substantially killed by the antagonistic arguments put forwards by the governments and the Advocate General), Trabucchi's civil law line, safeguarding the citizen's rights (and not those of the States, as sovereign, internal legislators), was the one that ultimately bypassed that primacy deadlock and steered the college towards the recognition of the autonomous, direct effect principle.

In other words, if for Michel Gaudet (the Commission Legal Service's General Director) the direct effect was the immediate consequence of the primacy principle implicit in the EC system (ie, a top-down perspective between two different, legal orders),[23] for Alberto Trabucchi, the direct effect was the immediate EU citizen prerogative (ie, a bottom-up perspective of the individual European rights over their own State's binding decisions of any kind) granting the economic operators in the European marketplace the right to react against any arbitrary national violation of an unconditional Community duty, so preserving also the effective functioning of the common market.[24]

[22] The English version – perhaps the first one so far available – is mine, as are the words between the square brackets that I have added so to preserve, as much as possible, the line of argument of Judge Trabucchi's proposal. For the original Italian version, see AA.VV., *La formazione del diritto europeo: giornata di studio per Alberto Trabucchi nel centenario della nascita* (n 2).

[23] See, the authors cited in footnote n 6 above.

[24] It is quite evident, already from the first words of Judge Trabucchi's note, that the Commission's 'primacy plus direct effect theory' did not convince any of the seven judges of the Court of Justice. And, as it can be seen from his own speech given before the Court of Justice when leaving this institution (see below section 5), Lecourt himself, who before the first tentative vote in the chamber was perhaps the judge closest to the Commission's arguments, finally aligned himself along Trabucchi's thesis. Moreover, when one year later the Costa/Enel case arrived before the Court of Justice, the Commission's contribution to the primacy principle's recognition was practically non-existent, its Legal Service having considered that the Milan court's preliminary question was inadmissible. The new EU legal history's argument that the Commission's Legal Service played a decisive role in dealing with these two cases appears therefore rather questionable. Instead, eight years later, in 1972, the Commission would be absolutely instrumental in officially codifying these two principles within the framework of the *acquis communautaire* clause (see below section 5).

5. PRESIDENT LECOURT'S TRIBUTE TO JUDGE TRABUCCHI AND THE MEMBER STATES' RECOGNITION OF THE VGL DIRECT EFFECT PRINCIPLE

On the day they together left the Court of Justice (6 October 1976), the two protagonists of the VGL and Costa/Enel cases, Trabucchi and Robert Lecourt (then President of the Court), revealed to the public, with tactful but clearly allusive and significant hints, their decisive involvement in the drafting and outcome of these two seminal judgments.

Let me quote, in particular, some words of the farewell speech President Lecourt addressed to his colleague Trabucchi, on the role he had in the VGL and Costa/Enel judgments.

> The person who arrived amongst us in 1962 – [he said during the abovementioned sitting of the Court of Justice, a solemn hearing crowded by the highest local authorities as well as ambassadors, eminent law professors and lawyers who came to Luxembourg from different European capitals to greet the departure of these two giants of the Court of Justice] – was a confirmed jurist, rich in experience and of well-deserved renown. What can I say about the judge that he was and the important role he played in giving direction to the case-law for which the Court is now famous? The secrecy of the deliberations prevents me from speaking about this at length. As far as I can go, let me say, my dear colleague, that your sense of the right word, which I dare say stems from your thorough knowledge of Roman law, has been the basis – and has been so since your first year here [ie, the year of VGL and Costa/Enel] – of the clarity and the precision of some of the most famous grounds for our judgments, which have become the classic "selected passages" of Community law. Even at the Court, the judge has never forgotten his vocation as a teacher. Here too you have remained the vigilant guardian of civil law, the '*juris civilis custos*' as Cicero put it.[25]

Despite the caution of these words, the reference to the central role played by Judge Trabucchi in giving direction to these two judgments and drafting their key reasoning's parts is undeniable.

It is also clear from President Lecourt's elegant words that these two judgments did not deviate from the legal framework of the Treaty – as Rasmussen argues – nor did they change the letter of these texts either. On the contrary, addressing his fellow judges during the same formal hearing, President Lecourt pointed out that with these two judgments 'you have identified from the treaties – and I underlined 'identified' as opposed to 'created' – the essential characteristics of what has become the [Community's] uniform law. A single law but for what purpose?', President Lecourt then asked himself. And his answer was: 'to protect the citizens and to preserve their community of destiny'.[26]

After this authentic interpretation of the main VGL and Costa/Enel principles given by the two 'tenors' leaving the Court of Justice on the same day, the academic views expressed until then on the various ins and outs of these

[25] Formal Hearings of the Court of Justice, 1976, 29.
[26] ibid., 50.

two rulings were therefore very politely set aside. And the same can be said of other, divergent views expressed more recently by the historians.[27]

Contrary to 'the new legal history of the EU' advocated by Rasmussen,[28] it must be said that no Member State has ever challenged the doctrines of these judgments or refused to codify them in the text of the Treaties. Indeed, these two judgments form the basis of the so-called *acquis communautaire* which constitutes – as I said above – *le bloc de legalité de la Communauté*, the overall Community's legal arsenal bringing together all the principles, the primary and secondary legal rules and the case-law established by the competent EU institutions. Well, this *acquis* has been officially accepted by the founding EC Member States since the first European enlargement, when three new European States joined the European Communities in 1972.

In its preliminary EC accession opinion (a mandatory legal text for the signature of any Accession Treaty) the Commission introduced, for the first time among the provisions of primary Community law, a clause that later became standard in all subsequent accession treaties (the *acquis communautaire* clause) that still exists today, and that stipulated the following:

> Whereas it is an essential feature of the legal system set up by the Treaties establishing the Communities that certain of their provisions and certain acts of the Community institutions are directly applicable, that Community law takes precedence over any national provisions conflicting with it, and that procedures exist for ensuring the uniform interpretation of that law; and whereas accession to the Communities entails recognition of the binding force of these rules, the observance of which is indispensable to ensure the effectiveness and unity of Community law.[29]

After the 1972 Treaty Accession, the *acquis* has been officially enshrined, first of all, in the Maastricht Treaty (1992)[30] and, later on, in the so-called 1993 Copenhagen criteria which, after the Lisbon Treaty, have been codified in Article 49 TEU, governing the EU's accession procedure. Finally, Article 20 TEU sets out, vis-à-vis the candidate European States, that the legal texts adopted by the Member States concerned through an enhanced cooperation procedure 'shall not be regarded as part of the *acquis*', thus confirming the binding nature of the *acquis* not only vis-à-vis the Member States involved in an enhanced cooperation but also in general, in the entire EU legal order.

In 1972, Trabucchi and Lecourt were still at the Court of Justice and, probably, they will have been quite satisfied with the excellent, institutional work realised in close cooperation between the Court of Justice (with the VGL and Costa/Enel rulings), the European Commission (with its crucial *acquis communautaire*

[27] See Section 2 above.

[28] See footnote n 8 above.

[29] See, EC Commission Opinion 19 January 1972, Treaty of Accession of Denmark, Ireland and the United Kingdom (1972), OJ L 73 27/3/1973, 3.

[30] Art. B, 5th indent, of the Maastricht Treaty, so provided: 'The Union shall set itself the following objectives: […] to maintain in full the *acquis communautaire* and build on it with a view to […] ensuring the effectiveness of the mechanisms and the institutions of the Community'.

clause) and the Member States (which ratified the United Kingdom, Denmark and Ireland Accession Treaty, with this new clause included).

Certainly, some national governments (as well as some supreme courts) have, particularly in recent years, not respected the rules contained in this legal heritage, by invoking the EU's duty to respect their own national identity.[31] This does not mean, however, that the Community legal arsenal has not been recognised as a whole. On the contrary, it could even be said that, hoisting the *acquis communautaire* flag at the mainmast of the first Accession Treaty, the governments of the Member States and the European Commission expressed their gratitude to the Court of Justice for having identified these two fundamental principles that the Member States themselves would otherwise probably not have been able to establish by a unanimous Treaty vote.

6. PROFESSOR TRABUCCHI AT THE COURT OF JUSTICE

When Trabucchi joined the Court of Justice, in March 1962, he didn't discover a completely new world, like most of the colleagues who arrived in Luxembourg before or after him.

On the contrary, he approached this new experience well suited for the job and with a clear European vision.[32]

In fact, in the five years prior to his appointment at the Court of Justice, from 1957 to 1961, professor Trabucchi acquired considerable experience in Community litigation as a lawyer for the ECSC High Authority in several cases brought by Italian coal and steel companies.

The importance of this experience did not lie, of course, in the controversial matters at issue, which essentially focused on the correct compliance with the European quota regime for scrap metal, but in his ability to assess and balance the rights and obligations at stake, between the supranational Community High Authority, having the power to directly regulate industrial activities, and the private undertakings concerned.[33]

[31] Consolidated Version of the Treaty on European Union [2008] OJ C115/13, Art 4.

[32] His appointment was due to the fact that his predecessor, Judge Nicola Catalano, had resigned in November 1961, 'for personal and family reasons', as he wrote in his letter to the President of the Court.

Perhaps, under the circumstances of that time, the addition of the word 'family' has something to do with it. Nevertheless, some historians argue that Catalano's resignation was actually due to a sort of conspiracy organised by the Italian government to force him to resign and consequently be replaced by Mr. Trabucchi (see especially, M Rasmussen, 'Agents of Constitutionalism, The Quest for a Constitutional Breakthrough in European Law, 1945–1964' in M M Payk and K C Priemel (eds), *Crafting the International Legal* Order (Oxford and New York, Oxford University Press, 2021) 273. These accusations against the Italian government are, however, supported by not even one concrete piece of evidence and are therefore, at this stage, definitely fanciful. Instead, it is well established that a few weeks before his decision to resign, on October 5, Judge Catalano had officially accepted his mandate's renewal for a six-year term, as decided by all the Member States, precisely on the Italian government's proposal.

[33] See, M Patrin, 'Meroni behind the scenes: uncovering the actors and context of a landmark judgment' (2021) 6(1) *European papers* 539–551.

In any case, during these five years as an attorney-at-law in Luxembourg, Trabucchi certainly became familiar, *affaire après affaire*, with the Court of Justice, its procedures, and its members. When he finally joined this jurisdiction as a judge, he was therefore warmly welcomed by the other members of the house almost as an 'old colleague'.[34]

In his welcome speech to Judge Trabucchi, André Donner, the then Dutch President of the Court of Justice, spoke as if he could already anticipate the positive outcome of his 'home-made' VGL case:

> [T]he person who is a thoroughbred lawyer and who, while being prepared to go beyond certain traditional conceptions, wants, above all, the law to be respected when applying the treaties of Paris and Rome, this hybrid semi-federal, semi-international regime, and the principles of a suitable and effective legal order to be safeguarded, has the best chances of finding himself in the right place in the more or less near future; he will therefore be able to work with satisfaction and success. The fact – dear colleague Trabucchi – that you have hitherto dealt with civil law, a discipline which is much less oriented towards this development than others, will undoubtedly give you the advantage of seeing things in perspective and will make it easier for you than for others to see cases in their true connections and in a larger legal context.'[35]

Now that we have Trabucchi's note and the VGL motivation in mind, I would say that this was indeed a prophetic, greeting message. Moreover, as I have already mentioned, President Lecourt confirmed, fifteen years later, the relevant professional qualifications of professor Trabucchi, as the first 'European' *juris civilis custos* at the Court of Justice.

Trabucchi and Lecourt arrived in Luxembourg just over a month apart, in March and May 1962, and they understood each other right away. Indeed, they had many similar traits in common: a deep European conviction, Christian Democratic political leanings, a great humanist culture and a strong personality.[36]

[34] Probably less well known, on his appointment at the Court of Justice, are the Council's minutes of the Conference of the Representatives of the Member States' Governments held in Brussels on 20 December 1961, in which the following has been recorded '*M. Segni* [the Italian Foreign Affairs Minister] *annonce à cet égard que le gouvernement italien présentera, dans un proche avenir, comme successeur de M. Catalano, M. Trabucchi, professeur de droit civil à l'Université de Padoue. En réponse à une question de M. Linthorst Homan ayant appelé l'attention sur les termes de la lettre du 15 décembre 1961 de M. Donner, Président de la Cour de justice, aux Présidents des Conseils, M. Segni précise que M. Trabucchi dispose de vastes connaissances dans le domaine du droit international*'. Translation: 'Mr. Segni [the Italian Foreign Affairs Minister] announced that the Italian Government would, in the near future, present as Mr. Catalano's successor Mr. Trabucchi, Professor of Civil Law at the Univeristy of Padua. In reply to a question from Mr. Linthorst Homan who had drawn attention to the terms of the letter of 15 December 1961 from Mr. Donner, President of the Court of Justice, to the Presidents of the Councils, Mr. Segni said that Mr. Trabucchi had extensive knowledge in the field of international law'. An answer, I would say, that speaks for itself, not only in French (See, Council document file CM 1/1961, archives of the European University Institute in Florence).

[35] Formal Hearings of the Court of Justice, 1962, 31.

[36] See W Phelan, *Great Judgments of the European Court of Justice* (Cambridge, Cambridge University Press, 2019); W Phelan, 'The Revolutionary Doctrines of European Law and the Legal Philosophy of Robert Lecourt' (2017) 28(3) *European Journal of International Law* 935.

To sketch a little difference between these two characters, Trabucchi was a committed pro-Europe civil law professor (that is why he upheld the EC citizen individual rights direct effect principle); Lecourt was instead a committed European federalist politician (and therefore more acquainted with the idea of an EC primacy law over the national one).

And, thanks to Trabucchi's *note en délibéré*, they identified in the Treaties, through these two 'queen' judgments, the real features of the new Community legal order.

It is true that, at the time of VGL, it was not easy to spot the real relationship between Community law and the citizens of this new legal order. Luckily enough, 'fate' asked a professor of civil law, and not a jurist of international law or a federalist, to look after this new legal system by guiding him towards what would become, with the subsequent official and unconditional consensus of Member States, the Europe of citizens.[37]

Thus, when, in January 1973, Trabucchi moved from his collegial seat of judge – a seat protected by the anonymity and the secret of the deliberations – to the public and individual pulpit of the Advocate General, he was the most experienced and authoritative Italian (and perhaps European) magistrate at the Court of Justice of that time. This made him able to guide this young jurisdiction towards new and fascinating European horizons.

Among the Opinions he delivered during this mandate, I would like to mention, in particular, the more 'civil-law' oriented ones, such as *Rewe Zentralfinanz*,[38] *Dassonville*,[39] *Centrafarm*[40] and, above all, *Defrenne*.[41]

7. CONCLUSION: TRABUCCHI'S POST-EUROPEAN PERIOD IN PADUA

Once he folded his vermilion toga of judge and Advocate General at the Court of Justice, professor Trabucchi gradually retired from the world of the Community law cenacles, bringing with him an unparalleled wealth of experiences and achievements, which is probably unmatched, so far, by any other member of

[37] In his article published only a few months after the VGL judgment (A Trabucchi, 'Un nuovo diritto' (1963) *Rivista di Diritto Civile* 229) he argued that, following the VGL judgment, the structure created by the Treaties would sooner or later open up 'an important path towards the recognition of a European citizenship, the ultimate consequence of the progressive fall of territorial barriers'. Almost thirty years later, the Maastricht Treaty (1992) officially introduced in this legal order the European citizenship. Furthermore, *l'Europe des citoyens* was also Judge Lecourt's indirect reply against *l'Europe des États*, the manifesto announced by Charles De Gaulle in his famous Press Conference on May 15, 1962, only a few months before the delivery, at the Court of Justice, of VGL's preliminary ruling.

[38] *Rewe Zentralfinanz v Landwirtschaftskammer Westphalen-Lippe* Case 39/73 ECLI:EU:C:1973: 98 [1973].

[39] *Procureur du Roi v Benoît and Gustave Dassonville* Case 8/74 ECLI:EU:C:1974:66 [1974].

[40] *Centrafarm BV and Others v Sterling Drug* Case 15/74 ECLI:EU:C:1974: 90 [1974].

[41] *Defrenne v Sabena* Case 43/75 ECLI:EU:C:1976: 39 [1976].

this jurisdiction. Civil law was then, once again, his main field of activity and interest.[42]

Trabucchi returned to Luxembourg from time to time, but only for personal reasons.

He retained, however, for quite a long time, a heartfelt nostalgia for the experiences he had at the Court of Justice as a lawyer, judge and Advocate General.

When I had the opportunity to visit him during those years, his first question to me was whether, despite the numerous accessions, the Court of Justice still had prestige in this enlarged Community and whether 'his' *Tariefcommissie* ruling was still the EU leading case.

And my answers were almost always reassuring.

If I were now to describe, concisely, the entire professional profile of Alberto Trabucchi, before and during his mandates at the Court of Justice, I would say – quoting moreover President Lecourt's words – that he has been, during these Community's roaring years, *the European juris civilis custos*, that is the defender of the individual rights of all the European citizens.

His role in, and intellectual contributions to VGL and Costa/Enel rulings tell us, therefore, a different story from the one advocated by 'the new legal history of the EU'.

Indeed, the story of these two judgments, as well as of the *acquis communautaire*, to which they gave birth, tells us that the European posterity should be grateful to Alberto Trabucchi for his *note en délibéré* and for his commitment in leading the majority of his colleagues involved in the *Van Gend & Loos* case towards this new, European, citizen legal order, which is the legacy this judgment has finally left for the benefit of all of us.[43]

[42] Nevertheless, he remained Director of the Centre for European Studies for several years, where he asked me to organize meetings and seminars with senior officials of the Communities, professors of Community law and also members of the Court of Justice for the benefit of the EU law students in Padua.

[43] Thanks also to the President of the Court of Justice who wisely authorised the disclosing of Judge Trabucchi's draft-note, thereby contributing to a better understanding of this landmark judgment (see, contra, Rasmussen (n 20) 163, regretting, in general terms, 'the lack of cooperation of the ECJ' with regard to access by historians to its judicial archives). Whether right or wrong, it is undisputed that as long as the authors of the Treaties will maintain the sacramental obligation provided by Art. 2 of the Court of Justice's Statute as well as a limited public access to the Court's administrative documents only (Art. 15 (3) 4th indent, TFEU), the internal working papers of the judges must remain protected by the secrecy of the deliberations and the CJEU's judicial documents not accessible to the public. By and large, the independence of the European judges and the autonomy of the European judicial function must be safeguarded, above all as a guarantee of the EU *justiciable* full trust in the European justice, a guarantee that takes precedence over the important work of the historians who, in my humble opinion as a jurist, do not have the monopoly of CJEU case-law's interpretation nor of the understanding of the dilemmas, successes and failures of its jurisprudence. The disclosure of Trabucchi's *note en délibéré* must therefore remain unique, being neither a dissenting nor a concurrent opinion but, unquestionably, the VGL 'winning note'.

6

Riccardo Monaco and the Doctrine of Supranationality in International Institutional Law

EDOARDO GREPPI

1. INTRODUCTION

THIS CHAPTER ENGAGES with Riccardo Monaco's work on the European integration process, by focusing on his insightful and articulated analysis of the legal nature of the European Communities and on the relationship between the supranational legal order and the national one. Monaco's thoughts on these two topics, which are closely interrelated, are strongly influenced by his international law background. At the same time, they reveal his capacity to cut loose from his roots and come to highly innovative conclusions. His theories on the idea of supranationality as something distinct from both the national and the international legal orders are highly revealing in this regard.

2. MONACO'S YEARS AT THE UNIVERSITY OF TURIN AS A STUDENT AND AS A JUNIOR PROFESSOR

Riccardo Monaco was born in Genoa in 1909.[1] After his first years in Genoa, he attended high school in Turin (Liceo Cavour) and then enrolled at the Faculty

[1] See R Monaco, *Memorie di una vita, memorie per l'Europa* (Rome, LEDIP, 1996); G Conso et al, 'Cerimonia commemorativa del Professor Riccardo Monaco' (2000) 4 *La Comunità Internazionale* 567; F Durante, 'Riccardo Monaco' (2000) 83 *Rivista di diritto internazionale* 481–485; U Leanza, 'Ricordo di Riccardo Monaco' (2000) 83 *Rivista di studi politici internazionali* 407–416; C Curti Gialdino (ed), *Riccardo Monaco, un giurista poliedrico al servizio della pace attraverso il diritto* (Milan, Giuffrè, 2009); S Marchisio, 'Monaco, Riccardo', in I Birocchi et al (eds), *Dizionario Biografico dei Giuristi Italiani (XII – XX secolo)* II (Bologna, Il Mulino, 2013) 1362–1363.

of Law at the city's University. In his memoirs, Monaco recounts that '[t]he four years of University were perhaps the most beautiful, the freest and the liveliest of my life [...]. The Turin Law Faculty was at the time one of the best in Italy, with Professors like Francesco Ruffini, Gioele Solari, Filippo Vassalli, Federico Patetta, Gino Segrè, Vincenzo Arangio Ruiz, and the three economists Luigi Einaudi, Achille Loria, and Pasquale Jannaccone'.[2]

In 1930, under the guidance of Giuseppe Ottolenghi,[3] Monaco graduated in Law from the University of Turin with a thesis on the relationship between international and domestic law, and obtained a professorship ('libero docente') in the same subject in 1933. This was the first step of an academic career.[4] In that same year, the number of Full Professors of International Law ('*professori ordinari*') in Italy was sixteen: a small academic community indeed. In 1939, Monaco won the competition for the chair of International Law at the University of Urbino (together with Rolando Quadri and Giorgio Cansacchi). The Committee was composed of Tommaso Perassi, Andrea Rapisardi Mirabelli, Bruno Breschi, Manlio Udina and Gaetano Morelli. He then taught first in Cagliari and then at the University of Modena. In the short period he spent at the University of Cagliari, Monaco was also asked to teach a course at the School of Economics of the University of Turin.

Finally, in 1942, he was called to Turin to the chair of Institutions of Public Law; however, there was no room for him at the Faculty of Law. The infamous racial laws of 1938 had forced Giuseppe Ottolenghi to leave the chair of International Law, which was then provisionally occupied by Alessandro Passerin d'Entrèves.[5] Monaco was therefore destined to the School of Economics and to the course of Political Sciences, which was at the time a separate part of the Law Faculty. In addition, the chair was not International Law, but Institutions

[2] Monaco (n 1) 12.

[3] See E Greppi, 'Ottolenghi, Giuseppe', in *Dizionario Biografico dei Giuristi Italiani (XII – XX secolo)* (n 1) 1474–1475.

[4] In 1981, at the Italian Society for International Organisation (SIOI) Piemonte, we organised a conference to celebrate Professor Giorgio Cansacchi di Amelia, at the time of his retirement from the University of Turin. Professor Monaco was a rapporteur, with Professors Benedetto Conforti and Georges Abi-Saab. On that occasion, Professor Monaco told me that he was happy to be in Turin again, since he had started his career at our University. He said that, at the time, International Law was not considered a good choice for a young lawyer. He had been summoned by the Dean of the Faculty of Law, who addressed him with these words: '*I have heard that you are brilliant. Why, then, do you choose International Law, which is not Law?*'. Many decades later, Riccardo Monaco was happy, and very proud of that choice.

[5] See L Grossio, 'Alessandro Passerin d'Entrèves' (*SIOI*) www.sioipiemonte.org/passerin.html, accessed 23 May 2023. Massimo Ottolenghi told me the true story of the appointment of Alessandro Passerin d'Entrèves. The plan was conceived by Luigi Einaudi, who told Ottolenghi: '*Appointing d'Entrèves – who is not an international lawyer – will leave the door open to your return on your chair. If a colleague of yours is chosen, you will never get your chair back*'. Monaco was obviously the natural candidate.

of Public Law. The same happened later to Giorgio Cansacchi in 1945, when Ottolenghi was finally reappointed.[6]

Monaco's aspiration was to get the chair of International Law at the University of Turin, his ancestral city of origin (in particular on his mother's side). However, the events of the racial laws of 1938, followed by the war, and the personal consequences on the life of Giuseppe Ottolenghi, had decisive effects on the choices of Riccardo Monaco.

3. THE MOVE TO ROME AND HIS MULTIFACETED CAREER

After World War II, Monaco decided to abandon his dream of a chair in International Law at the University of Turin. He seized the opportunities offered in Rome, were he was appointed to the Ministry of Foreign Affairs, the first of many appointments to national institutions.

From the earliest years of his activity as a scholar, Monaco's marked propensity to link his theoretical interests to the concreteness of legal relations emerged. The confirmation of this natural inclination to not limit himself to theoretical speculation as an end in itself, but, on the contrary, to pay attention to legal repercussions in practice, can be found in his career as a magistrate. This path saw him act as auditor at the Tribunal of Turin, praetor at Perosa Argentina, judge at the Tribunal of Cuneo and prosecutor again at the Tribunal of Turin.

During his years in Turin, drawing on Santi Romano's institutional theory,[7] Monaco enunciated his own systematic construction of public international law and deepened his study of private international law. During this period, he devoted several lectures to public law with Giorgio Cansacchi.[8] Cansacchi was Monaco's close friend, and they later wrote several books together.[9]

Monaco's vision of public international law was essentially institutionalist, as opposed to the contractualist one expressed by Gaetano Arangio Ruiz. 'For Arangio-Ruiz, the State 'in the sense of international law' represented a real institution, a 'given', presupposed entity comparable to a natural person, rather

[6] See E Greppi, 'Giorgio Cansacchi di Amelia' (*SIOI*) www.sioipiemonte.org/cansacchi.html, accessed 23 May 2023.

[7] See S Romano, *L'ordinamento giuridico* (1917–18), The Legal Order, translated into English by Mariano Croce (Abingdon-New York, Routledge, 2017).

[8] See, for example, *Istituzioni di diritto pubblico*, the first edition of which was published in 1945.

[9] See, for instance, R Monaco and G Cansacchi, *La nuova Costituzione italiana*, (Torino, Giappichelli, 1953); R Monaco and G Cansacchi, *Lo Stato ed il suo ordinamento giuridico: Istituzioni di diritto pubblico*, IX ed, (Torino, Giappichelli, 1962).

than a juridical one. [...]. Agreements were merely compulsory contracts and the assertion that the creation of a partial set of rules creating a new community may be based on an international agreement was wholly untenable. [...]. The existence of a 'rule of recognition' was upheld, instead, by other dualist authors who greatly contributed to the scholarly debate in Italy'.[10] Monaco, in line with other authors (Ago, Perassi, Morelli), instead identified the rule of recognition in the *pacta sunt servanda* rule. Under this basic rule, States establish international organisations through voluntary agreements. The use of an agreement to create an organisation has the double nature of a treaty (with the traditional set of rules on rights and obligations) and of the statute of the secondary legal entity.

However, Monaco's natural inclination to consider theoretical speculation inextricably linked with praxis led him to decide to return to the judiciary as *Consigliere di Stato* in 1949, in the Italian State Council. In fact, a fundamental reason for this decision was the task of monitoring the problems connected with the implementation of the peace treaties, which Monaco had taken on in 1947 at the Treaty Office of the Ministry of Foreign Affairs. He later became director of that office. The treaties connected with the negotiations for the creation of the European Organisation for Economic Cooperation were included in this monitoring work.

In 1953, Monaco took part as a member of the Italian delegation in the Rome Conference for the formation of a European Political Community. In 1955, he participated to the Messina Conference for the revival of European cooperation and the Brussels Conference preparatory to the 1957 Treaties of Rome establishing the European Economic Community (EEC) and the European Atomic Energy Community (EURATOM).

His almost twenty years of collaboration with the Ministry of Foreign Affairs in various offices had a considerable impact on Monaco's study interests.[11] Moving away from the classic approaches to public and private international law, the subject of his studies up to that time, he turned his attention to the new forms of cooperation between States that had developed after World War II. His sensitivity and attention to these new phenomena was confirmed by the fact that in 1956 Monaco was called upon to hold the first course in Italy on International Organisation, at the Faculty of Political Science of the University of Rome 'La Sapienza'. Monaco dedicated his 'Lezioni di organizzazione internazionale', the first volume of which was published in 1957, to this discipline. He was later called upon to teach a course at the Hague Academy of International Law entitled 'Les principes régissant la structure et le fonctionnement des organisations

[10] See E Milano, '*The Main International Law Issues Arising in the Aftermath of World War II*', in G Bartolini (ed), *A History of International Law in Italy* (Oxford, Oxford University Press, 2020) 406.

[11] Monaco worked in three different offices of the Italian Ministry of Foreign Affairs: Treaties Office, Diplomatic and Treaty Litigation, and Legislative Affairs.

internationales'[12] on the principles governing the structure and functioning of international organisations.

After having published some writings on the European Coal and Steel Community (ECSC), the birth of the two new communities (EEC and EURATOM) prompted further study that led him to found in 1961 the first Italian journal of European law, called the *Rivista di diritto europeo*, of which he was later also editor. These events also led to the publication of the volumes 'Primi lineamenti di diritto pubblico europeo' (1962), 'Commentario al Trattato istitutivo della CEE' (with Rolando Quadri and Alberto Trabucchi, 1965) and 'Manuale di diritto comunitario' (1983). As with his previous experiences, the speculative phase was followed by that of an operator immersed in the concrete reality of legal relations: from 8 October 1964 to 3 February 1976, Monaco served as a judge at the Court of Justice of the European Communities in Luxembourg.[13]

Riccardo Monaco's interest in multilateralism and international organisations also explains his strong commitment to the life and activities of the Italian Society for International Organisation (SIOI). He was a member of the SIOI board for fifty-two years, starting in 1947, he then became Secretary-General (from 1977 to 1983) and finally Vice-President, until his death in 2000. He was thus an active member of the SIOI managing office for twenty-two years.

He was also – with Umberto Leanza and Luigi Ferrari Bravo – one of the founders of the Italian Society of International Law (SIDI), and in 1995 became its first President.

Another important chapter in Monaco's life should be mentioned. Back in Rome after his time at the Court of Justice, Monaco was Secretary-General (1975–1984) and then President of the International Institute for the Unification of Private Law (UNIDROIT) from 1984 until 1994. In that period he played a decisive role in the drafting of the UNIDROIT Principles of International Commercial Contracts first published in 1994, and the 1995 UNIDROIT Convention on stolen or illegally exported cultural objects, which integrates the public international law approach of the 1970 UNESCO Convention.[14] Last but not least, he was an active member of the *Institut de Droit International*.

Together with a small group of academics at Italian Universities, Monaco played a decisive role in the creation and development of the departments of Political Sciences in Italian Universities. Originally, 'Political Sciences' was conceived and introduced in the Law departments as a separate bachelor's undergraduate degree '*corso di laurea*', aiming essentially at the training of diplomats

[12] Académie de droit international de La Haye. Recueil des cours, tome 156, 1977-III (Alphen aan den Rijn, Sijthoff et Noordhoff, 1980).

[13] See below para 5 of this Chapter.

[14] Both available at https://www.unidroit.org/.

and others seeking public service careers. When the Minister of education adopted the decision to create a separate Political Science department, Monaco was one of the leading academics in the planning and development of the project, together with some colleagues in Torino, such as Norberto Bobbio, Alessandro and Ettore Passerin d'Entrèves, Siro Lombardini and other professors.

This was a very relevant project as it led to the enlargement of the various branches of International Law, such as International Organisation (that is International Institutional Law), Diplomatic Law, International Economic Law, and then European Communities Law. In the 1960s, 1970s and 1980s there was no room for these subject areas in the Law Faculties. Monaco's strong commitment to the project explains the last period of his academic career, when he accepted a long appointment as Dean of the Faculty of Political Sciences of the University of Rome 'La Sapienza'.

The scientific activities of Riccardo Monaco started in 1932 with his first book, and ended 67 years later with a contribution to the essays in honour of Professor Valticos: some 20 volumes (books, manuals, courses) and more than 300 essays, book chapters, articles and notes.

4. THE DOCTRINE OF SUPRANATIONALITY AND THE EUROPEAN INTEGRATION PROCESS

Monaco's theoretical contribution to the understanding of the EU system was remarkable. He was the first international lawyer (not just in Italy) to realise that the phenomenon of European integration was unique in the panorama of institutionalised forms of cooperation between States. Indeed, Monaco realised that the three European Communities were not simply unions of States, but supranational communities in which the level of cooperation was much stronger and deeper than in other, more traditional, international organisations based on the contractualist vision of his colleague Arangio-Ruiz.

As far as the definition, nature and classification of international organisations are concerned, Monaco started by stressing the meaning of the word 'Community', indicating a union of States much more intense and of more strict institutional structure. The new feature of the Communities is that they are 'supranational', that is 'above the State'. From the fact that the Communities are supranational, they can directly bind – with their rules and the acts of their bodies – subjects of the domestic legal order. As a consequence, in this respect, the distinction between international law and municipal law vanishes. But, going further, the Community's legal order identifies itself with an autonomous legal system, distinct from both international and domestic law.

Monaco identified three elements that characterise these new supranational entities and that distinguish them from traditional international organisations. The first one is the presence of organs that are genuinely representative, as they are not the expression of governments, but are elected by the citizens of the polity. The second distinguishing feature is the adoption of decisions by majority voting rather than by unanimity. The third and last characteristic is the capacity of Community's organs to bind both the Member States and individuals (as well as legal persons). In this regard, Monaco also observed that the direct effect of Community law called into question the traditional principle of distinction and separation between international and domestic law, with the consequence that this principle no longer seemed to be applicable in the relationship between the two systems.[15]

Writing about the normative functions of supranational communities, quite remarkably, he went as far as to argue that 'the normative function performed by supranational communities is the one which is closer to the classic type of the federal State'.[16] Yet, he further added that it would be wrong to equate these Communities to federal States, as much as it is wrong to consider them as unions of States. It seems clear that here Monaco shares the view, albeit moving from a different theoretical perspective, expressed by the Court of Justice in *Van Gend en Loos* when it defined the Community as a 'new legal order of international law'.[17]

In this article originally published in 1953, Monaco argued that what distinguishes supranational communities from fully-fledged federal States was the former's 'lack of political quantity'.[18] To complete the transformation, it would therefore be necessary to fully integrate the technical functions entrusted to supranational communities into a political structure. This is a remark that still bears its relevance after almost seven decades of European integration if we look at the ongoing debate concerning the need to create a truly supranational political space.[19]

5. TWO TERMS AS A JUDGE AT THE COURT OF JUSTICE

In 1964, Riccardo Monaco was appointed as judge of the Court of Justice where he served for two terms, until 1976. His multifaced profile, combining high-level academic, judicial and diplomatic experiences, made him a well-suited candidate

[15] R Monaco, 'Le Comunità sopranazionali nell'ordinamento internazionale', in R Monaco, *Scritti di diritto europeo* (Milano, Giuffrè, 1972) 47–75 (originally published in (1953) 8 *La Comunità internazionale* 441, 441–453), 67–75.

[16] Monaco (n 15). The original Italian version reads as follows: 'la funzione normativa che le comunità sopranazionali esplicano è quella che, più di ogni altra, le avvicina al tipo classico dello stato federale'.

[17] See *Van Gend en Loos v Nederlandse Administratie der Belastingen* Case 26/62 ECLI:EU:C:1963:1 [1963].

[18] Monaco (n 15) 73.

[19] On this debate see D Hoeglinger, 'The Politicisation of European Integration in Domestic Election Campaigns' (2016) 39 *West European Politics* 44, 44–63.

for this position in Luxembourg.[20] In that period, he acted as judge rapporteur in 89 judgments and one Opinion adopted on the basis of current Article 218 of the Treaty on the Fuctioning of the European Union (TFEU). Roughly half the judgments concerned two subject-matters: staff regulations of EU officials and common agricultural policy. Another quantitatively significant field in Monaco's judicial activity was that of social security connected to the free circulation of workers, while a dozen of other judgments dealt with issues of competition law, free movement of goods and services, as well as transport policy. Lastly, in the early years at the Court, Monaco served as rapporteur for five judgments concerning the European Coal and Steel Community (ECSC) and, more specifically, actions for annulment brought by private undertakings against decisions adopted by the High Authority.

When reading these judgments, it is difficult to single out Monaco's individual contribution to the stance adopted by the Court, especially because of the institution's collegial method of deliberation.[21] However, although most of these judicial decisions concern highly specific and technical issues, they touched upon some of the elements of the sophisticated vision of the supranational legal order elaborated by Monaco in his academic capacity. *International Fruit Company* and *Aktien-Zuckerfabrik* represent two examples that stand out in this regard. These judgments, both concerning the common organisation of agricultural products, gave the Court the possibility to engage with one of the key aspects of Monaco's supranationality doctrine, i.e. the position of private parties in the supranational legal order and, more specifically, in its judicial system.[22]

The *International Fruit Company* judgment[23] represents a landmark in the definition of the standing conditions that private parties must satisfy in order to bring annulment proceedings against an act of the European legislator. The Court had traditionally taken a very restrictive approach on the matter, as epitomised by the *Plaumann* case.[24] Without overturning the previous case-law, in *International Fruit Company*, the Court shed light on the possibility for non-privileged applicants to challenge acts that are not directed to them, but to the State. The case concerned an annulment action brought by four Dutch undertakings against the refusal to grant them licences to import dessert

[20] See Curti Gialdino (n 1).

[21] See P Gragl, 'The Faceless Court? The Role of Individual CJEU Members' (2023) 30(1) *Maastricht Journal of European and Comparative Law* 15.

[22] R Monaco, 'Lo status dell'individuo nel diritto comunitario', in *Studi in onore di Manlio Udina*, vol. I (Milan, Giuffrè, 1975) 553–573.

[23] *International Fruit Company and Others v Commission* Case 41/70 ECLI:EU:C:1971:53 [1971].

[24] *Plaumann v Commission of the EEC* Case 25/62 ECLI:EU:C:1963:17 [1963]. For a comprehensive and critical analysis of the issue, see A Albors-Llorens, 'The Standing of Private Parties to Challenge Community Measures: Has the European Court Missed the Boat?' (2003) 62 *The Cambridge Law Journal* 72.

apples from third countries. The refusal was decided by the Commission on the basis of Regulation No 459/70 and notified to the undertaking by the competent national authorities. The Commission argued that the action should be dismissed, since there was no decision addressed to the applicants and their non-privileged status prevented them from challenge an act taking the form of a regulation and, thus, not being of individual concern to them as requested by then Article 173 TEEC. The Court disagreed and admitted the challenge on two grounds. First, it observed that the act, although taking the form of a Regulation, was to be regarded as a 'a conglomeration of individual decisions' that 'affects the legal position of each author of an application for a licence'.[25] Therefore, the Court concluded that it was an act of individual concern to the applicants. Second, it also held that the direct concern requirement was met, even though, according to the Regulation, the licences had to be issued by national authorities. Indeed, the Court observed that national authorities had no discretion in taking this step, which was just a way to give effect to the decision taken by the Commission on the basis of its own assessment of the situation. Therefore, the private undertakings could directly challenge the Commission's decision in front of the Court, since such act directly affected their legal position.[26]

Aktien-Zuckerfabrik[27] is another equally important decision, being the first case in which the Court defined the limits of the European Community's non-contractual liability for economic policy choices made by its institutions. The case concerned the action brought by a German undertaking running a raw sugar factory seeking to obtain compensation for damages allegedly caused by a Council regulation that affected the price of sugar without providing compensation to the affected economic operators. The measure was part of the process that led to the establishment of the common organisation of the sugar market at the supranational level. The Court approached the case by setting quite a demanding threshold which is still valid today. In particular, it held that '[w]here legislative action involving measures of economic policy is concerned, the Community does not incur noncontractual liability for damage suffered by individuals as a consequence of that action, by virtue of the provisions contained in Article 215, second paragraph, TEEC, unless a sufficiently flagrant violation of a superior rule of law for the protection of the individual has occurred'.[28] Although not explicit, the restrictive approach adopted by the Court aimed at avoiding that, as later clarified in *Bayerische HNL*, public authorities could be 'hindered by the prospect of applications for damages whenever it has occasion

[25] *International Fruit Company and Others v Commission* Case 41/70 ECLI:EU:C:1971:53 [1971] para 21.
[26] ibid., paras 23-38.
[27] *Zuckerfabrik Schoeppenstedt v Council* Case 5/71 ECLI:EU:C:1971:116 [1971].
[28] ibid., para 11.

to adopt legislative measures in the public interest which may adversely affect the interests of individuals'.[29]

Another set of proceedings in which Monaco served as *juge rapporteur* and that are worth taking into consideration in view of their broader constitutional relevance are those concerning the coordination of national social security systems with regard to mobile workers. Already in a chapter first published in 1963, Monaco duly pointed out the importance of this set of rules to ensure the free movement of workers and pleaded for swift and effective implementation by the Member States.[30] The Court has played a major role when it comes to strengthening this framework, by adopting a strongly integrationist approach in interpreting the relevant legal provisions, so to widen their reach and to bring about the most favourable conditions for mobile workers.[31] This pattern is evident with regard to all key aspects of the coordination framework, such as the definition of the material scope of application of the regulations or of the notion of workers in that context. The judgments adopted by the Court with Monaco serving as judge rapporteur fit perfectly in this mould. For example, in *Biason*[32] the Court was called upon to clarify whether the invalidity pension granted by France to an Italian lady and then withdrawn when she moved her residence to Italy fell within the scope of Regulation No 3. The French Government considered that the allowance was a social assistance benefit and, thus, did not fall within the matters covered by the Community regulations. While admitting that certain aspects of the allowance come close to the concept of assistance, the Court concluded that this could not lead to excluding it from the scope of application of the abovementioned regulation. The same approach was followed in the subsequent *Callemeyn* judgment,[33] concerning the refusal by Belgian authorities to grant to a French citizen a disability allowance. Belgium claimed that the refusal did not constitute a violation of the principle of non-discrimination, as codified in Regulation No 1471/68, since the allowance at stake was a social assistance

[29] *Bayerische HNL v Council and Commission* Case 83/76 ECLI:EU:C:1978:113 [1978] para 5. More generally on this issue, see C Hilson, 'The Role of Discretion in EC law on Non-Contractual Liability' (2005) 42 *Common Market Law Review* 677.

[30] R Monaco, 'Principi della libera circolazione dei lavoratori', in *Raccolta di scritti in onore di A.C. Jemolo* (Milano, Giuffrè editore, 1963) 453. Se also R Monaco, 'Politica sociale e giustizia sociale nella CEE' (1973) 1 *Affari sociali internazionali* 25.

[31] See S van Raepenbusch, 'The Role of the Court of Justice in the Development of Social Security Law of Persons Moving within the European Union', in Y Jorens (ed), *50 Years of Social Security Coordination Past – Present – Future. Report of the Conference Celebrating the 50th Anniversary of the European Coordination of Social Security, Prague 7 & 8 May 2009* (Luxembourg, Publications Office of the European Union, 2010) 29–54.

[32] *Caisse régionale d'assurance maladie de Paris v Giuseppina Biason* Case 24/74 ECLI:EU:C:1974:99 [1974].

[33] *Callemeyn v Belgian State* Case 187/73 ECLI:EU:C:1974:57 [1974].

benefit. Once again, the Court rejected this argument, restating its extensive conception of the notion of social security and, as a consequence, consolidating the expansion of the material scope of application of the rules on social security coordination.

The Court followed the same expansive approach in *Petroni*,[34] another decision in which Monaco served as judge rapporteur. The case concerned an Italian national who worked for seventeen years as a miner in Belgium and for seven years as an employee in Italy. The problem was that his pension would have been higher if calculated only on the basis of Belgian legislation than the one obtained by aggregating the Belgian and the Italian periods and then apportioning the amounts between the two States as imposed by Regulation No 1408/71. Answering the preliminary questions raised by the Belgian judge, the Court coined the so-called favourability principle (also known as 'Petroni principle') according to which a mobile worker could not end up in a worse position than a non-mobile one due to the application of social security coordination rules. This result would be in contrast with the objectives pursued by Articles 48 and 51 TEEC, that fostered workers' mobility.[35]

Beside the judgments examined above, it is worth taking into consideration Opinion 1/75,[36] the first case in which the Court exercised its advisory function with regard to the compatibility of an international agreement to be concluded by the EU with the Treaties. The Court seized the occasion to shed light on the rationale and function of a procedure that is advisory only in name, as well as on its objective scope of application. Furthermore, the Opinion is also remarkable with regard to the content of the answer given to the question raised by the Commission as to whether the European Economic Community had the competence to conclude an international agreement such as the OECD Understanding on a Local Cost Standard.

The first issue examined by the Court was whether the Understanding could be considered an international agreement and, consequently, whether the Court had jurisdiction to rule on the matter according to Article 228(1) TEEC or not. This is an issue that finds its definition under public international law and it is safe to assume that Monaco's deep and articulated knowledge of the field played a key part in steering the Court's course. Without expressly making any reference to it, the Opinion followed the anti-nominalist approach that the International Court of Justice had already adopted in its judgment on the *South West Africa*

[34] *Petroni v ONTPS* Case 24/75 ECLI:EU:C:1975:129 [1975].

[35] ibid., para 13.

[36] Avis 1/75 ECLI:EU:C:1975:145 [1975]. On this case, see recently M Cremona and K Jaka, 'Common Commercial Policy and the Determination of Exclusivity: Opinion 1/75 (Local Cost Standard)' in G Butler and RA Wessel (eds), *EU External Relations Law: The Cases in Context* (Oxford, Hart Publishing, 2022) 45–56.

Cases in 1962, in which it stated that '[t]erminology is not a determinant factor as to the character of an international agreement or undertaking'.[37] Moving from such premises, the Opinion concluded that the Understanding is an international agreement under Article 228(1) TEEC, also because it contained a binding rule of conduct for the Parties.

Next, the Court defined the scope of its review under the advisory procedure by looking at its rationale and function. Quite interestingly, the Opinion considered this procedure as having an exceptional nature: a term that is used to highlight the absence in most Member States' legal orders of a mechanism to allow a judicial body to exercise preliminary checks on the choices made by political organs in the exercise of their foreign policy prerogatives. The Court explained that the choice to include such a mechanism in the supranational legal order was an attempt to avoid that the conclusion of an agreement in violation of the Treaty could 'provoke […] serious difficulties and might give rise to adverse consequences for all interested parties, including third countries'. To be effective this control must therefore be as broad as possible, being 'open for all questions capable of submission for judicial consideration, either by the Court of Justice or possibly by national courts'.[38]

Coming to the answer given to the question raised by the Commission, the most relevant part concerns the nature of the EEC powers in the field of the common commercial policy. Here, the Court took a very bold stance, anticipating a solution that would find codification in the Treaties only with the entry into force of the Treaty of Lisbon in 2009. Indeed, it argued that the common commercial policy was an exclusive competence of the EEC, even though Articles 112 and 113 TEEC were silent on this point. The Court grounded its position on the necessity to preserve and reinforce the stability of the whole edifice of European law. Leaving the Member States free to act autonomously 'would thereby distort the institutional framework, call into question the mutual trust within the Community and prevent the latter from fulfilling its task in the defence of the common interest'.[39]

6. CONCLUSION

In all the positions Riccardo Monaco occupied in his remarkable career – the judiciary, the university, the State Council, the Court of Justice of the European Communities, the Higher Council of Public Education, the office of Dean of

[37] ICJ, *South-West Africa Cases [Ethiopia v South Africa; Liberia v South Africa] [Preliminary Objections]* [1962] ICJ Rep 319, 331. See generally J Klabbers, *The Concept of Treaty in International Law* (The Hague, Kluwer Law International, 1996).

[38] Avis 1/75 (n 36) 1361.

[39] Avis 1/75 (n 36) 1364.

the Faculty – his work was characterised by high professionalism and strong commitment, and accompanied by his elegant and lovable personality. He devoted his life to International Law, the Law of International Institutions and European Community Law and he put forward an innovative institutionalist approach to international organisations both in theory and in practice.

7

Francesco Capotorti: The Man, the Academic, and the Advocate General at the Court of Justice

LUIGI DANIELE

1. AN OUTLINE OF PROFESSOR FRANCESCO CAPOTORTI

TO THOSE WHO have been following the European Union's progress since the first decades of its existence, Francesco Capotorti is known mainly for his role as an Advocate General at the Court of Justice during the years between the 1970s and 80s. However, Capotorti was much more than that.

Capotorti was an eminent professor of International law, both Public and Private, and held a chair in several prestigious Italian universities, including the Sapienza University of Rome. He lectured extensively at both Italian and foreign universities, including the most distingued Academy of International law, at the Hague, where he delivered three courses (1963, 1971, 1994). Capotorti was a member of numerous international and Italian organisations and committees, and on many occasions acted as a member of the Italian delegations or as a representative of the Italian government in important international fora and negotiation rounds. He took part as a chairperson and as a rapporteur in many international and European conferences, including the FIDE conferences in the Hague (1984) and in Rome (1994). He earned numerous distinctions, including a degree *honoris causa* in law from the University of Liège in Belgium.

Additionally, Capotorti was a prolific writer in Public International law, Private International law and in European Community (now Union) law. His bibliography counts no less than 150 entries, including three monographs, two handbooks, several entries in prestigious Law encyclopedias, and an endless list of shorter essays, both in Italian and in other languages. Capotorti also co-edited several books and collections of case law and was the main editor and member of the editing board or of the scientific committee of important journals, such as *Rivista di Diritto Internazionale, Rivista di Diritto Internazionale Privato e Processuale, Rivista di Diritto Europeo*, and *Cahiers de Droit Européen*.

Capotorti enjoyed very high consideration and esteem as one of the individuals involved in the world of International law and European Union law.[1] Many younger scholars have benefited from Capotorti's guidance; even while he was in Luxembourg, he followed their steps and closely reviewed their writings.

Despite the time that has passed since his life came to an end in 2002, at the relatively young age of 77, Capotorti's memory and his personality continue to live on among those who had the chance to know him, either personally or through his opinions and writings.

Personally, I had a very close relation with Capotorti, both at a family and academic level. I dare say that I owe a lot of my university career and even my life trajectory to Capotorti's influence and to his encouragement and support. Capotorti's method of analysing legal issues and expressing his views set an everlasting example for many and, without a doubt, for me.[2] I am therefore very honored to be able to write this chapter and grateful to the editors of this volume to have chosen me from among the many students of Capotorti, for this task.

2. CAPOTORTI'S CAREER AS AN ACADEMIC

Francesco Capotorti was born in Naples in 1925. He studied law at the prestigious University of Naples, his hometown, where he graduated *magna cum laude* in 1945, at the unusually young age of twenty. At his graduation examination, he defended a dissertation in International law under the supervision of Professor Gaetano Morelli, one of the most eminent scholars in the field at the time, who, in the following years, served as a Judge at the International Court of Justice at the Hague.

Capotorti's university career was extremely quick and successful in the Italian context. Only a year after his graduation, he was appointed university 'assistente' (assistant lecturer) and, soon after, 'libero docente' (free lecturer), and was put in charge of holding classes in International law. In 1953, Capotorti

[1] This 'community' of colleagues and friends honored Capotorti two volumes of essays, 'Divenire sociale and adeguamento del diritto – Studi in onore di Francesco Capotorti', Milan, 1999'. The essays include a very detailed study of his life and career, authored by his first élève, Professor Vincenzo Starace, from the University of Bari, 'L'impegno scientifico, didattico e giudiziario di Francesco Capotorti', as well as a complete bibliography of Capotorti's published work.

[2] As an example of the widespread admiration Professor Capotorti enjoyed for his ability in approaching the most intricate questions of law, it is worth reporting two short passages drawn from the speech delivered on 8 October 1982, at the Court of Justice, by President Josse Mertens de Wilmars, on the occasion of the departure of Mr Advocate General Francesco Capotorti, First Advocate General, Judge Adolphe Touffait, President of Chamber, and Judge Fernand Grévisse. Referring to Capotorti's contribution to the work of the Court as a judge, President Mertens said that, when Capotorti took office as Advocate General, 'we regretted losing your contribution to our deliberations, your enlightened views and exemplary impartiality, your profound knowledge of the law, your exceptional analytical mind and the ease of your relations with your colleagues.' President Mertens also praised Professor Capotorti for his role as an Advocate General, with these remarkable words: 'More than once, when listening to you, I have been reminded of the expert hands of a brain surgeon, for you know how to handle with dexterity the most delicate threads of legal argument'.

earned his tenured Professorship in the same field and in 1954 was called to teach at the University of Cagliari. In 1955 he moved to the University of Bari, in 1968, to the University of Naples, and, finally, in 1976, to the Sapienza University of Rome. During his years in Naples, Capotorti acted as director of the Institute of Public law at the Faculty of Economics, which under his leadership soon became an important centre for legal studies and research in International and European Law.

3. CAPOTORTI'S APPOINTMENTS AT THE COURT OF JUSTICE

As already mentioned, Capotorti was well known within the Italian government and, especially, with the Ministry of Foreign Affairs, which very often availed themselves of his experience and knowledge in the international arena. He was a member of the '*Consiglio del Contenzioso Diplomatico*' (Diplomatic Litigation Council), an advising body composed of experts in International law, which was frequently called upon to advise the Ministry.

Moreover, Capotorti was a good acquaintance of Aldo Moro a prominent politician for Christian Democracy or *Democrazia Cristiana* (DC) who served as Prime Minister of Italy from 1963 to 1968 and then from 1974 to 1976. Before his assassination by the Red Brigades in 1978, Moro was possibly the most influential Italian politician, having been Minister for Foreign Affairs multiple times, and who also worked for other important ministries including Justice and Public Education. He held the position of Prime Minister five times, including, most significantly, during the year 1976. Capotorti and Moro had been colleagues both at the University of Bari and at the Sapienza University in Rome.

In 1976, Riccardo Monaco was serving as Judge at the Court of Justice.[3] His second mandate should have come to an end in October that year, however, for personal reasons, he wished to come back to Rome sooner and resigned about six months before the end of his term. The Italian Government, led at the time by Moro, was therefore called upon to propose a new person who should complete Monaco's mandate and the choice fell on Capotorti.

It is worth pointing out that Capotorti did not belong to the area of the Christian Democrats, Moro's political party, but was rather close to the other political party of the coalition cabinets of the time, the Socialists, although he was not particular in tune with Craxi, the strong man of that party. Therefore, there are grounds to assume that Capotorti's appointment to the Court of Justice from February 3 to October 6, 1976, then Advocate General from October 7, 1976 to October 6, 1982 was Moro's own decision, based on his merits.

[3] See E Greppi, 'Riccardo Monaco and the Doctrine of Supranationality in International Institutional Law', in this volume.

Less understandable is why, in October 1976, Capotorti was not confirmed as a Judge for a new entire mandate. Instead, the Italian Government proposed him as Advocate General, replacing Alberto Trabucchi.[4] Gacinto Bosco, another high ranked politician of *Democrazia Cristiana*, who, like Capotorti, was a professor of International law, but had devoted most of his life to the political arena, became the Judge at the Court representing the Italian nationality.[5]

I assume it is probable that Capotorti knew from the beginning that he would not hold the position as a Judge after October and that he would be appointed as Advocate General instead. Be that as it may, I believe that Capotorti was not unhappy with such an outcome. Being Advocate General, as opposed to being a Judge at the Court, assured him a lot more flexibility in terms of time, with fewer hearings and no long *délibérés* or collegial deliberations to attend. This allowed him not to give up completely his academic life and to travel very frequently between Luxembourg, Rome and Naples, where his family lived.

More importantly, the role of Advocate General allowed for much more independence of thought. Capotorti's Opinions were his own and he did not have to share them with his colleagues, whether fellow Advocates General or judges.

Unlike other Advocates General, Capotorti did not pay too much attention to whether his Opinions would be followed by the Court or not. His sense of individuality of thought was great and sometimes, I was witness to this, he even did not know exactly how the Court had ruled on the same case in which he had presented his Opinion, until, of course, he was called upon to work again on a similar or related case.

In this, I may say, Capotorti's attitude was more like that of an academic, whose position is to maintain his freedom of thought, than as a member of a court whose decisions were the result of secret and collegial deliberations.

Despite Capotorti perhaps not minding being 'downgraded', as some would have seen it, from Judge to Advocate General, he was very disappointed when, in 1982, the Italian Government decided not to confirm him as a candidate for a second mandate as Advocate General and instead nominated Federico Mancini for the position.[6]

Most people, at the time, knew perfectly well why this change had occurred. It is an embarrassing tale, which I do not wish to relate here. All what I can say is that everybody was disgusted by the fact that Capotorti only learnt of his 'fate' through some friends who heard the news on Italian television!

[4] See E Perillo, 'Alberto Trabucchi: the Defender of the European citizens' rights and the Van Gend & Loos ruling of the Court of Justice', in this volume.

[5] See J Ziller, 'Giacinto Bosco, a rather well-known politician in Italy, and one of the lesser-known Italian members of the Court of Justice of the European Communities', in this volume.

[6] See V Di Bucci, 'The Contribution of Giuseppe Federico Mancini as Advocate General (1982–1988) and Judge (1988–1999) to European Constitutionalism', in this volume.

4. CAPOTORTI'S LIFE AT THE COURT

The years Capotorti spent in Luxembourg at the Court, from 1976 to 1982, were very intense but also full of satisfaction for him. He enjoyed his role. His reputation grew very much. He was often invited to take part in conferences or to give lectures throughout Europe. Capotorti very generously hosted colleagues and all sort of people interested in the work of the Court and entertained them in a most friendly way.

Capotorti was on excellent terms with most of his fellow-members at the Court. His full mastering of the French language, together with his natural ability of engaging in pleasant conversation with anybody, made him a great company to his colleagues and staff at the Court. Among them, I may count Robert Lecour and Adolphe Touffait, respectively President and Judge of French nationality; Jean-Pierre Warner and Gordon Slynn, both Advocate General of British Nationality; Josse Mertens de Wilmars, Judge and later President of Belgian Nationality; Albert Van Houtte, the historic 'Greffier' of the Court; and, of course, Alexander Mackenzie-Stuart, Judge and later President of the Court. In fact, I remember that Mackenzie-Stuart and their family came to visit the Capotortis in Anacapri one summer and stayed a few days at their flat there.

While in Luxemborug, Capotorti worked hard and spent long hours in his chambers, remaining there even when the Court's building was nearly empty of people. The staff that worked with him were very reliable and attached to him, especially Carla Malnati, the 'senior' secretarial assistant of Capotorti's chambers.

Of his two *référendaires*, Paolo Gori had already been a legal secretary with Alberto Trabucchi.[7] Gori was a very learned and experienced jurist. He was associate professor of European Community law at the University of Padua. Capotorti had great respect for him. However, Gori, being a native of Prato in Tuscany, was of a somewhat 'cool' nature, which did not match completely with Capotorti's Southern, very talkative and open character.

On the other hand, the second *référandaire*, Antonio Saggio, who would later become the first President of the Court of first instance and Advocate General at the Court in the second, shared with Capotorti the same mindset and approach to people.[8] A native of Naples, he had studied and worked with Capotorti before they both came to Luxembourg. Saggio was a fine and extremely experienced jurist in Italy where he was a member of the judiciary and

[7] See P Gori, 'Souvenirs d'un survivant', in *Van Gend en Loos 1963–2013. Conference Preeceedings, Luxembourg 13 May 2013* (Luxembourg, Publications Office of the European Union, 2013) 29-35, available at https://curia.europa.eu/jcms/upload/docs/application/pdf/2013-12/qd30136442ac_002.pdf.

[8] See A Aresu and C Iannone, 'Antonio Saggio: A Major Contributor to the European Integration', in this volume.

had already reached to hold the position of President of Court of Appeals. Saggio was very friendly with everybody at the court and kept good relations with the Italian administration at home and at the Community institutions in Brussels. Many, including Capotorti himself, referred to him for information about what was happening in Luxembourg or in Brussels.

5. CAPOTORTI'S ACADEMIC LIFE DURING HIS TERM AT THE COURT AND AFTER

One is allowed to say that Capotorti's academic life went on irrespective of the heavy burden of his work at the Court.

As mentioned above, Capotorti went on teaching at the Sapienza University during the six and a half years that he spent at the Court. His routine was to lecture in Rome on Monday, fly to Luxembourg in the afternoon, work at the Court until Thursday afternoon, when he would fly back to Rome, lecture on Friday and then reach Naples, where is family lived.

Amid this 'frenetic' travelling, he still found time to take part in many academic conferences and to publish several essays.

For instance, when he was Advocate General, Capotorti wrote about the international protection of minorities, a topic on which Capotorti had worked extensively in the past. He had acted as a Special Rapporteur for the Sub-Committee at the United Nations on the suppression of discriminatory measures and for the protection of minorities, for which he drafted a report on the subject, which continues to be frequently quoted.[9]

In the field of European Community law, Capotorti wrote on the European Parliament and its first direct elections[10] as well as on the possible accession of the European Communities to the European Convention of Human Rights.[11] He also published as an article the text of an admirable presentation he gave at the Court to a group of members of the judiciary from all the Member States: European Communities law from the perspective of National courts.[12]

Obviously, after he left the Court, Capotorti had more time to accomplish his duties as an academic. His publications increased considerably in number. He published extensively on issues concerning Public International law and

[9] F Capotorti, *Ètude des droits des personnes appartenant aux minorités ethniques, réligieuses et linguisitques* (United Nations, New York, 1979).

[10] F Capotorti, *Le Parlement européen à la veille des élections directes, Thesaurus Acroasium, vol. VIII* (Thessaloniki, 1979) 177–144.

[11] F Capotorti, 'Sull'eventuale adesione della Comunità alla Convenzione europea dei diritti dell'Uomo' (1980) *Rivista di diritto internazionale* 5–28.

[12] F Capotorti, 'Il diritto comunitario dal punto di vista del giudice nazionale' (1977) *Rivista di diritto internazionale privato e processuale* 497–521.

Private International law, particularly on the new Italian law that reformed the Italian system of Private International law.[13] In fact, he took part in the drafting commission appointed by the Government to propose what became Law no. 218 of 1995.[14]

Among Capotorti's several contributions to European Community law, it is worth mentioning the two entries for the *Encyclopedia of Public International law*, which he devoted to *Supranational Organisations*[15] and to *European Communities: Community law and Municipal law*. He also wrote the long essay on the *Non-Written European law*;[16] a contribution on *The Law-Making Process in the European Communities*;[17] a presentation on the characteristics of the judgments of the European Court of Justice;[18] several entries for the *Enciclopedia giuridica*, each on one of the Community institutions.[19] Caportorti's goal was to include all these works in a Handbook on Community law, which, unfortunately, he never managed to publish.

In his last years, when his health began to deteriorate, Capotorti's energies were aimed at the preparation of the General Course in Public International law for the Academy of International law at the Hague, which he held in 1994. The Course was published in French[20] and was later translated into Italian as a Handbook of Public International law.[21]

6. CAPOTORTI'S WORK AS AN ADVOCATE GENERAL AT THE COURT

During his term as Advocate General, Capotorti delivered more than 150 Opinions, most on cases that were raising new and delicate issues and therefore are still quoted in the canon of European law as leading cases today.[22]

[13] F Capotorti (ed), *Commento coordinato sul nuovo sistema italiano di diritto internazionale privato – Legge 31 maggio 1995 n. 218* (Corriere giuridico 1995) 1225–1232.

[14] Law of 31 May 1995, No 218 (Reform of the Italian system of Private International law).

[15] F Capotorti, 'Suprantional Organisation' (1983) (Instalment 5) *Encyclopedia of Public International law* 262–268.

[16] F Capotorti, 'European Communities: Community law and Municipal law' (1983) (Instalment 6) *Encyclopedia of Public International law* 129–134.

[17] F Capotorti, 'Il diritto comunitario non scritto' (1983) *Diritto comunitario e degli scambi internazionali* 449–474.

[18] F Capotorti, 'Le sentenze della Corte di giustizia delle Comunità europee, in AA.VV., *La sentenza in Europa – Metodo, tecnica e stile* (Padova, CEDAM, 1988) 230–247.

[19] F Capotorti, 'Commissione delle Comunità europee', in *Enciclopedia giuridica*, VIII, (Roma, 1988) 9; 'Consiglio delle Comunità europee', in *Enciclopedia giuridica*, VIII (Roma, 1988) 11; 'Corte di giustizia delle Comunità europee', in *Enciclopedia giuridica*, IX (Roma, 1988) 8; 'Parlamento europeo', in *Enciclopedia giuridica*, XXI (Roma, 1990) 8.

[20] F Capotorti, 'Cours général de droit international public' (1994) 248 (IV) *Recueil des Cours de l'Académie de droit international de la Haye* 9–344.

[21] F Capotorti, *Corso di diritto internazionale* (Milano, Giuffrè, 1995).

[22] See A Vauchez, 'EU Law Classics in the Making Methodological Notes on Grands arrêts at the European Court of Justice', in FG Nicola and B Davies, *EU Law Stories; Contextual and Critical Histories of European Jurisprudence* (Cambridge, Cambridge University Press, 2017) 21–34.

Without going through the long list of cases in which Capotorti played the role as Advocate General, I will just mention a few which remain well known.

Starting with cases that touch on general or institutional issues of Community law, I will mention that Capotorti delivered his Opinion in *Défrenne III*[23] and in *Liselotte Hauer*.[24] Both are among the first cases in which the Court, after *Stauder*,[25] *Internationale Handelgesellschaft*,[26] *Nold*[27] and *Rutili*,[28] was still trying to imagine a precise role for the European Convention of Human Rights in the context of the protection of such rights under Community law.

In *Bayerische HNL*,[29] Capotorti and the Court, for the first time, had to deal with the problem of whether and under which conditions an individual may claim compensation for the loss caused by a Community regulation, which the Court had previously declared invalid. This was followed by many other cases on non-contractual liability, such as *Ireks-Arkady*[30] and *Interquell* in which also Capotorti acted as Advocate General.[31]

In *CILFIT*,[32] Capotorti offered his view on the problem of defining the scope and the limits of duty for national courts of last resort to apply to the Court for a preliminary ruling. It will be recalled that Capotorti was against admitting the exception of the so called '*acte clair*'. Under this principle, the duty of referral would not apply, when the answer to a question of Community law would raise no reasonable doubts. He did not consider it

[23] *Gabrielle Defrenne v Société anonyme belge de navigation aérienne Sabena* Case 149/77 ECLI: EU:C:1976:56 [1976] ECR 00455. In the judgment of 15 June 1978, the Court ruled in the same way as suggested by Capotorti.

[24] *Liselotte Hauer v Land Rheinland-Pfalz* Case 44/79 ECLI: EU:C:1979:290 [1979] ECR 03727. In the judgment of 13 December 1979, the Court ruled in the same way as suggested by Capotorti.

[25] *Erich Stauder v Stadt Ulm – Sozialamt* Case 29/69 ECLI: EU:C:1969:57 [1969].

[26] *Internationale Handelsgesellschaft mbH v Einfuhr- und Vorratsstelle für Getreide und Futtermittel* Case 11/70 ECLI:EU:C:1970:114 [1970].

[27] *J. Nold, Kohlen- und Baustoffgroßhandlung v Ruhrkohle Aktiengesellschaft* Case 4/73 ECLI:EU:C:1974:51 [1974].

[28] *Roland Rutili v Ministre de l'intérieur* Case 36/75 ECLI:EU:C:1975:137 [1975] ECR 01219.

[29] *Bayerische HNL Vermehrungsbetriebe GmbH & Co. KG and others v Council and Commission of the European Communities* Case 83/76 ECLI:EU:C:1978:113 [1978] ECR 01209. Contrary to what Capotorti was proposing, the Court, in the judgment of 25 May 1978, dismissed the application.

[30] *Ireks-Arkady GmbH v Council and Commission of the European Communities* Case 238/78 ECLI:EU:C:1979:226 [1979] ECR 02955. In the judgment of 4 October 1979, the Court ruled in the same way as proposed by Capotorti.

[31] *Interquell Stärke-Chemie GmbH & Co. KG v European Economic Community* Case 261/78 ECLI:EU:C:1982:329 [1982]. In the judgment of 6 October 1982, the Court ruled in the same way as proposed by Capotorti.

[32] *Srl CILFIT and Lanificio di Gavardo SpA v Ministry of Health* Case 283/81 ECLI:EU:C:1982:335 [1982] ECR 03415. The Court, in its ruling of 6 October 1982, accepted the principle of 'acte claire'. However, in order to avoid any abuse, it laid down some guidelines that the national courts of last resort should follow before reaching the conclusion that the answer to the question of Community law was really such as not raising any reasonable doubt.

appropriate to allow national courts to exempt themselves from their duty of referring to the Court in such vague conditions, as this might easily lead to abuses. With hindsight, one can say that Capotorti was right on this point. Indeed, the recent ruling in *Consorzio Italian Management*[33] is clear evidence of how difficult it still is for the Court of Justice as well as for national courts to come to terms with the notion of *acte claire* and the conditions in which it should apply.

In the case *Commisssion v. France*,[34] that concerned a French restrictive regime of imports for mutton and lamb of British origin, Capotorti and the Court were confronted with the first ever case of a request by the Commission for the indication of interim measures in the framework of an application against a Member State which had not complied with an earlier infringement judgment. This kind of request against a Member State has recently been made several times against Poland[35] but was unheard of at the time of Capotorti's tenure at the Court.

There are also many delicate cases that concern what is now referred to as the law of the Internal Market, in which Capotorti delivered his Opinion as Advocate General.

The most important of these cases is the landmark case *Cassis de Dijon*,[36] which asked the Court to rule on whether a non-discriminatory measure of a Member State, applying to both goods imported and of 'national origin', could be regarded as an obstacle to free movement and therefore fall under the prohibition of what is now Article 34 TFEU. On this trend of questions, I should also mention *Commission v. Ireland*,[37] the Irish jewelry and other souvenirs case, for which Capotorti served as Advocate General. Here, the Court drew a clear line that distinguished between discriminatory and non-discriminatory

[33] *Consorzio Italian Management and Catania Multiservizi SpA vs Rete Ferroviaria Italiana SpA* Case C-561/19 ECLI:EU:C:2021:799 [2021]. The ruling in this case is just the last of a series of cases in which the Court was asked to clarify the guidelines as laid down in the *CILFIT* case.

[34] *Commission of the European Communities v French Republic (Interim measures)* Joined Cases 24 and 97/80 R ECLI:EU:C:1980:107 [1980]. In his Opinion of 25 March 1980, Advocate General Capotorti proposed to the Court to reject the Commission's application for interim measures. The Court ruled in the same sense.

[35] *European Commission v Republic of Poland* Case C-619/18 R ECLI:EU:C:2019:575 [2019]; *European Commission v Republic of Poland (Independence of the Izba Dyscyplinarna (Disciplinary Chamber) of the Sąd Najwyższy (Supreme Court, Poland)* Case C-791/19 R ECLI:EU:C:2020:277 [2020]; *European Commission v Republic of Poland (Indépendance et vie privée des juges)* Case C-204/21 R ECLI:EU:C:2023:334 [2023].

[36] *Rewe-Zentral AG v Bundesmonopolverwaltung für Branntwein* Case 120/78 ECLI:EU:C:1979:42 [1979] ECR 00649. In its judgment of 20 February 1979, the Court ruled in the same way as suggested by Capotorti.

[37] *Commission of the European Communities v Ireland* Case 249/81 ECLI:EU:C:1982:402 [1982] ECR 04005. In the judgment of 24 November 1982, the Court ruled in the same way as suggested by Capotorti.

measures that hindered the free movement of goods, a clear line that, alas, the Court has occasionally not respected.[38]

Hoffmann La Roche[39] and *Centrafarm*,[40] both on the repackaging of pharmaceuticals, gave the Court the opportunity to assess the conditions under which only the use of Industrial Property rights could legitimately hinder the free movement of goods.

On the subject of the free movement of workers, Capotorti delivered his Opinion in two important cases, both of which concerned women of French nationality who were suspected of being prostitutes and risked being deported from Belgium on grounds of public policy: *Pecastaing*[41] and *Adoui*.[42]

Capotorti also dealt with *Casati*,[43] one of the first, if not the first, case of preliminary questions raised before the Court on the free movement of capital and on the possibility for individuals to rely on the corresponding Treaty provisions. One should remember that, in the original version, these provisions were much less precise and unconditional than the Treaty provisions that concerned the other freedoms of movement.

Capotorti examined the principle of equal pay for women and men in *Macarthys*[44] and in the already quoted *Defrenne III* case.[45]

Capotorti also offered his view on still well known cases in the area of State aid, such as *Philip Morris*.[46]

As a highly distinguished scholar and renowned expert in Private International Law, Capotorti naturally handled many of the early cases that involved the

[38] *Commission of the European Communities v Kingdom of Belgium* See Case C-2/90 ECLI:EU:C:1992:310 [1992] ECR I-04431, para 34; *Nicolas Decker v Caisse de maladie des employés privés* Case C-120/95 ECLI:EU:C:1998:167 [1998] ECR I-01831, paras 35–36; *PreussenElektra AG v Schhleswag AG* Case C-379/98 ECLI:EU:C:2001:160 [2001] ECR I-02099, paras 71–72.

[39] *Hoffmann-La Roche & Co. AG v Centrafarm Vertriebsgesellschaft Pharmazeutischer Erzeugnisse mbH* Case 102/77 ECLI:EU:C:1978:108 [1978] ECR 1224. In the judgment of 23 May 1978, the Court ruled in the same way as suggested by Capotorti.

[40] *Centrafarm BV v American Home Products Corporation* Case 3/78 ECLI:EU:C:1978:174 [1978] ECR 01823. In the Judgment of 10 October, 1978, the Court ruled in the same way as suggested by Capotorti.

[41] *Josette Pecastaing v Belgian State* Case 98/79 ECLI:EU:C:1980:69 [1980] ECR 00691. In the judgment of 5 March 1980, the Court ruled in the same way as suggested by Capotorti.

[42] *Rezguia Adoui v Belgian State and City of Liège; Dominique Cornuaille v Belgian State* Joined Cases 115 and 116/81 ECLI:EU:C:1982:60 [1982] ECR 01665. In the judgment of 18 May 1982, the Court ruled, in part, in the same way as suggested by Capotorti.

[43] *Criminal proceedings against Guerrino Casati* Case 203/80 ECLI:EU:C:1981:261 [1981] ECR 02595. In the judgment of the Court of 11 November 1981, the Court ruled in the same way as suggested by Capotorti.

[44] *Macarthys Ltd v Wendy Smith* Case 129/79 ECLI:EU:C:1980:103 [1980] ECR 01275. In the judgment of 27 March 1980, the Court ruled in the same way as suggested by Capotorti.

[45] See *Defrenne* (n 23).

[46] *Philip Morris Holland BV v Commission of the European Communities* Case 730/79 ECLI:EU:C:1980:209 [1980] ECR 02671. The judgment of the Court of 17 September 1980 ruled in the same way as suggested by Capotorti.

interpretation of the 1968 Brussels Convention on jurisdiction and enforcement of decisions in civil and commercial matters: *Mines de potasse d'Alsace*,[47] *Segoura*,[48] *Meeth*,[49] *Sanicentral*[50] and *Zelger*.[51]

Lastly, I should conclude this review of cases by mentioning the *Burgoa* case,[52] on fisheries. This case raised some very intricate questions concerning Article 234 of the Treaty on the European Community. Most interestingly, in this case, Capotorti had to make full use of his great skills in both mastering the interpretation of the 1969 Vienna Convention on the law of the treaties,[53] especially Article 30(4) (b), and in approaching the delicate question of whether Article 234 (now, Article 351 TFEU) could have direct effect.

7. CAPOTORTI'S ATTITUDE TOWARDS THE EUROPEAN INTEGRATION

Capotorti was a convinced supporter of European integration and wished it would develop towards a closer and closer union.

His pro-European integration attitude was well known. Indeed, he was among the members of the '*Comité des juristes*', which drafted the Treaty on the European Union, also known as the Spinelli Treaty, for the European Parliament Committee on Institutional Affairs.

Capotorti's commitment to this project is confirmed by the fact that he published two articles[54] on it and edited, together with the other members of the group (M Hilf, FG Jacobs and J-P Jacqué), a full Commentary of the draft, published both in English and in French.[55]

[47] *Handelskwekerij G. J. Bier BV v Mines de potasse d'Alsace SA* Case 21/76 ECLI:EU:C:1976:166 [1967] ECR 01735. In the judgment of the Court of 30 November 1976 ruled differently from what Capotorti had suggested.

[48] *Galeries Segoura SPRL v Société Rahim Bonakdarian* Case 25/76 ECLI:EU:C:1976:178 [1976] ECR 01851. In the judgment of 14 December 1976 ruled in the same way as suggested by Capotorti.

[49] *Nikolaus Meeth v Glacetal* Case 23/78 ECLI:EU:C:1978:198 [1978] ECR 02133. In the judgment of 9 November 1978, the Court ruled only in part in the same way as suggested by Capotorti.

[50] *Sanicentral GmbH v René Collin* Case 25/79 ECLI:EU:C:1979:255 [1979] ECR 03423. In the judgment of 13 November 1979, the Court ruled in the same way as suggested by Capotorti.

[51] *Siegfried Zelger v Sebastiano Salinitri* Case 56/79 ECLI:EU:C:1980:15 [1979] ECR 00089. In the judgment of 17 January 1980 the Court ruled in the same way as suggested by Capotorti.

[52] *Attorney General v Juan C. Burgoa* Case 812/79 ECLI:EU:C:1980:231 [1980] ECR 02787. In the judgment of 14 October 1980, the Court ruled in the same way as suggested by Capotorti.

[53] One should recall that Capotorti was one of the first authors to publish a full commentary on the Vienna Convention: F Capotorti, *Il diritto dei trattati secondo la Convenzione di Vienna: Studio introduttivo sulla Convenzione di Vienna sul diritto dei trattati* (Padova, CEDAM, 1969).

[54] F Capotorti, 'Dal Progetto Spinelli alla Costituzione europea (1994) *Unieuropa* 174; F Capotorti, 'Le funzioni dell'Unione europea nel progetto parlamentare di costituzione' in AA. VV., *Studi in ricordo di Antonio Filippo Panzera* (Vol. I, Bari, Cacucci Editore, 1995) 113.

[55] F Capotorti, M Hilf, FG Jacobs, J-P Jacqué, *The European Union Treaty: Commentary on the draft adopted by the European Parliament on 14 February 1984* (Oxford, Oxford University Press, 1986).

8. CONCLUDING REMARKS

Capotorti left the Court as an Advocate General on 6 October 1982.

In his final address, he expressed some very noble thoughts, which I believe are worth quoting here.

First of all Capotorti stressed the sense of unity and mutual respect that he experienced among all the Members of the Court. In his view, 'the quality of the relationship between the members, characterised by a deep respect for each individual's freedom to think independently and, at the same time, by the common commitment to defend the autonomy of the Court, as well as its quality of being truly and consistently "super partes".'[56]

These were remarkable features of the Court. On this point, Capotorti thought, 'the diversity of the professional origins of each one of us, the different legal traditions in which we were brought up and our different nationalities have not prevented us all from sincerely desiring to join together in making our diverse contributions serve the unity of the Court.'[57]

Secondly, Capotorti praised the Court for 'its consistency, its fidelity to certain principles, which are those proclaimed in the Treaties and whose numerous implications have been gradually clarified by the decisions of the Court.'[58]

According to him, 'this function is not discharged simply in order to comply with an obligation but rather with the aim of completing the edifice of European integration on the foundations of the Treaties.' The aim of integration, he added, 'which from the point of view of realpolitik must now be considered utopian, has been brought closer, in the field of law, by our Court and also by the large number of judges and lawyers of our countries who have adopted the same approach, with the result that the European legal community seems stronger today than the political community'.[59]

Finally, the Advocate General considered worth of special mention 'the discreet, reserved style' of the Court's activity, 'both internally and in its external relations'.[60] The Court's activity, Capotorti remarked, is such that it 'rarely attracts the attention of the mass media [...] is not subjected to the influence of approval or criticism. and .... does not involve any feeling of a need for wide publicity'.[61] He thought he could say that 'the most important decisions in the case-law of the Court were taken during the period in which the governments of the Member States were scarcely aware of its existence'.[62] The Court was

[56] Francesco Capotorti, Speech Delivered by Mr Advocate General, Translation (Formal sitting, 6 October 1982) 1.

[57] ibid., 1–2.

[58] ibid., 2.

[59] ibid., 3.

[60] ibid.

[61] ibid.

[62] ibid., 4.

therefore allowed to independently develop its case law in favour of integration, without asking itself whether the governments did 'really appreciate the role which the Court occupies in the Community structures and in the legal life of Europe' or not.[63]

One might point out that the situation is very different from the years Capotorti was referring to. Nowadays the most important of the Court's rulings are followed with great attention by the governments and are widely reported in the mass media. However, as Capotorti rightly observed in his speech, the Court had already acquired its authority during the first decades of its activity. The vast publicity it now enjoys does in no way jeopardise its prestige.

[63] ibid.

8

Giacinto Bosco, a Rather Well-known Politician in Italy, and One of the Lesser-known Italian Members of the Court of Justice of the European Communities

JACQUES ZILLER

1. GIACINTO BOSCO, AN ITALIAN LEGAL SCHOLAR MAINLY SPECIALISED IN INTERNATIONAL LAW

GIACINTO BOSCO WAS born on 25 January 1905 in Santa Maria Capua Vetere, a borough close to Caserta. The latter city is mainly known for the Reggia di Caserta (Royal Palace), the greatest palace erected in Europe during the 18th century. It was the residence of the House of Bourbon-Two Sicilies, who were Kings of Naples. Bosco died on 11 October 1997 at the age of 92.[1]

1.1. Academic Career

Bosco graduated at the University of Naples in 1925 with a Laurea in giurisprudenza, the highest[2] law degree. He was only 20 years old, a quite young age for such an achievement. He served as honorary judge in his native town before succeeding in a concorso (competitive examination) of the Ministry for Foreign Affairs in 1927. He served as Vicesegretario (Assistant Secretary) for five years.

[1] See especially the eulogy pronounced by the President of the ECJ Gil Carlos Rodríguez Iglesias at the solemn sitting of the Court on 14 January 1998 – Memorandum 001/98, the notices for each legislature are on the websites of the Senato della Repubblica and Camera dei Deputati, as well as *Enciclopedia Treccani* https://www.treccani.it/enciclopedia/giacinto-bosco/ and *Dizionario storico dell'integrazione europea* https://www.dizie.eu/dizionario/bosco-giacinto/.

[2] The dottorato di ricerca, equivalent to a PhD, was only introduced in Italy in 1984.

He also continued working for the Ministry of Foreign affairs as a legal adviser after he started an academic career.

In 1929, Bosco started teaching international law as Libero docente (free lecturer, without tenure) at the University of Rome 'La Sapienza'. He also taught international law, without tenure, at the University of Urbino, in the north of the present-day Region of Marche. At Urbino, he served as Dean of the Facoltà di giurisprudenza (law faculty), which had strong ties with the law faculty of Rome University. In 1933, he won a concorso per professore ordinario (competitive examination for full professor) of private and public international law at the University of Florence, where he continued teaching until 1940. In that year, Bosco was appointed at the Facoltà di economia e commercio (Faculty of economics and business) of La Sapienza University, where he remained a full professor until retirement in 1975, when he was appointed emeritus professor.

At Florence University, Bosco was a director of the 'Rivista di studi politici internazionali' (RSPI), founded in 1934, together with Jacopo Mazzei, a professor of economics. They were both attached to the 'Regio "Cesare Alfieri"', the oldest Italian Faculty of political and social sciences. RSPI's purpose was to disseminate international studies and to emphasise Italy's representation abroad, while moving toward a more decisive participation in the European political game. As a quarterly review, RSPI was one of the first publishing political and scientific contributions on current affairs, including essays, articles, profiles of statesmen and diplomats, briefings and documents, and reviews of books.

At La Sapienza University, Bosco set up the Scuola di perfezionamento degli studi europei della facoltà di economia e commercio (graduate school of European studies of the faculty of business and economics) in 1966. He was Director of the 'Rivista di Studi Europei', a quarterly journal of the Graduate school.

In 1962, Bosco was elected as a member of the Institute of International Law (IIL). The IIL is a learned society founded in 1873 in Ghent (Belgium) with the purpose of promoting the progress of international law, and which received the Nobel Peace Prize in 1904.

1.2. Publications

Bosco published a number of articles and handbooks in private and public international law and later in EC law, mainly in the Italian language.

Among several publications published before World War II are 'The current state of the question of the exemption of foreign states from domestic jurisdiction',[3] 'Relations and conflicts between international jurisdictions'[4]

[3] G Bosco, *Lo stato attuale della questione dell'esenzione degli stati esteri dalla giurisdizione interna* (Roma, Società Editrice Romana, 1929) 28 p.

[4] G Bosco, *Rapporti e conflitti fra giurisdizioni internazionali* (Vol 20, Pubblicazioni dell'Associazione italiana per la Società delle Nazioni; Roma, Anonima Romana Editori, 1932) 148 p.

and 'Private international aviation law'.[5] He also published in support of the Italian war against Ethiopia.[6] Bosco published a handbook of private international law in 1936[7] and handbooks on public international law in 1938 and 1942.[8]

A special mention has to be made of a publication on 'The Legal foundation of the compulsory value of international law',[9] because of the way in which AG Mancini refers to it in 1988 in his conclusions in *Greece v. Council* (Bosco was sitting in the Court):

> There is no doubt that in international law promissory declarations are binding. Giacinto Bosco made that assertion 50 years ago, basing his argument – which at the time was both original and heretical – on the power of States to enter into unilateral commitments – a power which is derived from a general norm relating to law-making and based on intention on the part of the States (see [...]). Subsequently that view has been taken by an increasing number of writers, even if they have used different arguments or, at times, less broad terms [...]. Today, the rule *promissio est obligatio* has been definitively confirmed by the International Court of Justice at The Hague in the judgment cited above concerning French nuclear tests in Polynesia.[10]

After World War II, Bosco published, among others, an essay on 'The plurality of legal orders in the unity of the Law of Nations',[11] often referred to by scholars. His theoretical stance is especially evident in the last eight words of that title. Bosco published a handbook of public international law in 1970 and 1972, with the same title as in 1938: 'Lectures in Public International Law'. The 1981 edition has an interesting complement to the title ie, 'with an introduction on the common law of mankind',[12] which also stresses Bosco's theoretical stance. Already in the 1970 and 1972 editions there was already a specific chapter entitled 'Diritto universal del genere umano e diritto internazionale' (universal law of mankind and international law). Bosco insists on criticising the

[5] G Bosco, *Il diritto internazionale privato aeronautico* (Società Editrice "Athenæum", 1934) 16 p.

[6] G Bosco, *L'iniquo processo di Ginevra: documenti sul conflitto italo-etiopico* (1936) 1 *Quaderni dello Studio fiorentino di politica estera* 128 p. See also T Scovazzi, 'The Italian Approach to Colonialism: The First Experiences in Eritrea and Somalia', in G Bartolini (ed), *A History of International Law in Italy* (Oxford, Oxford University Press, 2020) 205, 375, 377, 378, 380 and 389.

[7] G Bosco, *Corso di diritto internazionale privato: parte generale, diritto delle persone e diritto di famiglia* (Vol 1, Pubblicazioni dell'Associazione italiana per la società delle Nazioni; Firenze, Casa editrice poligrafica universitaria, 1936) 270 p.

[8] G Bosco, *Lezioni di diritto internazionale pubblico* (Castellani, 1938) 293 p; G Bosco, *Corso di diritto internazionale pubblico: anno accademico 1941–42* (Castellani, 1942) 320 p.

[9] G Bosco, 'Il fondamento giuridico del valore obbligatorio del diritto internazionale' (1938) *Rivista di diritto pubblico* 626.

[10] *Greece v Council* Case C-204/86 ECLI:EU:C:1988:259 [1988], Opinion of AG Mancini of 25 May 1988, 5350.

[11] G Bosco, *La pluralità degli ordinamenti giuridici nell'unità del diritto delle genti* (Firenze, F Le Monnier, 1961) 16 p.

[12] G Bosco, *Lezioni di diritto internazionale: con una introduzione sul diritto comune al genere umano* (Milano, Giuffrè, 1981) 564 p.

contemporary Italian scholarship for focusing solely on inter-state law, without sufficiently taking into account the sociological aspect of *ius gentium*. He concludes that chapter with the following statement:

> The establishment of a legal order proper to the society of states has not done away with the common law, otherwise known as the universal law of peoples, which is the order proper to the whole of humanity. This order (it must be admitted) has lost much ground with the formation of numerous particular orders, such as international law, the domestic law of the various states and the various autonomous international organisations, canon law, etc.; but it has not died out and manifests its presence both in customary norms and in general principles of law, which are applicable as long as inter-subjective relations are regulated by the specific sources of the individual particular orders, such as treaties, laws or other normative acts not contemplated by them.[13]

Bosco does not quote the French international lawyer Georges Scelle (1978–1961),[14] although he clearly shares some of the latter's analyses.

Bosco is considered by Italian scholarships as one of the promoters, with Gaspare Ambrosini (1886–1985) and Emilio Betti (1890–1968), of the so-called model of 'legal vacuum', rooted in an international private law model.[15] The 'legal vacuum' model has influenced the way the relationship between EU law and Italian law is considered, not only by Italian scholarship but also in the jurisprudence of the Italian Constitutional Court. That model is to some extent related to the legal pluralism and relativism of Santi Romano's masterwork 'L'Ordinamento Giuridico'.[16] Santi Romano (1875–1947), professor at the law faculties of Pisa and Milan, and President of the Council of State (1928–1944) has been one of the most influential scholars in Italian public law, together with Vittorio Emanuele Orlando (1860–1952), professor at the law faculties of Messina, Palermo and Rome, and politician and President of the Council (head of government) from 1917 to 1919. Differently from Romano and from

[13] G Bosco, *Lezioni di diritto internazionale* (Milan, Giuffrè, 1972) 17: 'Il costituirsi di un ordinamento giuridico proprio della società degli Stati non ha fatto venir meno il diritto comune, altrimenti detto diritto universale delle genti, che è l'ordinamento proprio dell'intera umanità. Questo ordinamento (bisogna riconoscerlo) ha perduto molto terreno col formarsi di numerosi ordinamenti particolari, quali il diritto internazionale, il diritto interno dei vari stati e delle varie organizzazioni internazionali autonome, il diritto canonico, ecc.; ma esso nondimeno non si è estinto e manifesta la sua presenza sia con le norme consuetudinarie che con i principi generali del diritto, che sono applicabili fino a quando le relazioni intersubiettive siano regolate dalle fonti proprie dei singoli ordinamenti particolari, quali trattati, leggi o altri atti normativi da essi non contemplati'. (My translation).

[14] See A Cassese, 'Remarks on Scelle's Theory of "Role Splitting" in International Law' (1990) *European Journal of International Law* 210.

[15] See G Itzcovich, *Teorie e ideologie del diritto comunitario* (Turin, Giappichelli, 2006) 387, according to whom the 'legal vacuum' model (Modello internazionalprivatistico del 'vuoto giuridicio') is 'based upon a pluralist institutionalist and Romanist imprint, develops a monism of jurs-naturalist inspiration, centred on the concept of the "common law of nations"'. (My translation).

[16] S Romano, *L'ordinamento giuridico – A cura e con un testo di Mariano Croce* (Reprint, Quodlibet, 2018). This major work of Italian legal theory has been translated into French, but not into English.

Bosco, Orlando was one of the few law professors to refuse to take an oath to the fascist regime; this being said, neither Romano nor Bosco can be considered as fascist scholars.

The 1970 edition of Bosco's handbook on Public International Public Law also contained a chapter on 'Le organizzazioni internazionali europee' (the European International organisations), which gave an account of the history of European integration after World War II, as well as of the organisation of the Council of Europe and the European Communities. The end of the chapter revealed both Bosco's views on the specific nature of the Communities and the fact that he wished further integration to be pursued. Bosco stressed the explicit mention of their supranational character in the treaties of the European Coal and Steel and European Defence Communities and further stated that:

> After the failure to ratify the [ECSC] Treaty, any allusion to the term supranational was avoided in the subsequent 1957 Rome Treaties, for understandable reasons of political expediency. But the omission of the term is, on closer inspection, of no decisive value, since the Union of the six Countries has in any case retained the Community character that is expressive of a solidaristic bond of a permanent and more incisive nature than that which binds ordinary Unions of states This element of supranationality that exists in the European Communities is not, however, such that it can be likened to a federal state.[17]

Quite logically, once he had become a judge in Luxembourg, Bosco's scholarly work centred on EC law. He published, amongst others, a comment on the Single European Act (SEA) in the French language.[18] As far as I know, he did not comment on sentences from the point of view of a Judge who was sitting in the Court when they were adopted.

Two books that were published after he finished his second term as a European Court of Justice (ECJ) judge are particularly worth mentioning.

'The Internal market of the European economic community'[19] published in 1990, is quite impressive with its extent of 775 pages; it is mainly a book of materials (that total 570 pages) that contain the relevant secondary law instruments and recommendations. The materials are preceded with a text that introduces the reader to the programme of completion of the internal market, as well as to the legal nature of regulations and directives (pages 9 to 46). There are then a series of comments on the most important normative acts that relate to the internal market (pages 49 to 202).

[17] Bosco (n 13) 258-259: 'Dopo la mancata ratifica del trattato [CECA], fu evitata nei successivi trattati di Roma del 1957, per comprensibili motivi di opportunità politica, ogni allusione al termine sopranazionale. Ma l'omissione del termine non ha, a ben vedere, alcun valore decisivo, in quanto l'Unione dei sei Paesi ha comunque conservato il carattere comunitario che è espressivo di un vincolo solidaristico di carattere permanente e più incisivo di quello che lega le normali Unioni di Stati Questo elemento di sopranazionalità esistente nelle Comunità Europee non è tale tuttavia da poterle assimilare ad uno Stato federale'. (My translation).

[18] G Bosco, 'Commentaire de l'Acte unique européen des 17-18 février 1987' (1987) *Cahiers de droit européen* 355–382.

[19] G Bosco, *Il mercato interno della Comunità economica europea* (Milan, Giuffrè, 1990) 775 p.

The preface reveals that the text was written before the adoption of the law of 9 March 1989, n 86 ('legge La Pergola'), as it includes the wish that a special act of Parliament be adopted to implement by means of Italian delegated legislation the secondary legislation commented on in the book. Bosco also points out that 'the reorganisation of the public administration must be carried out, also in order to make possible the timely preparation of the large number of implementing acts required for the future 'EC law' (*legge comunitaria*).[20] He concludes with a warning: 'It is not possible to remain in Europe without knowing and respecting its laws, which now regulate most of the economic and social relations of European citizens'.[21]

The second book, albeit taking over the former title of his handbook on Public International Public Law, is again a book of materials, as appears in its subtitle: 'Commentary of the Single European Act of 17–28 February 1986, Commentary on the Treaty on European Union of 7 February 1992'.[22] These two books amply demonstrate that Bosco, although retired from academia and the Court, remained fully committed to Italy's progress in implementing EC law even at the age of 87.

2. GIACINTO BOSCO, AN IMPORTANT MEMBER OF THE CHRISTIAN DEMOCRACY, MEMBER OF PARLIAMENT AND OF SEVERAL GOVERNMENTS, MEMBER OF THE HIGH COUNCIL OF THE JUDICIARY[23]

2.1. Member of Parliament and of the Core Groups of Christian Democrats

For somebody such as Bosco, who had been very active in the practice of foreign policy as a consultant to the Ministry of Foreign Affairs while developing an academic career, it was quite logical to become interested in politics after World War II; he became a member of the Democrazia Cristiana (Christian Democratic party). After the entry into force of the new Constitution on 1 January 1948, parliamentary elections were held on 18–19 April.

Bosco tried to be on the list of its candidates for the Camera dei deputati (lower house), in the constituency of Naples and Caserta: the elections were held with proportional vote. He was countered by other candidates of the party who slandered him, and he did not get a response to his appeal in the party structure. He thus decided to stand as an independent candidate for the Senato

[20] Bosco (n 19), XXII: 'occorre procedere alla riorganizzazione della pubblica amministrazione, anche per rendere possibile la predisposizione dell'ingente numero di provvedimenti di attuazione previsti dalla legge comunitaria, ancora in corso di approvazione'. (My translation).

[21] ibid., XXIII: 'Non si può restare in Europa senza conoscerne e rispettarne le leggi, che ormai regolano la maggior parte dei rapporti economici e sociali dei cittadini europei'.

[22] G Bosco, *Lezioni di diritto internazionale: commento all'Atto unico europeo del 17-28 febbraio 1986, commento al trattato sull'Unione Europea del 7 febbraio 1992* (Milano, Giuffrè, 1992).

[23] See above footnote n 1.

(upper house), where elections were held on the basis of a mixed system based upon proportional vote but with single-member constituencies for preferences. He was elected in the constituency of his hometown. He was excluded from the party for about one year even though he had supported the Christian Democrat candidates for the Camera dei deputati and had joined the Christian Democrat parliamentary group at the Senato when elected. He was readmitted to the party only two years later. It is clear that this episode gained him the trust and esteem of the party hierarchy, especially of its leader Alcide de Gasperi (1881–1954), as well as Amintore Fanfani (1908–1999), de Gasperi's successor, and Arnaldo Forlani (1925), another of the party's leaders, to both whom he remained always rather close.

Bosco was re-elected to the Senate for the five next parliamentary periods. He was Vice-President of the Senate from 12 June 1958 to 25 July 1960. He sat in European Parliament sessions as a senator of the Italian delegation from al 27 May 1959 to 19 December 1960.

2.2. A Long Experience as Minister in Several Cabinets

Bosco was a member of most Cabinets from 1953 to 1972. His career illustrates the governmental stability that is hidden behind the instability of Italian politics at the level of Presidente del Consiglio (head of government). Indeed, there has long been stability in some major portfolios, a factor that developed the capacity for politicians with high levels of education, such as Bosco, to increase their expertise in major fields.

Bosco was Sottosegretario di Stato (Junior Minister) at the Ministry of Defence from 1953 to 1958 in the De Gasperi-VIII Cabinet, and remained there in the Pella, Fanfani I, Scelba, Segni I and Zoli Cabinets.[24] This gave him increased practice of international relations and gave him experience in the field of European integration as he witnessed the preparation of the European Defence Community and the failure of its ratification due to the fact that the French National Assembly discarded the ratification of the Treaty that had been signed in May 1952 by a vote on a preliminary question that avoided its discussion in a highly divided house. The Benelux countries and Germany already held a positive vote on ratification, but the Italian government preferred to wait for the French ratification to occur before debating in Parliament. During the same parliamentary period, as is well known, Italy had a major role in helping, with Belgium, to resume the advancement of European integration, which led to the signature of the Rome treaties on 27 April 1957, which entered into force on 1 January 1958. After the elections of May 1958, Bosco was elected Vice-President of the Senate and thus did not participate in the Fanfani II, Segni II and Tambroni Cabinets.

[24] From 17 July 1957 to 12 June 1958.

Bosco was appointed Minister of Education in the Fanfani III Cabinet on 6 July 1960 and kept this position until 20 February 1962. He was then Minister of Justice in the Fanfani IV and Leone I Cabinets from 21 February 1962 to 3 December 1963. He was Minister for Labour and Social Security in the Moro I Cabinet from 4 December 1963 to 21 July 1964, and in the and Moro III and Leone II Cabinets and from 23 February 1966 to 11 December 1968. He was Minister without Portfolio in the Rumor I Cabinet from 12 December 1968 to 8 August 1969 and Minister for Finance in the Rumor II Cabinet that followed until 27 March 1970. In the Rumor III Cabinet that followed he was first Minister without Portfolio Ultimately, and Minister of Posts and Telecommunications from 9 June 1970, a position that he held in the Colombo and Andreotti I Cabinets, until the elections of 28 February 1972.

Especially noteworthy is the fact that he chaired the Conference of Ministers of Justice of the Council of Europe in 1962; he was Head of the Italian delegation at the General Assembly of the United Nations in 1965, and chaired the meetings of the EC Council of ministers of social affairs in 1968.

On the basis of his longstanding experience and knowledge of the EC institutions and of European integration, Bosco promoted the idea of a 'fourth European Community' dedicated to youth problems, to be established on the initiative of the six founding Member States and open for accession to all European States. He presented his idea on that fourth Community in his inaugural lecture at the Scuola di perfezionamento in Rome on 31 January 1969.[25] His speech is a passionate plea for further political integration from a typical Christian Democratic perspective in the tradition of de Gasperi, Schuman and Adenauer.

> The path taken [with the Rome treaties] has not been very productive from the point of view of the political development of European unity. There has been too much reliance on the driving force of mercantile activities, whereas the strengthening of cultural and spiritual values should have been tackled at the same time. This is perhaps the reason why not only the three Communities but also the state structures of the European countries are going through a crisis that many blame on the dominance of the consumerist aspects of modern society. Excessive reference to material interests fatally leads to new forms of nationalism, while it is indispensable to increase community participation, taking note of the wider dimensions of the modern world not only as a reflection of spatial conquests but also because of the emergence of new philosophical currents that take up the ancient Christian strand of the universality of spiritual values and the brotherhood of the human race.[26]

[25] The text has been sent by Bosco to Carlo Scarascia-Mugnozza MP, who was member of the Italian delegation at the European Parliament. It is available at the Historical Archives of the European Union. Bosco indicated that it would be published in the *Rivista di Studi Europei* in Spring 1969.

[26] 'La via percorsa non è stata molto produttiva dal punto di vista dello sviluppo politico dell'unità europea. Si è fatto eccessivo affidamento sulla forza propulsiva delle attività mercantili, mentre sarebbe stato necessario affrontare in pari tempo il rafforzamento dei valori culturali e spirituali. è questo forse il motivo quale nos soltanto le tre Comunità ma anche le strutture statuali dei Paesi Europei attraversano una crisi che molti addebitano al predominio degli aspetti consumistici della

Bosco had been Minister for Labour and Social Security during the student and workers protests that started in 1968 and went on into the following year. As Minister without Portfolio for Special Assignments from 12 December 1968 to 4 August 1969 in the Rumor I Cabinet, he had time to dedicate more attention to the questions he had encountered as a minister for Education eight years earlier. That attention appears in the inaugural lecture.

> The problem of the new frontiers is being addressed above all by young people who are not resigned to the disappointment of the failure to achieve European unity. [...] To this end, the possibility of establishing a new European Community for youth issues should be examined, to be proposed by the six countries of the current Communities but open to the unconditional accession of the other European states.[27]

Bosco then goes into details regarding the tasks of that new Community: exchanges and cultural encounters; university institutions (ie, the acknowledgement of European dimensions of higher education in member States' legislation); recognition of university degrees; scientific research; vocational education; organisation of sports; and improving the social welfare of young people in developing countries. On the institutional side, he proposed to adapt the EC institutions. Noteworthy is his proposal that the future direct election of MEPs should include voting rights for young people who had not yet reached the age of majority in their home countries.

2.3. Vice-President of the High Council of the Judiciary

After having been again elected to the Senate in May 1972, Bosco was elected by the Senators on 27 June for five years as one of the seven lay-members of the Consiglio superiore della magistratura – CSM (High Council of the Judiciary), the self-governing body for Italy's civil and criminal judges and prosecutors, which was also composed of members elected from among the judiciary – 14 at the time. His fellow councillors elected him as Vice-President. The Vice-Presidency of the CSM is particularly important because formally its President is the Head of State, who is not involved in the management of the institution. Having been an honorary judge before starting his professional career, and later on Minister of Justice for almost two years, Bosco thus complemented his

società moderna. L'eccessivo riferimento agli interessi materiali porta fatalmente a nuove forme di nazionalismo, mentre è indispensabile accrescere la partecipazione comunitaria, prendendo atto delle più ampie dimensioni del mondo moderno non soltanto come riflesso delle conquiste spaziali ma anche per l'affermarsi di nuove correnti filosofiche che riprendono l'antico filone cristiano della universalità dei valori spirituali e della fratellanza del genere umano.' (My translation)

[27] 'Al problema delle nuove frontiere guardano soprattutto i giovani che non si rassegnano alla delusione del mancato raggiungimento dell'Unità Europea. Bisogna incoraggiarli a procedere per nuove strade, più aperte ai valori universali della cultura e non ancorate ai ristretti limiti degli interessi economici e settoriali. [...] All'uopo si dovrebbe esaminare la possibilità di istituire una nuova Comunità europea per i problemi della gioventù, da proporsi dai Sei Paesi delle attuali Comunità ma aperta all'adesione incondizionata degli altri Stati Europei.' (My translation)

knowledge of law as an academic with his experience on the issue of the organisation of justice. Those qualifications and his experience of five years at the CSM thus predestined him to be a judge at the ECJ.

3. GIACINTO BOSCO, JUDGE AT THE ECJ[28]

3.1. Appointment and Duration of Mandate

Bosco's strong relations with the leadership of the Democrazia Cristiana explain why it was easy for him to be proposed as a Judge by the Italian Cabinet. His experience in the European Parliament sessions and in numerous sessions of the Council as an Italian minister gave him a solid internal knowledge of the EC institutions, which was then complemented by his two mandates as a judge.

When Ricardo Monaco resigned from office eight months in advance, the Italian Government – which was chaired by Giulio Andreotti – had already agreed to propose Bosco as his successor. It is most probably Bosco himself who suggested to Andreotti that he would like to go to the Luxembourg Court. Francesco Capotorti was proposed to finish Monaco's term with the understanding that he would then be appointed Advocate General when Alberto Trabucchi left the Court. As a result of Monaco's departure, there would be a short overlap with Bosco's mandate as Vice-President of the CSM, which finished on 10 January 1977, but he obtained the consent of the Court for this overlap when he started his term as a Judge.

By decision of the representatives Member states of 20 July 1976, Bosco was thus appointed as judge at the ECJ together with André M Donner (from the Netherlands) who had already served for three terms, Hans Kutscher (from Germany) who had already served for one term and Alexander J Mackenzie Stuart (from the United Kingdom) who had already served for three years, as well as Capotorti as Advocate General, for the period of 7 October 1976 to 6 October 1982 included.

Bosco was appointed for a second term in 1982 together with Mackenzie Stuart, Thymen Koopmans (from the Netherlands), Ulrich Everling and Kai Bahlmann (from Germany),[29] and Yves Galmot (from France), as well as Simone Rozès (from France) and Federico Mancini as Advocate Generals, and he served until the end of that second term. Bosco was thus 71 years old when he started as a Judge and 85 when he finished.

[28] Most of the details about Bosco's terms as a judge come from different documents of the Historical Archives of the European Union, and from the use of the case-law database of the CJEU https://curia.europa.eu/juris/recherche.jsf?language=en.

[29] Until the accession of Austria, Finland, and Sweden in 1995, there was one more Judge than the number of Member States, as illustrated also by the presence of Nicola Catalano and Rino Rossi during the same period.

Bosco served with three different Presidents of the ECJ: Hans Kutscher from 1976 to 1980, Josse Mertens de Wilmars from 1980 to 1984 and John Mackenzie-Stuart from 1984 to 1988. During his stay at the Court, Bosco was assisted by the following referendari (legal secretaries): Sergio Neri, Giovanni Gallo, and Luigi Daniele from 1983 to 1987, as well as Gian Michele Roberti in 1988.

Even though eulogies are inherently panegyric in nature, it is useful to quote President Gil Carlo Rodriguez's words at the solemn sitting of 6 October 1988, which are corroborated by those who worked with him:[30]

> Giacinto Bosco has left an indelible mark on our Institution and its jurisprudence. I belong to the minority of the current members of the Court who have still had the privilege of working with him and enjoying his friendship. For some years I was able to benefit from his incomparable experience and vast knowledge. I admired him above all for his inexhaustible capacity for work, his dialectical strength, his deep sensitivity and his open-mindedness, qualities which seemed to me to be particularly remarkable in a man of his age.
>
> His particularly firm convictions did not make him an easy opponent when one disagreed with him, but his warm and generous temperament earned him affection of his colleagues. It is significant in this respect that, when he left the Court last October, Advocate General Carl Otto Lenz had a special memory of him in his speech, in which he referred to him as a father.

3.2. President of Chamber

On 5 October 1977, Bosco was appointed President of the first Chamber of the Court; on 17 October 1981, he again was appointed President of the first Chamber; on 3 October 1985, he was appointed President of the first and fourth Chambers of the Court for one year, and again President of the first Chamber on 7 October 1987. Until 1979, the Rules of Procedure provided for the number of chambers. Following the amendments of 12 September 1979, the Court has been free to determine the number and composition of the chambers as it sees fit. As a Chamber President, Bosco chaired the sittings for 243 cases, yet another testimony to his working capacity.

Bosco also acted as delegate of the President of the Court, taking interim measures on 29 November 1982, in a rather simple civil service case. The interim measure was not granted because 'In this case the applicant has not adduced any evidence to establish prima facie that his application is well founded. In any event there is nothing to prevent any damage which might be suffered by the applicant from being properly made good'.[31]

[30] Historical Archives, CJUE -2616, Original Code A2-06-029. My translation from the French.

[31] *Gilbert Castille v Commission of the European Communities* Case 173/82 R ECLI:EU:C:1982:405 [1982] ECR 4047.

3.3. Judge Rapporteur

Bosco also acted as Judge rapporteur, for a total of 238 cases. These included 46 civil services cases from the period during which the Court of First Instance was not yet functioning. He acted as rapporteur in 106 cases on applications for Preliminary rulings, of which 5 originating from Italy; in 31 infringement procedures (none against Italy); in annulment procedures from natural or legal persons of which 3 were from Member States (none from Italy). Amongst all of these cases there were, for instance, 21 in the field of competition, 26 in the fields of social security and social policy, 38 in the field of free movement of goods, and 59 in the field of agriculture. It cannot thus be said that his previous experience as a member of the Italian government had any kind of influence on how cases were given to him.

Two cases in which Bosco acted as rapporteur are somewhat outstanding, ie, the Judgment of 30 April 1986, in *Lucas Asjes*, Cases 209 to 213/84[32] and the Judgment of the Court of 16 March 1983 in *Singer*, Case 290/81 and 291/81.[33]

Lucas Asjes is one of the very famous sentences of the Court in the 1980s, which led to apply competition rules to air transport and thus to lower the prices of that sector quite considerably. The central issue was whether the competition rules in the EEC Treaty were applicable to the fixing of the tariffs for Community and international air travel, albeit that Article 84 provided that the provisions transport would only be applicable to air and sea transport after a unanimous decision of the Council, which had not been done at the time. It is not possible to know if there were long discussions in the Court and thus what Bosco's influence on the decision was. As a matter of fact, the Court already had found that competition rules applied to sea transport in its Judgment of 4 April 1974 in *Commission v. French Republic*, Case 167/73[34] in which Mertens de Wilmars was rapporteur, so the Judgment in *Lucas Asjes* is in line with previous jurisprudence.

Singer is not especially important in substance: it is about the interpretation of the General Agreement on Trade and Tariffs (GATT) and protocols, which was an exclusive matter for Member States' courts before 1 July 1968, the date on which the Common Customs Tariff was brought into force, and of the competence of the ECJ after that date. The fact that the Italian judge was rapporteur in a question for preliminary ruling regarding the Italian government might seem noteworthy, but this was not unusual at the time. Here again it seems quite difficult, if not impossible, to understand to what extent Bosco had

[32] *Criminal proceedings against Lucas Asjes and others, Andrew Gray and others, Andrew Gray and others, Jacques Maillot and others and Léo Ludwig and others* Joined Cases 209 to 213/84 ECLI:EU:C:1986:188, [1986] ECR 1425.

[33] *Compagnia Singer SpA and Geigy SpA v Amministrazione delle finanze dello Stato* Joined Cases 290/81 and 291/81 ECLI:EU:C:1983:79, [1983] ECR 1983-847.

[34] *Commission of the European Communities v. French Republic* Case 167/73 ECLI:EU:C:1974:35, [1974] ECR 359.

an influence on the outcome as judge rapporteur. The same observation applies to Bosco's influence as judge rapporteur more generally.

As mentioned by his collaborators in interviews, Bosco put the same commitment and seriousness into all the cases he had to deal with – more than sixteen hundred – whether as rapporteur, President of Chamber, or a Judge amongst others.

According to the testimony of Daniela Amodeo in the preparatory workshop to this book on 24-25 June 2022, Bosco, as a politician, knew how to be respected and how to put the parties' lawyers in their place when they did not reply to his questions during the hearings. In dealing with colleagues as well as the Court's staff he was always a tough, but kind professional. Bosco, who as most educated Italians of his generation was fluent in French, gave much importance to the interpretation directorate of the Court and to the multilingual character of EU law. Indeed, he was sitting in the plenary when the Court decided on the CILFIT case, where the Court stated, following Advocate General Capotorti's Opinion, that 'to begin with, it must be borne in mind that Community legislation is drafted in several languages and that the different language versions are all equally authentic. An interpretation of a provision of Community law thus involves a comparison of the different language versions'.[35]

3.4. Member of the Working Party on the Court of First Instance

Last but not least, Bosco made an important contribution to the development of the ECJ as a very active member of the Court's internal working party that prepared the establishment of the Court of First Instance (CFI). Indeed, the Court worked on that project for almost the entire time of Bosco's presence as a Judge. It is quite clear that Bosco's experience as a former Minister of Justice and Vice President of the Consiglio Superiore della Magistratura ensured he would give a very valuable contribution to the elaboration of the Court's views on its own reform. Furthermore, his experience as a Chamber president and as a judge rapporteur gave him first-hand experience of the issues created by the development of the Court's workload in those areas that eventually evolved to the CFI. According to oral testimonies, Bosco was of the firm opinion that the Court itself would further develop the jurisprudence, but that the CFI would adjudicate on disputes.

In a memorandum of 21 July 1978,[36] the Court explained to the Council the problems that were caused by the increasing workload of the Court as a result of the growing number of cases brought before it and of the fact that, as a result

[35] *Srl CILFIT and Lanificio di Gavardo SpA v Ministry of Health* Case 283/81 ECLI:EU:C:1982:335, [1982], ECR 3430, para 19.

[36] See A Tizzano, 'La Cour de justice et l'Acte unique européen', in *Du droit international au droit de l'intégration : Liber Amicorum Pierre Pescatore* (Baden-Baden, Nomos, 1987) 705 and 706.

of the quantitative development of its litigation, the Court had to decide more and more often on cases that required a detailed examination of complex facts. On 4 August 1978, the Commission submitted to the Council a proposal for a regulation to establish an 'Administrative Court of the European Communities',[37] but the Court's request was not acted upon at the time for political reasons.[38] On 8 November 1985, the Court asked the Intergovernmental Conference in charge of revising the Treaties – which led to the adoption of the Single European Act – to insert the legal bases for the creation of the future CFI, which was done with Articles 4, 11 and 26 SEA.

To bring the CFI into existence as soon as possible, the Court sent a draft proposal for its establishment to the Council on 26 November 1986, with a copy to the European Parliament and the Commission. This draft was submitted with the express stipulation that it was only a working document corresponding to the Court's current state of reflection, as the SEA had not yet entered into force. The stated aim of this transmission was to obtain the Council's initial comments on the draft, so that the Court could present its final proposal as soon as the SEA entered into force.

On 25 September 1987, barely three months after the entry into force of the SEA, the Court transmitted to the Council a formal request to add a CFI under Article 168a of the EEC Treaty and the equivalent provisions of the other Treaties. On 13 June 1988, at the invitation of the President of the Council, the President of the Court, Lord Mackenzie Stuart addressed the Council to set out the Court's views on the scope of the jurisdiction to be given to the CFI and the number of judges it should comprise. At the end of this meeting, the Council instructed the Committee of the Permanent Representatives of the Governments of the Member States to the European Union (COREPER) to continue its work on these two issues, in the light of the opinions of the European Parliament and the Commission's opinions. The General Affairs Council of 25 July 1988 eventually decided on these two points and reached unanimous agreement on the creation of the CFI during its meeting.

After a final discussion in COREPER, the Council adopted its decision No. 88/591 establishing a CFI on 24 October 1988, ie, less than a month after the end of Bosco's term of office as judge.

[37] Proposal of the Commission of 4-8-1978, *Official Journal.* n° C 225, 22-9-1978, 6.

[38] See G Vandersanden, 'Considérations sur la perspective de créer un Tribunal de contentieux du personnel', in *Mélanges en l'honneur du professeur Constantinesco* (Bruxelles, Bruylant, 1978) 841.

Part I

C) Third Generation (1980–2000)

9

The Contribution of Giuseppe Federico Mancini as Advocate General (1982–1988) and Judge (1988–1999) to European Constitutionalism

VITTORIO DI BUCCI

1. INTRODUCTION

GIUSEPPE FEDERICO MANCINI – Federico as he was generally known – was appointed as an Advocate General at the Court of Justice in 1982. During the previous year, the Italian Socialist Party had put forward Mancini as a candidate to become one of the five judges of the Italian Constitutional Court elected by Parliament. In no less than six secret ballots, his candidacy missed the required supermajority by a handful of votes, not because of doubts on Mancini's personal qualities, but as a reaction to the positions of the Italian Socialist Party (PSI) led by the politician Bettino Craxi (1934–2000). Craxi was the leader of the Italian Socialist Party from 1976 to 1993 and he became Prime Minister between 1983 and 1987. His views on matters pertaining to the organisation of the judiciary and to the reform of the public prosecutor role were seen with skepticism as, according to him, judges 'were too inclined to interfere with the executive power and with any political action through legal procedures'.[1] Speaking about these events years later, Mancini used to say that his failed election as constitutional judge, leading to his appointment at the European Court of Justice (ECJ), had been an extraordinary piece of luck that had allowed him to live a unique professional and human experience.

While his nomination in the early 1980s by the Italian Government to become a member of the Luxembourg court may have been a solution to a political deadlock, Mancini was highly qualified for the position of Advocate General, a

[1] V Guizzi, 'Craxi's Italy' (1986) 20 *Government and Opposition* 166–177, 168.

key actor in influencing and improving the 'process of establishing the Court of Justice's decision making'.[2]

Born in 1927, Mancini belonged to the generation that had experienced the horrors of World War II without taking part in it. He studied at the University of Bologna, where he was a pupil of the renowned professor of civil procedure and labour law in the Faculty of Law, Professor Tito Carnacini (1909–1983). While he was initially active in different areas of civil and procedural law, in particular through his work for the *Rivista Italiana di Diritto e Procedura Civile* directed by Carnacini, he decided to devote most of his efforts to labour law. In post-war Italy, this area of law may not have been the most important one for academic purposes and scholarly writings. However, after the years of fascist corporatism and in the light of the new principles laid down in the Constitution of the Italian Republic, labour law was at the centre of political and social debate and in dire need of a radical refoundation.[3] Mancini's brilliant pupil at the University of Modena, Professor Marco Biagi (1950–2002), who was tragically killed in a terrorist attack, described Mancini as an innovator, a modernist, a protagonist, and a 'project-minded lawyer', who, in labour law, found fertile ground for his research and his reflections.[4]

As a young scholar, Mancini spent study periods in Vienna, Bordeaux, Paris and Chicago, which would contribute to his remarkable mastery of English, French, German, and, one must add, Spanish too. This knowledge and passion for languages served him well not only in his academic activities and personal contacts, but also in his work as a judge. For instance, when he was asked to sit in an English-speaking and then in a German-speaking chamber of the Court, Mancini could help to facilitate the integration of new judges with limited knowledge of French as this is the working language in Luxembourg. Mancini's foreign experiences as a young scholar also corresponded to his deep interest for comparative law, which allowed him to interact very effectively with lawyers educated in other legal systems. Over the

[2] L Clément-Wilz, 'The Advocate General: A Key Actor of the Court of Justice of the European Union' (2012) *Cambridge Yearbook of European Legal Studies* 587–613, 588.

[3] See The Costitution of the Italian Republic 1948. The Italian Constitution includes several fundamental principles referring to labour. Art 1 establishes that 'Italy is a Democratic Republic founded on labour.' Art 4 establishes a labour right, 'The Republic acknowledges the right of all citizens to work and shall promote conditions which will make this right effective.' Art 35 explains that 'The Republic shall protect labour in all its forms and practices available'.

[4] Among some of Federico Mancini's labour law contributions, see GF Mancini, *Il diritto sindacale* (Bologna, Il Mulino, 1971); GF Mancini, *Statuto dei diritti dei lavoratori (edizione universitaria)* (Bologna, Zanichelli, 1972); GF Mancini, *Costituzione e movimento operaio* (Bologna, Il Mulino, 1976); GF Mancini, 'Statuto dei lavoratori e movimento operaio 1970–1975', in AA.VV., *Lo Statuto dei lavoratori, un bilancio politico: nuove prospettive del diritto del lavoro e democrazia industriale* (Bari, De Donato, 1977) 11–22; GF Mancini, 'Possibili sviluppi del diritto del lavoro nella fase di transizione', in AA.VV., *Lo Statuto dei lavoratori, un bilancio politico: nuove prospettive del diritto del lavoro e democrazia industriale* (Bari, De Donato, 1977) 115–134; GF Mancini, *Terroristi e riformisti* (Bologna, Il Mulino, 1981).

years, he developed an informal network of labour lawyers active in different jurisdictions, contributing to the emergence of a common legal thinking and the laying of the intellectual ground for the development of European social law in the Single Market.

After working as a researcher in Bologna, Mancini started his teaching activities in Urbino in 1956, and was appointed professor there in 1961. He became a full professor of labour law at the University of Bologna in 1965. Mancini was considered to be the founder of the Bologna school of labour law and, since his first years in academia, he had nurtured many young talents who then became famous labor scholars and who deeply influenced the development of this area of law. He also taught at the University of Rome 'La Sapienza' between 1979 and 1982 and for twenty years at the Bologna Center of Advanced International Studies at Johns Hopkins University. Here, he lectured in English to an international audience about labour relations, and also Italian and European politics.

Federico Mancini was very active in Italian political and cultural life, well beyond purely legal matters. As early as 1951, he was among the founders of Il Mulino, which started as a journal published by a group of students in Bologna and which became one of the most important Italian cultural magazines of the latter part of the 20th century and a major publisher. Mancini was also involved in Italian political debate, in different areas: through party politics; the preparation of legislative initiatives; the training of trade union officials; and of course by writing numerous articles, including on current events, in newspapers and magazines. His ideas and his personal commitment were instrumental in the preparation of the Italian law on the Statute of Workers of 1970 and later in its implementation. He took pride in the widely shared observation that, if his friend Gino Giugni was the father of the Statute of Workers, Federico Mancini was its mother. He was a member of the Central Committee of the Italian Socialist Party between 1972 and 1982 and one of the most influential intellectuals of that political area, supporting the renovation of the party led by Bettino Craxi in 1976. Mancini was elected by the Italian Parliament as a member of the High Council of the Judiciary in 1976, where he served until 1981. This experience matched his acute interest in judicial activities and he maintained long-lasting connections with some members of the Italian judiciary he met in that period.

2. MANCINI AND HIS *CABINET* AT THE EUROPEAN COURT OF JUSTICE

Mancini arrived at the European Court of Justice in Luxembourg as an outsider, whose academic activity had not concerned Community law. Here, he very rapidly acquired a reputation for the intellectual depth of his reflections and for the quality, substantive and formal, of the Opinions he delivered as an Advocate General on very different topics – 200 Opinions over six years. When judge Giacinto Bosco left the Court in 1988, Mancini was appointed as a Judge, which corresponded to his wish to have a more direct influence on the development of the case-law. He served in that capacity until his death in 1999, for a total of nearly seventeen years at the Court, and was the judge rapporteur of more than 150 rulings. He narrowly missed the election to President of the Court in 1994, but in later years he used to say that this had probably been a blessing in disguise. Indeed, he profoundly enjoyed the independent role he managed to play both within the Court and in the discussions about the European polity, as a spearhead of integration and of 'the making of a constitution for Europe'.

While in Luxembourg, Mancini kept close contacts with the Italian academic world, not only in the areas of European and national labour law, but also with constitutionalists and with political scientists, who were increasingly realising how important European affairs had become for the Member States.[5] He also made a point of keeping links with the Italian judiciary, with the Constitutional Court, and with the highest authorities of the Italian State, paying a yearly visit to the President of the Republic to inform him about the activities of the Court and, all too often, about the difficulties that Italy encountered in complying with European law. However, in line with his independent role of a member of the Court, he only had occasional contacts with members of the Italian government, and never, to my knowledge, on cases pending before the Court.[6]

The composition of Mancini's Cabinet and the later careers of its members, particularly in judicial functions, testify to his exceptional qualities.[7] Mancini knew how to select bright lawyers and how to help them to further develop their skills. When he first came to Luxembourg in 1982, he kept as *référendaire* the Italian judge Antonio Saggio, who later became a member and then President of the Court of First Instance, as it was then known, and Advocate General at the Court of Justice. Following the advice of his predecessor Riccardo Monaco, who had been his colleague at the University of Rome (La Sapienza), Mancini also selected Monaco's pupil Carlo Curti Gialdino as a *référendaire*. Carlo Curti Gialdino was to remain with him for almost eighteen years, until Mancini's

[5] See for instance, GF Mancini, 'The Italians in Europe' (2000) 79 *Foreign Affairs* 122–134.

[6] See V Fritz, 'Judicial Biographies as a Methodology to Grasp the Dynamics inside the CJEU and Its Relationship with EU Member States', in M Rask Madsen, FG Nicola, A Vauchez (eds), *Researching the European Court of Justice. Methodological Shifts and Law's Embeddedness* (Cambridge, Cambridge University Press, 2022) 209–234, 232 explaining the 'personal proximity between judges and politicians' did not undermine 'the judges' internal practices,which are crafted independently from the member states'.

[7] See on the role of the référendaires H Schepel, R Wesseling, 'The Legal Community. Judges, Lawyers, Officials and Clerks in the Writing of Europe' (1997) 3 *European Law Journal* 165–88; AH Zhang, 'The Faceless Court' (2016) 38 *U. Pa. J. Int'l L.* 71–135.

death, as a close confidant and a trusted adviser, and later he became Professor of European Law at La Sapienza.

When Saggio returned to the Italian judiciary he was replaced by Ezio Perillo, who had been working with Antonio Trabucchi in Padova and who has authored the chapter on Trabucchi for this volume.[8] After 1988, Perillo went on to work in the European Parliament (EP), where he became director in the EP Legal Service, and was later appointed as judge of the Civil Service Tribunal and of the General Court. For a short period, the third *référendaire* was Lorenzo Salazar, an Italian judge, who later worked in the Italian Permanent Representation in Brussels before becoming Deputy General Prosecutor at the Court of Appeal of Naples. When Mancini ceased his activities as an Advocate General and became a Judge, Perillo and Salazar were replaced by Marc Jaeger and the author of this chapter, Vittorio Di Bucci. Marc Jaeger was a Luxembourgish judge who had already been the *référendaire* of Advocate General Mischo. He stayed for nearly eight years with Mancini before being appointed as a Judge to the General Court, becoming its President for 12 years and then continuing as a judge again, serving for more than 26 years total at the ECJ.

I was recruited when I was a very young official of the Court and spent two periods with Mancini, with an interval as a member of the Commission Legal Service. I reverted to that Service after Mancini's death, to become a director, and finally came back to Luxembourg as the registrar of the General Court. Between my two periods with Mancini, Guido Berardis became a member of the cabinet. He was a more senior official of the Commission Legal Service and after his time at the Court he became a director in the Commission's Internal Market Directorate General and in the Legal Service, and finally a judge of the General Court from 2012 to 2019. Last but certainly not least, Síofra O'Leary was a very young, brilliant Irish scholar when she was recruited to replace Marc Jaeger in 1996. After Mancini passed away, she stayed at the Court as a *référendaire* to Judge Macken, then as a member and Head of Unit of the Research and Documentation Service. In 2015 she was elected as Ireland's Judge at the European Court of Human Rights (ECtHR) and became its President on November 2022.[9]

3. MANCINI'S LEGACY

Mancini's outstanding career was recognised by the two impressive volumes of the *Festschrift* that he received on his 70th birthday, one on labour law and

[8] See E Perillo, 'Alberto Trabucchi: the Defender of the European citizens' rights and the Van Gend & Loos ruling of the Court of Justice', in this volume.

[9] See 'Síofra O'Leary, première femme à présider la Cour européenne des droits de l'homme' (La Croix in French, 1 November 2022), available at https://www.la-croix.com/Monde/Siofra-OLeary-premiere-femme-presider-Cour-europeenne-droits-lhomme-2022-11-01-1201240195.

one on European law. This was a fitting tribute to his own journey, which he described as going 'dal diritto di frontiera al diritto senza frontiere', from the frontier of the law to the law without frontiers. He could still savour that moment, before passing away less than two years later, after a shockingly rapid illness.

Notwithstanding the obvious difficulties linked to the confidentiality of the deliberations for the period he served as a Judge, I shall endeavour to provide an outlook on Mancini's judicial activities and on his contribution to the development of Union law. Over 17 years, first as an Advocate General and later as a Judge, Mancini dealt with virtually all subjects of Community law. Of course, as my former colleague Síofra O'Leary, explained so well in her remarks in Rome, one must not think of European law as it is today, but as it was in the 1980s and 1990s, with a strong economic focus that persisted even in the years immediately following the Maastricht and Amsterdam Treaties.[10] The effects of those Treaty changes on secondary legislation, or in certain fields, such as European citizenship, or asylum and immigration, were only beginning to be felt on the Kirchberg plateau where the buiding of the Court sits in Luxembourg.

I cannot refrain from briefly mentioning Mancini's role in the deepening of the internal market in the early 1990s, when the Court complemented the legislative efforts based on the Commission White Paper with an expansive reading of the Treaty provisions on fundamental freedoms and with an innovative use of the rules on special and exclusive rights. Mancini was the President of the Sixth Chamber, a very active chamber of five judges that sometimes acted as an *avant-garde* on important matters, when it delivered several influential cases. Examples of this include the *Säger* judgment,[11] which stated for the first time that the Treaty requires the elimination of non-discriminatory restrictions to the free provision of services. In another well known case, the *Höfner* judgment,[12] the Court found that a Member State could not keep in place an inefficient State monopoly for the activity of recruitment consultant. And, of course, he was judge rapporteur in the *Grogan* case,[13] which Síofra O'Leary describes as both a bold judgment and a skillful exercise in judicial restraint by the ECJ.[14] The Court recognised that the medical termination of pregnancy, lawful in the State

[10] As noted by Síofra O'Leary in her remarks at the Conference held at Luiss University on the 24 and 25 June 2022.

[11] *Säger v Dennemayer* Case C-76/90 ECLI:EU:C:1991:331 [1991].

[12] *Höfner and Elser v Macrotron* Case C-41/90 ECLI:EU:C:1991:161 [1991].

[13] *Society for the Protection of Unborn Children Ireland v Grogan* Case C-159/90 ECLI:EU:C:1991:378 [1991].

[14] See Síofra O'Leary's remarks at the LUISS conference manuscript on file with author. See also S Hennette-Vauchez, 'The Society for the Protection of Unborn Children v. Grogan: Rereading the Case and Retelling the Story of Reproductive Rights in Europe', in FG Nicola and B Davies (eds), *EU Law Stories: Contextual and Critical Histories of European Jurisprudence* (Cambridge, Cambridge University Press, 2017) 393–417.

where it was performed, constituted a service within the meaning of the Treaty. However, concerning the dissemination of information about that service in a country – Ireland – where abortion was illegal, the judgment deftly skirted the thorny issue that the Irish High Court had sent to the European Court. One may wonder whether or not such an approach would still be possible after the Lisbon Treaty and in light of the Charter.

One could say much more about the case-law concerning the internal market. However, to avoid this chapter being far too long, I shall focus on two topics that were particularly dear to Mancini's heart: social law and institutional affairs.

4. SOCIAL LAW

It was inevitable that one of the most prominent Italian labour lawyers should play a major role in the development of European social law. Yet, his first years as an Advocate General provided few opportunities to him in that respect. It was only in 1985 that Mancini delivered his Opinion in the *Pinna* case,[15] which concerned the right for migrant workers in France to receive family benefits for members of their family residing in another Member State. The case was atypical: the Community legislator itself had provided for an exception, applicable only to France, to the rule under which such family benefits were generally due at the rate of the Member State of employment, and even the European Commission was defending the legality of that exception. Mancini's conclusion demonstrated that this rule was incompatible with Articles 48 to 51 EEC Treaty (now 45 to 48 TFEU) because it violated the principle of equal treatment. After lengthy deliberations, the Court followed his suggestion and declared the provision invalid, while providing for a limitation in time of the effects of its judgment. It is interesting to note that this very question came up again in the course of the negotiations aimed at preventing Brexit and that the decision of the Heads of State or Government of 19 February 2016 on the so-called 'settlement' with the UK provided that 'conditions may be imposed in relation to certain benefits to ensure that there is a real and effective degree of connection between the person concerned and the labour market of the host Member State'. As we all know, the settlement never applied because of Brexit, but a few days before the Rome conference the Court of Justice considered that such an amendment would have been invalid under Article 45 TFEU, referring to the *Pinna* judgment.[16]

A similar constellation arose in *Roviello*.[17] The question concerned the validity of another provision of the regulation on the social security of migrant workers.

[15] *Pinna v Caisse d'allocations familiales de la Savoie* Case 41/84 ECLI:EU:C:1985:215 [1985].
[16] *Commission v Austria* Case C-328/20 ECLI:EU:C:2022:468, para 57 [2022].
[17] *Roviello v Landesversicherungsanstalt Schwaben* Case 20/85 ECLI:EU:C:1988:283 [1988].

Here again, both Advocate General Mancini and the Court found that the provision was invalid insofar as it provided that only activities exercised in Germany, to the exclusion of activities previously exercised in another Member State, could be taken into account in regard to the entitlement to a pension of invalidity or incapacity.

The *Heylens* case[18] provided Mancini, a notorious football fan and supporter of the Bologna team, with the first opportunity to deal with the application of Treaty rules on free movement of workers to football professionals. The legal issue was whether a football trainer qualified in another Member State could be denied access to this activity in France without any reasoning as to the lack of equivalence of his diploma and without a proper judicial review. Unsurprisingly, both Mancini and the Court gave a negative reply, enhancing the effectiveness of the rights based on Community law and laying the ground for further judgments on the recognition of professional qualifications such as *Vlassopoulou* or *Kraus*.

Mancini was even more active in the field of social law in his capacity as a Judge. He played a primary role in the development of the case-law on equal treatment between men and women, including in cases that raised fundamental societal problems. An example of this is *P v S and Cornwall County Council*[19] in which the Court ruled, in 1996, that the dismissal of a transsexual person for reasons arising from the gender reassignment was prohibited discrimination under the Directive on equal treatment as regards access to employment.

But let us look at some cases where Mancini was the judge rapporteur. Nearly 40 of the 150 rulings he drafted in this capacity concern social policy or free movement of workers, and many of them equal treatment between men and women. As Síofra O'Leary explains, in the latter sub-group of judgments, Mancini asserted and reasserted that the objective pursued by European gender equality law was real equality of opportunity. He deployed teleological interpretation and *effet utile* to protect part-time workers, victims of discrimination and those who, 20 years after *Defrenne*,[20] were still trying to obtain the equal pay to which that judgment entitled them. The most famous judgment in this area is certainly *Barber*,[21] in which the Court ruled that pensions paid under occupation schemes constitute pay within the meaning of Article 119 EEC (now 157 TFEU) and that it is contrary to the principle of equal treatment to deprive men of an immediate pension as a result of the application of an age condition that varies

[18] *Unectef v Heylens* Case 222/86 ECLI:EU:C:1987:304 [1987].

[19] *P v S and Cornwall County Council* Case C-13/94 ECLI:EU:C:1996:170 [1996].

[20] *Defrenne v SABENA* Case 43/75 ECLI:EU:C:1976:56 [1976].

[21] *Douglas Harvey Barber v Guardian Royal Exchange Assurance Group* Case C-262/88 ECLI:EU:C:1990:209 [1990].

according to sex. The judgment largely draws conclusions based on distinctions made in previous cases, such as *Defrenne*[22] and *Garland*,[23] but the Court was also aware of the considerable practical consequences of its judgment and that Directive 86/378/EEC had allowed Member States to defer the application of equal treatment in occupational schemes. On this basis, it decided to limit the effects of its judgment in time, unfortunately with a compromise formula that lent itself to different interpretations. This was the starting point of a number of further cases in which the Court clarified the meaning of the limitation. More importantly, this also let to one of the most formidable lobbying exercises in the history of the Community, which culminated in the adoption of the so-called *Barber* Protocol annexed to the Maastricht Treaty and now known as Protocol No 33 to the TEU and TFEU Treaties, based on a broad interpretation of that limitation.

Other notable judgments on equal treatment with Mancini as a rapporteur include: *Sutton*,[24] on State liability for the damages caused by a prohibited discrimination in the field of social security benefits; *Levez*,[25] declaring that national limitation periods cannot apply to a claim for equal pay where the employer misrepresented the level of the remuneration paid to persons of the opposite sex; and *Seymour Smith and Perez*,[26] in which the Court made a distinction between compensation for unfair dismissal, to be considered as pay, and conditions for reinstatement or re-engagement in the job, that fall under the Equal Treatment Directive. Such a distinction is reminiscent of the opposition between the traditional compensation for a breach of contract and the remedy of reinstatement established by Article 18 of the Statute of Workers in Italy (applicable since 7 March 2015 only to contracts concluded before that date), dubbed by Mancini himself as 'tutela obbligatoria' and, respectively, 'tutela reale'.

To conclude the chapter on social law, I must mention the *Bosman* case.[27] As a football aficionado, Mancini thoroughly enjoyed being the rapporteur of a procedure that put the Court of Justice under the spotlight of sports newspapers and of the general press, well beyond the attention of law journals. Much has been said and written about that case, so to avoid repetition I will just mention three points. First, while Advocate General Lenz examined both free movement of workers and competition rules, the Court decided to deal only

[22] *Defrenne* (n 20).

[23] *Garland v British Rail* Case 12/81 ECLI:EU:C:1982:44 [1982].

[24] *The Queen v Secretary of State for Social Security, ex parte Eunice Sutton* Case C-66/95 ECLI:EU:C:1997:207 [1997].

[25] *B.S. Levez v T.H. Jennings (Harlow Pools) Ltd* Case C-326/96 ECLI:EU:C:1998:577 [1998].

[26] *Regina v Secretary of State for Employment, ex parte Nicole Seymour-Smith and Laura Perez* Case C-167/97 ECLI:EU:C:1999:60 [1999].

[27] *Union royale belge des sociétés de football association ASBL v Jean-Marc Bosman* ECLI:EU:C:1995:463 Case C-415/93 [1995].

with the former, which Mancini actually welcomed, both for reasons of clarity and because this was well-suited to the labour lawyer he was. Second, although the case was technically very complex and the judgment very rich in content, the deliberation was incredibly smooth, as witnessed by the fact that the judgment was delivered less than three months after the Opinion of the Advocate General. Third, and exceptionally for those times, the Members of the Court realised that it was necessary to take steps so that the judgment would be followed in practice, failing which the Court's own credibility would take a hit. This can be seen in paragraph 136 of the judgment, with a harsh reprimand of the Commission for its previous, illegal arrangements with UEFA. Also, Mancini himself made efforts to (silently) attend conferences in which the judgment was discussed.

5. INSTITUTIONAL LAW: THE MAKING OF A CONSTITUTION FOR EUROPE

Institutional law of the Communities, or rather, 'the Making of a Constitution for Europe', to quote a seminal article of 1989,[28] quickly became the main topic of interest for Mancini after he came to Luxembourg. He saw both the difficulties of establishing a constitutional framework for such a diverse and articulated polity and the necessity for European countries to coalesce into a quasi-statal entity if they still wanted to play a role in the modern world.

5.1. Enhancing the Role of the European Parliament

The piecemeal definition of the Court's jurisdiction in the Treaties, and the limits on complete judicial control deriving from it, have always been a major concern for institutional lawyers. Already in one of his first Opinions, Mancini suggested that the Court adopt a wide approach to its own power to review the acts of the European Parliament. *Luxembourg v Parliament* concerned a Parliament resolution asserting its 'right to meet and work where it chooses' and, concretely, to hold all its plenary sittings in Strasbourg, discontinuing the practice of occasionally meeting in Luxembourg.[29] The Advocate General, followed by the Court, chose the simplest way to affirm the jurisdiction of the Court: given that Article 38 ECSC allowed the Member States to challenge the deliberations of the Parliament and given that the challenged act concerned all the activities of that assembly, it was unnecessary to determine whether this was also the case under the EEC and Euratom Treaties. However, Mancini took this occasion to refer to

[28] GF Mancini, 'The Making of a Constitution for Europe' (1989) 26 *Common Market Law Review* 595–614.

[29] *Luxembourg v Parliament* Case 230/81 ECLI:EU:C:1983:32 [1983].

the US experience, quoting a letter by Andrew Jackson to Benjamin Franklin, and 'to the system of checks and balances whereby the pluralist democracies govern themselves with their catalogue of fundamental rights'.

The next step was, of course, *Les Verts v Parliament*,[30] in which a political group challenged two decisions of the Bureau of the European Parliament concerning reimbursement of expenditures for participation in the European elections. As Mancini noted, while Article 173 EEC, interpreted literally, did not provide for judicial review of the decisions of Parliament, 'such an interpretation would conflict with the general scheme of the Treaties'.[31] After the Treaty changes that granted budgetary powers to the Parliament, 'the reasons for which the authors of the Treaty drafted Article 173 without mentioning the Parliament no longer exist'.[32] As we all know, the Court accepted this approach in a seminal judgment, in which it famously stated that the EEC 'est une Communauté de droit', 'is a Community based on the rule of law, inasmuch as neither its Member States nor its institutions can avoid the review of the question as to whether the measures adopted by them are in conformity with the basic constitutional charter, the Treaty'.[33] We can all see how much these words influenced the future evolution not only of the case-law, but of the European Union as we know it today.

Let us go back to the Opinion in *Les Verts* for a moment: to reply to the Parliament's argument that it would be inconsistent to allow proceedings to be brought against it without allowing it to bring proceedings itself, the Advocate General went on to explain the reasons that, in his view, also supported the proposition that the Parliament may attack the acts of other institutions. Thus, he was anticipating the next institutional battle, on the Parliament's *locus standi*, in which Mancini played a major role as a Judge.[34]

In a first case on the topic, *Parliament v Council* 'Comitology',[35] the Court declined to follow its Advocate General Marco Darmon, who had extensively quoted Mancini's Opinion in *Les Verts* to conclude that the Court should reject the Council's exception of inadmissibility. The Court ruled that the Parliament could not be recognised as having capacity to bring an action for annulment. It was not a 'privileged applicant' under Article 173 and its action did not fit into the system of actions brought by private applicants who are directly and individually concerned by the challenged act. The Court also rejected arguments based on the parallelism with the status of Parliament in other procedures, such

[30] *Les Verts v Parliament* Case 294/83 ECLI:EU:C:1985:483 [1985].
[31] ibid., para 36.
[32] ibid.
[33] ibid., para 23.
[34] The role of AG Mancini in this case was critical to establish the democratic role of the European Parliament as its 'capacity to sue and to be sued go hand in hand' as presented in A Caiola and FG Nicola, 'Defending Democracy Through Law: The Establishment of the Legal Service of the European Parliament' (2022) 46 *Fordham Int'l L.J.* 1–58, 42.
[35] *Parliament v Council* Case 302/87 ECLI:EU:C:1988:461 [1988].

as the action for failure to act or the intervention, or with the fact that its act could be challenged, as decided in *Les Verts*.

However, such a solution lasted for less than two years, until the spectacular and quite unique *revirement* in *Parliament v Council* 'Chernobyl'.[36] That case had already been pending when the judgment in 'Comitology' was delivered. However, the Court organised a new hearing, heard the Opinion of Advocate General Walter Van Gerven who urged it it to reconsider its previous judgment and finally decided that the Parliament had *locus standi* to bring an action for annulment in order to safeguard its prerogatives. The crucial passage in that judgment reads as follows:

> The Court, which under the Treaties has the task of ensuring that in the interpretation and application of the Treaties the law is observed, must therefore be able to maintain the institutional balance and, consequently, review the observance of the Parliament's prerogatives when called upon to do so by the Parliament, by means of a legal remedy which is suited to the purpose which the Parliament seeks to achieve.[37]

It was the first of many rulings in which the Court expanded its role beyond a literal reading of the Treaty, in an attempt to provide a full system of judicial remedies to support the European construction. While René Joliet was the judge rapporteur in 'Comitology' and Manfred Zuleeg in 'Chernobyl', it is fair to say that Mancini, the former Advocate General in *Les Verts*, played a major role in those deliberations and felt vindicated by the approach ultimately followed in 'Chernobyl'. As we know, the Court's solution, based on the safeguard of institutional prerogatives, was later accepted by the drafters of the Maastricht Treaty, before the Parliament was finally recognised as a privileged applicant on par with the Member States, the Council and the Commission under the Nice Treaty. That solution is still the one that applies to the Court of Auditors, to the ECB and to the Committee of Regions under Article 263, third indent, TFEU.

5.2. Enhancing the Preliminary Ruling Procedure

Another area in which Mancini left his mark is the procedure that concerns preliminary rulings under Article 177 EEC – now 267 TFEU. The case that immediately comes to mind is *Foto-Frost*, on the possibility for national courts to review the validity of Community acts.[38] Not only did Mancini, as the Advocate General of the case, successfully urge the Court to reply negatively and to rule

[36] *Parliament v Council* Case C-70/88 ECLI:EU:C:1990:217 [1990].
[37] ibid., para 23.
[38] *Foto-Frost v Hauptzollamt Lübeck-Ost* Case 314/85 ECLI:EU:C:1987:230 [1987].

that, as a result of the principle of uniform application of Community law, if a national court has doubts on the validity of an act of the institutions, it must stay the proceeding and ask the Court of Justice to give a preliminary ruling on the matter; but he also anticipated that a specific solution had to be found for summary proceedings, something the Court examined and admitted only years later, in *Zuckerfabrik Süderdithmarschen*[39] and *Atlanta*,[40] with Mancini involved as a judge.

A little-known example is the *Grimaldi* judgment, delivered by a small chamber of three judges with Mancini as the rapporteur, about an obscure recommendation on professional illnesses.[41] Here, the Court took an opportunity to define the system of remedies available in respect of recommendations. While such acts, not being binding, cannot be challenged through an action for annulment, the Court can assess their validity following a reference for a preliminary ruling. It is interesting to note that in recent years the Grand Chamber of the Court twice examined that issue again, in *Belgium v Commission*[42] and in *Fédération bancaire française*,[43] and fully confirmed the solution. *Grimaldi* also allowed the Court to expand, as much as possible, the effects of recommendations. It did so by stating that national courts are bound to take them into consideration, in particular where they cast light on the interpretation of national measures adopted to implement them or where they are designed to supplement binding provisions – another point confirmed by the Court in those later judgments.

An even more telling testimony of Mancini's quest to fully exploit the effects of Community acts is the *Foster* judgment, in which the Court, with Mancini as rapporteur, adopted a wide notion of emanation of the State for the purpose of the direct effect of directives after the *Marshall* judgment ruled out the so-called horizontal direct effect.[44] If the direct effect of directives cannot be invoked against individuals, the Court ruled that conditional and sufficiently precise provisions of a directive may be relied upon against organisations or bodies that are subject to the authority or control of the State or that have special powers beyond those that result from the normal rules applicable in relations between individuals. Once again, the Grand Chamber of the Court recently reviewed the issue and fully confirmed the solution in *Farrell*.[45] Still on the effects of directives, one should also mention *Marleasing*, a leading

[39] *Zuckerfabrik Süderdithmarschen and Zuckerfabrik Soest v Hauptzollamt Itzehoe and Hauptzollamt Paderborn* Joined Cases C-143/88 and C-92/89 ECLI:EU:C:1991:65 [1991].

[40] *Atlanta Fruchthandelsgesellschaft and Others (I) v Bundesamt für Ernährung und Forstwirtschaft* Case C-465/93 ECLI:EU:C:1995:369 [1995].

[41] *Grimaldi v Fonds des maladies professionnelles* Case C-322/88 ECLI:EU:C:1989:646 [1989].

[42] *Belgium v Commission* Case C-16/16 P ECLI:EU:C:2018:79 [2018].

[43] *Fédération bancaire française (FBF) v Autorité de contrôle prudentiel et de résolution (ACPR)* Case C-911/19 ECLI:EU:C:2021:599 [2021].

[44] *Foster and Others v British Gas* Case C-188/89 ECLI:EU:C:1990:313 [1990].

[45] *Farrell v Whitty* Case C-413/15 ECLI:EU:C:2017:745 [2017].

case on consistent interpretation of directives, ie, the obligation, for national courts, to interpret national law '*dans toute la mesure du possible*' in light of the wording and purpose of the directive in order to achieve the result pursued by it.[46] Mancini was the president of the bold Sixth Chamber that delivered that judgment.

In other decisions, such as *Peterbroeck*, the Court, with Mancini as *juge rapporteur*, mandated the national courts to raise questions of Community law of their own motion when procedural obstacles made it difficult for individuals to rely on the relevant provisions.[47] Once again, we find an echo of that solution in a recent judgment, *L v Unicaja*, delivered recently by the Grand Chamber.[48]

6. CONCLUSION

All of the cases mentioned in this chapter confirm what has become apparent to the reader of Mancini's writings about institutional law: that during his years at the Court he was the leading figure among those members who tried to give full effect to Community law. This meant increasing the protection granted to individuals and laying the constitutional foundations for a European political entity. To quote Síofra O'Leary again, in his extrajudicial activity he accompanied and frequently anticipated the transformation of an economic community into a monetary and, to an extent, political Union.[49] This is witnessed by the book that was published after his death and collects his writing about European integration: *Democracy and Constitutionalism in the EU*.[50] Some of these Articles, such as 'The Making of a Constitution for Europe',[51] 'Democracy and the European Court of Justice'[52] (1994) or 'A Currency in Search of a State'[53] (1999) show already in their titles Mancini's remarkable vision of future developments of the European Union and of the difficulties it would encounter.

[46] *Marleasing v Comercial Internacional de Alimentación* Case C-106/89 ECLI:EU:C:1990:395 [1990].

[47] *Peterbroeck, Van Campenhout & Cie v Belgian State* Case C-312/93 ECLI:EU:C:1995:437 [1995].

[48] *L v Unicaja Banco SA* Case C-869/19 ECLI:EU:C:2022:397 [2022].

[49] As stressed by Síofra O'Leary in her remarks at the conference held at Luiss University on the 24 and 25 June 2022.

[50] GF Mancini, *Democracy and Constitutionalism in the European Union: Collected Essays* (Oxford & Portland, Hart Publishing, 2000).

[51] GF Mancini, 'The Making of a Constitution for Europe' (1989) 26 *Common Market Law Review* 595.

[52] GF Mancini, 'Democracy and the European Court of Justice' (1994) 57 *The Modern Law Review* 175.

[53] GF Mancini, 'The Euro: A Currency in Search of a State' (1999) 22 *UNSW Law Journal* 205.

Mancini's academic production thus complements and clarifies the indications that can be found in the Advocate General's Opinions and, with more difficulty, in the judgments he authored as judge rapporteur. As Mancini frequently explained to outsiders, within the Court of Justice the real divide is not between Left and Right, but between more Europe and less Europe. We know where he stood: in his own words, *in dubio pro Communitate*.

10

Giuseppe Tesauro – Advocate General at the ECJ (1988–1998): A Paladin of Effective Judicial Protection

ROBERTO MASTROIANNI AND MASSIMO CONDINANZI*

1. GIUSEPPE TESAURO'S EDUCATION AND THE INFLUENCE OF HIS ACADEMIC BACKGROUND ON HIS APPROACH TO THE ROLE OF ADVOCATE GENERAL

Giuseppe Tesauro passed away on July 6th, 2021. He was one of the most influential Italian jurists of recent decades. Over the years, he held various high-level positions and, in each, left a highly recognisable personal mark due to the originality of his contributions and the depth of his analysis.

Born in Naples to a family of prominent academics and politicians,[1] Tesauro was academically raised in the University of Naples at one of the most important and productive schools of international and European law, led, at the time, by Professor Rolando Quadri.[2] He quickly progressed through his university

* This chapter is the outcome of a joint scientific effort by the Authors. Nevertheless, sections 1 and 2 were written by Roberto Mastroianni, while Massimo Condinanzi is the author of sections 3 and 4.

[1] His father, Alfonso Tesauro, was professor of Constitutional law at the University of Naples and Senator of the Italian Republic from 1948 to 1968; his uncle, Giuseppe Tesauro, was professor at the School of Medicine and Rector of the same University. His mother was Latvian. These double roots may explain why he was very attached to his hometown and at the same time extremely curious towards other 'foreign' environments and allergic to frontiers of any kind. In this regard, see also, for instance, A Tizzano, 'In Memoria: Giuseppe Tesauro', in *Giuseppe Tesauro: un uomo, un europeista – Atti del Convegno in memoria* (Naples, Editoriale Scientifica, 2023) XIII. To further deepen the figure of Giuseppe Tesauro and read the memories of his pupils and collaborators, see the contributions contained within this volume.

[2] Among the fellows of the same school it is worth remembering at least Professor Benedetto Conforti, member of the European Commission of Human Rights (1993–1998) and then judge at the European Court of Human Rights (1998–2001); Professor Luigi Ferrari Bravo, member

career and graduated, from the Law School (*Facoltà di Giurisprudenza*) of the University of Naples in 1964, with a dissertation on Public International law.[3] Tesauro started as an assistant professor of International law in 1965, following a period of study at the Max Planck Institute in Heidelberg, during which he broadened his language proficiency to include German in addition to French and English. In 1969 he obtained the *libera docenza* and in 1972 became a full professor.

He was an eminent professor of International law, European law, and International Organisations, and held chairs at various prestigious Italian Universities, such as the Universities of Catania, Messina, Naples, and Rome. In 2004, the University Paris II Pantheon-Assas awarded Tesauro the title of doctor honoris causa. He contributed, as a chairperson or rapporteur, to many International and European conferences including, for instance in 1992, his General Report at the 15th FIDE conference in Lisbon on *La sanction des infractions au droit Communautaire*. He held the Presidency of the Italian Association of European law scholars (AISDUE) from its establishment (2018) to the day of his death.

Before, during, and after his years as Advocate General in Luxembourg ('AG' hereinafter), he was the author of an incredibly rich series of books and articles published in the most influential legal journals in Europe, from International to European law, with the latter more present in the last decades of his academic activities. He was the author of one of the first handbooks[4] of the European Community (EC), then European Union (EU), law, first published in 1995, which is today still widely used in Italian universities.

Tesauro's scholarly approach distinguished his contributions to the various national and European institutions in which he was involved. First and foremost, this applies to his work in the European Court of Justice (ECJ) in Luxembourg. Appointed AG in 1988, during almost ten years (his second mandate was not completed because of his appointment as President of the Italian Competition Authority), he was the author of a rich series of Opinions (around 300) that, in many cases, led the Court of Justice to reach completely innovative solutions. These Opinions have influenced, if not driven, academic discussions beyond the boundaries of Luxembourg, even in the rare instances the Court did not 'follow' them, and are regarded in various fields of EU law, both substantive and institutional, as landmarks of legal analysis.

of the International law Commission of the UN and judge at the International Court of Justice (1995–1997); and Professor Antonio Tizzano, Advocate General (2000–2006) and then judge (2006–2015) and vice-president (2015–2018) at the Court of Justice of the European Union.

[3] It should be considered that, at the time of Tesauro's graduation from Law School and still for a few decades that followed, in the Italian Law Schools there was no specific course of EU law, the subject being included in the general courses of Public and Private International law.

[4] G Tesauro, *Diritto comunitario* (Padua, CEDAM, 1995).

His profound knowledge of EU law subsequently contributed decisive shifts of activity at the Italian Competition Authority (AGCM),[5] part of the European circuit of antitrust authorities, and at the Italian Constitutional Court (ICC), where he similarly attained the role of President.[6] At the latter, Tesauro was able to make a definite contribution as a rapporteur of cases and produced a tangible turning point in the ICC's jurisprudence regarding the relationship between domestic law and European Union law.[7]

In such a long and varied career, if asked to point out which of these highly prestigious institutional experiences had been the most significant and intense from both a professional and personal point of view, Tesauro would, without a doubt, answer: Luxembourg. As he underlined in an article published in a legal journal immediately after his period as AG, at the ECJ he espoused 'the fortune to enjoy the richness of this Court, which is the daily confrontation between different legal cultures. And, despite their diversity, so close, united by the same objective of finding a common result'.[8]

These phrases are indicative of the dual motivation that drove the passion and dedication with which Tesauro approached his work. On the one hand, Tesauro firmly believed in European integration. Certainly, he could not have achieved the extraordinary results of his career without a strong conviction of the virtues of the integration process, making it an obligatory point of reference not only in his work as AG but also in the – only apparently – more 'national' institutional roles mentioned above. On the other hand, he considered himself a professor of law – of International law and of European law – 'temporarily displaced' in other cities or offices. At the ECJ, he adopted an approach to his role as AG typical of an academic instructing his *référendaires* (including the authors of this chapter) to develop case analyses not solely based on the Court's prior judgments. Since, in his eyes, those judgments were not necessarily persuasive, he encouraged developing case analyses with typical academic research

[5] Giuseppe Tesauro was appointed President of the Italian Competition Authority on December 16, 1997, by accord of the Presidents of the two Chambers of the Italian Parliament, but assumed the functions only on March 12, 1998 to wait for the appointment of the new Advocate General. He held this office until 16 February 2005.

[6] Tesauro was appointed to the Constitutional Court by Italian President Carlo Azeglio Ciampi on 4 November 2005 and he was sworn in on 9 November 2005. He was elected President of the Constitutional Court on 30 July 2014 and served until 8 November 2014.

[7] For instance, Judgment No. 349 of 2007 was, together with Judgment No. 348 pronounced on the same day, the first to clarify the scope of application of the new Article 117 of the Italian Constitution concerning the relationship between domestic law, on one side, and European and International law, on the other side. The judgment clarified the difference between the European Treaties and other international treaties, including the ECHR, in a sense that only the former realize a *limitation of sovereignty* and therefore can be considered at the same level of the Constitution in the Italian legal system.

[8] G Tesauro, 'Riflessioni sull'esperienza di un Avvocato generale presso la Corte di giustizia' (1998) 3 *Il Diritto dell'Unione europea* 1.

involving books, articles, and case notes, as well as, of course, a fair share of original ideas.

Before his appointment, Tesauro was often asked whether he preferred the role of Judge or Advocate General.[9] In considering his reply, Tesauro consulted with Professor Alberto Trabucchi, another protagonist of this book, not only because of Trabucchi's recognised experience as a jurist but also because he was a Judge for ten years and an AG for three years. The answer, and the suggestion Tesauro followed, was clear: the role of Advocate General is more appropriate for an academic because it permits the contribution of original ideas to the development of EU law and '*in solitaire*', without the need to adapt and find compromises as is inevitable in a *college* of judges. The position of AG allowed Tesauro to perform an independent reflection of the legal problems posed by individual cases and to take full and complete responsibility for his role, then exposed to the assessment not only of the judges in charge of the case, but of the whole European legal community.[10]

It is worth noting that, coherent with this approach, during his years in Luxembourg, Tesauro always maintained close contact with the European legal community as he intended his participation in the work of the ECJ to be a form of 'representation' of the Italian tradition of EU studies. Far from wanting to be locked in an ivory tower, Tesauro always felt the need to 'provoke' exchanges with his university colleagues, who he contacted intensively,[11] and to be present in the most important seminaires and congresses that concerned European law, at least those who took place in Italy. The interaction with his colleagues was also fundamental in choosing his *référendaires*, from which he demanded, as mentioned, a particularly academic attitude towards work.

At the same time, prior to joining the Court, Tesauro had an intense practice as an attorney specialised in EU law, including internal market cases. Examining his approach to the different questions posed by single disputes – in particular in preliminary rulings procedures –reveals that he scrutinised case issues keenly, aware that the intervention of the Court, or any Court, is useless if not 'effective', particularly in regard to the protection of the rights of individuals or companies that 'knock at the door' of the Courts. Not surprisingly, the former President of the Court of Justice Vassilios Skouris, in his introduction to the Naples Conference organised in 2012 for the delivery of the essays dedicated to Giuseppe Tesauro, noted that:

> If I had only one sentence to describe the impact of his thought and analysis on the development of the jurisprudence of the Court, I would say that Tesauro exercised a

[9] Tesauro (n 8) 1.

[10] ibid.

[11] Just to name some of them, contacts were frequent for example with Antonio Tizzano and Ami Barav for the institutional aspects of EU law; with Sergio Maria Carbone for internal market and maritime law; with Riccardo Luzzatto and Paolo Picone for private international law; with Giorgio Gaia for public international law; and with Bruno Nascimbene for the law of citizenship.

> decisive influence in the process of taking the individuals into account by the law of the Union, and in the deployment of the effects of the jurisprudence of the Court on our daily life.[12]

This is especially reflected, as we will see in a moment, in his Opinions dedicated to the importance of the general principle of effective judicial protection.

2. THE INFLUENCE OF GIUSEPPE TESAURO'S OPINIONS IN THE DEVELOPMENT OF THE PRINCIPLE OF EFFECTIVE JUDICIAL PROTECTION OF INDIVIDUALS IN EU LAW

No writing, especially in the limited space at our disposal, could ever genuinely succeed in conveying the influence of Giuseppe Tesauro's work at the Court of Justice on EU law development. While selecting only a portion of his work is equally tricky, in this first part of the reflection, we will dwell on Tesauro's Opinions concerning the so-called 'institutional part' of EU law.

Whether fundamental rights or any other kind of rights, at the core of AG Tesauro's analyses are the interest of individuals. Widely known and cited still today are his Opinions in *Brasserie de pecheur*, of 17 May 1990,[13] which established some important principles and clarified the conditions of Member State liability for damages caused to individuals by breaches of Community law; or in *Hermès* (Opinion of 13 November 1997) where he tried – but this time without much success – to open a breach to the traditional, negative position of the ECJ with regards to the direct effect of World Trade Organization (WTO) rules in the EU legal order.[14] However, Opinions in more 'institutional' contexts cannot be ignored and include *Kleinwort Benson*,[15] on the limits of the Court's jurisdiction to give a preliminary ruling on the interpretation of the Brussels Convention; *Dorsch Consult*,[16] on the notion of 'national court or tribunal' within the meaning of Article 177 of the EC Treaty; *Kefalas*,[17] on the abusive exercise of a right arising from a provision of Community law; and *Metronome Musik*,[18] on the balancing of rights related to copyrights and the rights of free enterprise.

[12] V Skouris, *Discours d'ouverture*, in U Leanza, A Tizzano, T Vassalli di Dachenhausen, R Mastroianni, P de Pasquale, R Ciccone (Organising Committee), *Scritti in onore di Giuseppe Tesauro* (Vol 1; Naples, Editoriale Scientifica, 2014) 4.

[13] *Brasserie du pêcheur v Bundesrepublik Deutschland and The Queen v Secretary of State for Transport, ex parte Factortame and others* Case C-46/93 and C-48/93 ECLI:EU:C:1996:79 [1996].

[14] *Hermès International v FHT Marketing Choice* Case C-53/96 ECLI:EU:C:1998:292 [1998].

[15] *Kleinwort Benson v City of Glasgow District Council* Case C-346/93 ECLI:EU:C:1995:85 [1995].

[16] *Dorsch Consult Ingenieursgesellschaft v Bundesbaugesellschaft Berlin* Case C-54/96 ECLI:EU:C:1997:413 Case C-367/96 [1997].

[17] *Kefalas and others v Elliniko Dimosio and Organismos Oikonomikis Anasygkrotisis Epicheiriseon* Case C-367/96 ECLI:EU:C:1998:222 [1998].

[18] *Metronome Musik v Music Point Hokamp* Case C-200/96 ECLI:EU:C:1998:172 [1998].

It is impossible here to delve into all these Opinions. Instead, we will focus our brief analysis on the contribution of AG Tesauro's Opinions to the development of EU law, particularly in enhancing the effectiveness of judicial protection. Our preference lies in the Opinion delivered on 17 May 1990 in *Factortame*,[19] concerning access to interim relief before a national court in case of rights derived from provisions of EU law.

While *Factortame* remains, even today, one of the most famous Opinions authored by Tesauro, it was delivered, strikingly, only a little more than a year after his arrival in Luxembourg. Tesauro himself was rather conscious of the importance of the case. As he explained at the very beginning of the Opinion, 'The reply which the Court was called upon to give to two questions referred to it by the House of Lords certainly will rank amongst those which help to define the context of relations between national courts and Community law. And, I would add, on a point of unquestionable importance.'[20]

The questions posed by the House of Lords consisted, as Tesauro put it, of assessing whether:

> Pending a ruling by the Court of Justice on the interpretation of provisions of Community law having direct effect, and where United Kingdom law does not permit the national court to suspend, by way of interim relief, the application of the allegedly conflicting national measure and thus, provisionally, to acknowledge an individual's right claimed under Community law but denied by national law: (1) must (or may) the national court grant such relief on the basis of Community law, and (2) if so, applying what criteria?[21]

Tesauro added that the High Court had

> [C]onfirmed that as a matter of English law the courts have no power to suspend the application of an Act of Parliament on the ground of its alleged, but unproven, incompatibility with Community law, and referred to the Court of Justice for a preliminary ruling [on] the questions mentioned above, in order essentially to ascertain whether that which is not permitted by English law is required or permitted by Community law.[22]

Notoriously, Tesauro gave a positive answer to these questions, and the Court was of the same advice. Considering the state of the ECJ's jurisprudence at the time, this approach was revolutionary. It intended, first, to move rapidly towards a greater, *invasive* role of EU law *vis-à-vis* the sovereign choices made by Member States on how to rule the relationship between the individual and the

[19] *The Queen v Secretary of State for Transport, ex parte Factortame Ltd and others* Case C-213/89 ECLI:EU:C:1990:216 [1990].

[20] ibid, 1.

[21] ibid.

[22] ibid, 5.

administration ('the Crown', in that case), so to expand the power of national courts to set aside a national procedural provision incompatible with EU law. Secondly, it framed the power and duty of the national court in the broader context of the requirements of effective judicial protection, a fundamental right that, at the time, was slowly finding its way as one of the most important general principles of EU law, inspired by the ECHR and the constitutional traditions of many Member States.

In his Opinion, Tesauro focused on the critical role played by interim relief in any judicial system. He noted the gap between the point in time when a Community right comes into existence and later, when the existence of that right is definitively established, and stated that under the Article 177 TEC procedure,[23] judicial review only postpones the establishment of the right to a later point in time. Once established, the right is given retroactive effect. Tesauro observed that the very purpose of interim relief is to ensure that the time needed to establish the existence of a right does not irremediably deprive the right of substance. This applies especially where, as in that case, the determination of the right's existence involves the prior review of the validity, or compatibility, of one provision *vis-à-vis* another of a higher order.

Let us share a little anecdote about this case, from a conversation between AG Tesauro and Roberto Mastroianni. To convince the Court, Tesauro brought from Italy a book written by the famous jurist and Professor of civil procedure Pietro Calamandrei, entitled 'Introduction to the Systematic Study of Precautionary Measures' (*Introduzione allo studio sistematico delle misure cautelari*). He entrusted the Court of Justice's service with the translation of large sections of the book into English and had the translation distributed among the judges. In fact, it is clear to see, from the text of the Opinion, the legacy of the solid academic tradition of Italian scholars of civil procedure, in particular, Giuseppe Chiovenda and his last 'élève' Virgilio Andrioli, Professor at the University of Naples when Tesauro was a student. Chiovenda was the forerunner of the school of thought that attributed a decisive role to the protection '*ante causam*' via interim measures, including, if necessary, the suspension of the application of a national statute, to avoid that the rights invoked in proceedings are 'frustrated' by the delay in giving final judgment. As Chiovenda famously held, '*la necessità di servirsi del processo per ottener ragione non deve tornare a danno di chi ha ragione*' (the duration of the proceedings must not cause damage to the party in the right).

[23] Article 177 Treaty of the European Community Article 177 – EC Treaty extablished that: 'The Court of Justice shall have jurisdiction to give preliminary rulings concerning: (a) the interpretation of this Treaty; (b) the validity and interpretation of acts of the institutions of the Community and of the ECB; (c) the interpretation of the statutes of bodies established by an act of the Council, where those statutes so provide. […]'.

Not surprisingly, in Tesauro's Opinion it is rather easy to find traces of this academic heritage, which is expressly mentioned in a footnote to paragraph 18 of the text. Tesauro explains that

> Sometimes the right's existence is established too late for the right claimed to be fully and usefully exercised, which is the more likely to be the case the more structured and complex, and the more probably rich in safeguards is the procedure culminating in the definitive establishment of the right. The result is that in such a case the utility as well as the effectiveness of judicial protection may be lost and there could be a betrayal of the principle, long established in jurisprudence, according to which the need to have recourse to legal proceedings to enforce a right should not occasion damage to the party in the right.

This heritage of the Italian civil procedure school influenced the jurisprudence of the Court of Justice via Tesauro's Opinions. In a typical 'virtuous circle', such influence enriched the Italian legal order when the decision of the ECJ permitted the principle of the 'interim measures' to be integrated into sectors that, at the time, clearly suffered from limited access to judicial remedies, specifically administrative law and procedure.

3. GIUSEPPE TESAURO'S CONTRIBUTION IN SHAPING INTERNAL MARKET LAW

It would not be possible to speak fully about AG Tesauro's contribution to shaping EU law, and in particular internal market law, without primarily proposing a brief reflection on the nature (and the strategy) of the internal market in the decade in which he served on the ECJ.

We must take into account that Tesauro was in Luxembourg when the Maastricht Treaty entered into force (1st November 1993); Maastricht was a Treaty that, as is well known, 'gave life' to the internal market, starting from 31 December 1992 according to the relevant provision of the Single European Act (SEA). Indeed, after the Maastricht Treaty, the new Article 3(1)(c) of the EC Treaty states that the instrument of 'an internal market characterised by the abolition, as between Member States, of obstacles to the free movement of goods, persons, services and capital.' From the point of view of the free movement of persons, the abolition of such obstacles was clearly encouraged by the institution of European citizenship: the impact of this status on the interpretation of the market freedoms was clearly beyond the mere literal approach.[24]

In this framework, *freedom* represented the *raison d'être* of the internal market as it was initially conceived. The Community in which Tesauro was

[24] A Tryfonidou, *The impact of Union Citizenship on the EU's Market Freedoms* (Oxford, Hart, 2016) 23.

AG was a Community that yearned for freedom; the internal market aimed at achieving this freedom through a real process of liberalisation and mutual recognition. But freedom, under Tesauro's doctrine, is not just an abstract value; it is a fundamental right to be strictly connected to the needs of every human being.

As per today, the EU internal 'space', not only economic, is deeply different from what the internal market was during the Maastricht Treaty era. For instance, looking at the regulatory markets (banking services, telecommunications, energy, transports, etc.), the current EU legal system aims at regulating, at the *rule*, which, clearly, is the opposite of freedom. Of course, this is the consequence of a number of elements, namely, the enlarged competencies of the EU, the policy goals set-up in the Treaty, and basically, the transfer of the task of achieving certain political objectives from the Member States to the European Union. Finally, even if we still have the same definition of the internal market in paragraph 2 of Article 26 of the TFEU, the internal market as conceived during Tesauro's experience is just an element, and most likely, not the most important, of the current economic and social regulation in the EU. From a different point of view, the internal market, mainly achieved through the ECJ's case-law, to which the Opinions of our AG strongly contributed, will remain a 'cornerstone' of the 'ever closer union' as an unachievable target of the European integration process. Perhaps freedom is no longer the gravitational centre of contemporary European Union law, but is now the entire foundation of the European integration process; a process that wouldbe precarious without it.

Professor Tesauro was undoubtedly a proponent and a standard-bearer of principles and values of freedom, demonstrating a deep attention to the *substance* of problems rather than to the form and the 'frills'. After all, Professor Tesauro is the one who, for many years, rejected the use of the term 'union' and insisted on continuing to use the term 'community', in particular in the title of his already mentioned handbook ('Diritto comunitario'). He justified this choice in the light of the attention he wanted to reserve to the 'heart of the system', and the will to exclude what, for the citizen, belonged to the 'future or desirable', thereby showing a certain reluctance to purely formal matters.[25]

Cases on the internal market are perfectly suitable to his experience as lawyer and as a practitioner. This feature is recognisable and clearly visible in

[25] That justification (present in the 1995 edition) is present again in the 2000 edition's introduction, as well as in the 2003 edition. Still in the fourth edition, and even in 2005, after the failure of the so-called European Constitution, Tesauro entitled his work 'Community law'. And so again in the next edition, albeit after the signing of the Lisbon Treaty (2007). Only in the sixth edition (2010), finally, 'loyal to the Lisbon diktat', the handbook changes its name, in spite of its Author's disappointment, who, in the text, consciously continued to use the evocative, incisive and (maybe?) anachronistic word 'community'.

his approach to institutional law, described in section 2. Yet, it is even clearer in his approach to the internal market law and, more generally, to substantive law, which he defined as 'more complicated and demanding, but necessary to take seriously and understand the specificity of everything else'.[26] His distinguished approach was marked by a commitment to consistently revisiting principles and general categories, driven by an enthusiasm to find the coherence necessary for resolving the specificities of a case.

An emblematic case in this sense was *Kalanke*,[27] which grappled with the issue of equal treatment between men and women in access to work, a theme that Tesauro had already dealt with, providing a progressive attitude in the Opinions he delivered in the *Stoeckel*;[28] *Habermann-Bel Termann*;[29] *Minne*[30] and *Webb*.[31]

In *Kalanke*, the Bundesarbeitsgericht referred to the ECJ under Article 177 TEC on the interpretation of Directive 76/207/EEC, in particular to find out whether a national legislation under which women are given priority in recruitment and/or in obtaining promotion (provided that they had the same qualifications as the male applicants) was compatible with the principle of equal treatment for men and women laid down by the relevant Community legislation. Tesauro felt it necessary to broaden the perspective of the question with respect to the more general parameter of the principle of equal treatment, analysing the contrast between formal equality, 'in the sense of equal treatment as between individuals belonging to different groups, and substantive equality, in the sense of equal treatment as between groups'.[32] In this context, Tesauro – without neglecting that the ultimate goal of equal opportunities is undoubtedly to favour women's employment – courageously affirmed that the national legislation imposed only formal, numerical equality 'at the cost of an incontestable violation of a fundamental value of every civil society: equal rights, equal treatment for all'.[33] Formal (numerical) equality for Tesauro was '[...] an objective which may salve some consciences, but it will remain illusory and devoid of all substance unless it goes together with measures which are genuinely destined to achieve equality'. Instead, what was needed, according to Tesauro, was '[A]bove all a substantial change in the economic, social and cultural model which [was] at the root of the inequalities'.[34]

[26] G Tesauro, 'Il contributo di Antonio La Pergola all'affermazione e allo sviluppo del diritto comunitario' (2009) 4 *Studi sull'integrazione europea* 361, 366.

[27] *Kalanke v Freie Hansestadt Bremen* Case C-450/93 ECLI:EU:C:1995:105 [1995].

[28] *Stoeckel* Case C-345/89 ECLI:EU:C:1991:29 [1991].

[29] *Habermann-Beltermann v Arbeiterwohlfahrt* Case C-421/92 ECLI:EU:C:1994:29 [1994].

[30] *Office national de l'emploi v Minne* Case C-13/93 ECLI:EU:C:1993:924 [1993].

[31] *Webb v EMO Air Cargo* Case C-32/93 ECLI:EU:C:1994:215 1994.

[32] *Kalanke v Freie Hansestadt Bremen* (n 27) 7.

[33] ibid, 28.

[34] ibid.

Furthermore, in the context of the non-discrimination principle, the preceding Opinion delivered in the *Micheletti* case[35] is also grounded in the 'great' principles of the internal market. This case dealt with the issue of 'dual nationality' (one conferred by a non-member country and one conferred by a EU Member State) so to attribute to a dentist the right to settle in Spain, where he had never lived. Tesauro's Opinion invoked the principle of equality, of equal treatment, and rejected the internationalist 'romantic' notion of the concept of '[more] effective nationality' (point 5). In this way, he extended the scope of the fundamental right of freedom of establishment by stating that Mr. Micheletti, even though he had never lived in Spain, had the right to settle there because, otherwise, 'there would be discrimination between different categories of nationals': those who reside in an EU country and those who don't.[36] A secondary, but direct, consequence of the *Micheletti* judgment was the achievement that Member States' decisions in the field of nationality have to be compliant with EU law. In the more general context of the relationships between EU law and International law, and of the autonomy of the former vis-à-vis the latter, such a statement (clearly laid down later by the Court in the *Rottman* case[37]) was not without importance.

A hallmark of Tesauro's concept of the internal market was also the 'interdisciplinary reading' between freedoms, a perspective that aligns with a rather common approach in current doctrine. In particular, the interdisciplinary reading was between the free circulation of goods and services. Of course, Tesauro was not the very first to suggest this 'contamination' but he was building of the teachings provided by Advocate General Francis Jacobs in the *Säger* case,[38] as well as the Opinion by Advocate General Otto Lenz in the '*Tourist Guides*' case.[39] Nevertheless, Tesauro syntesthised these precedents and made a fundamental contribution to the extension of the jurisprudence on the free movement of goods and services.

For instance, in the Opinion he delivered in the *Collectieve Antennevoorziening Gouda* case[40] that concerned the imposition of certain conditions on foreign broadcasters regarding the re-transmission of programs containing advertising that was specifically intended for the Dutch public, Tesauro affirmed that the freedom to provide services 'corresponds to a large extent to that of the free movement of goods in view of its prohibition of all restrictions (Articles 30 to 34) and the derogations permitted by Article 36'.[41] On this basis, he held that 'as

[35] *Micheletti and Others v Delegación del Gobierno en Cantabria* Case C-369/90 ECLI:EU:C:1992:47 [1992].

[36] ibid, 6.

[37] *Janko Rottman v Freistaat Bayern* Case C-135/08 ECLI:EU:C:2010:104 [2010].

[38] *Säger v Dennemeyer* Case C-76/90 ECLI:EU:C:1991:72 [1991].

[39] *Commission v France* Case C-154/89 ECLI:EU:C:1991:76 [1991].

[40] *Stichting Collectieve Antennevoorziening Gouda* Case C-288/89 ECLI:EU:C:1991:157 [1991].

[41] ibid, 12.

in the case of the free movement of goods, any restrictions on the freedom to provide services (even if they are not discriminatory) are in principle incompatible with Article 59'.[42]

The *Veronica Omroep Organisatie* case,[43] instead, concerned the compatibility with the internal market rules of Dutch legislation that, to preserve a pluralistic and non-commercial broadcasting system, 'prohibit[ed] national broadcasting organizations financed out of public funds and not pursuing profit from engaging in economic activities which are unconnected with the tasks entrusted to them by their statutes'.[44] In balancing different interests (*ie*, free circulation of services and capital, and pluralism of the broadcasting system), Tesauro concluded that in principle the restrictions to the economic freedoms imposed by national law were compatible with the Treaty rules, since they were not discriminatory and were 'proportionate in relation to the aim pursued'.[45] Conversely, the abusive activities undertaken by Veronica, far from being functional to Articles 59 and 67 TEC, '[were] liable to undermine the pluralism which the law at issue was designed to safeguard'.[46]

With the same strong conviction with which he contributed to this 'contamination' between freedoms, Tesauro was a rigorous reader and interpreter of the Treaty: he rejected an 'interdisciplinary reading' between the free movement of goods and capital. Think, for example, about his Opinion in the *Safir* case,[47] which related to the compliance with the free movement of services and capital provisions of a Swedish law that subjected premiums for life insurance policies that were contracted with insurance companies not established in Sweden to tax payments. On this occasion, disregarding the *Svensson* case-law,[48] in which the Court had proposed an indiscriminate application of rules relating to capital and services, AG Tesauro stressed that 'indiscriminate application of the provisions of the Treaty governing services and capital might be further precluded by the fact that the scope of the prohibition laid down in Article 59, on the one hand, and that laid down in Article 73b of the Treaty, on the other, is different. While the freedom to provide services is, of course, subject only to the exceptional restrictions permitted or envisaged by Article 56 (and, on the conditions reviewed below, to restrictions justified by overriding requirements), free movement of capital, on the other hand, is subject to the broader restriction laid down in Article 73d(a), which expressly permits the enactment of fiscal provisions which distinguish between taxpayers on grounds of residence (even though, under the 'classic' formula, they must not constitute a means of

[42] ibid.
[43] *Vereniging Veronica Omroep Organisatie* Case C-148/91 ECLI:EU:C:1992:447 [1992].
[44] ibid, 11.
[45] ibid, 10.
[46] ibid.
[47] *Safir v Skattemyndigheten i Dalarnas län* Case C-118/96 ECLI:EU:C:1997:423 [1997].
[48] *Svensson and Gustavsson v Ministre du Logement e de l'Urbanisme* Case C-484/93 ECLI:EU:C:1995:379 [1995].

arbitrary discrimination or a disguised restriction). This is a subtle difference in the ambit of the two provisions, which makes it even more important for their respective scopes of application to be determined accurately'.[49]

The attention to the needs of individuals is always present in the Opinions of AG Tesauro. One can recall, for instance, the Opinions on the free movement of patients, inaugurated with the *Decker* case,[50] of which we still hear the echo today. In this case, Tesauro had to assess whether or not a national rule, which made the reimbursement of medical expenses incurred outside the national territory subject to the condition that the medical treatment (or the purchase of the medical products) were duly authorised by the competent social security institution, was compatible with Community law.

Tesauro was always searching for an 'anchoring' between the case, with its technicalities and limits, and the principles of the Community legal system considered as a whole. In the *Decker* case, he made this evident when he extended the scope of the fundamental right of free circulation, affirming that 'unjustified restrictions on the free movement of persons (establishment and services) and of goods are not permitted merely because the benefit conferred on individuals by the relevant Community rules conflicts with a national measure which in some way relates to social security'.[51] This field was under national competence, at least to the extent that it was not governed by specific Community legislation.

On this occasion, Tesauro began by saying that 'the implementation of the single market […] should […] constitute one of the cornerstones and hallmarks of the Community'[52] and that discouraging the free movement of patients, 'or of the less affluent among them at least', constitutes a negative factor in this sense.[53] He hoped for an 'Action by the Community legislature aimed at harmonizing the area in question so as to allow genuine and effective freedom of movement for patients, which would be a significant factor in the creation of a single integrated market'.[54] It is difficult not to glimpse Tesauro's legacy in this specific field, which saw (albeit with a certain delay compared with the wish of the Advocate General) the adoption of Directive 2011/24/EU of 9 March 2011 on the application of patients' rights in cross-border healthcare. Ultimately, Tesauro's approach in the *Decker* case is linked to values of health solidarity, an extensively discussed topic during the recent COVID-19 pandemic.[55]

[49] ibid, 16.

[50] *Decker v Caisse de maladie des employés privés* Case C-120/95 ECLI:EU:C:1997:399 [1997]; see also *Kohll v Union des caisses de maladie* Case C-158/96 ECLI:EU:C:1998:171 [1998].

[51] ibid, 22.

[52] ibid, 1.

[53] ibid, 2.

[54] ibid, 60.

[55] F Croci, *Solidarietà tra Stati membri dell'Unione europea e* Governance *economica europea* (Giappichelli, Torino, 2020) 325.

4. CONCLUDING REMARKS: GIUSEPPE TESAURO'S LEGACY

It is difficult to capture, in a few pages, the essence of the contribution of Tesauro in the evolution of EU law, as well as his legacy.

In addition to the three strands that we mentioned earlier (*i*) on the principle of non-discrimination, (*ii*) on the 'contamination' between freedoms, and (*iii*) on the free movement of patients, there have been many interventions of his that have strongly marked a step forward in EU law and, in particular, in the field of internal market law: for example in the *Gaal* case[56] on the notion of 'child of a migrant worker' pursuant to Reg. (EEC) no. 1968/1612, extensively interpreted by AG Tesauro, with a consequent extension of the related rights. Or, again, *The Queen-Surinder Singh* case,[57] where Tesauro believed that, to respect the principle of free movement of workers as well as the principle of non-discrimination, the right of a worker to enter and reside in his own Member State after a period of work in another Member State had to be extended to his relatives. Or, with respect to the free circulation of medicines, his important Opinions in *Schumacher/ Hautzollamt Frankfurt am Main-ost*;[58] *Delattre*[59] clarified the necessary balancing test between free circulation of goods and health protection made therein. What characterises the cases mentioned throughout these pages is the need, for Tesauro, to always 'bring back' his legal reasoning to fundamental principles of Community law. In reading the facts of a case in light of these principles, one can identify an analogy with the approach adopted by Advocate General Antonio La Pergola, remembered in these terms by Tesauro himself in a contribution to his colleague.[60] In these legal reasonings the great jurist always stands out, certainly, but so does his human side, 'not very commercial' (to use his words[61]) and sensibly attentive to individuals.

Finally, Tesauro's work at the ECJ was distinguished by his pioneering ability to anticipate key themes in Community law. His privileged position as an Advocate General, focused on 'defending the right and not the party', allowed him to address not only legal and scientific aspects but also cultural, social, and human dimensions.

One could conclude that Tesauro did not simply limit himself to 'shaping' EU law, but contributed, more than anything else, to the Union's ability

[56] *Landesamt für Ausbildungsförderung Nordrhein-Westfalen v Gaal* Case C-7/94 ECLI: EU:C:1995:29 [1995].

[57] *The Queen v Immigration Appeal Tribunal e Surinder Singh, ex parte Secretary of State for the Home Department* Case C-370/90 ECLI:EU:C:1992:229 [1992].

[58] *Schumacher v Hauptzollamt Frankfurt am Main-Ost* Case 215/87 ECLI:EU:C:1989:37 [1989].

[59] *Delattre* Case C-369/88 ECLI:EU:C:1991:17 [1991].

[60] See Tesauro (n 26) 366: 'Andava nei dettagli dei problemi e dei fascicoli. Aveva, tuttavia, pur sempre il gusto di risalire ai principi, alle categorie generali'.

[61] See G Tesauro, 'Alcune riflessioni sul ruolo della Corte di giustizia nell'evoluzione dell'Unione europea' (2013) 18 *Il Diritto dell'Unione europea* 483, 500.

to promote the protection and dignity of individuals belonging to the 'new legal order'[62] of the European Union legal system. It is of no surprise that the 1963 *van Gend & Loos* judgment and the 'culture of defending the rights of individuals',[63] enshrined therein also by Alberto Trabucchi, are for Tesauro the main connotations of European Union law.

[62] *Van Gend en Loos v Administratie der Belastingen* Case 26/62 ECLI:EU:C:1963:1 [1963].

[63] See F Pedrini, 'Colloquio sull'integrazione sovranazionale. Intervista al prof. Giuseppe Tesauro (Napoli, 20 giugno 2021)' (2021) 16 *Lo Stato* 183; see also P Mengozzi, 'Giuseppe Tesauro e l'integrazione europea come affermazione di una cultura di difesa dei diritti dei singoli' in *Giuseppe Tesauro: un uomo, un europeista – Atti del Convegno in memoria* (n 1) 89.

11

Antonio La Pergola: The Idea of Europe as an Objective to be Pursued, between Founding Values and Fundamental Principles

CHIARA AMALFITANO AND FILIPPO CROCI*

1. INTRODUCTION: ANTONIO LA PERGOLA'S MULTI-FACETED EXPERIENCE AND PERSONALITY AS A JURIST

VERY FEW PERSONALITIES have covered a variety of public functions, all of which of primary importance, comparable to those held by Professor Antonio La Pergola.

His academic career was brilliant. After graduating from the University of Catania in 1952 at the age of 21, he carried out research, first at the University of Edinburgh, and then at Harvard Law School, where he obtained a Master of Laws or LL.M. In 1959, he returned to Italy and became a lecturer (*libero docente*) at the University of Bologna; in 1962, he became full professor of American public law, subsequently teaching constitutional law as well, at the Universities of Padua, Bologna and Rome (La Sapienza).

His extraordinary institutional journey began with his appointment as a member of the Supreme Judicial Council (*Consiglio Superiore della Magistratura*) in 1976, a position from which he had to resign in 1978, when the President of the Italian Republic appointed him as Judge of the Italian Constitutional Court. In 1986, he was elected President of the same Court, until the end of his mandate of nine years in 1987.

* Although this chapter is the outcome of a joint effort by the authors, sections 1, 3.2 and 5 were written by Chiara Amalfitano, while Filippo Croci is the author of sections 2, 3, 3.1 and 4. The authors wish to thank Mr Carlo Zadra – currently Director at the Legal Service (Justice and Home Affairs) of the Council of the European Union – and Mr Giulio Cesare Rizza – currently Counsel at Cleary Gottlieb Steen & Hamilton, Rome – for all the information and memories shared with reference to their experience as former *référendaires* at the European Court of Justice, notably as members of the cabinet of (Judge and Advocate General) Antonio La Pergola.

He was then Minister for European Affairs under two different governments (1987–89), Member of the European Parliament for one term (1989–94) – where he was elected as member of the Italian Socialist Party, and then joined, at European level, the Party of European Socialists, founded in 1992 – and in 1994 he was appointed to the European Court of Justice. More precisely – as will be explained in para. 3 – he was appointed as Judge, then Advocate General and then Judge again. On his return to Italy in 2006, he became President of the Italian State Mint and Polygraphic Institute (*Istituto Poligrafico e Zecca dello Stato*). In parallel to all these activities, he was the 'founding father' (in 1989–90) and President (until his death in 2007) of the so-called Venice Commission (European Commission for Democracy through law) of the Council of Europe.[1]

In the different steps of such an outstanding institutional path, Antonio La Pergola could rely on (and make the best of) the *bildung* and the academic background he had developed through important cultural and scientific exchanges with personalities such as Costantino Mortati, his main mentor, as well as Paul Freund, Carl Friedrich, Hans Kelsen, and many others. Paul Freund once noted that La Pergola had 'a constructive fantasy', a definition which – according to Cesare Pinelli, one of his pupils – depicts the core of La Pergola's figure as jurist.[2]

Several authors have paid homage to Antonio La Pergola,[3] recalling his uncommon sensitivity, intelligence and sagacity, his oratorical elegance and his power of persuasion, his perfect knowledge of the English and Spanish languages, his deep culture and intellectual curiosity, his nobility of spirit, his openness to dialogue, and his sense of humour. Two of these homages are particularly relevant for the purposes of the present contribution, given that they gave particular consideration to the role of La Pergola in relation to European Union law: Giuseppe Tesauro[4] and Paolo Mengozzi.[5]

The present work, in line with the general topic of the book, will focus especially on the role played by Antonio La Pergola as a Judge and Advocate General at the ECJ. However, before examining the contribution given by La Pergola to the evolution of European Union law 'from Luxembourg', it seems appropriate

[1] P van Dijk and S Granata-Menghini (eds), *Liber Amicorum Antonio La Pergola*, 2nd ed (Lund, Juristförlaget i Lund, 2009), available at: https://www.venice.coe.int/files/articles/LiberAmicoriumLaPergola.pdf.

[2] C Pinelli, 'Professor La Pergola's "Constructive Fantasy"' in P van Dijk and S Granata-Menghini (eds), *Liber Amicorum Antonio La Pergola*, (n 1), 281, 281; see also C Pinelli, 'Antonio La Pergola, giurista-costruttore' (2007) 13 *Diritto pubblico* 571.

[3] In addition to the contributions gathered, the *Liber Amicorum* cited in the previous footnote, as well as the articles mentioned in the two following footnotes, see, for instance, A Reposo and N Olivetti Rason, 'In memoriam Antonio La Pergola' (2007) 9 *Diritto pubblico comparato ed europeo* XIII; the volume *Atti della giornata in ricordo del Presidente emerito della Corte costituzionale Antonio La Pergola*, Rome, 2009, available at: www.cortecostituzionale.it; G Caravale, 'Alla scuola di Costantino Mortati: Antonio La Pergola', 2014, available at: www.nomos-leattualitaneldiritto.it.

[4] G Tesauro, 'Il contributo di Antonio La Pergola all'affermazione e allo sviluppo del diritto comunitario' (2009) 4 *Studi sull'integrazione europea* 361 (also published in *Atti della giornata in ricordo del Presidente emerito della Corte costituzionale Antonio La Pergola*, (n 3) 33).

[5] P Mengozzi, 'Antonio La Pergola' (2008) 3 *Studi sull'integrazione europea* 489.

to make some considerations on the remarkable impact that he was able to have also 'from Rome', during his previous experiences.

2. ANTONIO LA PERGOLA AND THE RELATIONS BETWEEN THE EU AND ITALIAN LEGAL ORDERS: THE CONTRIBUTION GIVEN 'FROM ROME'

If it is true that Antonio La Pergola's contribution 'from Rome' in EU law matters was, to some extent, more indirect than what he could provide 'from Luxembourg', it is also true that his name is closely linked to the relations between the Italian legal order and EU law. Indeed, in performing his functions in the Italian institutions – notably, as a member of the Constitutional Court and as Minister for European Affairs – he played a fundamental role in innovating and systematising the ways in which the Italian legal order conceived, applied, and implemented EU law.

During his nine-year mandate at the Constitutional Court, La Pergola was the judge-rapporteur of 76 judgments and 63 orders:[6] several of those decisions were very important cases, a number of which related to issues pertaining to the then European Community law. The best-known judgment that he drafted as a Judge of the Constitutional Court is, by far, the so-called *Granital* decision of 1984. It is indisputable that the *Granital* judgment was (and still is) a real milestone in the case law of the Italian Constitutional Court. By substantially aligning its reasoning with the ECJ *Simmenthal* ruling, the Italian Constitutional Court recognised the possibility for 'ordinary judges' to set aside (ie, not apply to the case at hand) national norms that are contrary to EU provisions that are directly applicable (and/or have direct effect), without raising an issue of constitutional legitimacy. The involvement of the Constitutional Court remains necessary – as already clarified in *Frontini* – only when the EU provisions at issue are not directly applicable (and/or do not have direct effect), as well as in the exceptional cases known as 'controlimiti' (ie in the event that such provisions may call into question fundamental principles of the Italian constitutional legal order and/or inalienable rights of individuals), and when a national provision is alleged to be aimed at preventing or impairing the continuing application of the Treaty. Since the *Granital* judgment, the dynamics of relations between the EU and Italian legal orders remained largely unchanged – albeit with some adjustments – for more than thirty years until judgment no. 269 of 2017. This testifies to the importance of La Pergola's legacy in the field of relations between the Italian legal order and EU law.

La Pergola's role as judge rapporteur was essential to the outcome of the *Granital* case, according to other judges of the Constitutional Court.[7] His

[6] F Amirante, 'Apertura dei lavori', in *Atti della giornata in ricordo del Presidente emerito della Corte costituzionale Antonio La Pergola* (n 3) 1.

[7] See, for instance, L Elia, 'Ricordi di Corte', in *Astrid Online*, 2006, available at: www.astrid-online.it, 3.

contributions were especially vital to finding a positive compromise between the need to adapt the Italian legal order to the 'requests' of the ECJ, and the views held by some judges of the Constitutional Court who deemed it essential not to abandon the traditional 'dualistic' approach to the relations between the Italian and EU legal orders. In this regard, La Pergola was able to foster an evolution of that approach, introducing a solution that was defined as a 'temperate dualism', while confirming and enhancing the fundamental role of Article 11 of the Italian Constitution,[8] which is still the cardinal point of reference in relations between the national legal order and the EU today.[9]

Some authors highlight the connections between La Pergola's scientific contributions – in particular, his monograph of 1961,[10] in which he pleaded for a pragmatic approach to overcome the divisions between the 'monist' and the 'dualist' theories – and the effective and balanced solution adopted in the *Granital* judgment.[11] Others underline the references to La Pergola's studies on the theory of legal order elaborated by Santi Romano,[12] and even on the 'American Confederation'.[13]

Be that as it may, La Pergola's contribution (and that of the Italian Constitutional Court) to the *Granital* judgment was so important that it crossed Italian borders: for instance, the German Federal Constitutional Court, in its *Solange II* judgment, expressly mentioned an article written by La Pergola on the *Granital* judgment.[14] As already noted, La Pergola was not only the drafter, but also the main intellectual force behind *Granital* so that some refer to it as the 'La Pergola judgment'.[15]

[8] In this regard, see, inter alia, Mengozzi (n 5) 490.

[9] As emblematically recalled, for instance, in the judgment of the Italian Constitutional Court no. 227 of 2010, *M.K.P.*

[10] A La Pergola, *Costituzione e adattamento dell'ordinamento interno al diritto internazionale* (Milan, Giuffrè, 1961).

[11] See, for example, Pinelli, 'Antonio La Pergola, giurista-costruttore' (n 2) 578, according to whom the structure of the grounds of the *Granital* judgment was a 'miniature reproduction' of the reasoning developed in La Pergola's monograph of 1961.

[12] G Repetto, 'Pouring New Wine into New Bottles? The Preliminary Reference to the CJEU by the Italian Constitutional Court' (2015) 16 *German Law Journal* 1449, 1452.

[13] A Baldassarre, 'Intervento', in *Atti della giornata in ricordo del Presidente emerito della Corte costituzionale Antonio La Pergola* (n 3) 23, 25, who maintains that the famous statement of the *Granital* judgment on the fact that the Italian and the EU legal orders are 'autonomi e distinti, ancorché coordinati, secondo la ripartizione di competenza stabilita e garantita dal Trattato' (autonomous and separate, albeit coordinated, through the division of competences laid down and guaranteed by the Treaty) would be a homage paid by La Pergola to the motto of the stage of American history immediately preceding the foundation of the United States of America, in which the American States were a confederation. However, it should be noted that the statement at issue had already been made by the Italian Constitutional Court in the previous judgment no. 183 of 1973, *Frontini*.

[14] A La Pergola and P Del Duca, 'Community Law, International Law and the Italian Constitution' (1985) 79 *American Journal of International Law* 598.

[15] For this remark, see, inter alia, S Bartole, 'Intervento', in *Atti della giornata in ricordo del Presidente emerito della Corte costituzionale Antonio La Pergola* (n 3) 29, 31.

In a similar manner, his main achievement while serving as Minister for European Affairs after concluding his mandate at the Constitutional Court, law no. 86 of 9 March 1989, is commonly known as the 'La Pergola Act'. This Act was the first systematic piece of legislation adopted in Italy to regulate the relations between the EU and Italian legal orders, with particular regard to the proper execution of obligations under EU law. The most urgent need was to ensure full compliance with the obligation to implement Directives within the deadline set for their transposition: an obligation which, at the time, was systematically violated by the Italian Republic. This exposed the country to several infringement procedures brought by the Commission before the ECJ and compromised, to some extent, Italy's reputation in Europe.

The 'La Pergola Act' did not solve all of the problems of compatibility between the EU and the Italian legal order, and some regrettably persist to this day under the current, reformed, legislation. It was, however, a crucial step in modernising the Italian legal order and in improving relations with the EU.

More generally, as Minister for European Affairs, La Pergola had the merit – as observed by Giuseppe Tesauro – of perfectly understanding the nature of the governmental function entrusted to him and the contents of the activities he had to perform, in full consistency with his personality and with his scientific-institutional interests.[16]

3. ANTONIO LA PERGOLA AND THE DEVELOPMENT OF EUROPEAN UNION LAW: THE CONTRIBUTION GIVEN 'FROM LUXEMBOURG'

Following his institutional experience in Italy and his service as a Member of the European Parliament, La Pergola was appointed at the Court of Justice, first as Judge (October- December 1994), alongside Giuseppe Federico Mancini. He was then Advocate General (AG) (1995–1999), alongside Giuseppe Tesauro and later Antonio Saggio. Finally, he was appointed as Judge for a second time (1999–2006), while the 'Italian' AG was, first, Antonio Saggio, and then Antonio Tizzano.

According to people who worked in Luxembourg during those years, at the time the Court was profoundly different to what it is today, especially with regard to its working environment. First, there were very few institutions and buildings on the Kirchberg *plateau* other than the Court. Second, before the enlargements of the 2000s, the 'community of people' working at the ECJ and the then Court of First Instance was much smaller and, consequently, more cohesive – to some extent even friendly – compared with today.

La Pergola integrated perfectly into that context, thanks to his international experience and his capacity to get along with other people regardless

[16] Tesauro (n 4) 364.

of their cultural and professional backgrounds.[17] Indeed, in the words of Antonio Baldassarre, a former President of the Italian Constitutional Court, La Pergola was the first really cosmopolitan Italian jurist.[18] In the same vein, Paolo Mengozzi defined him as a '*brillant savant cosmopolite*'.[19]

3.1. Advocate General La Pergola

During his almost five years as Advocate General, La Pergola delivered around 130 Opinions, many of which became a point of reference for the Court's case law and, more generally, for all those who study and apply EU law.

It is debatable whether the influence of Advocates General on the ECJ is measurable or not,[20] and, if so, whether the number of cases in which an AG was 'followed' by the Court is a proper indicator in this respect.[21] It is, however, indisputable that Antonio La Pergola had a deep impact on the Court's activity and on the development of its case law.[22]

In his Opinions, one can always find a thorough and exhaustive legal analysis of the issues raised by the case at hand, developed and presented in a clear and elegant style, and complemented by extensive references to the relevant case law and contributions from legal scholars from several EU, and even non-EU, countries. At the same time, his capacity to delineate the theoretical framework underlying each file was never an aim in itself. He also devoted particular attention to the facts of the case, the arguments of the parties – which were summarised in detail, carefully considered, and often even challenged or endorsed – and, above all, he proposed concrete solutions to the Court. In this sense, La Pergola's 'constructive fantasy' mentioned above fits perfectly with the function he performed as an Advocate General, allowing him to make a

[17] Mengozzi (n 5) 492.

[18] Baldassarre (n 13) 24.

[19] Mengozzi (n 5) 489.

[20] Amongst the numerous studies dealing with such issues, see, for instance, T Tridimas, 'The Role of the Advocate General in the Development of Community Law: Some Reflections' (1997) 34 *CML Rev* 1349; K Mortelmans, 'The Court Under the Influence of its Advocates General: An Analysis of the Case Law on the Functioning of the Internal Market' (2005) 1 *YEL* 127; L Clément-Wilz, 'The Advocate General: A Key Actor of the Court of Justice of the European Union' (2012) 14 *CYELS* 587; U Šadl and S Sankari, 'The Elusive Influence of the Advocate General on the Court of Justice: The Case of European Citizenship' (2017) 36 *YEL* 421.

[21] For a clear answer in the negative, see, amongst others, G Tesauro, 'Riflessioni sull'esperienza di un avvocato generale presso la Corte di giustizia' (1998) 3 *Il Diritto dell'Unione europea* 1, 3.

[22] For example, U Šadl and S Sankari, 'The Elusive Influence of the Advocate General', (n 20) 437 state that, on the basis of their model and considering specifically the case law on European citizenship, 'AG La Pergola had a moderate to strong influence on the Court, but not a very strong overall influence (compared to, let us say, AG Jacobs)' and add that 'his imprint on the case law can be discussed more in terms of aspiration or "Court-whispering" than tangible influence'. Other authors support AG La Pergola's sizeable effect on the Court more boldly: see, in particular, N Burrows and R Greaves, *The Advocate General and EC Law* (Oxford, Oxford University Press, 2007) 277 and 292.

meaningful contribution to the ECJ's mission of 'ensur[ing] that in the interpretation and application of the Treaties the law is observed.' as stated in current Article 19(1) TEU.

Some of his legal clerks (*référendaires*), who worked in his cabinet when he was an Advocate General, remember La Pergola being very much appreciated and respected by the other Members of the Court. Even though at times the solutions he proposed were considered quite 'original' compared with the settled case law, the profoundness of his analyses was highly recognised and, usually, led the Court to follow the path he traced in his Opinions. It is also worth noting that proposing new and innovative solutions in interpreting EU law does not at all fall outside the tasks of the role of Advocate General.

An area of EU law in which his contribution was particularly significant is that of European citizenship. An important and well-known example is his Opinion in *Martinez Sala*,[23] a landmark case on the free movement and residence within the EU, as well as on the scope and effect of European citizenship. The Higher Social Court of Bavaria, Germany had referred the case for a preliminary ruling to the Court of Justice, focusing on secondary legislation and requesting the ECJ, inter alia, to interpret the notions of 'worker', 'family benefit' and 'social advantage' laid down in the relevant EU legal acts.

After having examined those issues in detail, AG La Pergola shifted his attention to the fundamental principle of non-discrimination enshrined in the Treaty and, most notably, to European citizenship, introduced by the Maastricht Treaty, including the related right of EU citizens to move and reside freely within the territory of all Member States other than the one of which they are nationals. In this regard, La Pergola highlighted the importance of the 'new' Article 8a of the EC Treaty (now Article 21 TFEU) and its consequences on the facts of the case. Following the entry into force of such provision, as pointed out by La Pergola

> the right to move and reside freely throughout the whole of the Union is enshrined in an act of primary law and does not exist or cease to exist depending on whether or not it has been made subject to limitations under other provisions of Community law, including secondary legislation. The limitations provided for in Article 8a itself concern the actual exercise but not the existence of the right.[24]

The Opinion continues stating that the novelty of Article 8a lies, in particular, in the fact of having extracted:

> the *kernel* from the other freedoms of movement – the freedom which we now find characterised as the right, not only to move, but also to *reside* in every Member State: a primary right, in the sense that it appears as the first of the rights ascribed to citizenship of the Union. That is how freedom of residence is conceived and systematised in the Treaty. It is not simply a derived right, but a right *inseparable* from citizenship

[23] *Martinez Sala v Freistaat Bayern* Case C-85/96 ECLI:EU:C:1997:335 [1997].
[24] ibid., para 18.

> of the Union in the same way as the other rights expressly crafted as necessary corollaries of such *status* […] – a new right, common to all citizens of the Member States without distinction.[25]

In this vein, the AG concluded that:

> Citizenship of the Union comes through the *fiat* of the primary norm, being conferred directly on the individual, who is henceforth formally recognised as a subject of law who acquires and loses it together with citizenship of the national state to which he belongs and in no other way. Let us say that it is the *fundamental* legal status guaranteed to the citizen of every Member State by the legal order of the Community and now of the Union.[26]

In its judgment,[27] the Court of Justice did not fully explore the reflections of AG La Pergola on the importance of European citizenship in relation to the right to reside in other Member States, nor did it endorse the definition of European citizenship as the 'fundamental status' of all the citizens of the Member States. The arguments developed by La Pergola were, however, 'followed' and duly considered by the Court in subsequent cases.[28] As effectively noted by two authors, 'the language and perhaps even the 'philosophy' of the AG Opinion in *Martinez Sala*' were adopted later on by the Court in *Grzelczyk*,[29] which, precisely in this vein, 'joins residence, equal treatment, and citizenship into the famous passage of fundamental status.'[30]

At the same time, AG La Pergola did not stress the importance of European citizenship 'at all costs', especially when it was not useful for the decision of the case. An example of this is his Opinion in *Calfa*[31] – a case that concerned the power of Member States to order the expulsion of EU citizens from their territory – in which he clearly stated that the provision laid down in Article 8a

[25] ibid.

[26] ibid.

[27] *Martinez Sala v Freistaat Bayern* Case C-85/96 ECLI:EU:C:1998:217 [1998].

[28] In this vein, see, inter alia, L Clément-Wilz (n 20) 596, according to whom, having regard to the Opinion in *Martinez Sala*, 'AG La Pergola was indeed a pioneer in "putting flesh on the bones of European citizenship"' (quoting S O'Leary, 'Putting Flesh on the Bones of European Union Citizenship' (1999) 24 *EL Rev* 68); U Šadl and S Sankari (n 20) 436 ff, who state that 'La Pergola is usually credited with the fundamental status formulation, spelled out in his opinion in *Martinez Sala*. Several AsG explicitly refer to this opinion […]. While the Court does not mention it at any point in later case law, the substance of points 18–22 of that opinion resonate with the Court's reasoning in *Grzelczyk*, *D'Hoop*, and *Garcia Avello* (normative relations of Art. 21 TFEU, the fundamental legal status, scope of EU law, and thereby non-discrimination), *Baumbast* (direct effect of Art. 21 TFEU), *Rottmann* (scope of application of Art. 20 TFEU), and is largely consistent with the Court's position in *Ruiz Zambrano* and even in *Dano*'. With particular regard to the influence of AG La Pergola's Opinion in *Martinez Sala* (as well as AG Jacobs's Opinion in Case C-274/96 *Bickel and Franz*) on the recognition of direct effect to the current Article 21 TFEU, see also M Condinanzi, A Lang and B Nascimbene, *Citizenship of the Union and Freedom of Movement of Persons* (Leiden-Boston, Brill, 2008) 26, footnote 98.

[29] *Grzelczyk* Case C-184/99 ECLI:EU:C:2001:458 [2001].

[30] U Šadl and S Sankari (n 20) 437.

[31] *Calfa* Case C-348/96 ECLI:EU:C:1998:64 [1998].

of the EC Treaty (now Article 21 TFEU) was not relevant. Indeed, according to La Pergola, the settled case law of the Court already afforded a complete answer to the preliminary questions at issue and Ms. Calfa's position was 'already properly protected by her status as a recipient of services as well as by the provisions of Directive 64/221/EEC', making recourse to the further protection offered by EU citizenship 'superfluous'.[32]

Equal treatment and non-discrimination – which, as noted above, played an important role in *Martinez Sala* – were also thoroughly scrutinised by La Pergola in the framework of the EU internal market rules. This is another field in which La Pergola gave a very significant contribution, first as an Advocate General, and subsequently as a Judge.

Considering the activity of La Pergola as an Advocate General, it is worth mentioning the Opinion he delivered in the *Kreil* case, in which he placed particular emphasis on equal treatment and non-discrimination.[33] This case dealt with the prohibition, laid down under the national legislation of a Member State (in the case at hand, Germany), against the recruitment of women into sectors of the armed forces other than the medical and military-music services. La Pergola carefully distinguished the case from the precedent *Sirdar*, in which he himself had delivered an Opinion as Advocate General,[34] noting that in *Sirdar* the exclusion of women concerned only the Royal Marines, which was a select marine commando corps that can be defined as the 'point of the arrowhead' of the United Kingdom's armed forces. In *Kreil*, the scope of the exclusion at stake was much wider. On this basis, following a profound analysis with an impressive set of bibliographic references, he concluded that the exclusion at issue was incompatible with Directive 76/207/EEC, of 9 February 1976, which concerned equal treatment for men and women on issues related to employment and, therefore, with the principle of equal treatment more broadly.[35] However, La Pergola also considered the possibility that the Court could disagree with his view. Consistent with his pragmatic approach, he therefore added further considerations concerning both the validity of the justification claimed by the German authorities and the proportionality of the system adopted by them, with a view to providing the national court with useful elements for applying the relevant principles and provisions to the case at hand. The ECJ eventually followed the approach suggested by La Pergola, declaring that the Directive precluded the application of national provisions such as those of German law at issue.

Another case that can be considered emblematic of the attention paid by La Pergola to general principles and the 'bigger picture'[36] is *Garonor*.[37]

[32] ibid., para 10.
[33] *Kreil* Case C-285/98 ECLI:EU:C:1999:525 [1999].
[34] *Sirdar* Case C-273/97 ECLI:EU:C:1999:246 [1999].
[35] *Kreil* (n 33) para 30.
[36] Tesauro (n 4) 366.
[37] *Dubois and Cargo v Garonor* Case C-16/94 ECLI:EU:C:1995:148 [1995].

In that case, the main issue at stake was the applicability, or lack thereof, of Treaty rules on charges having equivalent effect to a customs duty with regard to a 'transit charge' (*taxe de passage*) relating to customs. The peculiarity of that charge was that it was not imposed by the State but arose from an agreement concluded by a private undertaking with its customers, even if designed to compensate costs arising from performance of services in the public interest. AG La Pergola did not confine himself to proposing an answer to the questions raised by the referring French *Cour de cassation*. Instead, he also developed an in-depth reasoning on the EEC Treaty provisions at issue, examining their overall significance and legislative effect in upholding a fundamental principle of the common market – defined as a 'value' in the Italian (original) version of the Opinion – represented by the free movement of goods. In this context, he devoted his attention to the principle of loyal cooperation, at the time found in Article 5 of the Treaty, particularly its second paragraph according to which Member States are to abstain from jeopardising the attainment of the objectives of the Treaty.[38] In light of that obligation, AG La Pergola expressed the view that the fundamental principle of free movement of goods can be infringed by the Member States not only as a result of directly prohibited conduct, but also as a consequence of any other conduct which, 'although not displaying the characteristics of fiscal measures having equivalent effect to customs duties, is nevertheless liable to undermine the interest which those provisions protect'.[39]

In this latter regard, as pointed out by AG La Pergola

> Article 5 comes to the fore as a provision which makes the system watertight, guaranteeing in general that the values fundamental to the Community order are fully upheld where there is indirect non-observance of them, that is to say where a breach is not apparent from the literal wording of any specific provision of the Treaty. If that were not the case, it would have to be conceded that, in this and similar cases, the Community legal order is indifferent to conduct on the part of a State, whereby a prohibition is formally observed but in practice a prohibited result is arrived at. That is not the position.[40]

Garonor is a case that clearly reveals the special attention devoted by La Pergola not only to general principles, but also to the fundamental values underlying the EU legal order: an attention whose far-sightedness is evident in light of developments in recent years.

Finally, one cannot avoid mentioning the Opinion delivered by AG La Pergola in the notorious *Centros* case,[41] which was the first of a line of cases decided

[38] ibid, paras 9 ff. For some reflections on AG La Pergola's interpretation of the principle of loyal cooperation in *Garonor*, see, amongst others, F Casolari, *Leale cooperazione tra Stati membri e Unione europea. Studio sulla partecipazione all'Unione al tempo delle crisi* (Napoli, Editoriale Scientifica, 2020) 101 ff.

[39] *Dubois and Cargo v Garonor* (n 37) para 10.

[40] ibid.

[41] Case C-212/97 *Centros* ECLI:EU:C:1998:380 [1998]. Amongst the numerous comments, see, for a historical-legal perspective, M Gelter, '*Centros*, the Freedom of Establishment for Companies and

by the ECJ on the application of the freedom of establishment guaranteed to companies by the Treaty. That Opinion has been defined as a 'model' of the approach to the function of Advocate General[42] and serves as an example of the influence that Advocates General can have on the case law of the Court.[43]

Indeed, the complex issues related to the preliminary questions raised by the national court in the *Centros* case – involving aspects of private international law as well as fundamental principles of the internal market – were examined by AG La Pergola in depth and with uncommon clarity. The facts of the case are well known: Centros was a company that had been registered in England and Wales by two Danish spouses, who, without doing any business in the United Kingdom, had then immediately requested the registration of a branch of the company in Denmark, where the requirements on the minimum amount of paid-up capital were stricter. However, the Danish Companies Boards had rejected the application for registration, claiming in essence that the whole operation was aimed at circumventing the Danish rules. In the following judicial dispute, the question arose as to the applicability of the EU primary rules on freedom of establishment to the case at hand. The national court referred this question to the ECJ for a preliminary ruling.

Highlighting the importance of the right of establishment in the EU system, La Pergola thoroughly assessed (and then rejected) the arguments relating to the abuse of law, stating that a situation such as the one at hand, 'whether one likes it or not, is the logical consequence of the rights guaranteed under the Treaty'.[44] At the same time, he was the first Advocate General to state expressly that the prevention of abusive conduct 'is among the general principles of Community law', albeit recognising that '[i]t is however by no means easy to define the precise scope of that principle'.[45] He also added what has been defined as an

the Court's Accidental Vision for Corporate Law', in FG Nicola and B Davies (eds), *EU Law Stories. Contextual and Critical Histories of European Jurisprudence*, The Law in Context (Cambridge, Cambridge University Press, 2017) 309.

[42] Tesauro (n 4) 366.

[43] K Mortelmans, 'The Court Under the Influence of its Advocates General', (n 19) 168: 'In very many cases, Advocates General, through their meticulous interpretation of the Court's case law and their analysis of legal writing, have contributed to further refining the course taken by the Court. From this point of view the Advocates General were constructive commentators of the Court's judgments. Examples of this are provided by Advocate General Van Gerven's Opinion in *Vlassopoulou*, Advocate General La Pergola's Opinion in *Centros* and Advocate General Ruiz-Jarabo Colomer's Opinion in *Überseering*'.

[44] *Centros* (n 41) para 20.

[45] ibid. It should be noted that AG Tesauro, only a few months before, had expressed the opposite view, excluding the existence, in the then European Community legal order, of a 'general principle pursuant to which one could refuse to recognise as abusive the exercise of a right conferred by a Community provision': see Case C-367/96 *Kefalas* ECLI:EU:C:1998:41 [1998], para. 21. For further reflections on the positions of Advocates General on the question as towhether the abuse of law is a general principle of EU law or not (as well as on such question in broader terms), see S Vogenauer, 'The Prohibition of Abuse of Law: An Emerging General Principle of EU Law', in R de la Feria and S Vogenauer (eds), *Prohibition of Abuse of Law: A New General Principle of EU Law?*, Studies of the Oxford Institute of European and Comparative Law 13, 521, 589 ff.

elegant reflection[46] on the fact that 'in the absence of harmonisation, competition among rules must be allowed free play in corporate matters'.[47] Finally, providing once again a systematic interpretation of the EU rules and principles governing the issues under examination, he claimed that:

> The contested measure of the Companies Board is contrary to Community law precisely because it was adopted on the implicit but clear assumption that business activities conducted by Danish nationals and directed essentially at the Danish market must inevitably be carried on through their principal establishment in Danish territory. This view cannot however be sustained at the present stage of European integration, which is characterised by the almost full completion of a single market thanks to the abolition of national obstacles to freedom of movement for persons and capital [see Article 3(c) of the Treaty]. The interpreter must draw the necessary conclusions from the developments that have already taken place in the Community system; it is for the Court to ensure that the spirit of the Treaty prevails by applying the "*Cassis de Dijon*" doctrine on mutual recognition in a consistent manner, to corporate mobility *inter alia*.[48]

As recalled by one of La Pergola's *référendaires*, the case had initially been considered as a fictitious and non-serious one, in which the freedom of establishment should not have applied. The solution proposed by La Pergola, as seen above, was exactly the opposite: after considering all the peculiarities of the case, he concluded that the situation in *Centros* fell within the scope of application of the relevant rules of the Treaty. While at first the Court might have thought that La Pergola's interpretation was 'original' and went too far, in the end the Court followed the AG's approach, albeit with some additions on the possibility for national authorities to adopt appropriate measures to prevent or penalise fraud.[49]

As the selection of cases mentioned above shows, Antonio La Pergola was able to interpret his function as Advocate General in an exemplary way, providing the Court with insightful reflections, clear analyses, and original solutions. In this sense, he could draw together and build upon his previous experiences, rendering a very important service to the Court and to EU law at large.[50]

3.2. Judge La Pergola

In December 1999, La Pergola ended his mandate as AG and became Judge. In performing this function after having been Advocate General for several years, he maybe suffered – as noted by Giuseppe Tesauro – the more 'ordinary' and simplified activities related to the drawing up of judgments, compared with the articulated reflections that can be made and presented by an AG. He continued his efforts

[46] Tesauro (n 4) 366.
[47] *Centros* (n 41) para 20.
[48] ibid.
[49] *Centros* Case C-212/97 ECLI:EU:C:1999:126 [1999].
[50] In similar terms, Tesauro (n 4) 365 ff; Mengozzi (n 5) especially 492.

towards the improvement and development of case law, however, always giving an intelligent and relevant contribution.[51]

During more than six years as a Judge at the ECJ, La Pergola was the *judge-rapporteur* of approximately sixty-five judgments. While this number is not necessarily relevant by itself, due to the variability in complexity of the cases decided by the Court, it should be noted that La Pergola unfortunately suffered from serious health issues toward the end of his mandate.

Focusing on the cases in which La Pergola served as judge-rapporteur, many are very important and a few are worth mentioning. One example, which dealt with institutional issues, is *British American Tobacco*.[52] Here the ECJ tackled the delicate problem of setting the limits for review of compliance of an EU legal act with the principle of subsidiarity. Another example is *Commission v Parliament and Council* (case C-378/00),[53] on comitology and the criteria for choosing between different procedures for adopting implementing measures. Other landmark cases address the legal status of the European Central Bank(ECB)[54] and the European Investment Bank (EIB).[55] In these, the Court clarified that the independence recognised to those two entities does not make them completely autonomous and separate from the EU legal order. With particular regard to the ECB, this might seem an obvious conclusion today, after its inclusion in the list of the official EU institutions contained in Article 13(1) TEU. However, it was far from clear at the time, given that some interpreters even believed that the ECB was in fact an autonomous international organisation.

Other judgments drafted by La Pergola as *judge-rapporteur* touched upon procedural aspects. *Nachi Europe*[56] is one example. Through the framework of an anti-dumping dispute, the Court returned to the complex relationship between references for preliminary ruling on validity, and actions for annulment of EU law. It also touched on the effects that annulling an anti-dumping regulation had on other interested parties that did not take part in the judicial proceedings. Important procedural aspects, notably the extension of public powers in the context of antitrust investigations, were also dealt with by the ECJ in *Roquette Frères*.[57] In this case, the scope of a technical regulation raised questions related to fundamental principles, such as that of loyal cooperation and the division of competence between the EU and national authorities. The principle of loyal cooperation – already examined by La Pergola when he was an Advocate General, as noted above – was also mentioned and applied in an apparently 'minor' case; an infringement action brought against Luxembourg with reference to the choice of domicile with an approved agent in patent disputes.[58]

[51] Tesauro (n 4) 366.

[52] Case C-491/01 *British American Tobacco (Investments) and Imperial Tobacco* ECLI:EU:C:2002:741 [2002].

[53] *Commission v Parliament and Council* Case C-378/00 ECLI:EU:C:2003:42 [2003].

[54] *Commission v ECB* Case C-11/00 ECLI:EU:C:2003:395 [2003].

[55] *Commission v EIB* Case C-15/00 ECLI:EU:C:2003:396 [2003].

[56] *Nachi Europe* Case C-239/99 ECLI:EU:C:2001:101 [2001].

[57] *Roquette Frères* Case C-94/00 ECLI:EU:C:2002:603 [2002].

[58] *Commission v Luxembourg* Case C-478/01 ECLI:EU:C:2003:134 [2003].

As had been the case during La Pergola's mandate as an AG, many of the cases he dealt with as a judge-rapporteur related to internal market provisions and principles. A famous case concerned the application of freedom of establishment to the particular activity of prostitution, under the framework of association agreements concluded by the then Community with Poland and Czech Republic (which were third countries at that time).[59] Another line of case law had as its object the so-called free movement of patients, in relation to the freedom to provide services under the Treaty and other provisions of EU secondary legislation. Examples of this include *Smits and Peerbooms*,[60] *Vanbraekel and Others*,[61] *van der Duin*,[62] and *Inizan*.[63]

In some cases, La Pergola had the opportunity to return, as a Judge, to questions on which he had already left his mark as an Advocate General. This happened, for instance, with the principle of equal treatment and non-discrimination between men and women (*Lommers*,[64] *Schönheit*,[65] *Haackert*)[66] as well as European citizenship and the right to reside in Member State other than that of which one is a national (*Pusa*).[67]

In general terms, the judgments rendered by the Court in cases where La Pergola was *judge-rapporteur* often included more than one reference to the Advocate General's Opinion. This suggests that he, and the Court, had particular respect for the points made, and reflections developed, by the AG.[68]

Finally, as observed by Carlo Zadra, one of his *référendaires*, it should be noted that La Pergola used to examine in-depth all the cases in which he was involved. This was true even where he was not the *judge-rapporteur*, but a 'simple' member of the formation (*juge siégeant*, to use the Court's vocabulary). Indeed, especially when a case concerned issues that he had already tackled as an AG or as a Judge, he aimed at sharing his knowledge and reflections on the relevant matters with the other members of the formation, with a view to finding the best solution in the interest of the institution and, ultimately, EU law. As is well known, the latter kind of contribution is practically impossible to identify, given the secrecy of the deliberations of the Court and the absolute lack of concurring and dissenting opinions in the ECJ judgments. However, considering the remarkable role performed by La Pergola as Advocate General,

[59] *Jany and Others* Case C-268/99 ECLI:EU:C:2001:616 [2001].
[60] *Smits and Peerbooms* Case C-157/99 ECLI:EU:C:2001:404 [2001].
[61] *Vanbraekel and Others* Case C-368/98 ECLI:EU:C:2001:400 [2001].
[62] *van der Duin and ANOZ Zorgverzekeringen* Case C-156/01 ECLI:EU:C:2003:389 [2003].
[63] *Inizan* Case C-56/01 ECLI:EU:C:2003:578 [2003].
[64] *Lommers* Case C-476/99 ECLI:EU:C:2002:183 [2002].
[65] *Schönheit* Joined Cases C-4/02 and C-5/02 ECLI:EU:C:2003:583 [2003].
[66] *Haackert* Case C-303/02 ECLI:EU:C:2004:128 [2004].
[67] *Pusa* Case C-224/02 ECLI:EU:C:2004:273 [2004].
[68] See, for instance, *Commission v ECB* (n 54), in which the Court refers to the Opinion of the Advocate General (delivered, in that case, by AG Jacobs) for a total of eleven times (namely, at paras 90, 103, 110, 134, 137, 143, 161, 163, 177, 179, and 183 of the judgment).

as well as his previous institutional experience, it is not difficult to believe that his abovementioned 'hidden' contributions were as significant as the more visible ones.

4. ANTONIO LA PERGOLA AND THE STUDY OF EUROPEAN UNION LAW

Besides his unequalled experience in the Italian and European institutions, Antonio La Pergola was also deeply engaged in the study of EU law, with particular attention to its role in, and relevance to, the Italian legal order.[69]

La Pergola was not an EU law scholar, or a part of the so-called '*communautaristes*',[70] or even an international law scholar. He was, however, a constitutionalist with particular interest in the international and supranational dimensions of law. For that reason, he was intrigued by the legal system of the European Community (and then Union).[71]

His 1961 monograph on the Italian Constitution and the adaptation of the internal legal order to international law, as well as his 1985 article on the approach of the Italian Constitutional Court, published in the *American Journal of International Law*, have already been mentioned above. But La Pergola also authored several other scientific works on issues relating to EU law. He conceived the EU as a system that could be defined as 'Federalism by analogy',[72] having some features of a modern type of confederation.[73] He reflected in depth on the relations between the EU and Italian legal orders,[74] a reflection that he continued after the 1980s.[75] Additionally, he focused on

[69] For some reflections on the contribution given by Antonio La Pergola to the study of some aspects of the European Union, see, for instance, S Bartole, 'The European Union from the Perspective of the Contribution of Antonio La Pergola to the Doctrine of Federalism', in P van Dijk and S Granata-Menghini (eds), *Liber Amicorum Antonio La Pergola* (n 1) 73.

[70] See, in particular, A Tizzano, 'Quelques réflexions sur la doctrine du droit de l'Union européenne: les "communautaristes" et les autres' (2008) 13 *Il Diritto dell'Unione europea* 225.

[71] Tesauro (n 4) 365.

[72] ibid.

[73] For extensive considerations on this matter, see A La Pergola, 'L'Unione europea fra il mercato comune ed un moderno tipo di confederazione. Osservazioni di un costituzionalista' (1993) 47 *Rivista trimestrale di diritto e procedura civile* 1; A La Pergola, 'Sguardo sul federalismo e i suoi dintorni: una celebre dicotomia "Stato federale-confederazione", la confederazione di tipo antico e moderno, l'idea europeistica di comunità', in L Pegoraro, A Reposo and M Gobbo (eds), *Letture introduttive al diritto pubblico comparato* (Padova, CEDAM, 1998) 161.

[74] See, for instance, A La Pergola, 'Autonomia regionale "potere estero" dello Stato ed esecuzione degli obblighi comunitari' (1985) 13 *Diritto e società* 571; A La Pergola, 'Jurisdiccion ordinaria y aplicacion de reglamentos de la Comunidad europea', in A López Pina (ed), *Division de poderes e interpretacion: hacia una teoria de la praxis constitucional* (Madrid, Tecnos, 1987) 128.

[75] See, inter alia, A La Pergola, 'Il recepimento del diritto comunitario: nuove prospettive del rapporto tra norme interne e norme comunitarie alla luce della legge 9 marzo 1989, n. 86', in *La Corte costituzionale tra diritto interno e diritto comunitario: atti del seminario svoltosi in Roma, Palazzo della Consulta nei giorni 15 e 16 ottobre 1990* (Milano, Giuffrè, 1991) 9; A La Pergola, 'L'articolazione del diritto comunitario e di quello interno: l'esperienza italiana' (1994) 34 *Rivista di diritto europeo* 651; A La Pergola, 'Quale *Europa-Artikel* per l'Italia?', in *Scritti in onore di*

fundamental principles of EU law,[76] as well as institutional[77] and substantive[78] EU legal matters.

Albeit without a background as a 'pure *communautairiste*', Antonio La Pergola made significant and multifaceted contributions to the study of European Union law. For this, he was able to build on his wide-ranging constitutional and comparative law studies, as well as his broad institutional and professional experience. In this vein, La Pergola's scholarly works are extremely enriching and useful, not only to understand his views on the European integration process and his legacy in this and other fields of law, but also to have the opportunity to re-read traditional EU law debates from an original, fresh, and stimulating perspective.

5. CONCLUDING REMARKS: ANTONIO LA PERGOLA'S LEGACY

By being an excellent jurist, La Pergola had a significant influence on the ECJ's jurisprudence and the shaping of EU law, both as an Advocate General and as a Judge.[79] In approaching the cases assigned to him as a judge, La Pergola dove into the details of each dossier, while always bearing in mind the importance of general principles and fundamental categories, thereby showing an uncommon capacity to see the bigger picture in smaller details.[80]

He had a multifaceted, rich, and unique personality that contributed decisively to the development of EU law not only from a judicial perspective, but also from an institutional, political, scientific, and legislative one.

At the same time, he also left an important legacy on the framework of the Council of Europe, specifically the already mentioned Venice Commission of the Council of Europe.[81] Through the establishment of that Commission, before

Giuseppe Federico Mancini, Vol II (Milano, Giuffrè, 1998) 537; A La Pergola, 'Costituzione ed integrazione europea: il contributo della giurisprudenza costituzionale', in A Pace (ed), *Studi in onore di Leopoldo Elia*, Vol I (Milano, Giuffrè, 1999) 815; A La Pergola, 'Le système italien "à double voie" pour garantir le respect du droit communautaire: la protection judiciaire décentralisée et le contrôle centralisé de constitutionnalité', in N Fenger, B Vesterdorf and K Hagel-Sørensen, *Festskrift til Claus Gulmann* (Copenhagen, Thomson – GadJura, 2006) 381.

[76] A La Pergola, 'Il giudice costituzionale italiano di fronte al primato e all'effetto diretto del diritto comunitario: note su un incontro di studio' (2003) 48 *Giurisprudenza costituzionale* 2419.

[77] A La Pergola, 'L'Atto unico europeo: grande mercato interno e coesione comunitaria', in V Grementieri and A Papisca (eds), *Europa 1992: le sfide per la ricerca e l'Università* (Milano, Giuffrè, 1989) 25; A La Pergola, 'Dalla Comunità dei dodici alla Grande Europa: aspetti istituzionali della integrazione europea' (1990) 39 *Rivista della Guardia di Finanza* 1009.

[78] See, for example, A La Pergola, 'Integrazione europea e nuove prospettive dell'attuazione delle politiche comunitarie', in *Mercato europeo e diritto dell'energia. Atti del convegno di studi* (Milano, Giuffrè, 1990) 143.

[79] Mengozzi (n 5) 492.

[80] Tesauro (n 4) 366.

[81] For a historical reconstruction of the development of the Venice Commission, and the fundamental role played by Antonio La Pergola in this respect, see G Buquicchio, 'Vingt ans avec Antonio La Pergola pour le développement de la démocratie', in P van Dijk and S Granata-Menghini (eds), *Liber Amicorum Antonio La Pergola* (n 1) 29.

the fall of the Berlin Wall, he in some ways anticipated the developments that would occur in the following years and, especially, the pivotal role of law in particular during the Eastern enlargement process – and more importantly the rule of law – for the development of stable and enduring democracies throughout Europe. He was particularly proud of this achievement and continued to be strongly committed to supporting and promoting the Venice Commission's activities, through serving as its President.[82]

One of the aspects of Antonio La Pergola that is evoked in articles and memoires dedicated to him is his faith in European integration. Many of his lines of reasoning point to the idea of Europe as an objective to be pursued, ensuring its unity and conformity to fundamental principles.[83] Such faith and belief, together with his marked commitment and scientific rigour, as well as his capacity to effectively combine theory and practice, are probably the most significant and enduring legacies of Antonio La Pergola.

[82] See P van Dijk, 'Foreword', in P van Dijk and S Granata-Menghini (eds), *Liber Amicorum Antonio La Pergola* (n 1) 7, who, as member of the Venice Commission when Antonio La Pergola passed away, observed that: 'The Venice Commission lost its Founding Father and "*président éternel*", its prestigious standard bearer and effective liaison. The members of the Venice Commission and of the staff lost a wise and experienced mentor and patron, an unfailing source of inspiration, and a caring and fatherly friend in many respects. In several ways Mr. La Pergola *was* the Venice Commission, and the Venice Commission was *his* Commission'. In similar terms, see also many other homages collected in the same *Liber Amicorum*.

[83] Bartole (n 15) 31.

12

Antonio Saggio: A Major Contributor to European Integration

ANTONIO ARESU AND CELESTINA IANNONE

1. INTRODUCTION

THE ITALIAN MEMBERS of the Court of Justice and the General Court of the European Union have made an immense contribution to the evolution of the case law and, more generally, to the development of European Union law. This contribution is not only quantitative in nature – although the number of cases handled by Italian members remains highly impressive – but can be seen through the impact and importance of the judgments and Opinions they drafted. Antonio Saggio unquestionably holds a position of great distinction in this regard. His contribution lies in his tireless efforts to shape the European legal landscape. He was notably judge (1989–95), then President (1995–98) of the Court of First Instance, and also Advocate General at the Court of Justice (1998–2000). His vision, focused on individual rights and social protections, and his dedication to a borderless Europe, continues to inspire legal practitioners and scholars alike.

Those who have had the privilege of knowing and learning from Saggio are deeply moved when they reminisce about him, his teachings and values. While it was challenging to choose from the multitude of memories and testimonies, particular attention was given by people who shared a close relationship with him: his family members, his *référendaires* (legal secretaries), his colleagues and his devoted followers. Among them is Judge Guido Raimondi, former President of the European Court of Human Rights (ECtHR), who had the unique experience of being both a student and a friend of Saggio, making his perspective especially significant.

Before addressing his biography and his many contributions, it is important to frame the salient features of Saggio's work. He had a profound sense of justice, which was indeed a hallmark of Saggio's legal analysis. In the words of Raimondi, Saggio was an outstanding example of intellectual discipline, work ethic and absolute integrity. He always sought solutions that were not only appropriate and relevant to the case but that also furthered fundamental rights, took into account social factors, and embodied the sense of justice that should permeate every legal system.

Saggio also had the unique ability to state, in a meticulous, clear and concise manner, the rule at issue in the context of the particular circumstances of a case, seizing its inherent particularities to define an appropriate solution to the dispute. The transition from the analysis of the case to its resolution occurred almost instantaneously. He had an empirical, fact-based approach, mastered through his vast knowledge, experience and legal acumen. Saggio constantly sought, with surgical precision, to isolate, define and 'distil' the core of any dispute to its true essence. He could immediately identify the interests at stake with a vision that went beyond the material limits of the case itself.

In connection with Saggio's intense sense of justice, he never lost sight of the societal element of law, civic spirit, and above all, the Europeanist aspirations. The moral obligation to contribute to the development of a united Europe permeated his legal practice and his personal choices.[1] In this regard, one can fully understand his choice of Ventotene as a place of rest and reflection. Saggio felt completely imbued by the ideals of Altiero Spinelli's European project, envisioning a unified Europe as '*una casa per tutti*' ('a home for all'), especially for the most vulnerable and the underprivileged.[2] Simultaneously, Saggio championed a Europe without frontiers within which a free market could flourish in the spirit of fair competition between businesses.

In this way, his awareness and unwavering dedication to the protection of individual rights were intricately woven together with his firm conviction of the need to dismantle all visible and invisible borders that have existed in Europe. This fervent commitment shone through every one of his speeches and is reflected in each of his judgments and Opinions. It was the very cornerstone on which he orientated his interpretation of European law.

As regards his contribution to the legal edifice of the European Union, it is important to recall that Saggio played a pivotal role in the establishment of the Court of First Instance. He contributed greatly to the drafting of that court's first Rules of Procedure,[3] for which his judicial experience was invaluable. His discerning guidance provided it with a clear direction during its formative years. In that regard, his election as President of the Court of First Instance underscored this active and leading role in the establishment and functioning of that court. Furthermore, in 1994, Saggio, together with Professors Umberto Leanza

[1] See P Mengozzi, 'In memoria di Antonio Saggio' (2011) 5(2) *Studi sull'integrazione europea* 208–209.

[2] *Per un'Europa libera e unita. Progetto d'un manifesto* (For a free and united Europe. A draft manifesto was written by Altiero Spinelli with the assistance of Ernesto Rossi in 1941, during their period of exile on the island of Ventotene, to promote the objective of European integration. It was later published by Eugenio Colorni in 1944.

[3] The Rules of Procedure of the Court of First Instance of the European Communities of 2 May 1991 (OJ 1991 L 136, p. 1, and OJ 1991 L 317, 34).

and Pasquale Paone, published the first book in Italian entirely dedicated to the Court of First Instance.[4]

A concrete example of Saggio's foresight is provided by his reflections on the jurisdiction of the Court of First Instance. That court was originally established as a court to hear and determine factually-complex 'classes of action or proceeding brought by natural or legal persons', precisely to allow the Court of Justice 'to concentrate its activities on its fundamental task of ensuring uniform interpretation of Community law' in preliminary rulings on questions of the interpretation of Community law posed by national courts.[5] Nevertheless, already in 1990, only shortly after the establishment the Court of First Instance, Saggio raised the idea of extending that court's jurisdiction to preliminary rulings in certain regulatory fields.[6] In a finely-balanced conclusion, he ultimately expressed reservations on the matter.[7] However, he raised the issue a decade before the Treaty of Nice of 2001 amended Article 225 of the EEC Treaty to include the possibility of conferring jurisdiction to the Court of First Instance to give preliminary rulings under Article 234 of the EEC Treaty, and more than thirty years before the Court of Justice decided to initiate the process for implementing that extension of jurisdiction.[8]

2. AN OUTLINE BIOGRAPHY

2.1. The Formative Years

If we are to draw insight from the biographical notes of an individual to reveal his or her underlying motivations and passions, Saggio's career unequivocally

[4] U Leanza, P Paone and A Saggio, *Il Tribunale di primo grado della Comunità europea* (Naples, Editoriale Scientifica, 1994).

[5] Council Decision of 24 October 1988 establishing a Court of First Instance of the European Communities (OJ 1988 L 319, p. 1), in particular the twelfth, fourteenth and fifteenth recitals in the preamble thereto.

[6] According to Article 168-A of the EC Treaty requests for a preliminary ruling were excluded from the jurisdiction of the Court of First Instance.

[7] A Saggio, 'Quale futuro per il Tribunale di primo grado', Conference paper 'Il Tribunale di primo grado delle Comunità europee', Università Cattolica del Sacro Cuore, Milan, 15 November 1991, 29: 'It cannot be denied that there are certain categories of requests for a preliminary ruling that could reasonably, due to their very limited importance, be attributed to the jurisdiction of the Court of First Instance: suffice it to think of cases concerning the Common Customs Tariff. It is also true that a redistribution of preliminary rulings between the Court of First Instance and the Court of Justice, while it would have the advantage of lightening the Court of Justice's workload, would not respond to a criterion of rationality: the review that the Court of Justice exercises on the validity and scope of Community Acts under Article 177 of the EEC Treaty is in fact a typical task of constitutional courts and it is therefore consistent with the system that that function should be performed exclusively by the Court of Justice, which is the constitutional court of the Community.'

[8] Decision of the CJEU of 30 November 2022, Request submitted by the Court of Justice pursuant to the second paragraph of Article 281 of the Treaty on the Functioning of the European Union, with a view to amending Protocol No 3 on the Statute of the Court of Justice of the European Union, https://curia.europa.eu/jcms/upload/docs/application/pdf/2022-12/demande_transfert_ddp_tribunal_en.pdf. At the time of writing, the legislative procedure is ongoing.

demonstrates the profound influence that the study and practice of law exerted on his life. However, in this context, law should not be viewed solely as an austere reservoir of canons and sanctions. Rather it is here a compendium of those values and first principles that, when harmoniously intertwined within a specific historical and cultural context, form the idea of justice that only a noble soul has the ability to perceive and defend. Saggio's unwavering commitment to this understanding of law guided his actions and defined his purpose throughout all his life.

Saggio was born on 19 February 1934 in Naples, a city famous for its rich heritage of legal studies and their underlying spiritual ideals. The same ideals propelled Emperor Frederick II, a devotee of the powerful concept of earthly justice, to found the University of Studies that now bears his name. It was precisely at this university that Saggio gained a solid education in law. His brilliant academic career as a student culminated in 1957 with the defence of his thesis on international law with the provocative title 'War of peoples or war of armies?', for which he obtained a first-class honours.

2.2. Judge, Lecturer, Negotiator and Author

Having accomplished his aspirations, Saggio entered the Italian judiciary in 1960 as a trainee judge. His career developed rapidly. It led him first to the position of *praetor* in Frascati and Montalto Marche followed by that of judge of first instance in Sant'Angelo dei Lombardi and finally in Naples. He was then appointed as a court of appeal judge in 1973. In 1974, he was assigned to the prestigious legislative office of the Ministry of Justice, where he worked with considerable dedication until 1978, first with Francesco Saja,[9] and then with Antonio Brancaccio.[10]

During this period, Saggio cultivated another great passion: teaching. He had the conviction that law is not solely the domain of present-day jurists, but also a noble subject that moulds the minds of future generations who will confront ever more complex challenges in the days to come. After his initial experience as a young research assistant in the department of commercial law at the Faculty of Law of the University of Macerata from 1963 to 1967, Saggio became assistant lecturer in 1968 at the department of the law of international organisations at the Faculty of Law of the University of Naples, his home university. Here he resumed the journey in international studies that had so characterised his academic development. In 1971, Saggio began a long period of collaboration with the Faculty of Economics and Business at the University of Naples and with the Faculty of Political Science at the Oriental University Institute of Naples. Until 1985, Saggio dedicated himself to teaching courses on European

[9] President of the Constitutional Court of Italy from 1987 to 1990.
[10] First President of the Italian Supreme Court of Cassation from 1986 to 1995.

Community and International Law, leaving a lasting impact on many students. During this time, the European Economic Community held an air of intrigue and mystery, captivating the interest of those seeking to explore its evolution. Following that period, although Saggio's professional practice took precedence but he never completely abandoned his connection with teaching. Indeed, from 1985 to 1989, he was Professor of Community law at the Rome campus of the Higher School of Public Administration.

Furthermore, it is noteworthy to highlight Saggio's significant contribution as a governmental expert in various international conferences. He managed to balance these responsibilities alongside his roles as a judge and lecturer. Saggio's deep understanding of the critical significance of precise drafting in the formulation of treaties was evident in his meticulous and thoughtful approach. In addition to his involvement in the Copenhagen, Brussels and London conferences for the drafting of a convention on the extradition of persons accused of terrorist offences, he participated in the United Nations *ad hoc* Committee for the examination of a convention on terrorism and air piracy in the period from 1985 to 1988. Another noteworthy aspect of Saggio's career was his appointment as chairman of the working group of the Council of the European Union, responsible for negotiations with the countries of the European Free Trade Association (EFTA) for the adoption of a convention, parallel to the Brussels Convention on jurisdiction and the enforcement of judgments in civil and commercial matters. He was then appointed chairman of the general committee at the Lugano diplomatic conference, which adopted that convention.[11]

2.3. The European Commitment: From Rome to Luxembourg

During the 1970s, Saggio carried out his duties as a judge in Rome and, at the same time, maintained a solid link with his native Naples as a lecturer at the University of Federico II and at the Oriental University Institute. In Naples, he met a prestigious group of internationalists, which included, in addition to Benedetto Conforti, Chair of International Law at the Faculty of Law, Francesco Capotorti, Luigi Ferrari Bravo, Umberto Leanza, Antonio Tizzano, Paolo Picone and Giuseppe Tesauro.[12] The interactions and experiences within this elite group had a profound influence on Saggio, who was exposed to stimuli and observations that would influence his future work. In 1979, when Francesco Capotorti was appointed Advocate General at the Court of Justice of the then European Economic Community,[13] it was almost inevitable that he called Saggio

[11] Convention on jurisdiction and the enforcement of judgments in civil and commercial matters signed in Lugano on 16 September 1988 (88/592/EEC) (OJ 1988 L 319, p. 9).

[12] Among this group of Professors of International law from the 'Neapolitan School', Capotorti, Tesauro and Tizzano all became judges or Advocates General at the Court of Justice.

[13] See L Daniele, 'Francesco Capotorti: the Man, the Academic, and the Advocate General at the Court of Justice', in this volume.

to Luxembourg to be his *référendaire*. By obtaining a leave of absence from the judiciary, Saggio held this position in Luxembourg until 1984. This marked the beginning of a very fruitful season for him, during which he would make a fundamental contribution to the European judicial system.

In the meantime, in 1980, Saggio was appointed judge to the *Corte suprema di cassazione* (Supreme Court of Cassation). At the end of his time as a *référendaire* at the Court of Justice, he returned to Rome, where he took up the post of judge in the First Civil Division of the Court of Appeal, a post he held until 1988. It should be noted that in 1985 he was also assigned to the Report and Studies Commission of the Supreme Court of Cassation thanks to his valuable experience and study of fundamental rights.

In 1988, Saggio moved to the First Civil Division of the Supreme Court of Cassation. This would normally have marked the crowning achievement of a brilliant judicial career. For him, it became the launchpad for a new and prestigious appointment: the Italian Government nominated him as a judge at the newly established Court of First Instance of the European Communities.[14] There he served as President of Chambers from September 1989,[15] actively participating in the working group in charge of drawing up the draft Rules of Procedure of that court.

In 1995, Saggio was elected by his colleagues as President of the Court of First Instance in recognition of his exceptional leadership. This appointment brought a certain prestige to Italy which, before then, had had only one presidential appointment in the European courts, that of Massimo Pilotti, President of the Court of Justice of the European Coal and Steel Community from 1952 to 1958.[16] As President of the Court of First Instance, Saggio presided over both the 'First Chamber' and the 'Grand Chamber' of the court. Additionally, he had the exclusive power for the adoption of interim and emergency measures. These were years of great commitment in the field of an increasingly varied and complex Community law, and Saggio exercised these functions as *primus inter pares*. He prioritised the preservation of the freedom of judgment of each judge of the Court of First Instance. With a strong emphasis on collegiality, he fostered an environment in which diverse perspectives could be expressed and deliberated upon. He firmly believed in the importance of respecting differing ideas to ensure effective protection for litigants.[17]

In March 1998, at the end of Giuseppe Tesauro's term of office, Saggio was appointed by the Italian Government as the new Advocate General at the Court of Justice. In this position, which allowed him to express his own considerations

[14] That court was renamed the General Court of the European Union following the entry into force of the Lisbon Treaty.

[15] Although the Court of First Instance (of the European Communities) was established by Council Decision of 24 October 1988, its first members were not appointed until 25 September 1989.

[16] See V Fritz, 'Building the Foundations of the European Court of Justice: Massimo Pilotti (1879–1962)', in this volume.

[17] See Mengozzi (n 1) 208.

and analysis, he wrote exemplary Opinions that have often served as new inspiration for the interpretation and application of EU law.

Saggio was often confronted with complex interpretative choices on important issues in the articulation of legal rules. In resolving those issues, he drew not only from his extensive experience and culture, but also from the active collaboration and assistance of a team of enthusiastic, merit-selected *référendaires*. That team remained loyal to him for years to come. Indeed, during the eleven years of exercising his various judicial functions at the Court of First Instance and later at the Court of Justice, Saggio carefully selected the *référendaires* who accompanied him along his journey. In the selection of candidates, he ensured diversity of background and training to enrich his Chambers with a variety of voices and perspectives.

As *référendaires* of the judge, then President, of the Court of First Instance, Saggio selected officials with established experience at the Court (Dominique Thiaville and Celestina Iannone) and the Commission (Antonio Aresu). As Advocate General, he enriched the composition of his Chambers with high-profile academics (Roberto Mastroianni, Massimo Condinanzi and subsequently Criseide Novi) and a diplomat (Francesco Di Maio).

The diversity of the professional background of *référendaires* always found harmony in a unique style of expression and in the search for balanced solutions. The aim was to ensure the full realisation of the primary purpose of Saggio's contribution: creating the conditions for closer European integration. The well-known Opinion in *Océano Grupo*[18] is certainly an eminent example of that political will and belief.

The *référendaires* in Saggio's Chambers consistently felt the heartbeat of his vocation for the European project. The exchanges of views, his suggestions and advice were valuable messages that featured at various moments of daily meetings. The frank meetings in his Chambers were free of formalism and rich in content. Saggio was able to gain a thorough knowledge of the case and its legal implications quickly and accompanied the *référendaires*' reflections in a discreet but decided manner until the final drafting of decisions and Opinions. His *référendaires* had the pleasure of being granted intellectual freedom, guided by the clarity and lucidity that Saggio's path had established. This delicate balance allowed for an atmosphere of open-mindedness, where the *référendaires* could express their views while benefiting from Saggio's clear direction and guidance.

[18] See FG Nicola and E Tichadou, '20 – Océano Grupo: A Transatlantic Victory for the Consumer and a Missed Opportunity for European Law' in FG Nicola and B Davies, *EU Law Stories Contextual and Critical Histories of European Jurisprudence* (Cambridge, Cambridge University Press, 2017) 369. The authors point out that this ruling on the reliance on unfair clauses of a national court's own motion is the expression of the judicial activism led by Advocate General Saggio and his *référendaires* of that time. Indeed, the convergence in Luxembourg of independent, charismatic and intellectually committed judges and Advocates General had attracted a network of *référendaires* who shared the ambition of their mentors.

2.4. The Return to Italy

Towards the end of 2000, Saggio returned to Italy, to Rome, where he resumed his duties as a judge at the Supreme Court of Cassation. In 2001, he was appointed President of the First Civil Division – the most prestigious division – of the Supreme Court of Cassation, a position he held until his retirement in 2005.

Subsequently, Saggio enjoyed many joyful years of study and reflection in his beautiful house in Rome, filled with books and memories. Throughout this period, he was supported by his beloved wife Silvia, his children Valeria, Isabella and Fabrizio, and by his immense host of friends, colleagues and admirers, who made Saggio's Roman home an ideal centre for legal discussion. This inviting space facilitated the exchange of divergent opinions, particularly regarding the future of the European Union and the law upon which its unique nature is built.

While Rome became his cultural *locus standi*, during the summer period Saggio moved to his *buen retiro*, a picturesque villa on the island of Ventotene. Undoubtedly, the pro-European ideal, which was born on this island, serves as a constant and underlying driving force in his teachings and work. Whether as a national or European judge, lecturer, negotiator, or author, Saggio consistently saw the European Union as a harmonious collective of diverse peoples and cultures where fundamental rights are respected under the aegis of the 'rule of law'.

Saggio passed away surrounded by his loved ones on January 24, 2011. His departure marked a significant loss, felt deeply by all those who had the privilege of knowing and admiring him, but also for the European project.

In order to pay tribute to Saggio's legacy, in 2015 the Municipality of Ventotene and the Altiero Spinelli Institute established the Saggio prize. This award grants a scholarship to a deserving young participant in the Seminar of European Federalists, held annually on Ventotene. The prize serves as a testament to Saggio's enduring influence and commitment to European integration, nurturing the next generation of individuals dedicated to the ideals of peace and federalism.

3. SAGGIO'S CONTRIBUTION TO EUROPEAN CASE-LAW

Saggio's contribution to the case-law of the Court of First Instance and, subsequently, of the Court of Justice was remarkable. The issues he dealt with covered a wide array of fields of law. While it is not feasible to mention all the judgments and Opinions influenced or drafted by him, here we will highlight some of the most significant. We will first focus on his contribution to the Court of First Instance and subsequently explore some of his important Opinions at the Court of Justice.

3.1. Some Significant Judgments of the Court of First Instance

In the context of highlighting Saggio's significant contribution to the *acquis communautaire*, it is important to mention several landmark judgments. First of all, in the *Tetra Pak* judgment[19] of 10 July 1990 and the *RTE*, *BBC* and *ITP* judgments[20] of 10 July 1991, the Court of First Instance defined criteria for reconciling intellectual property rights and the principle of free competition. In particular, the question before the court in those cases was whether the ownership of an exclusive right can exempt an undertaking from the rules of competition. The Court of First Instance, with Saggio acting as Judge-rapporteur, reaffirmed the position of earlier, settled case-law according to which a refusal to grant a licence, even if exercised by a party in a dominant position, does not *per se* constitute an offence under Article 86 CEE (102 TFEU). However, Saggio went further, opening a window of opportunity for greater guarantee of market freedom. The Court of First Instance held that in 'exceptional circumstances' such a refusal may constitute abusive conduct, in particular where the exclusive right actually pursues the aim of unlawfully reinforcing the dominant position of the right-holder undertaking. Thus, the general interest in a free market may prevail, in some specific cases, over a dominant undertaking's exclusive right.

Also worthy of mention is the judgment in *Société générale des grandes sources*[21] of 27 April 1995, in which the Court of First Instance – again with Saggio as Judge Rapporteur – recognised for the first time the right of workers' representatives to bring an action for annulment against a Commission decision authorising a merger. In particular, the Court stated the following:

> [...] the position of the employees of the undertakings which are the subject of the concentration [operation] may in certain cases be taken into consideration by the Commission when adopting its decision. [Representative bodies are charged with defending the collective interests of the workers whom they represent and therefore have] a relevant interest with respect to the social considerations which may in appropriate cases be taken into account by the Commission in the context of its appraisal of whether the concentration is lawful from the point of view of Community law.[22]

[19] *Tetra Pak Rausing SA v Commission* Case T-51/89 ECLI:EU:T:1990:41 [1990] ECR II-309. See S Wheeler, 'The Relationship between Article 85(3) and Article 86' (1991) *European Law Review* 308–312.

[20] *RTE v Commission* Case T-69/89 ECLI:EU:T:1991:39 [1991] ECR II-485; *BBC v Commission* Case T-70/89 ECLI:EU:T:1991:40 [1991] ECR II-535; *ITP v Commission* Case T-76/89 ECLI:EU:T:1991:41, [1991] ECR II-575.

[21] *Comité central d'entreprise de la Société Générale des Grandes Sources* v *Commission* Case T-96/92 ECLI:EU:T:1995:77, [1995] ECR II-1213; see especially A Arnull, 'Case T-96/92, *Comité Central d'Entreprise de la Société Générale des Grandes Sources and Others* v *Commission*' (1996) 33(2) *Common Market Law Review* 319–335; A Saggio and C Iannone, 'Le informazioni riservate e i segreti commerciali nel diritto comunitario della concorrenza' (1999) *Rivista di diritto europeo* 547.

[22] *Grandes Sources* (n 21) para 30.

Finally, it is worth mentioning the judgment in the *Postbank*[23] case of 27 April 1995, which concerned the difficult balance to be struck between respect for business secrets and the guarantee of effective judicial protection. *Postbank* established the principle that EU law does not prevent undertakings, to which the Commission has provided documents in the course of an administrative procedure, from producing them before a national court. According to this principle, the use of such information does not impinge on the prohibition on using information gathered in the course of the same administrative procedure for a purpose other than that for which it was provided. This prohibition merely implies that the Commission and the national authorities, lawfully in possession of that information, may not use it for a purpose other than that for which it was gathered. To reach that conclusion, the Court relied in particular on the principle of 'loyal cooperation' between the Commission and the national courts, as the latter are in a position to assess the existence of possible infringements of competition rules and to protect any confidential information or business secrets.

3.2. Some Significant Opinions as Advocate General of the Court of Justice

During Saggio's time as Advocate General of the Court of Justice, his Opinion in 1999 in the *Eco Swiss*[24] case had a significant impact. This case involved proceedings brought for a stay of enforcement of an arbitration award ordering damages for breach of a licensing agreement on the ground that the award in question, which had become final, was contrary to public policy because the licensing agreement itself infringed Community competition rules. National law, in this case Dutch law, excluded this possibility, since competition rules were not considered to be part of public policy. Their violation could therefore not justify the annulment of the award. In this regard, Saggio expressed himself in his Opinions in a trenchant manner stating as follows:

> […] for the purpose of ensuring the correct and uniform application of Community law, courts […] called upon to determine whether arbitration awards are compatible with rules of law must be allowed to carry out an effective review of the award in question. In particular, the courts must be allowed to consider questions of Community law and, in so doing, to obtain the necessary guidance from the Court of Justice.[25]

[23] *Postbank v Commission* Case T-353/94 ECLI:EU:T:1994:288 [1996] ECR II-921; see especially, L Vasques, 'Limiti al diritto d'accesso e tutela delle parti nei procedimenti antitrust italiani e comunitari' (1997) IV *Il Foro italiano* 161–174; C Kerse, 'Case T-353/94, Postbank NV v. Commission, Judgment of the Court of First Instance of 18 September 1996, [1996] ECR II-921' (1997) 34 *Common Market Law Review* 1481; C Iannone, 'Art. 4 TUE', in A Tizzano (ed), *Trattati dell'Unione europea* (Milan, Giuffrè, 2014) 43–44.

[24] *Eco Swiss China Time Ltd v Benetton International NV* Case C-126/97 ECLI:EU:C:1999:269 [1999] ECR I-3055, Opinion of AG Saggio of 25 February 1999.

[25] ibid., point 32.

In his Opinion, Saggio emphasised the crucial importance of reviewing the compliance of arbitral awards with Community law, particularly in the context of competition law. For him, there is a broader interest in compliance with the rules to ensure the proper functioning of the internal market. This interest transcends that of the private parties and includes third-party companies, such as potential competitors and consumers. That analysis was fully endorsed by the Court in its final judgment.[26]

Saggio delivered another important Opinion in *Portugal v Council*[27] on the effects of the World Trade Organization (WTO) rules in the Community legal order. In this case, Saggio expressed the idea that the Community legal order should be regarded as autonomous and independent. He stated that certain rules of Community primary law and general principles had assumed the nature of constitutional rules within the Community legal order. In such cases, the Court was bound to apply Community law, even if it resulted in the Community being in breach of international law. To refrain from applying Community law in such cases would be contrary to the proper functioning and objectives of the Treaties. This approach reflected the Court's commitment to upholding the autonomy and supremacy of Community law within the EU legal framework.[28] It ultimately paved the way to the later *Kadi* judgment of 3 September 2008 in which the Court of Justice held that obligations imposed by an international agreement, such as a UN Security Council resolution, cannot have the effect of prejudicing the constitutional principles of the Treaties, in particular the principle that all Community acts must respect fundamental rights.[29]

[26] *Eco Swiss* (n 24); see, among numerous commentaries, L Idot, 'CJCE, 1er juin 1999, Eco Swiss, C-126/97' (1999) *Revue de l'Arbitrage* 639–653; S Bastianon, 'L'arbitrabilità delle controversie antitrust tra diritto nazionale e diritto comunitario' (1999) IV *Il Foro italiano* 471–483; L Radicati Di Brozolo, 'Arbitrato, diritto della concorrenza, diritto comunitario e regole di procedura nazionali' (1999) *Rivista dell'arbitrato* 665; A Komninos, 'Case C-126/97, *Eco Swiss China Time Ltd*' v *Benetton International NV*' (2000) 37(2) *Common Market Law Review* 459; N Shelkoplyas, 'European Community Law and International Arbitration: Logics That Clash' (2002) *European Business Organization Law Review* 569.

[27] *Portuguese Republic v Council of the European Union* Case C-149/96 ECLI:EU:C:1999:574 [1999] ECR I-08395, Opinion of AG Saggio of 25 February 1999. It is worth remembering that, given the evolution of the system from that of the GATT, in his Opinion, Saggio concluded in favour of the applicant being able to rely on WTO rules. This interpretation is still reflected in doctrinal analyses.

[28] *Portugal v Council* (n 27). See, among numerous commentaries, G Zonnekeyn, 'The status of WTO law in the Community legal order: some comments in the light of the Portuguese Textiles case' (2000) *European Law Review* 293; F Berrod, 'La Cour de justice refuse l'invocabilité des accords OMC: essai de régulation de la mondialisation. A propos de l'arrêt de la Cour de justice du 23 novembre 1999, Portugal c/ Conseil (accords textiles avec le Pakistan et l'Inde, aff. C-149/96, Rec. p.I-8395)' (2000) *Revue trimestrielle de droit européen* 419; P Mengozzi, 'La Cour de justice et l'applicabilité des règles de l'OMC en droit communautaire à la lumièrede l'affaire Portugal c. Conseil' (2000) *Revue du droit de l'Union européenne* 509; A Rosas, '*Case C-149/96, Portugal* v *Council*', (2000) 37(3) *Common Market Law Review* 797; S Griller, 'Judicial enforceability of WTO law in the European Union. Annotation to Case C-149/96, *Portugal* v *Council*' (2000) 3 *Journal of International Economic Law* 441.

[29] Joined Cases C-402/05 P and C-415/05 P, *Kadi and Al Barakaat International Foundation* v *Council and Commission*, EU:C:2008:461 [2008] I-06351, 285. See Mengozzi (n 1) 207–213.

Also of great impact was Saggio's Opinion in the joined cases *Océano Grupo Editorial* and *Salvat Editores*,[30] which provided the Court with an opportunity to set out its unequivocal orientation on the principle of procedural autonomy in consumer protection. This was the first time in which the Court was called upon to interpret Article 6 of Directive 93/13/EEC on unfair terms in consumer contracts.[31] In particular, the referring Spanish court asked if the system of consumer protection, guaranteed by that directive, meant that the court could assess of its own motion the unfairness of a term included in a contract between a seller or supplier and a consumer. In his Opinion, Saggio expressed himself forcefully and clearly in favour of this power, ruling out the possibility that decisive significance must be attached to the consumer' position:

> [...] the consumer might fail to invoke the unfairness of the term out of ignorance, or because he regards it as too expensive to defend himself in a court some distance from where he lives, as is the case with the term that is the subject of the dispute in the present case. In all these cases the objective which the [d]irective is seeking to pursue would not be attained if the term, although clearly harmful to the party to the contract who is in a weak situation, were to achieve its goal; the effectiveness of the [d]irective would be irreparably endangered.[32]

For the consumer, the term in question must not represent too great a legal burden in order to avoid a paradoxical situation whereby he is obliged to appear before a court in a place other than that where he resides and support all the associated costs in this regard, 'precisely in order to argue that the contractual term obliging him to do so is an unfair term!'.

That judgment of the Court fully adopted the approach taken by Advocate General Saggio, noting that:

> [...] the system of protection introduced by the Directive is based on the idea that the consumer is in a weak position vis-à-vis the seller or supplier, as regards both his bargaining power and his level of knowledge. [...] [This] imbalance between the consumer and the seller or supplier may only be corrected by positive action unconnected with the actual parties to the contract.[33]

[30] Joined Cases C-240/98 and C-244/98, *Océano Grupo Editorial and Salvat Editores*, ECLI:EU:C:1999:620 [2000] ECR I-4941, Opinion of AG Saggio of 16 December 1999. The question referred to the Court for a preliminary ruling arose from a series of disputes brought by the Spanish publishers Océano Grupo Editorial SA and Salvat Editores SA against several consumers for non-payment of the sums agreed in contracts for the sale of encyclopaedias on instalment credit terms.

[31] Council Directive 93/13/EEC of 5 April 1993 on unfair terms in consumer contracts (OJ 1995, L 95, 29).

[32] Opinion of AG Saggio, *Océano Grupo* (n 30) point 23.

[33] *Océano Grupo* Joined Cases C-240/98 and C-244/98 ECLI:EU:C:2000:346 [2000] paras 25–27. See, among numerous commentaries, L Bernardeau, 'Clauses abusives: l'illicéité des clauses attributives de compétence et l'autonomie de leur contrôle judiciaire (à la suite de l'arrêt CJCE, 27 juin 2000 Océano, aff. C-240/98)' (2000) *Revue européenne de droit de la consommation* 261; A Orestano 'Ricevibilità di ufficio della vessatorietà delle clausole nei contratti del consumatore' (2000) *Europa e diritto privato* 1179; J Stuyck, 'Joined Cases C-240/98 to C-244/98, Océano Grupo Editorial SA v. Rocio Murciano Quintero and Salvat Editore SA v. José M. Sànchez Alcón Prades et al., Judgment of

The interpretation that national courts are fully entitled to raise the invalidity of unfair contractual terms of their own motion then became settled case-law.[34]

Lastly, Saggio's Opinion in the *Bofrost*[35] case is of great importance because it addressed the crucial issue of workers' rights to participate in company decisions. Here, the Advocate General suggested an expansive reading of Article 11 of Directive 94/45/EC on the establishment of a European Works Council and the consultation of employees in Community-scale undertakings and Community-scale groups of undertakings.[36] Taking a pragmatic approach to ensure the effectiveness of the right guaranteed by the directive, Saggio emphasised the importance of recognising the right of workers' representatives, who are present in undertakings, to gather information necessary for initiating the establishment of a European Works Council. He highlighted that interpreting the directive in a manner that denied this right would undermine the aims and objectives of the directive itself. The refusal to grant workers such a right would be tantamount to a prohibition on access to any information, which would be clearly inconsistent with the purpose of the directive. The aim was to grant the right of workers to access information to acquire the means of ensuring their participation in the life of the company. The Court fully supported this approach in its final decision, recognising the importance of workers' access to information and their active involvement in the company's operations as stated in the directive.

4. SAGGIO'S CONTRIBUTION TO EUROPEAN LEGAL CULTURE IN ITALY

Saggio played a pivotal role in the Italian Association of European Jurists (*Associazione Italiana Giuristi Europei*, AIGE), making a significant contribution to its activities. He took on a leadership role and actively shaped the initiatives of the association, involving not only the Italian academic community but also judges, lawyers and legal practitioners. He was a member of the Board of Directors of AIGE from 1989 to 1999 and its President from 1999 to 2008. During his presidency, he organised conferences that left a mark on the legal

the Full Court of 27 June 2000' (2001) *Common Market Law Review* 719; M Van Huffel, 'La condition procédurale des règles de protection des consommateurs: les enseignements des arrêts Océano, Heininger et Cofidis de la Cour de justice' (2003) *Revue européenne de droit dela consommation* 79.

[34] See, among others, Case C-137/08 *VB Pénzügyi Lízing Zrt. v Ferenc Schneider*, ECLI:EU:C:2010:659 [2010] ECR I-10847, point 46; Case C-168/15, *Milena Tomášová v Slovenská republika*, ECLI:EU:C:2016:602, [2016], point 28; Case C-519/19 *Ryanair DAC v DelayFix*, ECLI:EU:C:2020:933, [2020], points 58–59.

[35] *Bofrost* Case C-62/99 ECLI:EU:C:2001:188 [2001] ECR I-2579, Opinion of AG Saggio of 26 September 2000. See especially, O Wéry, 'Les comités d'entreprise européens: à propos des arrêts de la Cour de justice des Communautés européennes en la matière' (2004) *Journal des tribunaux du travail* 365.

[36] Council Directive 94/45/EC of 22 September 1994 on the establishment of a European Works Council or a procedure in Community-scale undertakings and Community-scale groups of undertakings for the purposes of informing and consulting employees (OJ 1994, L 254, 64). This directive is no longer in force.

dissemination and analysis of EU law. Particular mention should be made of the conference on 'National Judges and Community Judges after the Treaty of Amsterdam: Collaboration and Cooperation' in 2000 and the conference on 'The European Community and the World Trade Organisation' in 2001. Under his stewardship, from 1999 to 2001 and in 2008, AIGE organised institutional courses on Community law, in collaboration with the *Ordine degli Avvocati* (Italian Bar Association), the *Procuratori di Roma* (Public Prosecutors of Rome) and the *Avvocatura dello Stato*.[37]

Remaining steadfast in his recognition of the significance of legal doctrine, Saggio continued to contribute actively to academic debate throughout his career, first on Italian law and, later in his career, on European law. To this end, he collaborated with prestigious Italian and foreign law journals[38] and participated in important international seminars, conferences and symposiums.

His initial début work was entitled *Civilians as Subjects of Military Aggression*.[39] Although from the title we can discern a clear reference to the work of Karl von Clausewitz,[40] the development of this monograph conveys to the reader a profound sense of distress regarding the escalating destructive nature of contemporary warfare. Gone are the conventional battles between soldiers, replaced instead by the ominous collision of entire communities locked in deadly conflict. This realisation evoked a sense of anguish, as Saggio vividly portrays the harrowing consequences of modern conflicts. Saggio's bibliography subsequently expanded considerably to encompass an extensive range of subjects.

Saggio authored numerous essays and articles of great significance, notably in the fields of European constitutional law,[41] Italian and European procedural law,[42]

[37] In the Italian legal system, the *Avvocatura dello Stato* is a body that forms part of the Office of the Prime Minister, tasked with providing legal advice and the protection and representation of the State and Italian public administrations in legal disputes in national and international proceedings.

[38] Suffice it to mention the following reviews: *Rivista di diritto europeo*, *Corriere giuridico*, *Diritto comunitario e degli scambi internazionali*, *Il foro italiano*, and among the foreign law journals, the *Journal of European Law*.

[39] A Saggio, *I civili come soggetti della violenza bellica* (Naples, Jovene, 1971), author's translation.

[40] K von Clausewitz, 'Vom Kriege', in *Hinterlasse Werke des Generals Karl von Clausewitz über Krieg und Kriegsführung* (Berlin, 1832) (Italian translation: *Della Guerra* (*On War*) (Milan, Mondadori, 1970)). His concept of 'absolute war' implies the active participation of the domestic population of the nations in conflict.

[41] See A Saggio, 'Rapports entre droit communautaire et droit constitutionnel italien' (1991) *Rivista di diritto europeo* 327; A Saggio, 'La protezione dei diritti fondamentali nell'ordinamento comunitario' (1993) (3) *Documenti giustizia* 275.

[42] See A Saggio, 'Aspetti problematici della competenza pregiudiziale della Corte di giustizia delle Comunità Europee messi in luce dalla giurisprudenza' (1987) *Rivista di diritto europeo* 179; A Saggio, *The Community Court of First Instance* (Naples, Editoriale scientifica, 1990); A Saggio, 'Il procedimento pregiudiziale di cui all'articolo 177 del trattato cee nell'esperienza delle giurisdizioni italiane' (1991) (2) *Mezzogiorno d'europa* 389; A Saggio, 'Prospettive di evoluzione del Tribunale di primo grado delle Comunità europee' (1992) *Rivista di diritto europeo* 3; A Saggio, 'Le Competenze', in Lenza, Paove, Saggio (n 4); A Saggio, 'Appunti sulla ricevibilità dei ricorsi d'annullamento proposti da persone fisiche o giuridiche in base all'art. 173, quarto comma, del Trattato CE' (1997) *Rivista di diritto europeo* 401; A Saggio, 'Incidenza della giurisprudenza della Corte di giustizia sulle norme processuali nazionali' (2001) *Il Corriere Giuridico* 114.

European competition law,[43] but also private international law.[44] In addition, he continued for years to write insightful commentaries, in close collaboration with Raffaele Foglia, on the most important judgments delivered by the Court of Justice and by the Court of First Instance in the 'Observatory of the Court of Justice' column of the journal, *Corriere Giuridico*.[45] He considered such commentaries not only a cultural exercise but also a moral obligation. The resulting invaluable doctrinal corpus stands as a testament to Saggio's unwavering dedication to his professional activities.

In particular, Saggio's studies on the Court of First Instance hold great significance, as his contributions played a crucial role in consolidating the jurisdiction of that court. In this regard, he published two articles on the subject in 1988 and 1992.[46] These articles offered valuable insight and analysis, and were included in the chapter on the jurisdiction of the Court of First Instance that appears in the aforementioned 1994 book for which he, Umberto Leanza and Pasquale Paone were the editors.[47]

Lastly, it is worth mentioning Saggio's 1998 paper, dedicated to Judge G. Federico Mancini (1927–1999),[48] in which he meticulously analysed the long-standing issue that has troubled the case-law of the Court of first instance: the admissibility of actions for annulment brought by natural and legal persons.[49] Even here, Saggio's focus extends beyond doctrinal approaches. Recognising the importance of protecting individuals' rights effectively, Saggio underscores the need for a system that facilitates citizens' access to justice. His perspective reflects a deep concern that EU citizens are afforded an unfettered access to justice within the EU legal order to protect their rights.

The discovery and publication of an unpublished and unfinished work by Saggio in 2019 can be seen as his swan song. This work, which focuses on the

[43] See A Saggio, 'Competenze rispettive delle autorità comunitarie e nazionali in materia di controllo e repressione delle attività anticoncorrenziali delle imprese', in Quaderni di ricerca giuridica della Banca d'Italia (Perugia, 1996); Saggio and Iannone (n 21) 547.

[44] See A Saggio, 'European judicial area for civil and commercial matters: the Brussels and Lugano conventions' (1991) *Rivista di diritto europeo* 617; A Saggio, 'Diritto internazionale privato e diritto uniforme nel sistema comunitario' in P Mengozzi (eds), *La riforma del diritto internazionale privato italiano: la legge 31 maggio 1995, n. 218* (2nd ed, Naples, Editoriale scientifica, 1997) 205; A Saggio, 'Riflessioni sulla legge italiana di riforma del diritto internazionale privato e sulla sua incidenza sul regime dello stato civile' (1997) (1–2) *Documenti giustizia* 13–28.

[45] Raffaele Foglia was Division President at the Supreme Court of Cassation, member of the Ministerial Commissions for the Reform of the Civil Process and Privacy Protection and a Professor of Labour Law and Trade Union Law at various Italian universities.

[46] See A Saggio, 'Il Tribunale comunitario di primo grado' (1988) *Diritto comunitario e degli scambi internazionali* 611; A Saggio, 'Prospettive di evoluzione del Tribunale di primo grado delle Comunità europee' (1992) *Rivista di diritto europeo*, 3.

[47] See footnote n 4.

[48] See V Di Bucci, 'The Contribution of Giuseppe Federico Mancini as Advocate General 1982–1988) and Judge (1988–1999) to European Constitutionalism', in this volume.

[49] See A Saggio, 'Appunti sulla ricevibilità dei ricorsi d'annullamento proposti da persone fisiche e giuridiche in base all'articolo 173, quarto comma, del trattato CE' (n 42) 107.

impact of social factors in competition law,[50] aligns with his previous scholarly contributions. It showcases Saggio's prowess as a legal scholar in comparing United States and European case-law in such a complex field. Although the paper was not updated, it retains the distinctive characteristics of an essay written by an authoritative figure. It demonstrates a meticulous and critical examination of significant United States and European jurisprudential trends, complemented by an objective analysis of the relevant legislation. This impressive piece of writing therefore serves as a crowning achievement, further solidifying Saggio's reputation as a prominent figure within the Italian legal establishment. It showcases his talents as a leading scholar and underscores his ability to delve into complex legal matters with precision and insight.

5. CONCLUSIONS: SAGGIO'S LEGACY

Lastly, a few closing remarks on the professional and human heritage that Saggio left and that he shared with all those who have had the privilege of walking at his side for a few moments or, as is the case for his affectionate *référendaires*, for several years.

Two words help to describe Saggio's legacy: honesty and discipline. The combination of these attributes epitomises his work and professional life. He shunned banality, preferring instead abstraction and the confrontation of ideas: a frank confrontation, devoid of frills and always profound and intelligent. For the *référendaires* in Saggio's Chambers, the opportunity to work with him was one of the great privileges that life offered them. An experience that was a transformative and enriching opportunity in which their understanding of the law was shaped by a true *maestro*.

Saggio was a model for his sharp legal reasoning, for his pragmatism, and for his wisdom: all qualities enhanced by a pure, noble and far-sighted manner of thinking that was a source of ideas and inspiration. His unique legal reasoning constantly guided his progress, dictated by a profound need to grasp the meaning of truth and justice, and by a vigorous and intense passion for the European project of integration.

[50] See A Saggio, 'L'incidenza dei fattori sociali nel diritto della concorrenza: appunti sulla giurisprudenza americana e su quella europea in materia', in A Aresu and C Iannone (eds), *Diritto comunitario e degli scambi internazionali* (2019) 329.

13

Concluding Remarks: An Insider's View on Italian Jurists at the CJEU

ANTONIO TIZZANO

I MUST CONFESS that I am not sure whether to breathe a sigh of relief at being, alongside my friend and colleague Paolo Mengozzi, the only surviving former member of the Court, or to lament not being among the honoured in this volume, which has featured commemorations of significant substance and rare depth. It is a small consolation to know that I will likely be among the protagonists at the next commemorative edition, assuming the scholarly practice initiated by this volume continues.

For now, my unique position compels me to write the conclusions for a volume of such high calibre on such fascinating topics. I begin by paying my compliments to the esteemed colleagues who wrote the chapters of this edited volume, and to the organisers for their conception and superb structuring of the book. Furthermore, their inspired decision to dedicate it to Professor Giuseppe Tesauro, to whom I wholeheartedly and affectionately pay tribute, is most commendable. This point is especially pertinent, as Tesauro has been a prominent figure in European law, who demonstrated that the history of European integration is carried forward by individuals. He has notably advanced this process, as have many others; each has contributed their own merits and limitations, whether as active protagonists or as firm supporters.

Indeed, the focus of this volume, which results from a conference held in June 2022 in Rome, is one that European Union (hereinafter EU or 'Union') law scholars often overlook. Indeed, they frequently discuss the European integration process as something propelled by historical forces, almost advancing inertially due to that momentum. Such a perspective, however, tends to overlook or insufficiently highlight the role of the institutions that embody this process and, consequently, the individuals that make up these institutions. This is equally true for the judicial bodies of the Union.

In this unconventional perspective, this volume has presented the experiences of the many Italian members of the Court of Justice of the European Union (hereinafter Court of Justice or Court) who have been part of this significant institution over the years; its chapters have analysed their respective contributions to the development of its jurisprudence. Remarkably, the aim of the contributions is not limited to examining the 'profiles' of the Italian members of the European judiciary; it also extends to consider the influence of these members on the activities of the Court and, more broadly, the *impact* both exerted by and upon these judges during their Luxembourg tenure.

The result is a comprehensive overview that fully shows the contributions that the Italian members of the Court have made over the years to the activities of the European judiciary. Whether as Advocates General or as judges, they have all endeavoured to express the essence and the uniqueness of a legal tradition rooted in ancient customs, which is, therefore, not inferior to those present in Luxembourg.

This is certainly significant because, although the influence of the nationality of the judges is relatively modest, as I will mention shortly, the jurisprudence of the Court of Justice does reflect the hybridisation of the various national traditions and cultures. This amalgamation makes it possible to express the whole of the European legal landscape and thus to be accepted by and within the Member States as a jurisprudence that is not alien to the common European spirit.

I must say that this comprehensive analysis constitutes the originality and the main merit of the volume since studies that systematically focus on the personal and professional history of the members of the Court of Justice of a given nationality and their overall contribution to its jurisprudence are not common.

That being said, it is nonetheless worth highlighting that the nationality of the Court's members is not, in itself, of significant relevance to its operations. What matters most is the judges' personal qualities, their prestige, expertise, and reasoning abilities. It is indeed rare for a ruling to be influenced by considerations tied to a judge's nationality, even in cases that specifically concern their country of origin. This reflects the provision that prohibits parties from objecting to the absence of a judge of their nationality in the panel. The judgment is, by definition and in reality, 'impersonal'; this is not only a tribute to the independence and impartiality of the Court but is also a reality evidenced by decades of its practice.

A different matter, however, concerns the *influence* of national laws on the Court's jurisprudence and vice-versa. This dialectical relationship has produced significant outcomes in both directions. Indeed, when considering the Union system as a whole, constituted by the ensemble of the Union and national legal systems, one observes that they have had important reciprocal effects, perhaps less conspicuous, but no less significant.

First and foremost, the law of the Union has had an extraordinary impact on the legal systems of Member States. A vast and penetrating legislative activity and a rich and intense jurisprudential practice have profoundly and decisively influenced many aspects of these systems, even challenging fundamental principles and traditional concepts, as well as solutions and situations that seemed – by necessity, conviction, or mental inertia – settled and unchangeable. Significant parts of many disciplines have fallen, and continue to fall, under the 'Union-law project'; likewise, substantive and interpretative principles or even a body of common norms have modified, integrated, or overlapped (and continue to overlap) the pre-existing national legislation.

What must be emphasised here, however, is that Union law impacts national legal systems profoundly because it can rely on the peculiar characteristics of the Union's legal system. Most notably, Union law can rely on the action of supranational authorities that preside over the formation of the EU norms and possess appropriate tools to monitor and enforce compliance, and on the primacy and direct applicability of said norms over those of Member States. Nevertheless, above all, it is worth stressing the significance of employing mechanisms of autonomous interpretation, reserved for an institution like the Court of Justice, whose actions reflect not only on the compactness and intrinsic coherence of the common normative body but also on its capacity to withstand national systems. Indeed, such mechanisms of autonomous interpretation extract Union law from the grip of national legal systems and thus prevent the weakening of its harmonising effects and reach.

The converse is also true, and this aspect deserves to be highlighted. Considering the context in which the Court operates and the absence of norms that guide and delimit the law it applies (unlike, for example, what happens for the International Court of Justice under Article 38, paragraph 1, of its Statute), it shall come as no surprise that the natural reference for the reconstruction and definition of legal concepts used by the Treaties has been primarily found in the Member States' domestic legal systems. Indeed, especially in the early days, some doctrine advocated that the Court should draw from such legal systems, and should resort to the general principles common to the legal systems of the Member States, which would come into play as a 'subsidiary source' of Union law. In truth, the Court's practice has not confirmed such an approach. Instead, it has maintained rigorous neutrality towards the national systems individually considered. This approach holds true even in the jurisprudential practice relating to the European Coal and Steel Community (ECSC) Treaty drafted, as is well known, only in French, which – contrary to what has been argued by some authors – does not entail the explicit use of legal concepts derived from French law. Conversely, even in this regard, it has proven necessary to consider the legal systems of all Member States and, in any case, the pursuit of an autonomous solution.

Of course, this approach does not mean that the Court considers – and considered – domestic legal systems irrelevant for reconstructing the meaning of a given legal notion. On the contrary, the Court itself, in its early years of activity, clarified that – in order not to give rise to a denial of justice – it was obliged to resolve the case submitted to it 'by drawing inspiration' from the legislation, legal doctrine, and case law of Member States. Nonetheless, the use of these 'sources of inspiration' has remained and remains, so to speak, in the shadows, without ever being formalised. Even when making use, usually without openly saying or developing it in specific cases, of the comparative method between national legal systems, the reference to them is normally generic and made 'in practice'. Hence, the reference to those national legal systems, when there is one, is only a very generic starting point, usually 'disguised' – especially in the first years of the Court's activity – by a generic reference to 'general principles of law', 'principles generally accepted', 'principles of administrative law admitted in all Member States of the EEC', and similar.

From the national legal systems, however, the Court does not hesitate to depart in the function of the needs of Union law and to adapt or modify it to these latter. In other words, the reference to national legal systems comes into play only as a means of interpretation, in the sense that from the examination of such legal systems (and of the connected legal doctrine and jurisprudence) one starts the analysis of the meaning of expressions used in the Treaties, to then arrive at the elaboration of an 'autonomous', 'community' notion of the same expression. This notion will be defined in the most conforming way to the specific characteristics and aims of the Union legal system. It is therefore a notion that becomes 'other' than that of the specific national legal systems. When, in short, the Union law itself does not contain the definition of a notion, nor explicitly refers to one or more national legal systems, the Court itself proceeds to elaborate the definition, naturally drawing more or less openly from domestic notions.

Such a process of 'Europeanisation' of the national legal systems develops not only through the direct influence of Union legislation but also, and in some respects principally, through less formal and institutionalised avenues, which are no less pervasive. This refers specifically to a sort of 'spontaneous' creation and dissemination of principles, methods, and legal practices that occur within the Union context as a consequence of the 'natural' process of reception, harmonisation, and sometimes even unification of national legal rules. This process is induced by the very development of the European legal system, facilitated by the diffusion of legal values that the uniqueness of the Union system greatly encourages. The system is indeed designed to operate as an integrative factor within the legal architecture of the Member States, and to compel the comparison, the coexistence, and the pursuit of maximum reciprocal compatibility among all the systems involved. This has resulted in a sometimes-inextricable intertwining of Union and national laws and regulations, which exist in a continuum, if not a blend. This phenomenon, in turn, continues to fuel the horizontal circuit that fosters legal integration among Member States and constitutes one of the most original and qualifying aspects of the Union legal system.

This blending process, which is also prompted by the doctrinal reflection and the working practice of legal experts, translates into the determination of common rules and principles, sometimes seemingly 'new', but more often defined or redefined, as just mentioned, on the basis of the national legal systems

Indeed, while at the legislative level, it is usually these latter that are influenced by the Union system, in turn, they constitute the 'humus' and source of inspiration for the values, principles, legal concepts, and legal practices at the core of the common Union law in the making. Against this backdrop, the Court has consistently sought to discover and delineate the legal rules and principles necessary for the Union legal system. Consequently, the Court has been frequently tasked with the identification or, as is sometimes imprecisely expressed, the 'creation' of these rules and principles.

It is clear then that this role has somewhat gradually dimmed over time as the Court's case law expanded and consolidated and the principles of Union law were affirmed or even inscribed in official legislative texts. However, once again, what is important to emphasise here is that this original and interesting 'synthesis' of different legal systems, which evidently serves as an authentic and decisive factor of integration, could not have been fuelled and would not have had such significant and profound impacts, such as those outlined so far, without the contribution of the Court of Justice.

Indeed, owing to its authority as the supreme interpreter of Union law and the guardian of compliance with such law and its application in Member States, the Court plays a pivotal role in ensuring the coherence of the overarching legal system upon which the European project is founded. From the standpoint of the issue at hand, the Court has wielded significant influence in the convergence of the legal traditions of the Union and national legal systems. A role that the Court has played without hesitation and sometimes even with a certain audacity, but whose utility has never really been called into question, notwithstanding some criticism occasionally directed at the so-called 'judicial activism'.

The Court's instrumental role could not have materialised without the valuable contributions of judges and advocates general from every Member State, including, naturally, those from Italy. They have brought their expertise in domestic law, general principles, and the rich heritage of the centuries-old civil law tradition to shape the construction of the Union system. Over time, they have managed to bring forth and indeed 'animate' the creation of a legal system that, also thanks to them, has never been alien to the sensibilities of European legal experts.

In this vein, the tribute paid in this volume to the Italian members of the Court of Justice seems a fitting recognition of their contribution to the construction of a generally accepted and shared Union legal system, which today appears to be of fundamental importance for the equilibrium and coexistence of the Member States.

Part II

Methodological Reflections on the Collective Biographies

14

Working at the Court of Justice of the European Union, in the Experience of a Judge

LUCIA SERENA ROSSI*

1. INTRODUCTION

THIS BOOK IS a successful synthesis of personal human stories (sometimes with some amusing gossip) and an institutional history of the European Court of Justice (ECJ / CJEU) from 1952 to the year 2000.

With its vivid portraits, this volume helps us to remember the protagonists of those stories, the Italian judges and Advocates General who are no longer with us. Indeed, when one of the editors asked me to write a brief account of my experience at the Court, my first objection was that contrary to all the other judges mentioned here, I am still alive. While the editors have promised me a new edition in due time, as it is better not to tempt fate, I won't insist on it and write instead about my own experience at the ECJ.

2. THE KNOWLEDGE OF ECJ JUDGES

In this book, we can read the stories of the men who, with their wisdom and legal knowledge, made relevant contributions to the working of the CJEU and the development of its case-law. While I would have happily added 'and women', I am the first Italian woman judge at the CJEU. In this respect, gender balance of the members of the Court still needs to improve. In my view, the agreement reached on the General Court, after the doubling of its members, that Member States should ensure that both sexes are equally represented should be extended at the CJEU, at least for those States that are entitled to designate the

* Judge at the Court of Justice of the European Union (CJEU). All opinions hereby expressed are personal and do not bind the institution in any way.

two posts of judge and Advocate General. The gender gap at the Court can be quite embarrassing in a European Union where gender equality is considered one of the founding values. Of course, the responsibility for such a gap must be attributed, not to the Court itself, but to the Member States. Regardless, I can assure you that once you arrive at the Court, your gender has no relevance. What counts, to earn the esteem and gain the agreement of the other judges on your position, is only your personal capability, your knowledge, and your experience.

As to a judge's knowledge, paradoxically, it is not very important to have a deep theoretical knowledge of the procedural aspects of the Court. Judges absorb very quickly all the procedural technicalities, strict timing, and terms that govern their daily lives: most of which others determine. To let the judges focus on the substance of the cases, the Registrar and an expert and dedicated staff at the Court have control of all the procedural steps. On the contrary, it is very helpful as judge at the CJEU to have excellent knowledge not only of the general principles, but also of the many different substantive fields of EU law. In fact, we are not preassigned to specific topics; our cases range between the most varied matters, exactly as it happens in the Constitutional Courts of the Member States. In this regard, our work differs from that of the judges of the General Court, currently divided into two groups, whose primary (of course, not only) specialisation is either public service or intellectual property. After the envisioned reform, the General Court will have two more specialised Chambers that deal with the specific matters attributed to the General Court in preliminary rulings.[1]

As to the experience, at the Court, there is a permanent – albeit always soft-toned and never too explicit – conversation as to whether it is better to arrive with a background as a national judge, as an academician, or (more rarely) from another legal profession. Of course, every member of the Court is sure that their background is the best one. The Italian tradition has, in most cases, been to designate University professors. Certainly, everyone has much to learn in their first mandate, although, in my view, it is easier to learn to become a judge than to learn the EU law if one has scarcely met that law in their previous life. Having to learn both would be of course very problematic. In any case, different experiences and approaches enrich the Court and contribute, in the same way as different origins and national legal cultures, to build a 'legal melting pot' that enables the Court to be a genuine European judiciary.

[1] See Commission Opinion on the draft *amendment to Protocol No 3 on the Statute of the Court of Justice of the European Union*, presented by the Court of Justice on 30 November 2022 Brussels 10.3.2023 COM (2023) https://www.europarl.europa.eu/RegData/docs_autres_institutions/commission_europeenne/com/2023/0135/COM_COM(2023)0135_EN.pdf; Report on the draft regulation of the European Parliament and of the Council amending Protocol No 3 on the Statute of the Court of Justice of the European Union (A9-0278/2023) https://www.europarl.europa.eu/doceo/document/A-9-2023-0278_EN.html.

Keeping a connection with academia is also an important aspect of my professional engagement as a judge. The Italian scholars specialised in EU law are numerous and very active in writing and organising conferences that I am often invited to as a speaker. Additionally, I make a concerted effort to engage with the training programs for national judges. These interactions offer an invaluable platform for the exchange of perspectives and ideas regarding the functioning of the preliminary ruling mechanism in Italy.

3. JUDGES *VERSUS* ADVOCATES GENERAL

What are the differences between the job of a judge at the CJEU and that of an Advocate General (AG)? One is that the work of AGs is more visible from the outside, as their Opinions are directly imputable to them. However, the main difference is that judges cannot master their schedule. This is due not only to the high number of cases that must be faced by only twenty-seven judges and to the constant effort to respect the deadlines to provide the citizens of the Union with an effective and rapid judicial review, but also to the complex and wholly collegial nature of all the steps of the decisional process. Each AG (there are eleven at the Court) has many cases; however, apart from the hearings of the cases in which they must present an Opinion and the General meeting (now, subject to exceptions, once every two weeks), they don't have to take part in any collegial event and so have greater freedom to organise their work. However, while less flexible and visible, the work of the judges is no less fulfilling. Collegiality helps to build friendships, mutual respect, and deeper knowledge of varied viewpoints.

The standard weekly schedule of the CJEU judges is as follows: hearings of the Grand Chamber on Monday and/or Tuesday mornings (often with an afternoon extension); hearings of the lower Chambers on Wednesday and Thursday mornings, the important General meeting and other administrative meetings on the second part of Tuesday afternoons, *deliberés* or *tours de table* of the Grand Chamber on Monday and Wednesday afternoons and the *deliberés* or *tours de table* of the lower Chambers on Thursday afternoons. Until 2022, Friday mornings were occupied by *deliberés* of the Grand Chamber, but it was decided to attribute to the Grand Chamber (which keeps 15 judges busy in hearing, *tour de table*, and *deliberés*) only those cases that really need it, allowing free mornings on Friday.

Even more importantly, of course, for each case, the reporting judge must find the time to write the preliminary report (*rapport préalable*) and to draft the judgment. All the other sitting judges (14, 4, or 2, according to the size of the Chamber concerned) have to study the report, almost always providing their opinion back to the others and suggesting amendments. So, when can a judge, who is continuously engaged in hearings, tours de table, and *déliberés* of the different Chambers they belong to, find the time to study and solve the cases? On Fridays, of course, but also exploiting time lapses that the abovementioned events may leave free when they don't last for too long. But when this isn't enough, we must exploit evenings at home, weekends, vacations, and travel time during our flights.

The envisaged reform of the Statute, which involves attributing the preliminary rulings in some specific matters to the General Court and slightly increasing the current filter of appeals, will lighten the schedule of the members of the CJEU. This remains to be seen as the trend for the Court has been to receive more and more appeals against the judgments of the General Court, as well as increasingly complex questions in the preliminary rulings that require the Grand Chamber. Luckily, all the members of the Courts are assisted by *référendaires* or legal clerks, who provide precious support in drafting different documents and in relating with their colleagues from the other cabinets of the Chamber to clarify the respective positions of the members in view of the *deliberé*. However, even if their help is precious and necessary, it is only the judge that can take part in the collegial decisional process in *tours de table* and *deliberés*, and it is the judge who must write the report.

At times, I come across the misconception that Advocates General are responsible for drafting their preliminary reports. This, however, is far from accurate. Even if the first document seen by the public is the Opinion of the AG, which is released some weeks after the hearing, the first in-depth study and conceptual framing of the case is done by the reporting judge, well before the hearing. This preliminary report is sent to the AG, who can make observations only on the procedural treatment of the case – the size of the chamber, if there should be a Hearing, and whether or not there should be an Opinion. It is then sent to the General meeting, in which a final decision on the procedural treatment is adopted. Of course, the Opinion of the AG can differ from the preliminary report, in the same way as the judgment of the Court may diverge from the Opinion.

4. THE INTERNAL WORKING LANGUAGE

Finally, I would like to make some remarks on the debated issue of the internal working language at the Court, which is French. There is a strong lobby to push the Court to change to English or German, the former option is supported by law firms and part of the academic world, while the latter is, after *Brexit*, supported by a group of Member States. What is essential to stress is that all hearings and external activities of the Court take place in the language of the national case. Multilingualism is so important that it absorbs, notably through interpretation and translations, the greatest part of the Court's budget. A testament to its importance is that the new public garden next to the formal piazza of the Court has been named 'the Garden of Multilingualism'.

AGs are allowed to present their Opinion not only in French but also in English, German, Italian, Spanish, or Polish. Judges, however, work collegially and need to have one single working language to exchange internal documents, and deliberate in only one language, which, by tradition, happens to be French. The reason for this is historical: the Court was founded in 1952 as the judiciary of the Steel and Coal Community, while the accession of the UK took place in 1972, ie, twenty years later. After *Brexit*, the only EU member States that asked to keep English as an official language were Ireland and Malta, albeit with no waiver to their national languages.

Crucially, French is a more structured language than English, and its structure has permeated the reasoning of the Court. For the Italian members – as well as for the members of other countries, the use of French is of course very simple, as grammatical structures and legal jargon are very similar to those of the national language. But, despite the differences between their national languages, the level of French used by the judges at the Court of Justice is very high and usually better than the English they speak. Moreover, there are technical reasons to continue the use of French, as all the databases, procedures, and working instruments are in French.

Yet many colleagues at the Court speak, understand, read, or study Italian; many are even able to follow hearings of Italian cases with no interpretation. Why, they say? Because Italian is beautiful. The 'Italian touch', from a cultural point of view, spreads at the Court even beyond the activity of its Italian members.

This volume having the merit to add to the current literature on the Court of Justice a comprehensive view of such activity allows the reader to understand what has been, in more general terms, the 'Italian touch' at the Court.

15

An Institutional View on the Influence of Italian Judges and Advocates General

LAURE CLÉMENT-WILZ

1. INTRODUCTION: PURSUING CLARITY AS A RESEARCH AGENDA

A LACK OF transparency necessitates a call for greater clarity. The secrecy and the collegiality of the deliberation at the Court of Justice of the European Union (CJEU), the globally opaque judges' nomination process and the challenging access to cases' *dossier de procédure*, have paradoxically sparked a growing body of research in law, sociology, and history. This avenue of research aims to unveil the political and sociological embeddedness of the CJEU.[1] In simpler terms, some have argued that a public political opinion of candidates for the position of judges and Advocates General as well as public dissenting opinions would enable a more straightforward response to the questions raised by keen observers of the Court. Moreover, the famous quote 'Tucked away in the fairyland Duchy of Luxembourg […]' of Eric Stein has created a misguided image of the Court as detached from national political life.[2] However, the Treaty of Lisbon provides that judges and Advocates General 'shall be appointed by common accord of the governments of the Member

[1] J Bailleux, 'Penser l'Europe par le droit – L'invention du droit communautaire en France' (2014) 46 *Politique Européenne* 178 ; A Vauchez, *L'Union par le droit – L'invention d'un programme institutionnel pour l'Europe* (Paris, Les Presses de SciencesPo, 2013); FG Nicola and B Davies (eds), *EU Law Stories – Contextual and Critical Histories of European Jurisprudence* (Cambridge, Cambridge University Press, 2017); M Rask Madsen, FG Nicola and A Vauchez (eds), *Researching the European Court of Justice: Methodological Shifts and Law's Embeddedness* (Cambridge, Cambridge University Press, 2022); A Boerger-De Smedt 'La Cour de justice dans les négociations du traité de Paris instituant la CECA' (2008) 14 *Revue d'histoire de l'intégration européenne* 7, 17; M Rasmussen 'Revolutionizing European Law: A history of the Van Gend en Loos Judgment' (2008) 12 *International Journal of Constitutional Law* 136; A Cohen, *De Vichy à la Communauté européenne* (Paris, Presses Universitaires de France, 2012).

[2] V Fritz, *Juges et avocats généraux de la Cour de Justice de l'Union européenne (1952–1972): une approche biographique de l'histoire d'une révolution juridique* (Frankfurt, Klostermann, 2018).

States',[3] thereby leaving each state the freedom to choose the most suitable candidate. Empirical studies have already demonstrated the constant links of judges with their national States.[4]

Opacity also fuels suspicion. Nevertheless, as correctly highlighted, 'in the euro-fatigue and euro-crisis, removing the information barriers on the political opinions, political involvement and political influence of the members of the Court helps at reducing academic speculations'.[5] Indeed, 'lifting the veil, at least a bit'[6] on the political influence of Italian judges and Advocates General does not weaken the Court but, on the contrary, it seeks to shed light on both the foundations of its legitimacy and its profound humanity. By shedding light on biographies and national influences, this book follows another research agenda – one based on the assumption that law is highly dependent on judges, emphasising that law and case law are, above all, human creations.[7] As highlighted by the editors, in engaging with the 'hermeneutic of suspicion,' legal historians, just like lawyers, will have to grapple with the fact that law remains indeterminate and that every actor in their story will attempt to exploit every wiggle room in it.[8]

2. MEASURING INFLUENCE: IS IMPOSSIBLE NOT AN ITALIAN TRAIT? EMBRACING THE HUMAN FACTOR

Exploring influence raises significant methodological challenges, and presents even greater obstacles for legal experts. They need to reconcile the fact that individuals, with their own peculiar biographies and cultures, are asked once in Luxembourg to interpret European law in an equal and common way. Furthermore, legal scholars often grapple with a seemingly contradictory stance when addressing the question of influence.

On one hand, legal practitioners readily and spontaneously acknowledge the decisive role of human factors. However, when delving into the study of these factors, legal scholars frequently conclude that the individuals or groups

[3] Consolidated Version of the Treaty on the Functioning of the European Union [2016] Article 253 (hereinafter the TFEU).

[4] As stated by M Rasmussen, during the conference entitled 'Italian Judges and Advocates General Shaping European Law (1952–1990s)', jointly organised by LUISS University, American University Washington College of Law and University of Naples Federico II and held at Luiss University (Rome, Italy) on 24 and 25 June 2022; see Fritz (n 2).

[5] M Bobek, 'Prologue: The Changing Nature of Selection Procedures to the European Courts', in M Bobek (ed), *Selecting Europe' Judge – A Critical Review of the Appointment Procedures* (Oxford, Oxford University Press, 2015) 1.

[6] ibid.

[7] O Jouanjan, 'Les scènes du droit – Recension de Jacques Krynen, Le théâtre juridique. Une histoire de la construction du droit, Gallimard' (La vie des idées, 9 November 2019), available at www.laviedesidees.fr/Les-scenes-du-droit-4417.

[8] See D Gallo, R Mastroianni, FG Nicola and L Cecchetti, 'Introduction: Tracing the Italian Influence on European law through Judicial Biographies', in this volume.

under scrutiny played a significant role or contributed an 'enormous input'.[9] This paradoxical dynamic poses its own risk: the potential collapse of research interest through mutual cancellation. If numerous studies assert that everyone is influential, it necessitates further research to determine degrees of influence among individuals.

On the other hand, law seeks certainty and lawyers often seek refuge behind 'the Court', a unique and enduring entity. When elucidating legal concepts, principles, exceptions, and norm articulations, they lean on the legal fiction that the Court remains unchanged, consistent in 2022 as it was in 1952. This narrative conveniently overlooks the reality that the Court has been dominated by (old) white men for four decades. Within the CJEU, the General Court, responsible primarily for hearing and determining actions brought by natural or legal persons against acts of the institutions, bodies, offices or agencies of the European Union,[10] has benefited from the 2015 reform of its composition and now adheres to gender equality.[11] In contrast, the Court of Justice, tasked mainly with responding to references for preliminary rulings, addressing actions for failure of Member States to fulfil obligations, and handling some action for annulment and failure to act of EU institutions, is still predominantly composed of males judges and Advocates General (along with registrars) and has never been chaired by a woman.

Scholars have acknowledged law as 'a third language'[12] because its foundation and function rely on its presumed neutrality. A notable example of this conception of law is the case of AG Lagrange (1952–1964), who applied his legal expertise uniformly to both the Jewish Statute during Vichy's period in France[13] and the European law.[14]

[9] G Butler and A Lazowski, 'Introduction', in G Butler and A Lazowski (eds), *Shaping EU Law the British Way – UK Advocates General at the Court of Justice of the European Union* (Oxford, Hart Publishing, 2022) 1, 2.

[10] For instance, actions brought by Member States against the Commission; also actions brought by the Member States against the Council relating to acts adopted in the field of State aid, trade protection measures (dumping) and acts by which it exercises implementing powers; actions seeking compensation for damage caused by the institutions or the bodies, offices or agencies of the European Union or their staff; actions based on contracts made by the European Union that expressly give jurisdiction to the General Court; actions relating to intellectual property brought against the European Union Intellectual Property Office and against the Community Plant Variety Office; and disputes between the institutions of the European Union and their staff concerning employment relations and the social security system.

[11] Regulation (EU, Euratom) 2015/2422, European Parliament and the Council [2015] (amending Protocol No 3 on the Statute of the Court of Justice of the European Union).

[12] A Supiot 'Il n'est pas de paix durable sans justice sociale', Conférence at Académie royale de Belgique (28 January 2020); F Ost, *Le droit ou l'empire du tiers* (Paris, Dalloz, 2021) 348.

[13] M O Baruch, *Servir l'Etat français. L'administration en France de 1940 à 1944* (Paris, Fayard, 1997); see generally regarding Lagrange's carreer path M Mangenot (ed), *Un légiste de Vichy à la Communauté européenne. Maurice Lagrange : une biographie professionnelle*, dossier, *Civitas Europa* 50 (forthcoming).

[14] M Lagrange 'The Court of Justice as a factor in European Integration' (1966–1967) 15 (4) *American Journal of Comparative Law* 709; see L Clément-Wilz, 'La Cour de justice de M. Lagrange', in M Mangenot (ed), *Un légiste de Vichy à la Communauté européenne. Maurice Lagrange: une biographie professionnelle* (2023) 50 *Civitas Europa*.

European lawyers encounter three distinct methodological challenges in measuring the influence of a particular group of individual judges or Advocates General on EU law. This book on Italian judges and Advocates General is designed to address all three challenges. Firstly, as underscored by numerous authors of this book, measuring the influence of judges proves to be a challenging task, approaching the realm of impossibility. This challenge arises as a result of the secrecy of deliberations and the enduring single judgment rule. The opening of the ECJ archives in Fiesole has not altered this situation significantly.[15] In matters involving secret deliberation, the Court retains the power to 'blacken' or to 'redact' the *dossiers de procédure* because 'under no circumstance shall access be given to documents relating to the secrecy of deliberation'.[16] The editors of the recently published book, *Shaping EU Law the British Way*, even deem it 'impossible'.[17]

From the Italian perspective adopted here, this volume endeavours to achieve the seemingly impossible. A noteworthy initiative of Paolo Gori, *référendaire* of the Judge Alberto Trabucchi, consisted in publishing his 'note du délibéré' in the notorious *Van Gend en Loos* case, admittedly overcoming the barrier of the secrecy of deliberation. This publication became an invaluable source for research on the Euro-lawyers that were shaping European integration.[18] In a parallel effort to open the door of the *delibéré*, connections are drawn between key case outcomes and judges' publications. For instance, Amedeo Arena contends that the main output of the Plaumann case, which regarded individual challenges against EEC legal acts, is 'certainly aligned with extra-curial writing' of Rino Rossi, who served as the nominated judge rapporteur in this case.[19] Additionally, Edoardo Greppi argues that certain Court decisions align with Riccardo Monaco's (judge from 1964 to 1976) vision of the supranational order developed in his academic capacity.[20] Finally, as highlighted by Síofra O'Leary in her remarks to Vittorio Di Bucci's chapter on Federico Mancini (Advocate General in 1982–1988 and judge in 1988–1999), in his extrajudicial activity, 'accompanied and frequently anticipated the transformation of an economic community into a monetary and, to an extent, political Union'.[21]

[15] M Pollak 'Learning from EU Law Stories', in FG Nicola and B Davies (eds), *EU Law Stories – Contextual and Critical Histories of European Jurisprudence* (Cambridge, Cambridge University Press, 2017) 577–602.

[16] FG Nicola, 'Waiting for the Barbarians: Inside the Archive of the European Court of Justice', in C Kilpatrick and J Scott (eds), *New Legal Approaches to Studying the Court of Justice* (Oxford Oxford University Press, 2020).

[17] See Butler and Lazowski (n 8) 1.

[18] See generally, M Rasmussen, 'Law Meets History: Interpreting the Van Gend en Loos Judgement', in FG Nicola and B Davies (n 16) 103–120.

[19] See A Arena, '"Notre Nestor, Monsieur le Juge Rossi" (1889–1974): an Internationalist's Contribution to the Making of a Supranational Legal Order', in this volume.

[20] See E Greppi, 'Riccardo Monaco and the Doctrine of Supranationality in International Institutional Law', in this volume.

[21] See V Di Bucci 'The Contribution of Giuseppe Federico Mancini as Advocate General (1982–1988) and Judge (1988–1999) to European Constitutionalism', in this volume (O'Leary and Di Bucci were former référendaires of Federico Mancini).

The second obstacle, unique to European Studies, lies in the generation of 'aficionados', devoted enthusiasts of European integration.[22] European lawyers have played a prominent role in brokering European integration.[23] As articulated by Walter Hallstein, a jurist and former president of the European Commission, in 1972, 'The European Economic Community is a remarkable legal phenomenon. It is a creation of law; it is a source of law; and it is a legal system'.[24] Furthermore, 'a certain form of thought has been developed, a style unique to EU legal studies'.[25] Jurists created a new language, composed of principles and formulae in order to promote the continuation of the integration process through law.[26] Lawyers, judges and scholars constructed this novel language to advance the ongoing integration process.

Once again, this book intriguingly constructs an alternative narrative. As revealed by Vera Fritz, at the commencement of his term, the first President of the Court, Massimo Pilotti, did not emphasise the Court's novelty but rather followed the International Court of Justice path with respect to the procedural rules. Archives show that he became a 'contentious president,' frequently absent from the Court, despite his 'very much appreciated legal culture', as stated by Vera Fritz in this book. Additionally, Tommaso Pavone provides a nuanced portrait of Nicola Catalano, who served as a judge from 1958 to 1961, after serving on the Tangiers international tribunal. Regarded as one of the main architects of the preliminary ruling procedure during the Rome Treaty negotiations, Catalano paradoxically did not significantly shape the Court and European integration during his tenure, arguably due to his temperament. Interestingly, he remained an activist Euro-lawyer after his mandate at the Court and brought several cases to Luxembourg voiding Italian protective regulations from the restriction of free movement.

The third methodological challenge arises from the opacity of the nomination process, particularly during period covered by this volume, when the so-called '255 committee' did not yet exist.[27] Once again, the editors' ambition to unveil the nomination condition introduces a salutary 'hermeneutic of suspicion' to European Studies. This approach does not inherently undermine the quality of impartiality – referring to the human qualities and personal convictions of judges and Advocates General whose biographies are under scrutiny – given that independence depends on their legal status. As affirmed by the European Court of Human Rights, what must be objectively justified are the doubts on the impartiality.[28] For instance, being a freemason, in

[22] See D Caruso, 'EU Law in U.S. Legal Academia' (2011) 20 *Tulane Journal of International and Comparative Law* 175.

[23] A Vauchez, *Brokering Europe – Euro-Lawyer and the Making of Transnational Polity* (Cambridge, Cambridge University Press, 2015).

[24] See quote by L Azoulai, 'Solitude, community, and critique. Motives for a reshaping of EU Legal Studies' (2015) 50 *Politique européenne* 82–98.

[25] ibid, 50.

[26] ibid.

[27] Article 255 TFEU.

[28] ECtHR, *Morel v France* (Application No 34130/96) [2000].

and of itself, does not limit impartiality. Membership in such organisation is not a determining factor in one's eligibility to be judge.[29] In his chapter, Jacques Ziller unveiled the nomination's reason that determined the choice of Giacinto Bosco (judge from 1976 to 1988) as a candidate by the Italian cabinet.[30] In his view, this choice was linked to his strong connections with the leadership of the *Democrazia Cristiana* (Christian Democratic party), his experience in the European Parliament sessions, and his involvement in sessions of the Council of Ministers in Brussels as an Italian minister.

While this book navigates the inherent methodological challenges confronted by a study on influence in the European legal field, it also provides another layer of inquiry into a recent avenue of research on the CJEU. This 'institutional take' on the CJEU analyses the Court as an institution,[31] namely as it presents itself on its *Curia* website.[32] This research entails a deeper focus on procedural and organisational choices of a legal institution and their connections to legal substance.[33] As further detailed below, this focus enables researchers to explore the legal fabric of the Court of Justice.

3. EXPLORING THE LEGAL FABRIC OF THE COURT OF JUSTICE AND ITS ITALIAN ESSENCE

The above-mentioned research has delved into the Court's legal framework, conducting a meticulous analysis of statutes, rules, internal procedures, and procedural practices, including their historical evolution. These studies argue, for example, that the Court of Justice has experienced a diminishing institutional autonomy over time, particularly when compared with its European counterpart in Strasbourg.[34] A noteworthy example is the significant role played by the Council in the 2015 reform of the General Court, illustrating the Council's decisive influence. The European Parliament also exerted substantial influence,[35] particularly regarding gender equality in the General Court's

[29] ECtHR, *Grande Oriente d'Italia Di Palazzo Giustiniani v Italy* (Application No 35972/97) [2001] 34 EHRR 629.

[30] See J Ziller, 'Giacinto Bosco, a rather well-known politician in Italy, and one of the lesser-known Italian members of the Court of Justice of the European Communities', in this volume.

[31] L Clément-Wilz, *La Cour de justice de l'Union européenne* (Paris, Librairie Générale de Droit et de Jurisprudence, 2020).

[32] CURIA, 'General Presentation on the Institution, Court of Justice of the European Union' curia.europa.eu/jcms/jcms/Jo2_6999/en/.

[33] ibid.; C Krenn, *The Procedural and Organisational Law of the European Court of Justice – An Incomplete Transformation* (Cambridge, Cambridge University Press, 2022).

[34] L Clément-Wilz, 'Autonomie et transparence des cours européennes', in D Petrick, M Bobek, JM Passer and A Masson (eds), *Evolution des rapports entre les ordres juridiques de l'Union européenne, international et nationaux – Liber Amicorum Jiri Malenovsky* (Bruxelles, Bruylant, 2020) 607–624.

[35] C Krenn, 'The European Court of Justice's Financial Accountability – How the European Parliament Incites and Monitors Judicial Reform through the Budgetary Process' (2017) *European Constitutional Law Review* 13, 453.

composition, thanks to an amendment of the preliminary referrals of the Regulation 2015/2422.[36]

The choice of French as the *langue du délibéré* is a recurring subject of discussion, with academics and/or members of the Court questioning the relevance of maintaining this language[37] or raising concerns about a perceived 'French capture' over the ECJ.[38] The persistence of French as a working language in today's globalised world carries a certain mystery. The Court's inherent conservative role, coupled with the need to develop a coherent and stable case law based on legal concepts shaped in French, contributes to this specificity.[39] Importantly, no empirical data has thus far demonstrated that the dominance of the French language implies a cultural French domination within the Court. The Court of Justice stands as a temple of multilingualism, with the language of the case corresponding to one of the twenty-four official languages of the European Union.[40] In a similar vein, the Italian portraits presented in this book stress the challenge of connecting the 'Italian-ness' of an institution such as the CJEU to the Italian legal culture. It guides the reader through these individuals' lifelong professional trajectories and also sheds light on and humanises the legal architecture, organisation, and composition of the Court.

The 'Italian-ness' of the organisation of the Court is logically attributed to the pioneering role entrusted to individuals appointed to the institutions established in 1952, to individuals in charge of drafting the new procedural instrument created in 1958, and with the creation of the then Court of first instance in 1988. As nationals of a founding Member of the Communities, Italian judges and Advocates General stood as pioneers, alongside their counterparts from Germany, France, Luxembourg, the Netherlands, and Belgium. Notably, as the President of the first Court of Justice, Massimo Pilotti played a pivotal role in drafting the initial version of the Rules of Procedure. During this period, the ECJ did not require the agreement of the Council to adopt these

[36] Regulation (EU, Euratom) 2015/2422, European Parliament and the Council [2015] (amending Protocol No 3 on the Statute of the Court of Justice of the European Union).

[37] K Schiemann, 'La langue de travail de la Cour', in *La Cour de justice de l'Union européenne sous la présidence de Vassilios Skouris* (Bruxelles, Bruylant, 2015) 569; M Bobek, 'Epilogue: Searching for the European Hercules', in Bobek (n 5) 309.

[38] M Cohen, 'On the Linguistic design of multinational courts: the French Capture' (2016) 14 *International Journal of Constitutional Law* 1.

[39] L Clément-Wilz, 'Les Français, la France et la francophonie, réflexions sur la fabrique du droit européen' (2020) 4 *Rivista di diritto europeo* 701; B Nabli, 'Le français, une langue intégrée ?', in B Nabli (ed), *L'Etat intégré, un nouveau type d'Etat – le cas de la France* (Bruxelles, Bruylant, 2022).

[40] K McAuliffe 'Language and the Institutional Dynamics of the Court of Justice of the European Communities: Lawyer-Linguists and the Production of a Multilingual Jurisprudence', in M Gueldry (ed), *How Globalizing Professions Deal with National Languages: Studies in Cultural Conflict and Cooperation* (Lewiston, The Edwin Mellen Press, 2010) 239; see also C Mendez, M Gazzola, L Clément-Wilz, V Triga, F Mendez, C Djouvas, A Charamboulos and J Bachtler *Study for the EP CULT Committee: The European Union's approach to multilingualism in its own communications policy* (Brussels, European Parliament, Policy Department for Structural and Cohesion Policies, 2022) 22.

rules, and Pilotti guided discussions, drawing inspiration from his experience at the International Court of Justice in the Hague.[41]

While pioneering members, such as Maurice Lagrange, or well-known judges, such as Pierre Pescatore may not have initially grasped the significance of this new legal instrument in the integration process,[42] Pavone explains that archival evidence suggests that Nicola Catalano intentionally designed the Rules of Procedure. Catalano, leveraging the perception that the issue was overly technical, played a crucial role in shaping this procedural tool with foresight, contributing to its importance in the integration process. His vision encompassed the primacy of EU law, its immediate effect, its constitutional and federal nature, and the shared authority to interpret European law with national courts. Following the end of his mandate at the Court, Catalano, as a practising Eurolawyer, assumed the role of the 'referral's central choreographer' in a number of cases brought before the Court, demonstrating a continuation of his legal architectural work.

Lastly, it emerges that Giacinto Bosco played an active role as a member of the Court's internal working group that was responsible for preparing the establishment of the Court of First Instance (CFI). His former position as the Minister of justice and vice president of the *Consiglio superiore de la Magistratura* positioned him in a leadership role during the process.[43] Subsequently, as analysed by Antonio Aresu and Celestina Iannone in their chapter on Antonio Saggio, he was one of the initial members of the CFI who actively contributed to the drafting of its first rules of procedure.[44] In 1994, Saggio authored a book on the CFI and in 1995, he became President of that court. Notably, he proposed the idea of expanding the Court's jurisdiction to preliminary rulings in specific regulatory fields. While this transfer has not always been viewed favorably,[45] the proposal is currently under discussion by the European legislator, nearly 30 years after it was initially introduced by the Court of Justice.[46] In the aftermath of the reform of the General Court and the suppression of the Civil Servant Tribunal, the ECJ has finally taken the plunge. Substantially, the transfer would concern technical issues that should not raise issues of principle. In this way, the Court of Justice paves the way to becoming a true Constitutional Court.

[41] See V Fritz, 'Building the Foundations of the European Court of Justice: Massimo Pilotti (1879–1962)', in this volume.

[42] P Pescatore, 'Les travaux du groupe juridique » dans la négociation des traités de Rome' (1981) 34 *Studia diplomatica* 1.

[43] See J Ziller (n 30).

[44] See A Aresu and C Iannone, 'Antonio Saggio: A Major Contributor to the European Integration', in this volume.

[45] On the evolution of the position, see R Rousselot, 'Tribunal: une réforme du statut de la Cour de justice de l'Union européenne en demi-teinte' (Insight of 16 April 2016) 1 *European Papers* 1 European Forum 275–285.

[46] Request submitted by the Court of Justice pursuant to the second paragraph of Article 281 of the Treaty on the Functioning of the European Union, with a view to amending Protocol No 3 on the Statute of the Court of Justice of the European Union, 30 November 2022.

4. EBBING AND FLOWING: AN ITALIAN PERSPECTIVE ON THE JURISPRUDENCE OF THE COURT

This section will delve specifically into the Opinions of Italian Advocates General. These Opinions are believed to breathe life into the legal framework of the decision-making process, revealing how the final judgment is reached. However, measuring the influence of an Advocate General's Opinions on ECJ judgments introduces a distinct set of methodological challenges, particularly with regards to the practical issue of providing evidence. When comparing both the judgment and the Opinion, even when they align, establishing that it is the Advocate General who influenced the judges poses a challenge. Differentiating it from a similar argument presented by a party or even stemming from the judge's individual perspective on the case becomes a critical consideration. Furthermore, the question arises: should we measure the utility of Advocates General in their capacity to be influential at all?

Despite the debate surrounding their influence, Advocates General offer valuable and unique insights into the judicial fabric of the law.[47] While attempting to quantify influence in legal fields may seem like a dead end for lawyers, the intellectual approach taken to assess it provides useful insights. Beyond the discussion of the Opinions of Advocates General versus dissenting opinions, the Opinions of Advocates General currently serve the crucial function of providing transparency in each case. Moreover, they vividly illustrate the dynamic ebb and flow of the case law of the Court of Justice. The fabric of European case-law consists of a flow of judgments (also referred by B Bertrand as 'case law blocks' or 'series of rulings').[48] It broadly aligns with the four-stage cycle previously identified in a 2011 research on Advocates General published in 2011:[49] foundation (1950s and early 1960s), consolidation (1960s, 1970s and 1980s), challenge/criticisms (1990s), and a search for consistency (2000s).[50] Since the time Italy gained a position of Advocate General, individuals nominated during the studied period include Alberto Trabucchi in 1973, Francesco Capotorti in 1976, Federico Mancini in 1982, Giuseppe Tesauro in 1988, Antonio La Pergola in 1995 (serving until 1999), and Antonio Saggio in 1998 (serving until 2000). The roles played by these Italian Advocates General since the 1970s provide a valuable lens for a comprehensive analysis within the broader study on the role of the Advocate General.

[47] B Latour, *La fabrique du droit- une ethnographie du Conseil d'Etat* (Paris, La Découverte, 2004).

[48] B Bertrand, 'Les blocs de jurisprudence' (2012) *RTD Eur.* 741 (Translation of 'blocs de jurisprudence' and 'séries d'arrêts').

[49] L Clément-Wilz, *La fonction de l'avocat général près la Cour de justice de l'Union européenne* (Bruxelles, Bruylant, 2010).

[50] See also A Arnull, The European Union and its Court of Justice (Oxford, Oxford University Press, 1999).

The role of these Italian AGs since the 70s can be analysed in the overall study on the role of the Advocate General. Since the first case,s and especially since the 60s, the Advocates General helped to establish and to develop a European *acquis*. They always took the previous decisions of the Court into consideration and never contested their authority, especially in the field of the nature and specificity of the European legal order. Because of the quest for continuity in AG Opinions, CJEU cases became actual jurisprudence relied on and examined by future cases, rather than a mere collection of decisions. In this context, the Advocates General carried on and strengthened this approach throughout the seventies and eighties.

In the 70s, when the first Italian AG was nominated, Advocates General helped to bring European case law into existence, by establishing a level of coherence between different cases. They never ventured out of the mainstream opinion conveyed by the European Court of Justice. Italian AGs followed this movement. For example, in the *Factortame* case (1990), AG Tesauro relied on paragraphs 14 and 16 of the *Simmenthal* judgment (1977).[51] He stated that provisions of Community law having direct effect 'must be fully and uniformly applied in all the Member States from the date of their entry into force and for so long as they continue in force' (para 14) and that 'this consequence also concerns any national court whose task it is as an organ of a Member State to protect, in a case within its jurisdiction, the rights conferred upon individuals by [then] [Union] law' (para 16).[52] More importantly, Tesauro '[does] not consider it useful […] to enter into a sterile dialectical discussion on the theoretical basis of *such a firmly established principle*' (para 13).[53] Although the Court of Justice and the Advocates General were going in the same direction, it does not mean that they were in absolute agreement on every issue. In reality, the European Court of Justice and Advocates General did not always follow the same rhythm, jurisprudence appearing as a tide, following ebbing and flowing movement. For instance, in the field of external competences, the Advocate General Trabucchi in the *Kramer* case did not give any opinion leading the Court to take the decisive step.[54] However, in 1975, the same Trabucchi suggested to retain, in his Opinion in the *Cristini* case,[55] a broad interpretation of the notion of 'advantage' provided by Regulation No 1612/68 on free movement of workers. Trabucchi underlined that: 'one of the objectives of Regulation No 1612/68 is de jure and de facto equality of treatment

[51] *Amministrazione delle Finanze dello Stato v Simmenthal* Case 106/77 ECLI:EU:C:1978:49 [1977] ECR 629.

[52] *The Queen v Secretary of State for Transport, ex parte: Factortame* Case C-213/89 [1990] ECR I-2433, Opinion of AG Tesauro, para 13.

[53] ibid.

[54] *Cornelis Kramer and others* Joined Cases 3/76, 4/76 and 6/76 ECLI:EU:C:1976:96 [1976] Opinion of AG Trabucchi.

[55] *Anita Cristini v Societe National Des Chemins de Fer Francais* Case 32/75 ECLI:EU:C:1975:120 [1975], Opinion of AG Trabucchi.

for a worker including its application to the right to be joined by his family and the conditions under which his family is integrated within the community in the host country.'[56] Such a broad definition appears in the ECJ decision.[57] Respectively in the *Hoffman Laroche* and *CILFIT* cases, which raised the question about the obligation to ask questions of last instance national courts, AG Capotorti (1977 and 1982) gave Opinions with a more restrictive approach than the Court concerning the doctrine of *acte clair*.[58]

From the early 1990s onward, Advocates General began to provide their own interpretations of EU case law and to criticise its outcome. This phenomenon can be attributed to two main factors: the more established doctrines of EU law through the case law of the ECJ and the diverse background of Advocates General, many of whom come from academia with a robust understanding of European Law. This critical perspective is evident in the case law concerning the admissibility of references for preliminary rulings; especially in instances where national law unilaterally refers to EU law in both internal situations and more broadly. Notably, Advocates General, including Mancini, Tesauro, and Saggio, have been highly critical in their analyses of these 'internal' situations. In the early 1990s, Advocate General Van Gerven (in the *Sunday Trading* cases, 1989, 1991, 1993) and Advocate General Tesauro (in the *Hünermund* case, 1993) criticised the broad definition of 'restriction' given by the Court. Advocate General Tesauro raised the following issue:

> Is Article [34] of the Treaty a provision intended to liberalize intra-[Union] trade or is it intended more generally to encourage the unhindered pursuit of commerce in individual Member States?[59]

He also put the Court's responsibilities into sharp focus, arguing that:

> The inconsistency and contradictions pointed out increase the need to achieve clarity by means of criteria that are as precise and unambiguous as possible and, even more importantly, of a conscious and explicit basic choice regarding the need for (or expediency of?) review of the type of measures in point here for their conformity with Article [34].[60]

Even if the ECJ did not follow the new definition of 'restriction' given by Advocate General Van Gerven and Tesauro, it did modify its approach in *Keck and Mithouard* (1993) in which the distinction was made between a restriction on 'certain selling arrangements' and on 'product requirements'.

Finally, at the end of the twentieth century, the Court case law has become increasingly complex in part due to the expansion of European Union

[56] ibid, para 2.
[57] *Anita Cristini v. Societe National Des Chemins de Fer Francais* Case 32/75 ECLI:EU:C:1975:120, [1975], para 13.
[58] *Hoffmann La Roche AG v Centrafarm* Case 107/76 ECLI:EU:C:1977:89 [1977] 957.
[59] *Ruth Hünermund* Case C-292/92 ECLI:EU:C:1993:932 [1993], Opinion of AG Tesauro, para 1.
[60] ibid, para 25.

competence and jurisdiction of the CJEU in new sensitive areas. In this context, Advocate General La Pergola, along with Advocate General Cosmas, decided to strengthen the legal effect of the concept of European Union citizenship when mentioning it in their main argument. In *Martínez Sala*, La Pergola considered that freedom of residence was 'not simply a derived right, but a right inseparable from citizenship of the Union' (1998). He added that:

> Citizenship of the Union comes through the fiat of the primary norm, being conferred directly on the individual, who is henceforth formally recognised as a subject of law who acquires and loses it together with citizenship of the national state to which he belongs and in no other way. Let us say that it is the fundamental legal status guaranteed to the citizen of every Member State by the legal order of the [Union] and now of the Union.[61]

AG La Pergola was indeed a pioneer in 'putting flesh on the bone of European citizenship'.[62] He was then followed by the Court in the *Martínez Sala* case that embraced his rights-based approach to EU citizenship. In turn, AG Saggio was the first to inaugurate a stream of AG Opinions, followed by the Court, that aimed at increasing consumers' protection by clarifying the power of domestic courts to determine of their own motion whether a term inserted in a contract is unfair.[63]

In conclusion, the Italian Advocates General, all of whom came from an academic background (with the exception of Saggio, who was nevertheless teaching in University) and began serving in the early 1970s, navigated the ebb and flow of the ECJ jurisprudence tide alongside their colleagues. Much like their counterparts, they exhibited varying degrees of integrationism, occasionally surpassing the stance of the Court or lagging behind. At times, they proved to be innovative, while at other times, they did not. Regardless, they consistently upheld the *acquis communautaire*, treating case law as precedent, thereby reinforcing the legitimacy and authority of the ECJ.

5. CONCLUSION: THE EUROPEANISATION OF ITALIANS MIND AND *ESPRIT DE CORPS* AT THE COURT OF JUSTICE

In the same way that the study on the role of the Advocate General has revealed both the institutional framework of the Court and the decision-making

[61] *Maria Martínez Sala* Case C-85/96 ECLI:EU:C:1997:335 [1997], Opinion of AG La Pergola para 18; See also *Rui Alberto Pereira Roque* Case C-171/96 ECLI:EU:C:1997:425 [1997] ECR I-4607 Opinion of AG Tesauro, para 48.

[62] O'Leary, 'Putting on the Bones of European Union Citizenship' (1999) 24 *European Law Review* 68–79.

[63] *Océano Grupo Editorial SA v RocióMurciano Quintero*, *Salvat Editores SA v José M. Sánchez AlcónPrades*, *José Luis Copano Badillo*, *Mohammed Berroane* and *Emilio Viñas Feliú* Joined Cases C-240/98, C-241/98, C-242/98, C-243/98, and C-244/98 ECLI:EU:C:1999:620 [1999], Opinion of AG Saggio; see FG Nicola and E Tichadou, 'Océano Grupo: A Transatlantic Victory for the Consumer and a Missed Opportunity for European Law', in FG Nicola and B Davies (eds), *EU Law Stories: Contextual and Critical Histories of European Jurisprudence* (Cambridge, Cambridge University Press, 2017) 369–390.

process,[64] this book navigates both institutional and substantial realms in EU law. It not only sheds light on the legal framework of the institution but also examines the tangible outcomes, offering a nuanced perspective on the Court's identity over this significant period of almost half a century. Through in-depth analyses of the personalities, career paths, and the quest for Italian influence on EU Law, this research presents a novel, embodied, and national perspective on the legal architecture of the Court of Justice.

Irrespective of their pre-existing commitment to European integration before assuming roles at the Court, it becomes evident that they all embraced the *esprit de corps* of the Court of Justice once in Luxembourg. This *esprit de corps*, at times rooted in past experiences such as serving as *référendaire*, as seen in the case of Antonio Saggio, transcended personal histories. Their robust connection with the Court and their unwavering commitment to the European project is vividly illustrated in Ezio Perillo's tribute to Trabucchi and 'his' Court of Justice.[65] Similarly, Chiara Amalfitano and Filippo Croci emphasise La Pergola's enduring 'faith in European integration.'[66] These instances not only signify a personal bond with the Court but also underscore a dedication to the broader goals of European unity and integration. Highlighted by Luigi Daniele's chapter, Francesco Capotorti (judge in 1976 and Advocate General from 1976 to 1982), embraced the sense of unity and mutual respect he encountered at the Court.[67] Furthermore, Capotorti underscored the imperative for the Court to maintain consistency and unwavering loyalty to the principles proclaimed in the EU Treaties. This commitment reflects the Court's dedication to upholding the core values enshrined in Treaties. A particularly noteworthy example is Giuseppe Tesauro, who served as a constitutional judge from 4 November 2005, and later assumed the role of President of the Constitutional Court in 2014. As stated by Roberto Mastroianni and Massimo Condinanzi:

> [I]f asked to point out which of these highly prestigious institutional experiences had been the most significant and intense from both a professional and personal point of view, Tesauro would, without a doubt, answer: Luxembourg.[68]

Giuseppe Tesauro attributes this to the unique opportunity to engage daily in the rich exchange of ideas within the Court, where diverse legal cultures converge to the same objective of finding a common result. The deep integration of Italians within the Court of Justice brings about a reciprocal effect, leading to the institutionalisation of the minds of Italian judges and Advocates General.

[64] Clément-Wilz (n 49).

[65] See E Perillo, 'Alberto Trabucchi: the defender of the European citizens' rights and the Van Gend & Loos ruling of the Court of Justice', in this volume.

[66] See C Amalfitano and F Croci, 'Antonio La Pergola: The Idea of Europe as an Objective to be Pursued, between Founding Values and Fundamental Principles', in this volume.

[67] See L Daniele, 'Francesco Capotorti: the Man, the Academic, and the Advocate General at the Court of Justice', in this volume.

[68] R Mastroianni and M Condinanzi, 'Giuseppe Tesauro – Advocate General at the ECJ 1988–1998: A paladin of effective judicial protection', in this volume.

16

Italian Ways of EU Law: Rooting Italy in European Legal Integration

ANTOINE VAUCHEZ

1. INTRODUCTION: FILLING THE GAP

THIS MUCH AWAITED volume provides an important addition to the growing literature on Euro-lawyers, the Court of Justice of the European Union (CJEU) and the process of European legal integration. After decades during which the process of the emergence of EU legal order had been thought of as a product of the sole case-law of the Court, this stream of research has pointed out the critical contribution of lawyers in feeding, promoting and authenticating the Court's legal accomplishments, acting as both a breeding ground (of former students, research assistants, law clerks or interns) and as a vigilant custodian of its authority against a variety of external criticisms. While this lively research pathway has now explored in great detail the role of *transnational* networks of professionals, in particular the role of the *Fédération International pour le Droit Européen* (FIDE), as a critical support-structure for the continuous development of a pan-European case-law in Luxembourg, it has for a large part ignored the *national roots* of these pan-European legal networks. This volume is an important redress to this scholarly gap through its reconstitution of the biographies of the eleven Italian judges and Advocates General who have worked at the Court from 1952 to 2000, thereby delineating the contours of Italian ways of EU law.

The issue of national legal traditions of EU law is not new. It has even been a central concern in a European project haunted by the return of forms of national hegemony. While the European Communities emerged out of an attempt to overcome the power politics of national powers, the field of European law – like other fields of European construction – has developed a particular interest in its own 'European-ness' –that is its capacity to produce authentically 'European' norms that are not just a mask for new forms of domination, influence or hegemony. Big Member States, such as France or Germany, have been under continuous scrutiny for their propensity to disproportionately weigh upon the making of EU law and to establish a variety of forms of capture, whether they be linguistic, methodological, doctrinal or even ideological.

For instance, for France, while the role of *Conseil d'Etat* members and of French administrative law in the early years of European Community law, often represented by figures such as Maurice Lagrange and Michel Gaudet, has been thoroughly analysed over the past decade,[1] the monopolistic position of French as the *langue du délibéré* of the CJEU has been described as favouring the recruitment of judges and *référendaires* trained in France or Belgium. This favourite position of the French language, it is argued, has ultimately led to a situation in which 'Francophones have a disproportionate influence over the shaping of EU law'.[2] Similarly, scholars have pointed out how German conceptions of economic constitutionalism have permeated EU competition law, just as the usage of the proportionality method drawn from the German legal tradition has deeply influenced the reasoning of the Court of Justice to a point that the German constitutional court abruptly objected to the misapplication of the principle by the CJEU in the *Weiss* decision.[3] Since the 1980s, other viewpoints have insisted on the domination of English (and English-speaking publishing venues) as the vector of *transnational* communication among EU Law scholars – with the related risk of the marginalisation of otherwise lively domestic legal scholarship that end up being prevented from weighing in on Europe's doctrinal conversation.[4] In the years after 2000, at the peak of the debate over the European Constitution, some scholars have also regretted forms of doctrinal capture by American ways of law, as identified in the interdisciplinary, contextual and constitutionalist paradigm of EU law that had found a particularly welcoming place on the hills of Fiesole.[5]

2. ITALIAN-NESS AT THE CJEU

The issue of 'national legal traditions' is not only important intellectually speaking, it also plays a critical part in the sensitive doctrinal and judicial

[1] See L Clément-Wilz, *La fonction de l'avocat general près la Cour de justice de l'Union européenne* (Bruxelles, Bruylant, 2011); J Bailleux, 'Michel Gaudet a law entrepreneur: the role of the legal service of the European executives in the invention of EC Law and of the Common Market' (2013) 50 *Common Market Law Review* 359.

[2] See A Huyue Zhang, 'The Faceless Court' *(VerfBlog*, 3 June 2020) www.verfassungsblog.de/the-faceless-court/.

[3] See T Marzal, 'Is the BVerfG PSPP decision "simply not comprehensible"?: A critique of the judgment's reasoning on proportionality' (*Verfassungsblog*, 9 May 2020), available at www.verfassungsblog.de/is-the-bverfg-pspp-decision-simply-not-comprehensible/; *Weiss* Case C-493/17 ECLI:EU:C:2018:1000 [2018].

[4] A Vauchez, 'Vicarious Hegemony. The German Crisis of European Law' (*Verfassungsblog*, 6 October 2020), available at https://verfassungsblog.de/vicarious-hegemony/.

[5] A Arnull, 'The Americanization of EU law scholarship', in A Arnull, P Eeckhout, and T Tridimas (eds), *Continuity and Change in EU law – Essays in Honour of Sir Francis Jacobs* (Oxford, Oxford University Press, 2008) 415–431; B de Witte, 'European Union law: A Unified Academic Discipline?' [2008] *EUI Working Paper-RSCAS 2008/34*, available online.

debates over the supremacy of EU law and in the relationship between the CJEU and national supreme courts.[6] While the CJEU makes increasing references to national constitutional traditions, some national supreme courts have used the notion to contain the development of EU law and the realm of its supremacy. Suffice it to consider here the wording of the *Weiss* decision by which the German constitutional court contested the CJEU interpretation and application of EU law on the ground that 'the traditional European methods of interpretation or, more broadly, the general legal principles that are common to the laws of Member States are manifestly disregarded',[7] thereby claiming to be acting as the authentic spokesperson of national constitutional traditions.[8]

Yet, the *Italian-ness* of EU law as assessed here through the collective contribution of Italian law and lawyers to the making of EU case law has rarely been questioned. Wrongly so, one would think, after reading this volume. Italian judges played important institutional roles as presidents of the European Court of Justice (Massimo Pilotti from 1952 to 1958) and of the Court of First Instance (Antonio Saggio from 1995 to 1998), or acted as vice-president (Antonio Tizzano from 2015 to 2018) or presidents of chamber (eg, Federico Mancini). They have also been instrumental in shaping EU law at some of its turning points: as members, *juges rapporteurs* or as Advocates General, taking an active part in the 'making of a Constitution for Europe'[9] in some of the key constitutional cases from *Van Gend en Loos* (Antonio Trabucchi) to *Les Verts* (Federico Mancini), but also in many of the critical debates of EU law, whether that be one of the recognition of 'European citizenship' as the 'fundamental status' of all citizens of the Member States, as per Antonio La Pergola in *Martinez Sala* (1996), or an attempt to enhance the effectiveness of judicial protection, as per Giuseppe Tesauro in *Factortame* (1990) and others. As such, the book reads like an Italian journey into the *grands arrêts* of EU case law.

3. BEYOND THE ELEVEN OFFICIAL PORTRAITS

While these eleven *vitae* can certainly be read as an homage to important legal figures, bringing back to light a lively gallery of portraits of notable lawyers,

[6] See FG Nicola, 'National Legal Traditions at Work in the Jurisprudence of the Court of Justice of the European Union' (2016) 64 *The American Journal of Comparative Law* 865; S Rodin, 'Constitutional Relevance of Foreign Court Decisions' (2016) 64 *The American Journal of Comparative Law* 815.

[7] German Federal Constitutional Court, Weiss 2 BvR 859/15 ECLI:DE:VBerfG:2020:rs20200505.bvr085915 [2020].

[8] See M Claes and J Reestman, 'The Protection of National Constitutional Identity and the Limits of European Integration at the Occasion of the Gauweiler Case' (2015) 16(4) *German Law Journal* 917. On the Conseil d'Etat, see L Azoulai, 'L'État, c'est moi ! Le Conseil d'État, la sécurité et la conservation des données' (2021) 57 *Revue trimestrielle de droit européen* 349.

[9] F Mancini, 'The Making of a Constitution in Europe' (1989) 26(4) *Common Market Law Review* 595.

they also open an interesting methodological pathway into using judicial biographies in the study of EU law. So far indeed, the historical and sociological turn of EU law has been for the most part focused about 're-discovering' CJEU landmark cases. A series of collective undertakings have re-opened the black box of landmark cases and have unearthed the various legal and political stakes and contexts in which these decisions had been framed and interpreted.[10] To a certain degree, this volume pursues a similar agenda with biographies. Just like cases cannot be reduced to the sole moment of deliberation but have to be repositioned in a long trajectory before and after the verdict, biographies of CJEU judges and AGs cannot be limited to their time at the Court but must be situated within their life-long professional trajectories. If one considers that EU law is not just a set of acontextual legal answers to acontextual legal questions about the authentic nature of law, then both cases and judicial biographies are essential levers to reposition the social, political and legal ramifications in which the Court and its case law have developed.

Truly enough, biographies have never been absent from Luxembourg. Unlike other EU institutions, the Court has always published in its *Recueil* and later, on its website, short notices providing biographical details on current as well as former judges' and AGs' professional trajectory. And, ever since the 1970s, the Court's most prominent judges and Advocates General have been offered *Festschriften* and Mélanges that magnify individual contributions to the Court's case law.[11] However, the issue in this volume is not to identify new heroes or 'founding fathers' to Europe's legal project. The editors have not brought their *preferred* list of judges but *all* Italian judges and AGs between the creation of the Court in 1952 and 2000. Drawing from the two decades of scholarly *acquis* of historians and sociologists, complemented with new empirical material and first-hand testimonies from former colleagues and *référendaires*,[12] the contributions go beyond official portraits, thereby displaying the increasing maturity and cross-fertilisation of a field of research developing in-between Law, Sociology and History.

[10] FG Nicola and B Davies (eds), *EU Law Stories. Contextual and Critical Histories of European Jurisprudence* (Oxford, Oxford University Press, 2017). Relating to two special issues of European Papers, and some methodological insights, see also A Vauchez, 'The Court of Justice in the Archives Project: An Initial Reflection' (2021) 6 *European Papers* 533; A Vauchez, 'EU Law Classics in the Making. Methodological Notes on *Grands Arrêts* at the European Court of Justice', in Nicola and Davies (n 10) 21; see also W Phelan, *Great Judgments of the European Court of Justice. Rethinking the Landmark Cases of the Foundational Period* (Cambridge, Cambridge University Press, 2019).

[11] A Vauchez, 'Keeping the Dream Alive. The European Court of Justice and the Social Fabric of Integrationist Jurisprudence' (2012) 4 *European Political Science Review* 51.

[12] See in particular the important archival work by V Fritz, *Juges et avocats généraux de la Cour de justice de l'Union européenne (1952–1972). Une approche biographique de l'histoire d'une révolution juridique* (Frankfurt, Klostermann, 2018) 396.

4. THE COURT'S EMBEDDEDNESS IN THE ITALIAN LEGAL FIELD

While the literature has brought back to light some individual biographies, the particular richness of this volume is in its provision of a collective biography of all Italian judges and Advocates General up until 2000,[13] thereby allowing the reader to draw more general conclusions on the Court's embeddedness in the Italian legal field. What may be striking at first sight is the relative diversity of profiles, even if it is within the limited social, gender and ethno-racial boundaries of the Italian legal profession of the times.[14] Under the European judicial robe, one finds a variety of breeding grounds and career paths to 'European legal glory': former ministers and seasoned politicians, treaty negotiators, high magistrates, professors, etc.; this diversity of backgroundsmaps out an Italian field of European law that goes beyond the Italian judiciary. Yet, while judicial nominations depend on many factors and contingencies (political majorities of the time, personal connections to ministers and *Presidente del Consiglio*, social networks, etc.), there are continuities and regularities that can be identified.

First of all, among the continuities, it is not difficult to identify the central role of legal academia, as only very few Italian judges or AGs have not been full time professors. Their specialisations may be quite diverse: one can find, at least in the early generations, specialists in labour law, competition law, civil law, civil procedure, etc. However, the Naples School of International Law occupies a special place in this map as it has brought various generations of international law professors into the field of EU Law and later at the court, just as it did for the European Court of Human Rights and for the International Court of Justice: Francesco Capotorti, Antonio Saggio, Antonio Tizzano, and Giuseppe Tesauro. The over-representation of legal academia (compared with French or German judges) entails the under-representation of other groups or institutions such as the members of the *Consiglio di Stato* (with the exception of Riccardo Monaco, who was also a much esteemed professor of International law), and more strikingly from the legal profession (with the late exception of Nicola Catalano, who served as State attorney at the time of his appointment at the Court of Justice). As the years pass, the Court itself becomes a breeding ground as the first generations of *référendaires* working for Italian judges or AGs move to academia or

[13] In addition to the work by Bailleux (n 1) and Vera Fritz (n 12) quoted supra, see: A Arena and A Losanò, 'Nicola Catalano (1910–1984): Eurolawyer Extraordinaire' (HEC Working Paper 2022/05, Alcide de Gasperi Centre for Research at the EUI), available online; A Boerger, 'At the Cradle of Legal Scholarship on the European Union: The Life and Early Work of Eric Stein' (2014) 62(4) *American Journal of Comparative Law* 859–892; W Phelan, 'The Revolutionary Doctrines of European Law and the Legal Philosophy of Robert Lecourt' (2017) 28(3) *European Journal of International Law* 935–957; and the homage to Pierre Pescatore in the symposium: 55(4) *Revue de la Faculté de droit de l'Université de Liège* (2010).

[14] S Hennette-Vauchez, 'More Women – But Which Women? The Rule and the Politics of Gender Balance at the European Court of Human Rights' (2015) 26(1) *European Journal of International Law* 223–227.

to EU institutions' legal services and become potential nominees (following the model of Antonio Saggio who had been initially called upon to join Capotorti's cabinet at the Court in 1979 and would be nominated judge at the Court of first instance ten years later).

5. THREE DISTINCTIVE TYPES AND ONE MISSION AT THE COURT

This mapping allows us to draw a tentative typology of Italian judges and AGs with three distinctive attributes – the balance of which has changed over time. First come the legal diplomats who have been historically dominant in the early years of the Court, sometimes with a passage at the *Consiglio del Contenzioso Diplomatico* or some expertise on behalf of the Ministry of Foreign Affairs. Among them, one can think of figures such as Massimo Pilotti, who had famously been an important State lawyer in the interwar period, negotiating treaties and acting a deputy secretary general of the League of Nations in its last and infamous years, but also individuals as different as Rino Rossi or Nicola Catalano who had acted under a variety of guises in representing Italy.[15] Then come the statesmen politicians of the law who lacked the legal specialisation in international or European law, such as Federico Mancini, a prominent professor in labour law and close collaborator of Bettino Craxi, and Antonio La Pergola, a highly esteemed professor of constitutional law but also a former member of the European Parliament and Minister of European Affairs: both of them had strong entrepreneurial conceptions of the law. One should also mention the less cosmopolitan Giacinto Bosco, who came to the Court after a longstanding ministerial career as a Christian-Democrat. The third and last category is that of the specialists, most of them law professors who, like Francesco Capotorti or Giuseppe Tesauro, were appointed at the Court in light of their legal expertise in the field of European law.

What is striking beyond the diversity of Italian Euro-lawyers involved at the CJEU is their brokering role in the defence of European legal integration.[16] As the essays in this volume present their entire career before and after the Court, one is able to assess the variety of roles they have played, many of them in the field of EU law. These include working successively as law clerks (Saggio) legal agents representing the Italian government (Catalano, Monaco, Rossi etc.), litigants pleading in EU law affairs (Catalano, Trabucchi), members of the European Commission's Legal service, and law professors committed to the establishment of EU law as a new academic discipline. These figures were able

[15] See in particular M Eperlding, 'Juristes internationalistes, juristes mixtes, Euro-Lawyers: l'apport de l'expérience semi-coloniale à l'émergence d'un droit supranational' (2022) 22 *Clio@Themis. Revue électronique d'histoire du droit* 1, 8.

[16] A Vauchez, 'Communities of International Lawyers', in CPR Romano, K Alter and Y Shany (eds), *Oxford Handbook of International Adjudication* (Oxford, Oxford University Press, 2013) 65[illegible]

to move across the private-public, national-European, legal-political, practice-academic borders of EU law. In other words, when contextualized in the judges' biographies, the Court appears as just one moment in entire lives often (even if not always) devoted in large part to the development of EU law. Some would use their passage at the Italian Constitutional Court to get involved in the hard cases of accommodating EU law in the Italian legal order.

As an example of this accommodation, in the *Granital* judgment (1984), Antonio La Pergola pushed for the possibility for ordinary judges to set aside national norms that were contrary to directly applicable EU provisions without involving the Constitutional court, thereby opening the way for deeper legal integration. Others contributed as professors to the writing the first treaties, teaching the first courses and formalising the principles of a new body of law. For instance, Capotorti also took part in many expert bodies, such as the European Parliament committee on institutional affairs in charge of drafting the treaty on the European Union, also known as the 'Spinelli treaty'. Others worked for the EU institutions' legal service, as Nicola Catalano had done before joining the Court, or as Ezio Perillo, Mancini's former *référendaire*, was a jurisconsult at the European Parliament legal service and then a judge at the *Tribunal* or General Court since 2016. Others engaged in strategic litigation before the CJEU, bringing no less than 16 preliminary references to Luxembourg from Italian lower courts, thereby acting as 'transmission belts'.[17] Last but not least, there were some who acted within the Ministry of European Affairs in negotiating EU treaties, such as Antonio La Pergola, who served after his mandate at the Italian Constitutional court and promoted the so-called La Pergola Act, which attempted to ensure a swift compliance with the obligation to implement Directives in due time, thereby avoiding the risks of infringement procedures, etc. In other words, the collective of Italian Euro-lawyers acted as 'double agents', shaping EU law in Luxembourg while receiving and promoting it in the domestic legal order, contributing 'from Rome' as much as 'from Luxembourg'. As such, the collective legacy of this group is to have firmly rooted Italy in a European law path.

6. CONCLUSION

Today, this collective portrait of an Italian way of EU law that is deeply enmeshed in academia and, for the very first generations, well connected with the Ministry of Foreign Affairs may appear more as a representation of the past rather than the present. Not just because all these members of these early years have now passed away (most recently Giuseppe Tesauro in 2021), but

[17] T Pavone, *The Ghostwriters: Lawyers and the Politics Behind the Judicial Construction of Europe* (New York, Cambridge University Press, 2022).

also because the conditions for the nomination to the CJEU have profoundly changed since that time. There are indeed good reasons to believe that, just like for many other countries, the establishment of the 255 Panel in the selection of the judges,[18] and the rise of its *de facto* veto power 'on candidates' suitability to perform the duties of Judge and Advocate-General of the Court of Justice and the General Court' and their 'legal expertise, experience, suitability for the office of Judge, independence and impartiality' is progressively transforming the profile of the CJEU community.[19] It's all the more interesting as the panel under the lead of former *Conseil d'Etat* vice-president, Jean-Marc Sauvé from 2010 to 2018, has favored a more court-oriented definition of what it takes to be a good European judge in Luxembourg (judicial professionalism, impartiality) in contrast with the historically strong academic backgrounds and frequent diplomatic ties of this early Italian way of EU Law.

[18] Ever since its creation in 2010, two Italian lawyers have taken part on this panel: Luigi Berlingue in representation of the Parliament (2014–2018) and Silvana Sciarra, (since 2022) as President of th Italian Constitutional Court.

[19] See M Lasser, *Judicial disappointments. Judicial Appointments Reform and the Rise of Eurc pean Judicial Independence* (Oxford, Oxford University Press, 2020).

17

Comparative Legal Reasoning (Overt and Covert) in the Work of the Advocate General

ELEANOR SHARPSTON KC*

1. INTRODUCTION

LET ME BEGIN by echoing the neat observation of my colleague and friend, former Advocate General Michal Bobek, 'It is indeed very strange to listen to a marine biologist's description of what fish are like if you happen to be a fish!' He and I have both had the privilege of being 'fish' inside the very public goldfish bowl that is the Court of Justice of the European Union (the CJEU). Like fish in such a bowl, we have spent some of our time gazing thoughtfully out of the bowl at the outside world. Much of the time, however, we have been swimming around observing the fellow inhabitants of our little universe.

I would also warmly endorse Michal Bobek's statement, 'I was happy when I wasn't followed but I obliged people to think'.[1] I respectfully agree with the sentiment behind that very important statement. It is the job of the Advocate General to sit down and really think through the issues raised by the case about which they are writing. Having done that, it is then the Advocate General's job to lay the choices available to the Court squarely before the judges and require them, if they disagree with the solution being proposed, to think carefully about why they are disagreeing. I am tempted to add here that, where the Court decides not to follow its Advocate General, it would do everyone a service if it explained clearly in the judgment why it has made that choice. That is normally not the case, however. Where the Court expressly references the Advocate General's Opinion, it usually confines itself to some anodyne statement with which it

* Eleanor Sharpston served as an Advocate General at the CJEU from 2006 to 2020. She is the Arthur Goodhart Visiting Professor in Legal Science at the University of Cambridge for the academic year 2023–2024.

[1] Comment made during Michal Bobek's oral presentation at the conference whose proceedings have been collected in the present volume.

agrees. Although it is naturally pleasant for the Advocate General, reading the judgment, to see a reference to their earlier work, such a reference does little to advance one's understanding of the interplay between the Opinion and the ensuing judgment.

Thus, for example, in Case C-64/16 *Associação Sindical dos Juizes Portugueses v Tribunal de Contas* the Court says,

> In the present case, as the Advocate General observed in point 32 of his Opinion, the dispute before the referring court in the main proceedings concerns the annulment of the administrative measures under which the remuneration of members of the Tribunal de Contas (Court of Auditors) was reduced and the reinstatement of sums withheld pursuant to Law No 76/2014.[2]

That information comes straight out of the order for reference. It does not represent some special flash of inspiration or legal insight on the part of the Advocate General. Indeed, in the very next paragraph the Court goes on to refer to the file submitted to the Court,[3] from which it was 'apparent' that the amounts withheld from the remuneration of the persons concerned had not been repaid to them, to conclude that 'the main proceedings have not become devoid of purpose' and that the order for reference was therefore admissible.[4] That was not, however, exactly the point that Advocate General Saugmandsgaard Øe was making in the passage from his Opinion cited by the Court in its judgment.[5]

In that case, there were two challenges to admissibility: from the Commission, relating to the adequacy of the content of the order for reference,[6] and from the Portuguese Government, relating to whether the request for a preliminary ruling had become devoid of purpose.[7] Both the Advocate General and the Court concluded that the reference *was* admissible.[8] Had the Court wished to show clearly that it agreed with the Advocate General's reasoning and conclusion on both challenges to admissibility, it could have said so in a single sentence.[9]

[2] See *Associação Sindical dos Juizes Portugueses v Tribunal de Contas* Case C-64/16 ECLI:EU:C:2018:117 [2018], para 24.

[3] That is, the file sent to the CJEU by the national court making the reference for a preliminary ruling, which often contains useful additional background information.

[4] See paragraphs 25 and 26 of the judgment.

[5] Point 32 of the Opinion reads, 'In fact, contrary to the Portuguese Government's contention, the dispute before the referring court does not relate to judicial independence as such, as the principle of judicial independence is relied on solely as a plea in law, for the purpose of securing the annulment of the allegedly unlawful administrative measures under which the remuneration of the persons represented by the [Associação Sindical dos Juízes Portugueses] ASJP was reduced and the reinstatement of the sums improperly withheld from their salaries in application of Law No 75/2014.' At point 33 (not point 32), the Advocate General went on to say that an amending law had not fully put an end to the contested reductions and that when the order for reference was submitted 'the referring court was still under an obligation to adjudicate on the subject matter of the action'. Like the Court, the Advocate General concluded that the request for a preliminary ruling was admissible (point 34).

[6] See points 18–24 of the Opinion and paragraphs 19–12 of the judgment.

[7] See points 25–33 of the Opinion and paragraphs 22–25 of the judgment.

[8] See point 34 of the Opinion and paragraph 26 of the judgment.

[9] There is a rare precedent for the Court having done just that: *Hauptzollamt Hamburg-St Annen v Ebbe Sönnichsen GmbH* Case C-59/92 ECLI:EU:C:1993:167 [1993] (a case about determining the customs value of defective goods).

2. BEING YOURSELF AS AN ADVOCATE GENERAL

Is there an 'Italian way' of doing the job of judge or Advocate General? I do not venture to express a view as to whether there is a particularly 'national' way of being a reporting judge (a *juge rapporteur*). If I am qualified at all to offer an opinion, it is only in relation to the job that I had the pleasure and honour of doing: that of Advocate General. I do not think there is an Italian (or British, or Croatian, or Czech …) way of being an Advocate General. It is the only job at the CJEU in which you are allowed, quintessentially, to be yourself.

If you are a *juge rapporteur*, you spend your professional life trying to put together a text with which your judicial colleagues sitting with you in the chamber are going to be prepared to agree. That inevitably requires you at some point – perhaps, at many points – to submerge your own personality and your own culture and your own quirky ideas in the interests of getting a collective text through the *délibéré*. The glory of being an Advocate General is that you have freedom. You can have intense and passionate discussions with your nice, intelligent *référendaires*. They can alert you to the likelihood that, if you go down a particular path, the Court will probably not follow you. And at the end of the day, you can thank them for their valuable input, agree that they are probably right about what the Court will do, and then say, with a gentle smile, 'And now we will finalise the text the way round that I want it to be'.

Part of 'being yourself' is, of course, related to your background: to your personal career path but also to the legal culture in which you were educated. Judges and Advocates General are not programmed automatons. The way that we do the job to which we were appointed reflects those aspects of ourselves. It also reflects our perception of what doing that job should properly imply. What I shall be saying therefore reflects my perception of what an Advocate General 'should' do, coloured in turn by my own background and my own professional career prior to joining the Court. It is therefore neither objective nor value-neutral.

3. SELECTING THE ADVOCATE GENERAL FOR A CASE

What about comparative legal reasoning and the Advocate General's work? Maybe we should start by asking, 'Who is going to be giving an opinion in this case, and why is the opinion going to be by this particular Advocate General?' You might think that there are (or at least that there should be) some guiding principles so that – for example – in a case in which understanding how the common law works is going to be fundamental, the case will be allocated to an Advocate General who has some knowledge of common law systems.

As far as I am aware, the case allocation system does not work like that. The actual allocation is made by the First Advocate General after the President has selected from amongst their colleagues the judge who is to act as *juge rapporteur*. There are a few house rules that are fairly self-evident and that are naturally respected. Thus, for example, infringement proceedings brought by the Commission under Article 258 TFEU are not allocated to an Advocate General from that same Member State. Although members of the Court are independent of the Member State that put them forward for appointment, it would be invidious to have to 'take sides' (very publicly) for or against one's own Member State in such circumstances. For a similar reason, a reference for a preliminary ruling from Member State X will not normally be allocated to an Advocate General from that Member State, unless it is so similar to a case that they are already handling that it would be an inefficient waste of resources to give it to a different Advocate General. Beyond that, case allocation is based upon a combination of aligning with known preferences and strengths of individual Advocates General, avoiding allocating a case to an Advocate General who is from the same Member State as the reporting judge,[10] and trying to distribute both legally uninteresting cases and the overall workload in a way that is fair and equitable.[11] Sometimes the resulting case allocation is inspired; sometimes it is rather curious.[12] I am not sure that you can discern a golden thread that consistently matches appropriate Advocates General to appropriate cases.

I should also like to ask the follow-up (perhaps slightly provocative) question: what is 'an appropriate Advocate General' for a particular case, anyway? Perhaps Advocate General X often does cases relating to a particular subject area (possibly because they have a *référendaire* who is tacitly acknowledged within the Court to have special expertise in that field). Where there is a 'chain' of cases in a specialist area – for example, milk quotas – it makes sense (in terms of resource allocation) to allocate further cases in that sequence to the same Advocate General. But that should not mean that a different Advocate General is barred from exploring that subject area and making their views known. After a while both the Court and the wider public outside the Court can probably make an educated guess, based on past pronouncements, as to what Advocate General X will opine in the next case in the sequence of cases attributed to them. It is no bad thing to hear from a fresh voice with a fresh perspective on the topic. So, that may sometimes also be a consideration in case allocation.[13]

[10] There is obvious good sense behind this informal house rule. Diversity of legal tradition normally promotes a wider view of the issues. However, the informal 'rule' is not always adhered to in practice. Thus, for example, in *Inuit Tapiriit Kanatami* Case C-583/11 P ECLI:EU:C:2013:625 [2013] Judge Thomas von Danwitz was the reporting judge and his compatriot Juliane Kokott the Advocate General.

[11] Even though the legally uninteresting case may eventually proceed to judgment without their public contribution, the Advocate General will still have expended precious time and effort analysing the case in depth before agreeing with the recommendation of the reporting judge to the '*réunion générale*' (the weekly general meeting of the Court) that the case does not need an Opinion.

[12] For example, the first two cases dealing with dismissals of female Muslim employees for wearing the Islamic hijab (judgments given by the Grand Chamber on the same day) were allocated to two different Advocates General: Case C-157/15 *G4S Secure Solutions* to my colleague Juliane Kokott and Case C-188/15 *ADDH* to myself. We reached radically different conclusions. How should we categorise that allocation decision?.

[13] Particularly if the topic is a sensitive one: see preceding footnote in relation to the first two hijab cases.

Against that background, let me turn to the impact of comparative law on an Advocate General's legal reasoning.

4. OVERT USE OF COMPARATIVE LAW

Sometimes a case includes a comparative law aspect because (bluntly) that is what the case requires. Sometimes, by its very nature, a case requires one to examine what solutions have already been explored in various legal systems. If one is fortunate, the analysis may be (greatly) assisted by a lovingly crafted research note, prepared at the direction of the Court's *réunion générale* for that specific case by the Court's own research and documentation division.

In former times, when the European Union (then the European Community) comprised fewer Member States and its Court of Justice was much smaller and much less burdened with cases, such a request would generate an exquisite piece of comparative law scholarship that covered *all* the legal systems of *all* the Member States and then offered a magisterial synthesis of the conclusions to be drawn from that exercise. Alas, those days are long past. There are many more legal systems. The other pressures on the research division are extraordinary.

Thus, nowadays even if there is a research note, it will only cover a cross-section of legal systems in the hope of giving the reader a flavour of how the problem is addressed in the various legal traditions across the European Union. Say to any self-respecting comparative lawyer, 'The note covers a cross-section of legal systems', and the natural response will be, 'What on earth do you mean? You cannot just pick a random civil law system and a random common law system! Each system has its own individual features.' But that is perforce what the Court now does – and of course, it is not perfect.[14]

If there is no research note but you decide, nevertheless, that you need to do your own investigation, there are obvious limitations. First, there are limitations of space. What are you going to want to fit into the Opinion (given that there is an informally agreed average page limit for each Opinion and that using more pages in this Opinion means using less in another Opinion to stay roughly on target overall)? Next, there are limitations of time – because as sure as the sun rises in the east, someone will always be chasing you to get the Opinion out as quickly as possible. Then, there are limitations of language. It would be lovely if one were able to access all the material that was relevant so that one could read it and research it all. Yet, even if you are blessed – as I was – with

[14] Sometimes elements of such research notes do indeed find their way into Opinions. Sadly, Advocates General are not meant to acknowledge such contributions openly and to thank the colleagues in the research and documentation division for their thorough work. Instead, we pretend that it is all attributable to our own unaided brilliance. However, recently these comparative law notes are being made available to the wider public on the CJEU's website albeit only in French (full text) and English summary only): see https://curia.europa.eu/jcms/jcms/p1_2170124/en/.

a very talented and very hardworking team of *référendaires* who have a lot of different languages between them, that does not mean that you can access everything.

5. COVERT USE OF COMPARATIVE LAW

So much for the overt comparative law. What about the covert comparative law?

By 'covert comparative law' I mean the input that comes from the Advocate General's own legal tradition and their own legal and professional background. I thoroughly endorse the view already expressed by Michal Bobek that those factors are likely to have a significant and useful predictive value in foreseeing the direction in which a particular Advocate General is likely to go in any given case. The individual's personal background should also not be overlooked.

Perhaps the most insidious effect of such factors is their impact upon the assumptions that we make. As lawyers, we all bring to the reading of a legal file certain assumptions: assumptions that were hard-wired into us during our own legal training. The problem is that my legal background may lead me tacitly to assume 'white' whereas your legal background may lead you tacitly to assume 'black'. Unless we both make our assumptions explicit, putting them out there in the open, some very strange things may happen in the subsequent discussion between us.

One's perception of the case is a very personal perception, as is (indeed) the shape that one gives to the text that one is preparing. True, all Opinions have a similar generic structure. Thus, in an Opinion in a case that arises out of a reference for a preliminary ruling, there will be an initial section that explains why the case is important and what the Court is going to have to decide when ruling upon it. That will usually be followed by an exposition of the relevant EU law and national law, a summary of the facts, and a recital of the questions referred by the national court. But what happens thereafter will depend very much on your professional background, your writing style and – above all – what you personally regard as important and unimportant amongst the issues that you feel that you need to address. Here, I can only reiterate that the Advocate General has so much more freedom than his counterpart, the *juge rapporteur*.

To my mind, at least, there are two overarching constraints. On the one hand, as the Advocate General you want to write an Opinion that is intellectually respectable: a text that can decently take its place in the theoretical and academic literature in that area of EU law. On the other hand, what you write must be operationally sound. At a strictly practical level, what you are recommending needs to be capable of being put into effect by an overworked official in a small provincial town in a distant region of a different Member State from the one from which the reference to the Court was made.

6. CONCLUSION

An Advocate General is writing for many different audiences. They are (of course) writing for the Court, to assist the Court in deciding the case.[15] But the Advocate General is also writing for the Member States' legal advisers, for the European Commission, for the lawyers working in private practice, and for the wider academic audience. The Advocate General must not, therefore, write an Opinion that is intelligible only to those who share their legal background. That may influence whom they choose to work in their team of *référendaires*. Throughout my time at the Court, I made sure that my team was balanced in terms of legal background (not all British, not all common lawyers but also civil lawyers) and professional experience (academic, civil servant, practitioner).

Above all, however, it is the Advocate General (the team leader and the Member responsible for assisting the Court) who must learn on the job what to do, and how to do it, to offer the maximum assistance and the maximum value-added in the Opinion that is being prepared.

[15] That is precisely how Article 252 TFEU defines the job of being an Advocate General: 'The ourt of Justice shall be assisted … by Advocates-General'. The second sub-paragraph amplifies the b-description by stating that, 'It shall be the duty of the Advocate-General, acting with complete npartiality and independence, to make, in open court, reasoned submissions on cases which, in ccordance with the Statute of the Court of Justice of the European Union, require his involvement'. rticle 20(5) of the Statute then sets out the criteria for when an Opinion is required.

18

Impact of the National Legal Traditions on the Role and Activity of the EU Judges

SINIŠA RODIN*

IT IS NEARLY self-evident that the activities of the Court of Justice of the European Union (the CJEU) amalgamate the legal traditions of its Member States. The question as to whether or not the CJEU has, over time, forged a distinctive legal tradition in the realm of EU law remains a subject of ongoing debate.

The way how the Court is composed, structured and how it operates in practice is unique and barely comparable to any other court of highest jurisdiction. When addressing the question as to whether or not national legal traditions affect the work of the Court it is only rational to expect a positive answer. After all, the judges and Advocates General have national legal educations, have extensively practiced national law, and are embedded in cultural traits of their respective States of origin and education.

In this chapter, I will explore several key questions. Firstly, I will provide an explanation of my interpretation of tradition, encompassing the concept of legal tradition. Additionally, I will examine whether traditions possess an inherent quality of goodness. Secondly, I will endeavour to identify the actors or agents involved in shaping a tradition, with particular consideration given to the role of the CJEU. Lastly, assuming the existence of a distinct EU legal tradition fostered by the CJEU, I will explore its interactions with national legal traditions and discern the evolving trends within it.

1. WHAT IS A TRADITION?

In its plain meaning, the English word 'tradition' originates from the Latin word *traditio*, meaning a surrender, delivery of possession, but also a teaching,

* Judge, CJEU, ideas and opinions expressed in this text in no way express those of the CJEU and are presented as an academic contribution unrelated to the author's judicial position.

instruction or a saying handed down from earlier times. From there on, tradition is also understood as a transfer of social practices and culture from one generation to another. I take tradition to emerge from documented reiteration of certain human actions or behaviours.[1] Reiteration becomes practice, while documented description of that practice, often contextualised by normative claims or value judgements, stabilises as a tradition and ultimately, once the density of social artifacts becomes significant, – as a culture.

In the realm of law, such social artifacts include material and immaterial objects such as constitutions, treaties, laws, bar associations, individual (including fundamental) rights, faculties of law, law societies and courts of justice. Tradition and culture go hand in hand. Culture is hardly imaginable without a tradition and traditions operate within the context of a culture.

In the legal sphere, we speak about legal tradition and legal culture.[2] Eugen Ehrlich described how law emerges from individual cases. *Leges Barbarorum* emerged as codification of penal practice. 'Judicial decrees begin to awaken general interest. There are people who write them down, gather them, arrange them, and at the same time on all sides there arises a demand that every new legal case that is at all similar to an older one shall, so far as possible, be decided according to the same Legal Provisions […] In this way judicial decisions become Legal Provisions for they contain the norms for the decision of future cases'.[3]

An early representation of legal tradition, the transfer of God's laws to humanity and its stabilisation in form of the written word can be found in Christian iconography in which the motive of *traditio legis* represents '… Christ standing on a mountain holding an open scroll flanked by the apostles Peter and Paul', '… the composition, also referred to as the "*Dominus legem dat*" scene […]'.[4] Such laws of divine origin are not supposed to be questioned and are subsequently transformed in practice, tradition, and culture. Similarly, in a court of law, once a judicial decision is stabilised by repetition it becomes practice, well-established practice, jurisprudence constante, tradition and finally, a culture.

Participants of national traditions, being immersed in them, historically do not often look outside their own tradition. While it may be different for legal comparatists or internationalists, the fact remains that tradition develops through repetitive practice which is dominantly local, that is, being formed by

[1] Documented orally or in written forms.

[2] Among rich literature on legal tradition see e.g. F Wieacker and E Bodenheimer, 'Foundations of European Legal Culture' (1990) 38(1) *The American Journal of Comparative Law* 1; FG Nicola 'National Legal Traditions at Work in the Jurisprudence of the Court of Justice of the European Union' (2016) 64(4) *The American Journal of Comparative Law* 865; HJ Berman, *Law and Revolution: The Formation of the Western Legal Tradition* (Cambridge, Massachusetts, Harvard University Press, 1983).

[3] E Ehrlich, 'Sociology of Law' (1922–1923) 36(2) *Harv. L. Rev.* 130, 134.

[4] AF Bergmeier, 'The Traditio Legis in Late Antiquity and Its Afterlives in the Middle Ages' (2017) 56(1) *Gesta* 27.

local courts, applying local law, where local attorneys represent local clients. In such situations, a specific legal tradition may appear objective, as the inherently subjective descriptions provided by participants within that tradition are presented in an impartial or objective manner. This is possible as Paul Feyerabend would suggest '[...] because the participants and the tradition they project are nowhere mentioned in them. They are subjective because they depend on the tradition chosen and on the use the participants make of it.'[5] Feyerabend assumes that traditions are unaware of their historical grounding. For him, traditions are neither good nor bad, they just are. They assume desirable or undesirable properties only when compared with another tradition.[6]

2. AGENTS OF A TRADITION

2.1. Participants and Observers

Who are the agents of the legal tradition of the EU? Most generally, everyone taking part in practices that contribute to its formation. Eric Stein referred to lawyers and judges[7] but Advocates General, law clerks (*référendaires*) at the CJEU, legal academics, jurist linguists and experts, parties before the CJEU but also national courts and other actors can be included too. Some of them affect the formation of the European legal tradition directly as participants and some of them indirectly as observers.

The distinction between participants in and observers of a tradition was introduced by Feyerebend. In his words, '... [o]bservers want to know what is going on, participants what to do. An observer describes a life he does not lead (except accidentally), a participant wants to arrange his own life and asks himself what attitude to take towards the things that may influence it.'[8]

This difference is relevant on two counts. First, as traditions are developed by practices of their participants, the participant/observer distinction makes it possible to identify who the direct agents of a tradition are. Second, the distinction makes it possible to recognise that someone can be participant to more traditions than one and even a participant to one tradition and observer of another. For example, someone can simultaneously be a participant of tradition of liberal democracy, Christianity, and Mediterranean cuisine. Likewise, a judge of the CJEU is a participant of a tradition of EU law as they actively contribute to practices that are constitutive of it and, at the same time, can be an observer of the tradition of the law of the United States.

[5] P Feyerabend, *Against Method* (3rd ed, London, Verso, 1993) 225.
[6] ibid., 226.
[7] E Stein, 'Lawyers, Judges, and the Making of a Transnational Constitution' (1981) 75(1) *The American Journal of International Law* 1.
[8] Feyerabend (n 5) 217.

The distinction is not purely academic. As Vera Fritz has demonstrated in her chapter of this volume,[9] Massimo Pilotti, the first President of the Court of Justice of the Coal and Steel Community in 1952 was a participant to multiple traditions, including those of colonialism and fascism but also a participant in the traditions of internationalism and supranationalism. Furthermore, what appears to be pertinent regarding his appointment to the Court of Justice, and ultimately his presidency, is his association with the legal and juridical tradition that evidently was perceived as autonomous and independent from other traditions in which he had also taken part.[10]

2.2. Explicit and Covert Practice

Another distinction I would like to make is one between explicit and covert practice that contributes to the formation of a tradition. While the former manifests in a form that is presented to observers of the tradition, for example, in form of a formalised judicial ritual, such as a public hearing, or published judicial decisions and rules of judicial procedure, the latter comprises internal workings and communications of participants. In other words, participants of a tradition are familiar only with overt practices. On the other hand, covert practices and artifacts[11] are typically not fully documented nor publicly accessible but incline to stabilise and consequently to affect the formation of explicit ones. They may reflect institutional hierarchy (formal or informal), the nature of a discourse (eg, guided exchange versus open exchange)[12] or simply avenues of communication among participants (formal/informal, bilateral/collective

[9] V Fritz, 'Building the Foundations of the European Court of Justice: Massimo Pilotti (1879–1962)', in this volume.

[10] Being the President of the Supreme Court of the fascist-administered Province of Ljubljana and thus participant (or at least an observer) of the fascist tradition was apparently separable from being a participant in the Italian and international legal tradition as a judge of the Trieste Court of Appeal or international tradition of the League of Nations where he served as a Deputy Secretary General respectively. It is precisely the separability and discontinuity of traditions that made Pilotti's post World War II ascent to the presidency of the Court of Justice possible. Transition from one tradition to another entails an important legitimising function not dissimilar to the legitimisation of Jesus by reference to Melchizedek, a clear repudiation of Leviticus according to which only descendants of Levi can be entitled to priesthood. (Hebrews 7.17 – King James Version): 'For he testifieth, Thou *art* a priest for ever after the order of Melchisedec'. Pilotti embedded himself in the judicial tradition separate from any other. In his own words, by reference to Dante Alighieri, '… wherever there was dispute, a judge must be present to settle it. Ubicunque potest esse litigium ibi debet esse iudicium. Figuratively, Dante plays the role of Melchisedec, an ancient authority that pre-dates the undesirable tradition and legitimises agents of the new one. See Address given by Massimo Pilotti (10 December 1952), available at https://www.cvce.eu/obj/address_given_by_massimo_pilotti_luxembourg_10-december_1952-en-d6970fd1-3640-4ae8-b413-36807af803d0.html, accessed on 27 September 2023.

[11] Periodical informal meetings of judges (forum des membres) followed by a lunch (déjeuner des membres) is example of such an artifact.

[12] P Feyerabend, *Science in a Free Society* (London, Verso, 1978).

horizontal/vertical, etc.).[13] For example, an informal agreement (covert practice) concerning the order of speakers in a discussion may shape the explicit practice that crystalises in a form of judicial decision.

What is more, such covert practices or artifacts may serve as an invisible transporter of traditions that a judge is or used to be a participant in or an observer of. For example, a judge who simultaneously belongs to judicial and academic traditions and a judge who belongs to judicial and administrative traditions may entertain different habits when it comes to collegiality of discourse, organisation of work, or use of specific professional jargon. In other words, in shaping the tradition of EU law, the presence of multiple traditions that judges participated in or observed is a reality that must be recognised. While a large part of that process remains obscure, that obscurity appears to be more than a coincidence given the attitude of some judges, according to which they should speak only through their rulings.[14] It will probably never be known from the judicial decisions themselves to what extent and by what means the Italian constitutional choice of priority of international law, enshrined in Article 10 of the Constitution of the Italian Republic,[15] influenced the evolution of jurisprudence of the Court of Justice in *Costa v. ENEL*. However, research of individual agency discloses the pivotal role of judge Trabucchi, who understood the EEC Treaty as a foundation of a new legal order.[16]

2.3. Individual and Institutional Agency

There is a difference between the individual agency of actors within the CJEU and the institutional agency of the Court.

When judges, *référendaires* and other actors interact within the workings of the Court they act as agents of their respective traditions. On the other hand, when the Court acts as an institutional actor, by deciding cases and publishing its decisions, it acts as an institutional agent in a broader social context.

Feyerabend introduced a distinction between guided and open exchange. The former is such a form of communication in which '[…] some or all participants adopt a well specified tradition and accept only those responses that

[13] At the CJEU, judges communicate formally by written notes or during recorded meetings but also informally, at social occasions or in the corridors. Such communication can be bilateral or collective and may entail hierarchical relationships, such as between a judge and the référendaires, or between a president of a chamber and its member(s), or can be horizontal, ie, among peers. Such communication can, and often does, serve as a pretext to formalised practice.

[14] See A Arena, '"*Notre Nestor*, Monsieur le Juge Rossi" (1889–1974): an Internationalist's Contribution to the Making of a Supranational Legal Order', in this volume.

[15] Article 10: 'L'ordinamento giuridico italiano si conforma alle norme del diritto internazionale generalmente riconosciute'.

[16] See E Perillo, 'Alberto Trabucchi: the Defender of the European citizens' rights and the Van Gend & Loos ruling of the Court of Justice', in this volume.

correspond to its standards'. In contrast, in context of open exchange '[…] [t]he tradition adopted by the parties is unspecified in the beginning and develops as the exchange goes along. The participants get immersed into each other's way of thinking, feeling, perceiving to such an extent that their ideas, perceptions, world views may be entirely changed – they become different people participating in a new and different tradition'.[17]

Speaking about individual agency, the question is how those different traditions interact through the agency of individual actors. In other words, is the result of that interaction placed within an already existing tradition or is it an entirely new European legal tradition? As I have suggested at another place, '[…] it is impossible to deny that judges of the CJEU are educated in one (or more) of the Member States' legal traditions. It is only natural that their respective referential frameworks are based in and permeated with national legal culture, reasoning, and methodology. After all, the entire institutional edifice, including the CJEU did not fall from the sky but was devised by national jurists. In that sense, national legal tradition is not at all foreign to the European Union law but, on the contrary, represents its main cognitive source.[18] And it goes almost without saying that all Member States and all judges of the CJEU being co-equals, the discourse among them takes form of an open exchange, resulting in crystallisation of European legal tradition.

However, once the European legal practice becomes stabile and once the tradition has crystallised, the nature of the exchange becomes guided. It is guided by general principles of law, the values of the EU and the well-established case law of the CJEU which can be altered only exceptionally and only by a larger judicial formation such as the Grand Chamber or Plenary Assembly of the Court. In essence, judicial activity is dedicated to the reduction of initial complexity in which, at the beginning, many outcomes are possible while the completion of judicial work results in singular solutions.[19]

The question concerning institutional agency is the following: given the European legal tradition,[20] what is its specific contents and to what extent, if at all, should the Court actively and consciously promote it, as opposed to just deciding cases according to legal rules and rules of interpretation? Should the CJEU act as an institutional agent of the European tradition? I have already

[17] Feyerabend (n 12) 29–30.

[18] S Rodin, 'Constitutional Relevance of Foreign Court Decisions' (2016) 64(4) *American Journal of Comparative Law* 815.

[19] For an elaboration of judicial reductionism, see P Schlag, 'Spam Jurisprudence, Air Law, and the Rank Anxiety of Nothing Happening (A Report on the State of the Art)' (2009) 97 *Geo. L. J.* 803, 815.

[20] For elements of European legal tradition see S Rodin, 'Liberal Constitutionalism, Rule of Law and Revolution by Other Means' (2021) 26(2) *Il Diritto dell'Unione Europea* 203, 230–231 in which I suggested the following: supranational structure, separation of powers, independent judicial review, fundamental rights, liberties and values, legal protection of the weaker party (minorities, workers, consumers and individuals in general), and EU law as a vehicle of European integration.

indicated at another place that the attitude of the Court in defending the values enshrined in Article 2 TEU and the constitutional liberalism on which those values are based are a deliberate constitutional choice.[21] As a matter of fact,[22] the Court does protect those values as they make up part of the tradition of the EU.[23]

3. HOW THE TRADITION OF EU LAW INTERACTS WITH NATIONAL LEGAL TRADITIONS AND WHAT ARE THE TRENDS OF ITS CHANGE?

3.1. Interaction with National Legal Traditions

Talking about tradition of EU law means talking about the practice of the CJEU. It is a dialectical process in which the practice of decision-making stabilises in form of *jurisprudence constante* and evolves into a specific EU judicial culture where participating agents and artifacts define the creation of new practices, new traditions and, ultimately, new cultures.

However, considering the division of work between different levels of jurisdiction, EU and national, in which the CJEU interprets and national courts apply EU law, we should not forget that national courts, when applying EU law, operate by necessity within purely national legal traditions. It appears clear that national and EU legal traditions and legal cultures not only diverge in the procedural, ontological and hermeneutical sense but that the parallel existence of national and European courts by necessity permanently creates differences and possible conflicts between them.

The European Union is a meeting place of different national legal traditions. Being the Union of Equals it is understood that all national traditions of the Member States are, at least *prima facie*, legitimate.[24] This

[21] Rodin (n 20).

[22] See *Republic of Poland and Hungary v European Parliament and the Council* Case C-157/21 ECLI:EU:C:2022:98 [2022].

[23] Rodin (n 20) 240: '… there must be at least some awareness, within the tradition, of the world-outside-tradition, a notional hors-tradition, or an imaginable absence of one's own tradition. In that way a tradition (re-)constitutes itself in opposition to a notional hors-tradition, without having to be aware of particulars of any other specific tradition. In such circumstances [the] criterion for determining desirable and undesirable outcomes is tradition itself and only those outcomes that perpetuate the tradition are desirable. That is why the judiciary belonging to the tradition of constitutional liberalism defends and perpetuates that tradition when it delivers outcomes viewed as neutral from the liberal point of view. For, the absence of such outcomes is perceived as a threat to the tradition itself'.

[24] This is enshrined in Article 4(2) TEU: '2. The Union shall respect the equality of Member States before the Treaties as well as their national identities, inherent in their fundamental structures, political and constitutional, inclusive of regional and local self-government. It shall respect their essential State functions, including ensuring the territorial integrity of the State, maintaining law and order and safeguarding national security. In particular, national security remains the sole responsibility of each Member State'.

is, however, subject to the respect of values enshrined in Art 2 TEU.[25] As the CJEU has stated,

> The values contained in Article 2 TEU have been identified and are shared by the Member States. They define the very identity of the European Union as a common legal order. Thus, the European Union must be able to defend those values, within the limits of its powers as laid down by the Treaties.[26]

Art 2 values are themselves a result of evolution of EU law, starting from early judgments of the CJEU in *Internationale Handelshesellschaft*[27] and *Nold*[28] according to which '... the Court is bound to draw inspiration from constitutional traditions Common to the Member States ...'.[29] Together with principle of primacy/supremacy of EU law and facilitated by the process of comparative distillation[30] performed by the CJEU, European values on the one hand and national legal traditions on the other ideally amalgamate into what the CJEU has named the identity of the European Union, that is, its 'good tradition'. It is against that identity and that tradition that desirability or non-desirability of all other traditions is measured, including the undesirable elements of national legal traditions.

Interestingly, while there is a general obligation of national courts to interpret national law in conformity with EU law,[31] in the area of fundamental rights conform interpretation works in the opposite direction. Graziadei suggests that making reference to common constitutional traditions amounts to an invitation to comparative law and draws attention to the obligation to interpret the Charter of Fundamental Rights of the EU in harmony with those traditions.[32]

[25] According to Article 2 TEU: 'The Union is founded on the values of respect for human dignity freedom, democracy, equality, the rule of law and respect for human rights, including the rights o persons belonging to minorities. These values are common to the Member States in a society i which pluralism, non-discrimination, tolerance, justice, solidarity and equality between women an men prevail'.

[26] *Republic of Poland and Hungary v European Parliament and the Council* (n 22) para 145.

[27] *Internationale Handelsgesellschaft mbH v Einfuhr- und Vorratsstelle für Getreide und Futtermittel* Case 11/70 ECLI:EU:C:1970:114 [1970] ECR 01125, para 14.

[28] *J. Nold, Kohlen- und Baustoffgroßhandlung v Commission of the European Communities* Cas 4/73 ECLI:EU:C:1974:51 [1974].

[29] For discussion of constitutional traditions common to Member States see S Cassese, 'Th "Constitutional Traditions Common to the Member States" of the European Union' (2017) 4 *Ri Trim. Dir. Pub.* 939 and M Graziadei and R De Caria, 'The "Constitutional Traditions Common t the Member States" in the Case-law of the European Court of Justice: Judicial Dialogue at its Fines (2017) 4 *Riv. Trim. Dir. Pub.* 949.

[30] The term forged by J H H Weiler. See JHH Weiler, 'The Transformation of Europe' (1991) 10 *The Yale Law Journal* 2403.

[31] *Sabine von Colson and Elisabeth Kamann v Land Nordrhein-Westfalen* Case 14/8 ECLI:EU:C:1984:153 [1984], para 26: 'national courts are required to interpret their national law i the light of the wording and the purpose of the directive in order to achieve the result referred to i the third paragraph of Article 189'.

[32] M Graziadei, 'The European Court of Justice at Work: Comparative Law on Stage and Behin the Scenes' (2020) 13(1) *Journal of Civil Law Studies* 1, 28 referring to Article 52(4) of the Charte

The case of delimitation of legal traditions is far from being closed and the process of amalgamation has not always been smooth. National legal traditions from time to time overtly rub against EU law and case law of the CJEU and take part in formation of EU tradition. Three prominent examples can be mentioned.

First, the agency of high national courts, notably the Italian *Corte Constituzionale*, which introduced what can be described as a theory of countervailing power that limits transfer of national sovereignty to supranational level. The concept of *controlimiti*[33] and the *Frontini* reservation draw the line according to which the transfer of sovereignty, which is inherent in the Founding Treaties, cannot include the transfer of powers to Community institutions to 'violate the fundamental principles of the Constitution or the inalienable rights of man'.[34] A similar attitude was being expressed by the German Federal Constitutional Court in three well-known constitutional cases, commonly known as Solange I., Solange II. and Maastricht.[35] These reactions of high national courts not only facilitated fundamental rights standards to the review performed by the CJEU but also instigated the adoption of the Charter of Fundamental Rights of the EU as a source of primary EU law.

Second, in the *Taricco* cases[36] the CJEU accepted the principle of legality as interpreted by the Italian Constitutional Court by adding an exception to obligation of national courts to set aside national law incompatible with EU law. According to the CJEU, such an exception obtains where: '… disapplication entails a breach of the principle that offences and penalties must be defined by law because of the lack of precision of the applicable law or because of the retroactive application of legislation imposing conditions of criminal liability stricter than those in force at the time the infringement was committed.'[37]

Readiness of the CJEU to soften its stance in respect of fundamental principles of the Italian legal order is remarkable but not surprising. After all, the CJEU has a task to interpret EU law to ensure its uniform application in all Member States and, in that way, equality of Member States under the Treaties. However, this task does not include the harmonisation of national legal traditions beyond what is necessary to protect the values enshrined in Article 2 TEU.[38]

[33] See A Oppenheimer (ed), *The Relationship between European Community Law and National Law: The Cases* (Cambridge, Cambridge University Press, 2005); M Cartabia, 'Nuovi sviluppi nelle competenze comunitarie" della Corte costituzionale, nota a sentenza n. 232 del 1989' (1989) 34 *Giurisprudenza costituzionale* 1012.

[34] Italian Constitutional Court, Judgment of 18 December 1973, No 183, *Frontini v Ministero delle Finanze*.

[35] *Solange I*, BVerfGE 37, 271; *Solange II*, BVerfGE 73, 339; *Maastricht*, BVerfGE 89, 155.

[36] *Criminal proceedings against Ivo Taricco and Others* Case C-105/14 ECLI:EU:C:2015:555 [2015]; *Criminal proceedings against M.A.S. and M.B. (Taricco II)* Case C-42/17 ECLI:EU:C:2017:936 [2017]; Italian Constitutional Court, Judgment of 14 December 2017, No 269.

[37] *Taricco II* (n 36), operative part.

[38] For discussion of Taricco dialogue between the CJEU and Italian Constitutional Court see A Scaccia, 'The Lesson Learned from the Taricco Saga: Judicial Nationalism and the Constitutional

The third example concerns judgment of the CJEU in *Weiss*,[39] following which the BVerfG contended that:

> The Court of Justice of the European Union exceeds its judicial mandate, as determined by the functions conferred upon it in Article 19(1) second sentence of the Treaty on European Union, where an interpretation of the Treaties is not comprehensible and must thus be considered arbitrary from an objective perspective.[40]

In *Weiss*, the CJEU had to decide about the validity of certain decisions of the European System of Central Banks and of the European Central Bank, including, among other legal issues, the proportionality of such decisions in relation to objectives of monetary policy. Without entering into debate on the merits, I would like to focus on the methodological disagreement between the BVerfG and the CJEU, which concerns the application of the principle of proportionality. In German doctrine, a fully developed proportionality test comprises four elements, notably, legitimacy, appropriateness, necessity and balancing *stricto sensu*.[41] In the judicial practice of the CJEU the proportionality test is not always performed *in toto*. Reasons for that may be different but they boil down to judicial economy. If a regulatory measure fails the appropriateness test, ie, if it is not suitable for achieving the legitimate aim, there is no need to perform other steps, such as a test of necessity.

One of the principal objections that the BVerfG addressed to the CJEU in that respect was the absence, in *Weiss* of the fourth step of proportionality analysis – the proportionality *stricto sensu*. In the words of the BVerfG:

> When applied in this manner, as undertaken by the CJEU, the principle of proportionality … … cannot fulfil its corrective function for the purposes of safeguarding the competences of the Member States … As a result, the review of proportionality is rendered meaningless, given that suitability and necessity of the PSPP are not balanced against the economic policy effects – other than the risk of losses -arising from the programme to the detriment of Member States' competences, and that these adverse effects are not weighed against the beneficial effects of the programme aim to achieve.[42]

Review of E.U. Law' (2020) 35 *Am. U. Int'l L. Rev.* 821; D Gallo, 'Challenging EU Constitutional Law: The Italian Constitutional Court's New Stance on Direct Effect and the Preliminary Reference Procedure' (2019) 25(4) *European Law Journal* 434.

[39] *Proceedings brought by Heinrich Weiss and Others* Case C-493/17 ECLI:EU:C:2018:1000 [2018].

[40] BVerfG, Judgment of the Second Senate of 5 May 2020–2 BvR 859/15, paras 1–237.

[41] For a lucid analysis of German doctrine see J Bomhoff, 'Making Legal Knowledge Work: Practising Proportionality' (2023) 32(1) *German Repetitorium, Social & Legal Studies* 28.

[42] BVerfG, Judgment of the Second Senate (n 40) para 133.

Subject matter of the *Weiss* controversy aside, the CJEU has started to apply a fully developed four-pronged proportionality test in other areas of EU law, such as freedom to provide services[43] or protection of personal data.[44]

These three examples witness important developments in the evolution of practice of the CJEU; the protection of fundamental rights; deference to national legal traditions within boundaries of Art 2 TEU; and the evolution of proportionality tests more akin to those of the German legal tradition.

3.2. Current Trends of Change

The above-mentioned examples demonstrate the role of highest national (constitutional) jurisdictions as institutional participants in overtly shaping the legal culture of the EU. This kind of judicial dialogue requires judges to be knowledgeable about both EU and national laws and legal traditions, which is clearly the case. While national legal traditions do influence the practice of the CJEU in different ways (eg, shaping important legal concepts such as proportionality, or through the intellectual background of judges), there is yet another, covert, dimension of tradition formation. I would like to outline four trends of this covert type of change.

The first trend indicates an increased reference to national law. Whereas the CJEU is not competent to interpret national law, the fact remains that extensive parts of its judgments, notably the *cadre juridique*, extensively cite national legal provisions relevant to the case. In this way, a discussion of facts and law is narrowed to the circumstances of a case that may create an impression that the judgment is restricted to that specific national legal framework only.

The second trend, which is related to the first one, can be described as legal detailing, in which justifications are increasingly sought in legal authority, both black letter and *praetorian*, and less in the legal context and purpose that inform legal interpretation. This is partly as a result of the detailed nature of references for preliminary ruling, which are focused on solving the case at hand under the

[43] *AS 'PrivatBank' and Others v Finanšu un kapitāla tirgus komisija* Case C-78/21 ECLI:EU:C:2023:13 [2023], operative part of the judgment '… measure which is justified on grounds of public policy, referred to in Article 65(1)(b) TFEU; secondly, is appropriate for ensuring attainment of those objectives; thirdly, does not go beyond what is necessary for attaining them; and, fourthly, does not lead to an excessive impairment of the rights and interests protected under Articles 56 and 63 TFEU, which are enjoyed by the credit institution concerned and its customers'.

[44] *WM and Sovim SA v Luxembourg Business Registers* Joined Cases C-37/20 and C-601/20 ECLI:EU:C:2022:912 [2022]: 'According to settled case-law, the proportionality of the measures which result in interference with the rights guaranteed in Articles 7 and 8 of the Charter requires compliance not only with the requirements of appropriateness and of necessity but also with that of the proportionate nature of those measures in relation to the objective pursued (see, to that effect, judgment of 5 April 2022, Commissioner of An Garda Síochána and Others, C-140/20, EU:C:2022:258, paragraph 93)'.

specific facts and law which, when answered by the CJEU may not be applicable in all 27 Member States.

The third trend concerns an increased interpretation of EU law '*à la lumière*' of the Charter of Fundamental Rights of the EU. The Charter has been interpreted as binding not only on the institutions of the EU and on the Member States in vertical situations, but also in horizontal situations as well. What is more, the Charter is increasingly pleaded by the parties in attempts to re-interpret EU law.[45]

The fourth trend is of a procedural nature and concerns internal organisation of work and the implicit docket control that the Court performs when allocating cases to different formations of the Court. According to Article 60 of the Rules of *Procedure* of the Court of Justice, allocation to the Grand Chamber is warranted where 'difficulty or importance of the case' require so, or where a Member State or an EU institution require so pursuant to the third paragraph of Article 16 of the Statute. This clearly creates a pressure on the Court as an ever-increasing number of legal issues important for fine-tuning national and EU law are being presented as difficult or important to seize the Grand Chamber. In this way the Grand Chamber has established itself as a prominent institutional agent of amalgamation of national and EU legal traditions.

[45] For interpretation in the light of the Charter of Fundamental Rights of the European Unic throughout the text and the operative part see eg, *Ligue des droits humains ASBL v Conseil d. ministres* Case C-817/19 ECLI:EU:C:2022:491 [2022].

19

Judicial Biographies and Judicial Decision-Making: A Fish Reflects on the Work of Marine Biologists

MICHAL BOBEK*

1. INTRODUCTION: A TALKING FISH

HOW COULD ONE measure influence in judicial decision-making that takes place behind closed doors, in a world that wishes not to be seen? How could one evaluate the effects, whether they be individual, or cul-ural, in an environment carefully structured to dilute individuality for the sake of collegiality, wherein highly standardised outcomes conceal individual prefer-ences? Is there, in fact, any traceable, and thus potentially equally predictable, connection between a judicial biography and the decision-making of the given person on the bench? Furthermore, is it even possible to aggregate and analyse individual judicial profiles at a national-cultural level, implying that there is a distinct Italian, British, Czech or Finnish way of adjudicating, and hence such representatives of that culture are bound to exercise some form of synergic impact that amounts to national influence within an international institution, uch as the Court of Justice of the European Union (the 'Court')?

These questions emerged in my thoughts while I read the objectives outlined by the editors of this volume, and while having the privilege of listening – over two days – to the life stories of the past Italian members of the Court. It was a fascinating experience to witness the familiar names that, but for two of them, I reviously encountered only through their signatures at the bottom of past judg-ments, or their charcoal portraits hanging in the gallery of the former members at the Court, to suddenly come to life right before my very eyes. Names ceased to be just names. They became personalities imbued with human stories.

* Justice, Supreme Administrative Court of the Czech Republic; Visiting Professor, Institute of European, International and Comparative Law, University of Vienna Faculty of Law. Between 2015 and 2021 Advocate General at the Court of Justice of the European Union.

At the same time, the more inhuman, scientific part of me kept wondering: how exactly can one measure or single out the '*Italian Influence on European Law*', as the main title of this volume promises? In a similar vein, how can one account for '*Shaping EU Law the British Way*', as the title of another recently published volume states?[1] Is it genuinely possible to substantiate such propositions?

What I am about to undertake in this contribution may seem unorthodox. It essentially entails a fish, venturing out of its bowl to offer a collection of disjointed remarks to a group of marine biologists writing about the life of the fish. There is naturally a considerable danger of introspection bias on the side of that fish, which might only be mitigated by the fact that, despite a former (European) fish, it happens to be (naturally, only to its immense regret) a non-Italian variety, and thus with no vested interest in portraying any particular Italian fish in a specific light. Therefore, adhering to the constraints of respecting one's oath, collegiality, and institutional loyalty, what I offer here are observations that a scientifically minded fish with inside knowledge might make about the study of individual or collective influence of certain fish species on the life within the bowl and beyond.

2. JUDICIAL BIOGRAPHIES GOING CONTINENTAL

As has often been the case historically, the wind of inspiration towards Europe blows, at least partially, from U.S. scholarship. Across the 'pond', the drawing up of judicial biographies has served not only as a means of literary pursuit, but also for recounting the life and judicial views of a judge as evidence of his or her era and times. A prominent focus within the study of judicial biographies has been to draw connection(s) between individual personality and decision-making on the bench. As one contribution put it: 'while different balances may be struck between the classic biographical goals of portraying character and career, the prime object is to describe and relate the judge's personality, background, and belief system to his conduct on the bench and impact on the law and politics of his time',[2] adding that this 'highlights the one common denominator of the leading biographies: each illuminates relationships among a personality (independent variable), his court or institution (intervening variable), and his polity (dependent variable)'.[3]

[1] G Butler and A Łazowski (eds), *Shaping EU Law the British Way: UK Advocates General at the Court of Justice of the European Union* (Oxford, Hart, 2022).

[2] H Woodford Jr., 'Judicial Biography and the Behavioral Persuasion' (1971) 65 *The American Political Science Review* 704, 704–705.

[3] ibid., 705, footnote no 8, relating those goals and approaches to older contributions dating back to 1948.

Certainly, different authors may pursue distinct goals in drawing up biographies of individual judges.[4] Yet, in most judicial biographies, there is often an implied or even explicitly stated connection between the person and their decisions. After all, if that were not the purpose, why write a *judicial biography* in the first place? A judge is usually not chosen as the object of biographical study for his or her expertise in miniature gardening or groundbreaking inventions in cryptocurrency trading, which could warrant a biography in its own right, but rather *because* of his or her judicial role. That is inherent in the very connection between the words 'judicial' and 'biography'.

More recently, critical streams of legal studies push the same logic further. Individual biographies are transformed into data points for larger, aggregated data sets, which allow for an explanation of the past, or sometimes even promises of the prediction of judicial behaviour in the future. A specific social variable, extracted from individual judicial biographies, can be paired with the outcomes of past cases to explain judicial decision-making.[5] The same type of endeavour can naturally be attempted regarding international courts and international adjudication.[6]

Coming back to the level of *individual* judicial biographies, it is clear that the explicit or implicit promise with which those biographies come is *making the connection between the person and their judicial output*. Those promises are indeed less frequently put in hard or direct form, where anybody would be making causal claims or connections between a biography and concrete decisions. More frequently, the connections are being asserted at a higher level of abstraction: certain ideas or ideological background, that found their reflection in a judicial decision or line of case law, are being traced back to the individual judicial biographies. While naturally being more general and abstract, the nature of the claim remains essentially the same: because of a certain ideological background stemming from the biography, certain decision(s) were reached.

However, establishing such type of connection in the world of continental (civil) high courts, characterized by their distinct style and inner functionings, represents a challenge.

In a *common law* high court, the court consists of personalities who traditionally express their individual views through their own, distinct voice, by delivering individual judicial opinions (speeches). Internal (dis)agreement and

[4] Critically, see, RA Posner, 'Judicial Biography' (1995) 70 *New York University Law Review* 502, 512, who suggested that a great number of judicial biographies are essentially *ideological* pieces of prose, just as a tool for expounding the biographer's (own) judicial philosophy.

[5] See, for illustration, eg, O Ashenfelter, 'Theodore Eisenberg and Stewart J Schwab, Politics and the Judiciary: The Influence of Judicial Background on Case Outcomes' (1995) 24 *Journal of Legal Studies* 257.

[6] See, for instance, G Maučec and S Dothan, 'The effects of international judges' personal characteristics on their judging' (2022) 35 *Leiden Journal of International Law* 887 or L Epstein and J Knight, 'How social identity and social diversity affects judging' (2022) 35 *Leiden Journal of International Law* 897.

voting patterns are fully disclosed, and the reasons for them are made explicitly. While in many high common law jurisdictions, a collective judgment (*per curiam*) has become more prominent in recent decades, the option for judges to express an individual judicial view through concurring, separate or dissenting opinions remains available. Additionally, high judges from common law backgrounds have traditionally not been shy in making their views known to the outside world, whether it be (for continental standards) in a somewhat relaxed judicial style or writing extra-judicially. Overall, there has always been a legible (that is to say, in the sense of publicly known) person and personality, who leaves quite a clear, individualised paper trail, that encompasses both their judicial and personal views.

By contrast, in a high *continental* jurisdiction, to the outside world, there is *the court*, but not individual judges. Indeed, the traditional picture is one of '*des êtres inanimés*',[7] who are unknown to the broader public, or even kept anonymous.[8] A decision is by default collegiate, with (except for constitutional courts) no possibility for dissenting opinions.[9] That structural setting fosters internal consensus, which often comes at the cost of subtle to significant dilution of individual voices, including naturally the voice of the reporting judge. The language, and the style of collegiate decision, is significantly determined by the respective legal tradition. The strength of that conventional straitjacket may differ among the various continental traditions, but the product is the judgment of the court, not the personal judgment of judge X or Z. Upon arrival, the judicial acolyte is informed that this is the court's drafting practice and is given explicit instructions to set to one side his or her personal preferences and literary proclivities and leave them at the courtroom door, together with their coat and other belongings. Finally, within the same tradition, a judge is heavily constrained in what he or she may state publicly outside of the exercising of the judicial function.

Views might certainly differ on where, between these two indeed sharply articulated ends, one should place the present Court.[10] If not taking the traditional notional escape route of calling it a 'sui generis', to escape further need for classification, in my view, the Court today as to its inner functioning is certainly much closer to the continental high jurisdiction model.[11]

[7] Montesquieu, *De l'esprit des lois I* (Paris, Garnier Flammarion, 1979) 301.

[8] Going as far as in some Continental legal traditions, such as the French one in the not so recent past, not even disclosing the names of judges sitting in a given formation of the court in the decision but indicating that to be the decision of the 'court', or just giving the name of the president of the section, but not all the judges participating in the decision.

[9] Leaving aside the '*votum separatum*', which allows a judge in some continental systems, who voted against the judgment, not to sign the voting protocol. But that dissent is only recorded in the judicial file. There is no 'public' dissent in whatever form.

[10] See, for illustration, eg, FG Nicola, 'Luxembourg Judicial Style with or without the UK' (2017) 40(5) *Fordham International Law Journal* 1505 or P Gragl, 'The faceless court? The role of individual CJEU members' (2023) 30(1) *Maastricht Journal of European and Comparative Law* 15.

[11] As already suggested and explained in M Bobek, 'The Court of Justice of the European Union' in A Arnull and D Chalmers (eds), *The Oxford Handbook of European Union Law* (Oxford, Oxford University Press, 2015) 153–177.

All of this creates a 'hostile environment' to the promise that the study of judicial biographies holds: to establish a credible connection (in the logic of empirical scientific discovery, which is therefore to some extent verifiable)[12] between the personality of the individual judge and the outcome in the form of a decision. In other words, while the fascination with judicial biographies has successfully traversed the Atlantic, the legal culture and context necessary for drawing up, for examining and evaluating these biographies, have not made the same journey. This disparity renders the task of forming propositions about judicial behaviour, based on such biographies in the same manner as in the common law context, a somewhat perilous endeavour.

3. TRACING INFLUENCE: MISSION (IM)POSSIBLE?

Despite these challenges, there emerged a group of bold social scientists, mostly historians,[13] who chose to subtly infiltrate that forbidden territory and dared to peek behind the curtain into a world that does everything in its might to remain hidden from view. They are acutely aware of the issues of access and lack of primary sources for their study, when studying the decision-making of the Court. For that reason, for instance, in her ground-breaking work on early members of the Court,[14] and later on, with regard to the specific issues of the methodology of that study condensed into a chapter,[15] Vera Fritz has attempted a certain step to the side. As a result of the recognised scarcity of primary sources, she initially suggests that 'the biographies are not a goal in themselves, but rather a means to craft primary material which can be explored to study different aspects of the functioning of the court'.[16] Moreover, in terms of methodology, her work 'does not aim at producing any quantitative statistical analysis, nor does it seek to

[12] K Popper, *The Logic of Scientific Discovery* (London, Routledge Classic, 2012) 17 ff. Without opening that can of worms (on the nature of history and historical research), the alternative, naturally, is not to claim to carry out any empirical research at all, just to capture the larger context and social field. That is certainly possible; but, as will be discussed in the immediately following section, such promises are rarely kept.

[13] See, amongst others, eg, M Rasmussen, 'The Origins of a Legal Revolution – the Early History of the European Court of Justice' (2008) 14 *Journal of European Integration History* 77; the individual contributions in (2012) 21 (3) *Contemporary European History* 305; and B Davies, *Resisting the European Court of Justice* (Cambridge, Cambridge University Press, 2012). For the broader context, see also A Vauchez, *Brokering Europe: Euro-Lawyers and the Making of a Transnational Polity* (Cambridge, Cambridge University Press, 2015). More recently, cf. eg, C Kilpatrick and J Scott (eds), *New Legal Approaches to Studying the Court of Justice* (Oxford, Oxford University Press, 2019) or MR Madsen, FG Nicola, A Vauchez (eds) *Researching the European Court of Justice: Methodological Shifts and Law's Embeddedness* (Cambridge, Cambridge University Press, 2022).

[14] V Fritz, *Juges et avocats généraux de la Cour de Justice de l'Union européenne (1952–1972): Une approche biographique de l'histoire d'une révolution juridique* (Klostermann, Frankfurt, 2018).

[15] V Fritz, 'Judge Biographies as a Methodology to Grasp the Dynamics inside the CJEU and Its relationship with EU Member States', in Madsen, Nicola, Vauchez (n 13) 209–234.

[16] ibid., 213.

draw up correlations between the professional profiles present at the court and its judicial behaviour'.[17] Therefore, no direct connection, not even a correlation, between a judicial profile and certain judicial behaviour or decision-making patterns is said to be attempted.

However, later on in the same chapter, some kind of connection nevertheless begins to take shape. First, with the statement that 'the biographical approach generates a better understanding of why it [the Court] produced so ambitious case law in the first place',[18] then through setting out a sort of "collective biography" for the judges of the Court of the early 1960s, revealing that a majority of them were national politicians or high civil servants, whose 'arrival at the Court of Justice was mainly the result of a low point in their political careers',[19] but who kept good political connections back home,[20] and, with respect to their own political convictions, were 'militants of European integration'.[21] This not only led to their specific decisions in the early case law of the Court, but apparently also in navigating the repercussions of those choices back home: 'This ideological background, which was the result of the member states' judge recruitment choices, clearly explains why the Court of Justice became outright provocative in its case law in the 1970s, and considerably expanded the key legal principles established in 1963 and 1964.'[22]

In eventually moving beyond the mere description of an environment, network, or social field, quite solid *causal* propositions end up being made: a particular group of individuals made specific choices *because* of who they were and *due to* their original background, they got away with it. The Member States acquiesced to the revolutionary ideas concerning the new legal order.

I do not dare to offer any comment on that hypothesis, because I do not know. There is the obvious hindsight problem and the lack of a comparative sample, as is indeed the case with most propositions about historical events: today, we now know how history turned out. Would it have turned out differently if the Court in the late 1960s and early 1970s were not composed of what has been just described as a group of exiled national politicians, who were inexperienced in applying the law (as they had little judicial experience), but who were ready to make bold political proclamations instead?

The proposition that acceptance of the Court's decisions back home was facilitated by good political bureaucratic connections is equally hard to confirm. Is it possible to argue that, because a particular judge was well-received in their home country, and frequently travelled there to deliver lectures and to explain

[17] ibid., 216.
[18] ibid., 217.
[19] ibid., 226.
[20] ibid., 228. The arrival of the second Italian judge, Alberto Trabucchi, features prominently in the discussion, as an example in which political ties join family ties in making a selection.
[21] ibid., 230.
[22] ibid., 230.

the Court's early, indeed radical case law (which was later labelled as 'revolution' or even a 'coup d'Etat'),[23] such rulings were embraced?

These are again bold propositions, on which opinions might differ. Intuitively, personal contacts and good relations in the Member State certainly cannot hurt in communicating and clarifying the developments in Luxembourg. But would those contacts alone, together with a couple of FIDE Congresses, do the trick of convincing all the necessary national audiences back home? Or, could the reasons rather have been the higher degree of social cohesion and the social/professional landscape of the 1960s and 1970s, together with the fact that EEC law was at that time perceived to be a branch of administrative law, coupled with limited knowledge of what was in fact going on in Luxembourg and what that would eventually entail. Did all this help to create the initial absence of open resistance towards the emerging key doctrines of EEC law, irrespective of the social background of the (then) members of the Court?

The inherent challenge in evaluating any such propositions is that we view them with the lenses of our present social experience. In our contemporary setting, the answer would likely be 'no'. However, this perspective is again pre-determined by the present social context, in which a judge having too many lunches with the minister of justice might be viewed with some suspicion, and also the overall discourse is fragmented and particularised, with the basic issues being heavily contested, and ensuing in minimal social consensus and cohesion.

In any event, not only does fortune favour the brave, but so does a scarcity of data: those who pioneer into uncharted territory have the privilege of laying the first claim to it. The absence of data presents them with both methodological headaches and a distinct advantage over subsequent explorers. The first narrative to occupy this space tends to become entrenched. Whoever comes next, wishing to establish an alternative narrative, will have to rebut the already existing one without the benefit of data to support their challenge.

It remains nonetheless clear that, even if the authors of juidicial biographies are aware of methodological issues and the scarcity of primary sources, even if they initially proclaim to merely be setting out the social context, environment, or just the individual story of a judicial life, it rarely stops there. The temptation to make broader, essentially causal claims that connect the biography to the decision-making on the bench, becomes hard to resist, especially in view of the material already compiled and the effort invested.

In the remainder of this chapter, therefore, I will offer some additional thoughts on the study of judicial biographies and their influence, focusing on the two main roles that judicial biographies are supposed to fulfil: firstly, (collective) judicial biographies as a celebration, and secondly, (collective) judicial

[23] Cf. the various contribution titles on *Costa v ENEL* and other founding judgments in e.g. M Poiares Maduro and L Azoulai (eds), *The Past and Future of EU Law: The Classics of EU Law Revisited on the 50th Anniversary of the Rome Treaty* (Oxford, Hart, 2010).

biographies as an explanatory or even predictive tool for understanding judicial decision-making.

4. JUDICIAL BIOGRAPHIES: CELEBRATING THE CONTRIBUTION

Assembling judicial biographies is undeniably a worthy endeavour in and of itself. Such biographies are compiled not only because the individual held a notable position, but also because that person was a remarkable jurist. That said, the ultimate picture taken is there to document that person's life and their era, serving as a sort of time capsule or a snapshot in history. They do not necessarily make further assertions about the impact of that person on their choices within the judicial realm. When these biographies are put together, certainly along the lines of nationality, such collective biographies (like those of the Italian members of the Court in this volume, or the previously mentioned volume concerning British Advocates General) is drawn up to commemorate and to celebrate the achievements of those people, to pay tribute to their lives and their work.

For the reasons outlined in the previous parts of this chapter, such biographies are rarely able to identify *outward* concrete judicial influence (by the individual judge at the European level). However, if compiled in a collective biography, they may very well be able to map the *inward* influence, capturing the national patterns established within a given Member State as regards their nominations to the Court. In this way, and rather intriguingly perhaps, a volume that originally focuses on the national influence on the European law may in fact reveal itself to be a testament of the European (non) influence on national ways by disclosing that in spite of being a long-time member of the club, it is evident that discernible national patters persist, repeated over and over again, immune to any top-down European influence.

Beyond that, such collective biographies encounter the inherent challenge of pinpointing, let alone substantiating, the individual or cultural impact at the European level itself. That is quite understandable, given that international judiciaries are a complex social system, as well as the above-outlined nature of continental high courts, which conceal the influence of its individual members. However, this inherent limitation may pose a more significant problem in the case of a volume entitled '*The Italian Influence on European Law*' or '*Shaping EU Law the British Way*', because exploring the manner in which something was specifically shaped or influenced by a given national culture appears to be the key promise of the volume.

For instance, how exactly was EU Law 'shaped' the British Way? The already cited volume[24] contains primarily a collection of case notes in which the British Advocates General delivered Opinions, with accompanying comments as to how

[24] Butler and Łazowski (n 1).

the case eventually turned out, placing its outcome in the broader context of the development of EU law within the given area. In the cases reported, there was no doubt the *individual* shaping of EU law by somebody holding a UK passport, simply by virtue of such a person exercising the role of Advocate General in the given case. Yet, was there anything distinctively British about that influence? That puzzling question becomes more apparent when pushed to the *collective* level, in searching for a distinct British contribution to emerge from the various individual case studies, but not being able to identify much: was it an increased use of oral hearings in Court's proceedings,[25] or perhaps the well-known 'British sense of humour' in the Opinions of British Advocates General?[26] In the same volume, other contributors even seem to contest that there is a specific 'British way' of being an Advocate General.[27] '*Shaping EU Law the British Way*' thus eventually becomes a shorthand for singling out and celebrating the work of four extraordinary jurists nominated by the United Kingdom, while, in the same vein, gently affirming that 'being British does not exclude being European'.[28]

If understood in this broadest sense, making a 'contribution', 'shaping' or 'influencing' EU law essentially boils down to being there and participating in the decision-making. The problem with such a diplomatic proposition is that it lacks analytical depth and borders on being tautological – being there and contributing naturally entails contribution. Similarly, individuals nominated by one Member State made contributions on behalf of that Member State, because they were in Luxembourg and participated to the collective decision-making. The crucial unanswered question that remains, however, is the genuinely interesting one: to what degree, and how, did they in fact influence the case?

In sum, if the purpose is to pay homage by assembling biographies, one should focus solely on that: acknowledge the exceptional work of a group of jurists, but without promising much broader or structural discoveries in terms of concrete outward influence at the European level. What such type of assembled collective judicial biographies might nonetheless be better at providing is the mapping of the inward impact of the incoming European influence: all relevant national samples are there, and the national introspection might thus commence.

[25] G Butler and A Łazowski, 'Neither Advocates, Nor Generals: The UK Advocates General and the Shaping of EU Law', in Butler and Łazowski (n 1) 607, 609.

[26] ibid., 609-610. However, whatever the famous British humour might be, if it were to mean including the occasional artistic or literary reference, or even a joke, into an Opinion, that does not appear to be anything distinctively British – see examples in M Bobek, 'La Cour casse mais ne rit pas: Law and Laughter in the Opinions of Advocates General,' in C Barnard, A Łazowski, Sarmiento (eds), *Pursuit of Legal Harmony in a Challenging World: Essays in Honour of Eleanor Sharpston* (Oxford, Hart, 2024).

[27] For critical remarks in this regard, see AM Collins, 'Foreword', Butler and Łazowski (n 1) xxxiii, r N Fennelly, 'Shaping EU Law: Ireland and the Common Law in Europe', *ibid*, 29. See also the contribution of E Sharpston, 'Comparative Legal Reasoning (implicit and explicit) in the work of the CJEU', in this volume, not herself believing that there is any distinct 'British Way' of being an Advocate General.

[28] Butler and Łazowski (n 25) 621.

5. JUDICIAL BIOGRAPHIES AND THE STUDY OF JUDICIAL DECISION-MAKING

In the realm of judicial biographies, it was already outlined that authors frequently draw various types of connections, ranging from social fields or context, correlations, and even to outright causal claims. However, when it comes to continental courts, and in particular, the Court of Justice of the European Union, *who* and *what* can in fact be studied? In the closing section of this contribution, a couple of rather unassorted remarks on this theme are offered.

In view of the structure of the Court and its procedures, the study of Advocates General and their Opinions has traditionally been seen as a more fertile ground for empirical research[29] than those of judges. With regard to an Advocate General Opinion, a clear connection between a given person and his or her views expressed in an Opinion can indeed be made. However, in terms of evaluating the genuine impact of that one document, entitled 'Opinion of an Advocate General', there is both an upstream and downstream problem that a researcher is bound to immediately face.

In order to see genuine influence and shaping of the law by an Advocate General, one would have to consult at least some documentation *upstream* in the proceedings, which was there before the Advocate General in question wrote an Opinion (such as, the order for reference of the national court, the parties' submissions in the case), to see what the particular Advocate General was reacting to. If an academic observer were to study the 'influence of Advocates General' by examining only the Opinion against the Judgment, such an observer might too easily succumb to the temptation of overstating the importance of the contribution of an Advocate General's Opinion. Certainly, if one is left to believe that it was the Advocate General who came up with all the brilliant points themselves, then the picture becomes distorted. However, a much more nuanced picture emerges if one does not see the Opinion as the starting (or even the central) piece, but just as one stepping stone in a much more complex story called judicial proceedings, in which the views and positions of the Advocate General rarely emerge out of the blue, but are responses to the arguments and ideas put to the Advocate General by the referring court, the parties, or the previous case law of the Court itself.

Even with all of that knowledge, the key question then is the qualification of what takes place *downstream*, once an Opinion has been delivered. Even if an Opinion is not followed, in part or in its entirety, by the Judgment of the

[29] From the many contributions, see in particular N Burrows and R Greaves, *The Advocate General and EC Law* (Oxford, Oxford University Press, 2007) as well as the various contributions contained in the Vol. 14 (2011–2012) *Cambridge Yearbook of European Legal Studies*. For a more normative discussion of the role, see L Clément-Wilz, *La fonction de l'avocat général près la Cour de justice* (Brussels, Bruylant, 2011).

Court, does that imply that the Advocate General did not exert intellectual influence? There is no shortage of cases, including a number of my own, in which an Opinion was delivered that was neither referred to, nor, in substance, followed by the Court. However, from the structure of the Judgment, points raised, and the way in which that Judgment was eventually reasoned, I would consider that the Opinion did in fact play a considerable role in the deliberations of the Court. Such a 'problem of silence'[30] can only be overcome with an in-depth qualitative study of the substance of the case. Conversely, if an Opinion is partially or fully followed, is this genuinely due to the analysis of the Advocate General, or is it rather a natural and logically expected outcome, given the context of the case and the options on the table before the Court? All in all, a binary box of followed/not followed, based on (absence of) direct reference or the textual overlap in the operative part of the judgment, will provide but a skewed understanding of the true impact of an Advocate General.

Turning to the individuals within the judicial black box, the judges themselves, the challenge of accessing sources to study the influence becomes even more acute. Was there any measurable influence of an *individual* judge exercised in a given case? As a rule of thumb, naturally, one is right to assume that an increased level of influence is likely to be exercised by the reporting judge and the president of a given formation deciding the case. However, again, to what exact extent? In drafting for sure, but as far as the individual result is concerned? Three factors emanating from the continental judicial tradition and practice, ie, not specific just to the Court, are worth singling out in this regard.

First, the greater the number of cases a given court deals with, the stronger the role of the reporting judge is likely to be in 'his or her' cases, for the simple reason that other members of the same formation (that is to say, the other member of the deciding formation but for the reporting judge or the presiding judge) have plenty of work with their own cases. *In extremis*, in situations in which courts are overwhelmed, a reporting judge might effectively function as a solo judge in disguise, with the other members of the chamber of three or five judges simply mutually checking each other's outcomes but having no residual capacity in normal cases to contribute much to the actual thinking and drafting. Even in such situations, the president of the given formation should exercise greater involvement and oversight. Yet, in some jurisdictions, the reporting judge is, at the same time, allowed to act as the presiding judge in the cases where he or she is the *judge rapporteur*, thus uniting both functions in one person.

[30] Explicit judicial references to the Advocate General's Opinions tend to be 'positive' only, ie, approving. But not every positive citation of the sort 'as the AG has already stated in point X of their Opinion' automatically means that the Opinion was decisive for the Court. It can equally mean that the Court referred in this way to an ancillary point or detail, which it itself did not really wish to deal with. By contrast, 'negative' references to Advocate General's Opinions, with the Court stating that the Advocate General was mistaken, and it does not agree with the Advocate General's Opinion, are very rare. See, for illustration, *bpost* Case C-117/20 ECLI:EU:C:2022:202 [2022], paras 52 and 53.

Second, the larger the decision-making formation, the less substantive impact each individual member of that formation is likely to have on the reasoning of the final collegiate decision. From a certain number of judges onwards, it is difficult to have a meaningful, substantive discussion about a case with say 13 or 17 or even more people in the room. The dynamics of such a process can occasionally be somewhat paradoxical. The main reason for "going larger" in apex courts is to secure additional input and legitimacy for a given outcome: more members of a given jurisdiction embraced the solution. This provides a judgment by a grand chamber or a division of a continental jurisdiction, or a full court in a common law jurisdiction, with greater formal authority, essentially based on political legitimacy (the number of votes given in favour of a solution). At the same time, however, this often comes at a price in the form of a decrease in substantive, persuasive authority, as the final judicial product becomes too truncated as a consequence of the need to reach a sufficiently large voting majority, or even a consensus.[31] It also means that, unless a really exceptional case comes along, most of the individual members of the larger formations do not contribute much to the actual (positive) drafting process, but rather collectively engage in the process of elimination of propositions on which there is no general agreement.[32]

Third, in the continental tradition, in which true internal deliberation within a given formation do occur (ie, the first scenario just outlined has no materialised), the reporting judge remains a reporting judge: he or she submit the first draft, but then the case is partially out of their hands. Naturally, a strong reporting judge might be better at preventing their 'intellectual baby' from being altered beyond recognition, or at the very least, even if everything else is basically eliminated because somebody disagrees with a proposition, there remain some coherent line of argument. But in courts that do not allow for the swapping of the role of reporting judge based on the outcome of the deliberations and in the absence of concurring or dissenting opinions, one cannot state for sure that the reporting judge in a given case in fact agreed with the outcome tha he or she must eventually write up. It might also be that the reporting judge wa in the minority and ended up drafting a judgment he or she disagreed with.

In terms of the object of study, beyond the Judges and Advocates General, further level of complexity in making valid connections between a judicial biography and a judicial decision is the fact that, in a number of high jurisdiction today, including the Court, the drafting of a judgment (as well as, of course, a Opinion of an Advocate General) is a collective endeavour. 'Collective' refers t

[31] In detail see M Bobek, 'What Are Grand Chambers for?' (2021) 23 *Cambridge Yearbook of European Legal Studies* 1, 5–7.

[32] Eventually arriving indeed at what Stephen Weatherill once poetically called with the help of Charles Dickens as 'A Circumloquacious Statement of the Result, Rather than a Reason for Arriving at It' in his contribution to M Adams et al. (eds), *Judging Europe's Judges: the Legitimacy of the Case Law of the European Court of Justice* (Oxford, Hart, 2013) 87.

the fact that it is not only the judges that take part in the decision, but rather judicial teams of assistants, legal secretaries and clerks. While those genuine ghost-writers fall normally out of the picture in the study of judicial biographies and judicial influence on individual cases,[33] their contribution to the decision-making and final decision, in particular as far as its actual reasoning is concerned, can hardly be understated. In addition, it is precisely that level which hides potential for the study of collective national influence, beyond the study of Advocates General, judges, reporting judges, or chamber presidents. The projection of national legal thinking may not hinge so much on the court members themselves, but equally on a level below, specifically that which involves experienced legal secretaries (*référendaires*).

Finally, is it possible to shift the biographical focus from the individual to a group and conduct a study on their *collective* influence? Propositions that concern the influence exerted by a group of individuals nominated by the same Member State, might in fact be more difficult, and at the same time, easier to make.

On the one hand, those propositions may be easier to establish because the assertion to be made is less precise and clear-cut: it is not stated that Professor X turned a case in a given direction by his or her influence, but rather that a certain solution or approach came from a given legal system or culture. To support such a claim, what is needed is to establish the result and the origin – this is an approach that evidently came from system Z and is now part of EU law. What needs to be excluded, at the same time, is that the same approach could not have come from a different legal system, and that it was in fact sneaked into EU law by the representatives of that legal system, that is to say, it was not a purely comparative inspiration inserted by a third party.[34]

On the other hand, where the proposition regarding the collective influence of a specific group of individuals becomes more complex is about two implicit assumptions that are crucial to even be able to talk about 'cultural' influence. First, there must be a distinctive and recognisable national method, say Italian, British, or Finnish, of approaching cases and reasoning, or even 'legal thinking', which then also transpires at the European level, when approaching cases there.

[33] For one of the rare peeks behind the curtain, see eg, S Gervasoni, 'Des référendaires et de magistrature communautaire', in *Etat souverain dans le monde d'aujourd'hui: Mélanges en honneur de Jean-Pierre Puissochet* (Paris, Pedone, 2008) 105.

[34] It has been well-known that the Court relies on comparative scholarship as well on a dedicated research and documentation department providing it with research notes on given legal issue. A fraction of those studies are publicly accessible (at https://curia.europa.eu/jcms/jcms/p1_2170124/en), with a greater selection accessible within the Judicial Network of the European Union platform that is accessible only to the highest national courts united in the Judicial Network of the EU). The knowledge gained from such studies, as well as from comparative research carried by the members of the Court or their chambers, might lead to a situation in which the Court uses comparative inspiration that came from a given (national) system, without however that fact being in fact in any way distinctively attributable to the member from that given Member State (who might not have even sat in that case).

Second, the individuals selected to be members of the Court by that given Member State then ought to be in fact genuine representatives of that culture and way of thinking, which they then collectively and synergically project at the European level.

I shall deliberately refrain from engaging in a discussion about national legal culture.[35] Certainly, being socialised (if nothing else, by university studies of the law) within a given legal culture clearly bears an imprint on the way a lawyer thinks. There is likely to be a difference in approach to the law if a student in a law school learnt the law just by memorising definitions in a rather abstract way, or he or she was led to believe that law is a coherent system of rules discovered by dutifully following neatly packed algorithms and almost mathematical schemes for solving a case in their *Klausuren* (written exams), or was effectively left to swim from the very beginning in a chaotic sea of precedents, being great at rhetoric and advocacy, but never seeing the law as either a dogmatic nor a coherent system. The same is even more true for the overall outlook that comes with that socialisation in terms of preferences for certain interests, beliefs, or values, that often directly translate into institutional or constitutional choices within a given Member State.[36] Finally, it is equally true that in the absence of a distinct 'European solution', the natural reaction for any individual is likely to be to carry out, at a subliminal or even advised level, 'self-projection' of own thought processes and patterns at the European level and labelling that the 'European way'.[37]

Such propositions are intriguing to make, but are extremely difficult to genuinely establish without falling rather quickly into the realms of cultural stereotypes.[38] Moreover, the notion of legal culture competes with other variable

[35] Referring the reader instead to the contribution by Siniša Rodin in this volume, see S Rodin 'Impact of the national legal traditions on the role and activity of the EU judges'.

[36] For illustrations of such response structures of national constitutional provisions and othe examples of historically conditioned value differences between the East and West of the Union, se M Bobek, 'Fundamental rights and fundamental values in the old and new Europe', in S Douglas Scott and N Hatzis (eds), *Research Handbook on EU Law and Human Rights* (Cheltenham, Edwar Elgar, 2017) 309.

[37] For an example of such a projection of national solutions onto the European level, one ma for instance contrast the three options in terms of substantive solutions that lay in the front c the Grand Chamber of the Court in Case *Gottfried Heinrich* Case C-345/06 ECLI:EU:C:2008:20 [2008], coming from different legal traditions in Europe: German (and CEE European one), Frenc and English as far as the status of non-published (secret) legislation was concerned. But then, in h Opinion of 10 April 2008 (ECLI:EU:C:2008:212), AG Sharpston pleaded very convincingly for t (principled) German approach, and in this way (presumably) was not at all '*shaping EU law the Bri ish Way*', but very much '*the German Way*' in fact. The Grand Chamber of the Court in its judgme of 10 March 2009 chose the (rather deferential) French approach. In greater detail, see my case no in (2009) 46 *Common Market Law Review* 2077.

[38] It is certainly widely believed, for example, that the Germans like their proportionality and t protection of personal data, while the Nordic countries are champions of transparency and acce to documents, and Southern countries including Italy or Spain hold dear their culinary delights a their protection (not only of origin). But making the connection between such cultural stereotyp and individual cases, on the one hand, and each and all individual persons coming from those cou tries, on the other, is a different task.

for establishing any behavioural patterns. For example, what I experienced as being equally important in making some sort of guess as to how a person will think as a lawyer, was the professional background and previous experience of that person. A professor of law who has never seen a courtroom from the inside in his or her life is likely to think along different lines than an attorney, and the approach of a diplomat or a politician to a case put before them is likely to be different from that of a career judge. They are likely to think along different lines, primarily focusing on different issues, seeing different problems, and placing emphasis on slightly different elements contained in the case file.

Finally, another issue for assuming any collective influence is the question of representativeness: are the persons sent to Luxembourg genuinely the best representatives of a *national* legal tradition? Perhaps the answer to that question might differ in time.[39] Nowadays, with increasing demands for specialisation and linguistic skills, often even assessed at the national levels in a form of open competition, and later tested before the 255 Panel,[40] the profile of successful candidates tends to be much more international and, in this regard, perhaps less purely the product of their national legal culture and their domestic socialisation. More often than not, the persons nominated to the European jurisdictions are not always a national representative embedded that deeply within the national legal culture, but rather a European or international professional, who might have spent the majority of their previous career in EU or other international institutions, or abroad, and might have never even practiced at home in whatever legal profession. What that might mean for the legitimacy of the European judicial institutions, in view of the historical emphasis on the 'national envoys' to Luxembourg being well-known back home and having solid ties there,[41] is an intriguing question for another discussion.

[39] Even if not necessarily: for instance, as far as nominations by the Italian Republic discussed in is volume are concerned, starting with Massimo Pilotti, the common theme of a number of nominations made was because the proposed person was a renowned 'internationalist' or 'comparative wyer', therefore would be a suitable candidate for Luxembourg, but not because he would have en (at least publicly) selected for being a 'true Italian lawyer'.

[40] See already M Bobek (ed), *Selecting Europe's Judges: A Critical Review of the Appointment ocedures to the European Courts* (Oxford, Oxford University Press, 2015) and then in much eater convincing detail M de S-O-l'E Lasser, *Judicial Dis-Appointments: Judicial Appointments eform and the Rise of European Judicial Independence* (Oxford, Oxford University Press, 2020).

[41] As set out by Vera Fritz (above n 15).

20

Conclusion: Four Traits of the Italian Influence on European Law

FERNANDA G. NICOLA, DANIELE GALLO, ROBERTO MASTROIANNI, AND LORENZO CECCHETTI

1. INTRODUCTION: NO LONGER A FACELESS COURT?

THE PORTRAYAL OF the CJEU as a 'faceless court', a distant institution detached from the people in the Member States, its judges and bureaucracy shrouded in anonymity yet with considerable authority over the nterpretation of European Union (EU) law, has been a prevalent theme in cholarly discourse on European law for quite some time.[1] Contributing to his narrative, Eric Stein described the Court in the 1980s as 'Tucked away in he fairyland Duchy of Luxembourg and blessed, until recently, with benign eglect by the powers that be and the mass media, the Court of Justice of he European Communities has fashioned a constitutional framework for a ederal-type structure in Europe'.[2] This constitutional framework mentioned by tein entailed a doctrinal revolution led by the Court in the 1960s through the idge-made doctrines of direct effect and primacy of Community law. If this evolution triggered an avalanche of scholarship on the Court's institutional ole and political power, the attempt to open the 'black box' of the individual idges who participated to its secret deliberations took relatively a long time in U law scholarship.[3]

[1] See critical work debunking the idea of the 'faceless court', AH Zhang, 'The Faceless Court' 016) 38 *U. Pa. J. Int'l L.* 71 and P Gragl, 'The faceless court? The role of individual CJEU members' 023) 30(1) *Maastricht Journal of European and Comparative Law* 15.

[2] See E Stein, 'Lawyers, Judges, and the Making of a Transnational Constitution' (1981) 75(1) *merican Journal of International Law* 1. Cf V Fritz, 'Building the Foundations of the European ourt of Justice: Massimo Pilotti (1879-1962)', in this volume.

[3] While some of the early work appeared in the 1970s, N Condorelli Braun, *Commissaires et ges dans les Communautés Européennes* (Pichon, Paris, 1972), only recently, EU scholars have gun focusing on the role of individual judges and Advocates General beyond the long practice

A significant impediment to redirecting attention from the abstraction of the faceless court to the individual judges at the CJEU, as pointed out by some critics, is the institution's inherent secrecy and dearth of public scrutiny.[4] The secretive nature of deliberations within its judicial chambers not only poses a challenge in discerning the specific judicial reasoning of each individual judge, but has become part of its *raison d'être*. In fact, the Court's Statute protects the secrecy of its deliberations by affirming that '[t]he deliberations of the Court of Justice shall be and shall remain secret',[5] and every member of the Court of Justice and of the General Court reaffirms this commitment at the moment of their oath.[6] Because secret deliberations are central to the Court's own identity, they are not publicly accessible even after the opening of the CJEU historical archives that allows access after thirty years to the *dossiers de procédure* of the cases.[7] Nevertheless, recent scholarship underscores the historical significance of revealing the process and outcomes of judicial deliberations. It is now widely acknowledged that the fundamental *Van Gend en Loos* ruling of 1963 was decided by a narrow margin of 3-4, which highlights the alliances and divisions among the seven judges, as well as their distinct roles in the decision-making process.[8]

Another reason, advanced by comparative lawyers, on why focusing on the role of individual judges is not relevant to grasp collegial decision-making processes and the institutional culture of judges working in Luxembourg is that similar to a continental or civil law court, individual voices disappear in judicia

of Festschrifts that have been mostly addressed to a specialised and legal audience, for a larger EU studies audience, such as V Fritz, *Juges et avocats généraux de la Cour de Justice de l'Union euro-péenne (1952–1972): Une approche biographique de l'histoire d'une révolution juridique* (Frankfurt, Klostermann, 2018).

[4] See A Alemanno and L Pech, 'Thinking Justice Outside the Docket: A Critical Assessment of the Reform of the EU's Court System' (2017) 54(1) *Common Market Law Review* 129.

[5] Consolidated Version of the Statute of the Court of Justice of the European Union (2016), Article 35.

[6] Consolidated Version of the Statute of the Court of Justice of the European Union (2016), Article 2. Rule of Procedure of the Court of Justice (2019), Article 4. Rules of Procedure of the General Court (2023), Article 5.

[7] FG Nicola, 'Waiting for the Barbarians: Inside the Archive of the European Court of Justice' in C Kilpatrick and J Scott (eds), *New Legal Approaches to Studying the Court of Justice* (Oxford, Oxford University Press, 2020) 72 that explains 'When the secret deliberations are at stake, whether in their preliminary or final versions, the Court retains the power to 'blacken' or 'redact' the *dossiers de procédure* because 'under no circumstance shall access be given to documents relating to the secrecy of deliberation''.

[8] If Alberto Trabucchi and Robert Lecourt were the main advocates, supported by the Commission in favour of direct effect, the opposition to their views was not only expressed by the governments of Germany, Belgium, and the Netherlands but also by the *juge rapporteur* from Luxembourg, Charles-Léon Hammes, supported by German judge Otto Riese and Andreas Donner, President of the Court. See M Rasmussen, 'Revolutionizing European Law: A history of the Van Gend en Loos judgment' (2014) 12 *International Journal of Constitutional Law* 136, 153. See also P Gori, 'Souvenirs d'un survivant', in A Tizzano, J Kokott, and S Prechal (eds) *50th Anniversary of the Judgment in Van Gend en Loos, 1963–2013* (Luxembourg, European Union, 2013).

deliberations.[9] However, as recent scholarship has pointed out, the CJEU is a supranational constitutional court at the intersection of an international and domestic court. As comparative lawyers have pointed out, the hybridisation of civil and common legal traditions has produced a unique blend that can no longer fit into traditional comparative law taxonomies.[10] By working in constant dialectic among different legal traditions, through its legal doctrines and procedural norms, the CJEU has created a new dynamic legal tradition that cannot be reduced to a continental or civil law one.[11] This is also expressed by the self-understanding of the judges of a supranational court[12] that have become agents of the European tradition[13] in the process of creating a 'transnational fabric of integrationist jurisprudence'.[14]

An excellent example of this new European legal tradition is found in the rulings rendered by the CJEU under Article 267 TFEU, within the context of the preliminary reference procedure,[15] which do not constitute precedent in the strict sense, the overall structure of the EU legal order being different from the anglo-saxon or common law system.[16] As a matter of fact, two components of a precedent-like system are missing: the hierarchical relationship between the CJEU and domestic courts, and the duty to openly justify the reasons in case a *revirement* is made. In addition, there is no provision in either primary or

[9] M Bobek, 'Judicial Biographies and Judicial Decision-Making: A Fish Reflects on the Work of Marine Biologists', in this volume.

[10] See M Graziadei, 'The European Court of Justice at Work: Comparative Law on Stage and Behind the Scenes' (2020) 13 *J. Civ. L. Stud*. 2.

[11] See FG Nicola, 'National Legal Traditions at Work in the Jurisprudence of the Court of Justice of the European Union: Symposium: Foreign Law in Constitutional Courts'(2016) 64 *American Journal of Comparative Law* 865. See also Graziadei (n 9).

[12] See S Caserta and M Rask Madsen, 'The Situated and Bounded Rationality of International Courts: A Structuralist Approach to International Adjudicative Practices' (2022) 35 *Leiden Journal of International Law* 935, 935–7.

[13] See S Rodin, 'Impact of the National Legal Traditions on the Role and Activity of the EU Judges', in this volume.

[14] See A Vauchez, 'Keeping the Dream Alive: The European Court of Justice and the Transnational Fabric of Integrationist Jurisprudence' (2012) 4 *European Political Science Review* 65.

[15] Nicola Catalano played a pivotal role in the drafting of what is now Article 267 TFEU. In this regard, see T Pavone, 'Making the European Court Work: Nicola Catalano and the Origins of European Legal Integration', in this volume; A Arena and A Rosanò, 'Nicola Catalano (1910–1984): padre del rinvio pregiudiziale d'interpretazione e apostolo del primato del diritto comunitario' (2024) *Eurojus* 89; and M Rasmussen, 'Between contraints and innovation: the role of the Groupe de Rédaction and the legal shape of the EEC Treaty (2023) Jean Monnet Working Paper No 1/23, available online.

[16] As explained by G Bebr, *Development of Judicial Control of the European Communities* (The Hague/Boston/London, Martinus Nijhoff, 1981) and AG Toth, 'The Authority of Judgments of the European Court of Justice: Binding Force and Legal Effects' (1984) 4 *Yearbook of European Law* 1, 2–3. See also J Barceló, 'Precedent in European Community Law', in N MacCormick and S Summers (eds), *Interpreting Precedents – A Comparative Study* (London, Routledge, 1997) 416, and G Martinico, 'Retracing Old (Scholarly) Path. The Erga Omnes Effects of the Interpretative Preliminary Rulings', in D Gallo and L Cecchetti (eds), 'The Preliminary Ruling Procedure, Today: Revisiting Article 267 TFEU's Constitutional Backbone' (2023) 15 *European Journal of Legal Studies* 37, 42–43.

secondary law that provides that preliminary rulings are an autonomous source of law, separate from the provisions that they interpret, as would instead be the case if it were a formal system of precedents. On the other hand, there is no doubt that preliminary rulings produce *erga omnes* effects[17] and that, for this reason, the CJEU tends to avoid, at least openly, overrulings.[18]

Another significant institutional impediment to spotlighting individual judges in Luxembourg stems from the Court's complex organizational framework characterised by both visible and more concealed hierarchies. The CJEU is composed by the Court of Justice (CJ) and the General Court (GC, formerly the Court of First Instance) that are led by their respective Presidents who wield the authority to propose the distribution of the judges among the Chambers and allocate cases to reporting judges. The chambers play a crucial role in workload distribution and in fostering collegiality among judges. In the GC, these chambers consist of five judges, while in the CJ, they comprise three or five judges. For more intricate cases, convening a Grand Chamber with 15 judges, or exceptionally the entire court of 27 judges, is crucial to ensure the 'amalgamation of domestic and EU legal traditions'.[19] Finally, the Opinions of 11 independent Advocates General serve to bolster and guide the interpretative efforts of the Court. This institutional architecture renders it challenging to discern the distinct contributions of individual judges.

Not surprisingly, in addition to the individual roles of the Advocate General, the spotlight on judges has primarily revolved around reporting judges or *judges rapporteurs*, as well as Chamber Presidents who fulfill specific institutional and intellectual functions at the Court, and who aim to maintain consistency among the various chambers. Consequently, judges require time to acclimate to the Court's style and to the goal of maintaining a sense of 'common purpose' for the institution.[20] Conversely, a multi-term tenure holds significance for ascending its invisible hierarchy, not necessarily reflected by the formal *ordre protocolaire*, and potentially attaining positions such a

[17] See, amongst early commentators, AM Donner, 'National Law and the Case Law of the Court of Justice of the European Community' (1963) 1 *Common Market Law Review* 8, 15; see again Martinico (n 16).

[18] See D Sarmiento, 'The 'Overruling Technique' at the Court of Justice of the European Union in D Gallo and L Cecchetti (eds), 'The Preliminary Ruling Procedure, Today: Revisiting Article 267 TFEU's Constitutional Backbone' (2023) 15 *European Journal of Legal Studies* 107.

[19] See S Rodin, 'Impact of the national legal traditions on the role and activity of the EU judges' in this volume.

[20] See the groundbreaking quantitative and qualitative work on the role of the Chamber Presidents and judge rapporteurs, handpicked by the Court President, in shaping the jurisprudence of the Court and in creating a sense of 'common purpose' by C Krenn, 'A Sense of Common Purpose: On the Role of Case Assignment and the Judge-Rapporteur at the European Court of Justice', in M Rask Madsen, FG Nicola, and A Vauchez (eds), *Researching the European Court of Justice* (Cambridge, Cambridge University Press, 2022) and C Krenn, *The Procedural and Organisational Law of the European Court of Justice: An Incomplete Transformation* (Cambridge, Cambridge University Press, 2022).

President or Chamber President, or reporting judge in a Grand Chamber case, thereby influencing its *jurisprudence constante*.[21]

Given the pivotal role of judicial tenure in judges' aspirations to maintain influence within the CJEU, increasing scholarly focus has shifted towards the nomination and confirmation of judges following their six-year mandates. This attention aims to illuminate the opaque and non-uniform aspects of what is predominantly a decentralised process mainly within the executive branches of the twenty-seven Member States,[22] although with specific nuances according to national rules and traditions. In theory, Member States' governments could confirm the same judges indefinitely once they are initially nominated and have received a favorable opinion from the 255 Committee.[23] This Committee, established by the Treaty of Lisbon, aims to exercise tighter control over national candidate selections, which often lack transparent procedures.[24] Apart from the 255 Committee at the EU level, the sole means for judges to serve multiple mandates and ascend the formal hierarchy of the CJEU – eventually becoming Chamber President, Vice-President, or President of the Court of Justice or the General Court – is confirmation by their respective Member State government.[25]

Nevertheless, the turnover of CJEU judges has prompted some scholars to redirect their attention towards the permanent staff at the Court, notably the *référendaires* or law clerks in judges' offices or *cabinets*. These personnel, who often continue their service at the court beyond the judges' mandates, assume a crucial behind-the-scenes role, ensuring continuity in the work of the CJEU.[26]

[21] See A Lazović, 'Structuring perception: how structures of practice influence decision-making at the Court of Justice of the European Union' (PhD thesis, Florence, European University Institute, 2023) 74.

[22] See M Bobek (ed), *Selecting Europe's Judges: A Critical Review of the Appointment Procedures to the European Courts* (Oxford, Oxford University Press, 2015).

[23] See the 255 Committee, https://comite255.europa.eu/en/ explaining that 'The Judges and Advocates General at the Court of Justice and the General Court of the European Union are appointed by mutual agreement of the Governments of the Member States, after consulting the panel provided for in Article 255 of the Treaty on the Functioning of the European Union. That panel was created by the Treaty of Lisbon, which entered into force on 1 December 2009. Its task is to 'give an opinion on candidates' suitability to perform the duties of Judge and Advocate-General of the Court of Justice and the General Court before the governments of the Member States make the appointments'.

[24] See M Lasser, *Judicial Dis-Appointments: Judicial Appointments Reform and the Rise of European Judicial Independence* (Oxford, Oxford University Press, 2020) 371, which addresses that, with the looming enlargement of the Eastern and Central European countries, the 255 Committee responded to anxieties of both a neoliberal and intergovernmental nature: 'The resulting desire to control judicial activism can (and should) of course be read as demonstrating a fear of the horde of new European judges descending from the East'. But to attribute the fear entirely to this Eastern peril would be to oversimplify. At its core, this anxiety was arguably as neoliberal as it was intergovernmental in nature: the danger of judicial activism (ie, judges disrupting settled expectations via aggressive judicial decision- making) was every bit as pressing as the danger of judicial hack-tivism (ie, judges acting under governmental orders)'.

[25] Bobek (n 22) 1–23.

[26] See Zhang (n 1). M Cohen, 'Justices or Hostages?', in FG Nicola and B Davies (eds), *EU Law Stories: Contextual and Critical Histories of European Jurisprudence* (Cambridge, Cambridge University Press, 2017). A recent phenomenon in this respect is the increasing trend of appointing

On the other hand, for some scholars, the new focus has taken a more contextual approach. This entailed that each individual Advocate General and judge must be understood within their historical context and cultural background, the process of assimilation into the new transnational judicial network, and the need to become familiar with the European legal tradition, the Court's judicial style, processes, and its *esprit de corps*.[27] This approach, which informs the research beyond this volume, entails a deeper exploration of the linkages between the cultures of the Member States and the enduring contributions of legal professionals who bring with them diverse prior professional experiences to Luxembourg.[28]

2. THE FOCUS ON ADVOCATES GENERAL AND JUDGES

Despite the multiple impediments that have delayed the research on individuals at the CJEU, social scientists, lawyers and historians have begun delving into collective portraits of judges and Advocates General as part of a broader legal community in European law.[29] Among the pioneers, the work that traces the judicial path to the judgeship in the work of Sally Kenney,[30] Antonin Cohen[31] and more recently Mitchel Lasser should be remembered for highlighting the increasing 'professorialisation' in the path to the Court.[32] EU legal scholars such as Alan Dashwood, Noreen Burrows and Rosa Greaves, Takis Tridimas, Iyiola Solanke, Michal Bobek, Eleanor Sharpston and Laure Clément-Wilz have focused on the role of the Advocates General and how their professional backgrounds shaped their individual opinions as key players in the Court's

members of the CJEU that had previously served as *référendaires*. This choice presents the advantage of having scholars that have already assimilated the peculiarities of the work at the CJEU and are familiar with the procedures and the case-law.

[27] See A Vauchez, 'Keeping the dream alive: the European Court of Justice and the transnational fabric of integrationist jurisprudence' (2012) 4 *European Political Science Review* 1.

[28] See for instance G Butler and A Lazowski (eds), *Shaping EU Law the British Way: UK Advocates General at the Court of Justice of the European Union* (Oxford, Hart Publishing, 2022); see also W Phelan, 'The Revolutionary Doctrines of European Law and the Legal Philosophy of Robert Lecourt' (2017) 28 *European Journal of International Law* 935 and W Phelan, 'The Constitutional Audacity of Robert Lecourt' (2024) 3 *European Law Open* (forthcoming).

[29] See H Schepel and R Wesserlin, 'The Legal Community. Judges, Lawyers, Officials and Clerks in the Writing of Europe' (2002) 3 *European Law Journal* 2.

[30] SJ Kenney, 'The Members of the Court of Justice of the European Communities' (1998) *Columbia Journal of European Law* 101, 101–34.

[31] See A Cohen, 'Ten Majestic Figures in Long Amaranth Robes:The Formation of the Court of Justice of the European Communities', in A Vauchez and B de Witte (eds), *Lawyering Europe. European Law as a Transnational Social Field* (Oxford, Hart Publishing, 2013) 21–43; See also A Cohen 'The European Court of Justice in the Emergent European Field of Power: Transnational Judicial Institutions and National Career Paths', in Y Dezalay and B Garth (eds) *Lawyers and the Constitution of Transnational Justice* (New York, Routledge, 2012) 245–46.

[32] See Lasser (n 24) 380.

jurisprudence.[33] More recently, the most comprehensive biographies on judges and Advocates General (between 1952 and 1972) is the collection of materials in Vera Fritz's book,[34] who undertook the Herculean task with the intent to 'craft primary material that can be explored to study different aspects of the functioning of the Court'.[35] Focusing on individual judges, the work of William Phelan and Laure Clément-Wilz has shed new light on long-serving Presidents of the Court, such as Robert Lecourt and Koen Lenaerts.[36] Additionally, the project led by Stefan Vogenauer and Sigfrido Ramírez Pérez has begun collecting oral histories and testimonies of the Court's members and their staff through semi-structured interviews of 'those who worked at the Court in its formative years'.[37] This interdisciplinary approach between social scientists and lawyers in focusing on individual judges and Advocates General has been key to paving the way for new insights into the decision-making process at the Court and highlighting the underlying political struggles behind the text of the case-law.[38] This approach contrasts with the traditional focus on black-letter law and doctrinal analyses of cases, which often overlook the structural, historical, and material factors that influence judicial decision-making.

One could speculate why, despite some of the most revolutionary doctrines of direct effect and primacy in EU law having been articulated in the CJEU jurisprudence,[39] that a close look at the individuals who were actually making the 'transnational constitution', as Eric Stein called it, did not become a subject of

[33] See AA Dashwood, 'The Advocate General in the Court of Justice of the European Communi-ies' (1982) 2(2) *Legal Studies* 202; N Burrows and R Greaves (eds), The Advocate General and EC aw (Oxford, Oxford University Press, 2007); T Tridimas, 'The Role of the Advocate General in the evelopment of Community Law: Some Reflections' (1997) 34 *Common Market Law Review* 1349; Solanke, 'Independence and Diversity in the European Court of Justice' (2009) 15 *Columbia Jour-al of European Law* 89; M Bobek, 'A Fourth in the Court: Why Are there Advocates General in the ourt of Justice?' (2012) 14 *Cambridge Yearbook of European Legal Studies*, 529–561; E Sharpston, 'he Changing Role of the Advocate General', in A Arnull, P Eeckhout, and T Tridimas (eds), *Conti-uity and Change in EU Law: Essays in Honor of Sir Francis Jacobs* (Oxford, Oxford University ress, 2008) 20-33; L Clément-Wilz, *La Fonction de l'Avocat Général près la Cour de Justice de Union européene* (Bruxelles, Bruylant, 2010); I Solanke, 'The Advocate General: Securing Trust in e CJEU of Art 13 TFEU' (2012) 14 *Cambridge Yearbook of European Legal Studies* 698.

[34] See Fritz (n 3).

[35] V Fritz, 'Judge Biographies as a Methodology to Grasp the Dynamics inside the CJEU and Its elationship with EU Member States' in MR Madsen, FG Nicola, and A Vauchez (eds), *Research-g the European Court of Justice: Methodological Shifts and Law's Embeddedness* (Cambridge, ambridge University Press, 2021).

[36] See W Phelan, *Great Judgments of the European Court of Justice* (Cambridge, Cambridge niversity Press, 2019); Phelan (n 28) 935-37. See also L Clément-Wilz, 'La Bonne Europe du presi-nt Koen Lenaerts', in A Bailleux, E Bernard, S Jacquot and Q Landenne (eds) *Les récits judiciaires l'Europe, Diffusion, réception et coproduction (vol. 3)* (Bruselles, Larcier Intersentia, 2023) 169.

[37] See 'An Oral History of the European Court of Justice', available at www.lhlt.mpg.de/research-oject/an-oral-history-of-the-european-court-of-justice.

[38] See P Bourdieu, 'The Force of Law: Toward a Sociology of the Juridical Field' (1977) 38 *The astings Law Journal* 805, 818.

[39] See W Phelan, 'Robert Lecourt: The ECJ Judge as Journalist and Political Organiser' (2020) RiSS Working Paper Series; Phelan (n 28).

interest for the general public. With some recent exceptions today, in respect to Robert Lecourt, Pierre Pescatore and the first French Advocate General, Maurice Lagrange,[40] most bibliographical information has been relegated to the practice of *Liber Amicorum* for an expert audience. Our edited volume aimed at gathering data, often neglected, or dispersed in *Libri Amicorum*, about the background of individual judges and Advocates General. In following the German tradition of *Festschrift*, the practice of *Liber Amicorum* at the CJ and the GC has been an increasing celebratory way to portray the life and the contribution of the judges and Advocates General at the end of their tenure, with chapters written mostly by their colleagues, *référendaires* and professionals connected to the Court. In Italian legal academia these are called *Scritti in Onore* or *Studi in Onore* (studies in honour of) and they are written about the Italian judges and Advocates General at the Court who, for the most part, are also Italian scholars.[41] While not well-known among the general public, thanks to this practice, the portrait of an individual judge or Advocate General is very familiar to judicial, academic and diplomatic circles. The practice of *Scritti in Onore* or *Liber Amicorum* has not only concerned ECJ Presidents with a long mandate,[42] but also judges and Advocates General with one term tenure at the court.[43] As a result, between 198 and 2007, there were at least fourteen *Libri Amicorum* published about cour members.

Our volume draws on a variety of data to offer a 'collective biography' o Italian male judges and Advocates General, across a limited period of tim between 1952 and 2000.[44] In fact, no Italian women were nominated to the cour until Lucia Serena Rossi was appointed as a judge at the CJ in 2018, followe by Ornella Porchia who was appointed to the GC in 2019. Nevertheless, it i notable that the Italian government has never nominated a woman to serve as a Advocate General. This underscores the challenges inherent in the appointmen and confirmation procedures in Italy.[45]

[40] See V Fritz, 'Activism on and off the bench: Pierre Pescatore and the law of integration' (202 57(2) *Common Market Law Review* 475; L Clément-Wilz, 'La Cour de justice de Maurice Lagrange in M Mangenot (ed), *Un légiste de Vichy à la Communauté européenne. Maurice Lagrange: u biographie professionnelle* (2023); MO Baruch, *Servir l'Etat français. L'administration en France 1940 à 1944* (Paris, Fayard, 1997).

[41] See *Scritti in onore di Giuseppe Federico Mancini: Vol. 1 Diritto del Lavoro* (Milan, Giuffr 1998); *Studi in onore di Francesco Capotorti* (Milan, Giuffré, 1999); P Van Dijk and S Granat Menghini (eds), *Liber Amicorum Antonio La Pergola* (Roma, Instituto Poligrafico e Zecca del Stato, 2008); and U Leanza, A Tizzano, T Vassalli di Dachenhausen, R Mastroianni, P de Pasqua R Ciccone (Organising Committee), *Scritti in onore di Giuseppe Tesauro* (Naples, Editoriale Scie tifica, 2014).

[42] See 'The Court of Justice of the European Union under the presidency of Vassilios Skou (2003–2015)', available at https://curia.europa.eu/jcms/jcms/P_170283/en/.

[43] See D O'Keefe and A Bavasso, *Judicial review in European Union law: Liber amicorum Honour of Lord Slynn of Hadley* (Kluwer Law International, The Hague, 2000).

[44] For a definition of collective biographies see Bobek(n 9).

[45] See J Guth and S Elfving, 'Court of Justice of the EU and Judicial Politics', in G Abe A Krizsan, H MacRae *et al* (eds), *Routledge Handbook of Gender and EU Politics* (London, Rou ledge, 2021) 273.

3. THE ROLE OF JUDICIAL BIOGRAPHIES

The emphasis on judicial biographies is not novel in common law jurisdictions, given the central role of judge-made law and the significant attention paid to courts bound to their own precedents through the principle of *stare decisis*. For example, in the United States, Supreme Court rulings are frequently associated with the judges who deliver them, even though they require a majority to reach a decision, and even when delivered *per curiam*. This focus on the judge as the author of majority, dissenting or concurring opinions justifies the considerable interest in the biographies of individual judges, as they are perceived as accountable to public opinion. In common law countries, therefore, judicial biographies are often crafted for a general audience intrigued by Supreme or Constitutional Court Justices who, owing to their lengthy or even lifelong tenure,[46] have played crucial roles in their institutions during tumultuous periods, serving as Associate Justices, Presidents, or Chief Justices.[47] These biographies serve to illuminate not only their legal contributions but also their personal journeys and impacts on the course of legal history.[48]

While some biographies delve into the private lives of the judges,[49] others seek to show how the intellectual legacy of these justices, influenced by their past experiences, before their tenure at the Court, has shaped constitutional decisions.[50] Some of them have put forward new legal ideas or have promoted progressive or conservative notions about racial justice and gender equality that were embraced by Court's jurisprudence.[51] This large biographical literature goes beyond the United States, especially when addressing judicial trailblazers

[46] When judges have longer mandates they can have more influential institutional roles. For instance, life tenure has been famously justified as an effective way to ensure judicial independence even in *Federalist No. 78* by Alexander Hamilton. However, critics have shown that life tenure can become a source of anxiety when judges lack precise accountability mechanisms and there is no mandatory retirement age so that they can sit on the bench for decades with little oversight. See M Clark, 'Judicial Retirement and Return to Practice' (2011) 60 *Catholic University Law Review* 841.

[47] See, for instance J Biskupic, *The Chief: The Life and Turbulent Time of Chief Justice John Roberts* (New York, Hatchette Book Group, 2019); E Thomas, *First: Sandra Day O'Connor* (New York, Random House, 2019).

[48] See, for instance, some of the volumes of Library of Congress series, such as M Marcus (ed). The Oliver Wendell Holmes Devise History of the Supreme Court of the United States (George Washington School of Law). See also R Post, *The Taft Court: Making Law for a Divided Nation, 1921–1930* (Cambridge, Cambridge University Press, 2014) and MV Tushnet, *The Hughes Court: From Progressivism to Pluralism, 1930 to 1941* (Cambridge, Cambridge University Press, 2022).

[49] See 'Sandra Day O-Connor: First Woman on the Supreme Court', available at www.supremecourt.gov/visiting/exhibitions/SOCExhibit/Section1.aspx#SOCExhibit1.

[50] See Clarence Thomas' recent biography that explains his aversion towards affirmative action, C Robin, *The enigma of Clarence Thomas* (New York, Henry Holt, 2019); and S Sotomayor, *My Beloved World* (New York, Penguin Random House, 2013).

[51] See F Michelmann, *Brennan and Democracy* (New Jersey, Princeton University Press, 2005); J de Hart, *Ruth Bader Ginsburg: A Life* (New York, Knopf, 2018), which highlight how her advocacy for women rights shaped the intermediate scrutiny doctrine in the Equal protection jurisprudence, see Robin (n 50) and Sotomayor (n 50).

on constitutional and international courts ranging from Canadian, Australian and African tribunals.[52]

Our approach to judicial biographies diverges from in-depth individual portraits, opting instead for a collective biographical approach focused on a group of jurists connected through a professional network during a limited period of time.[53] This method aims to illustrate how Italian judges and Advocates General have influenced the development of EU law before, during, and after their mandates at the CJEU. Our volume examines both legal and non-legal facets of their careers, encompassing their geographical origins, legal educations, professional backgrounds, and political affiliations prior to their appointment. We aimed to discern how these factors influenced their symbolic authority within the Court and their standing within their respective communities upon returning home.

The collective biographies of the Italian jurists highlight the professional, personal and contextual differences that characterise the lives and careers of each judge during their time in Italy, in Luxembourg and when they go back home. As a result, this volume presents collective biographies that delve into the shared traits and unique characteristics of eleven individuals who were judges or Advocates General at the Court, exploring their diverse cultural and geographical backgrounds, legal expertise, political preferences and professional affiliations. It also examines how these factors contributed to the acquisition of their symbolic capital once they assumed their roles at the CJEU. Additionally, the volume explores how their acquired knowledge, authority, prestige and reputation at the Court influenced their standing upon returning to Italy, during or after their mandate.

What our collective biographical endeavour reveals is that at various historical junctures and by employing diverse methodologies, these Italian jurists have skillfully intertwined their local expertise and professional culture, deeply rooted in their legal language, juridical style and social norms. In doing so, they have played instrumental roles in the ongoing process of hybridisation and transfer of the evolving Italian style into the fabric of European law, subsequently serving as conduits for the Europeanisation of Italian law.[54]

4. TRACING THE ITALIAN INFLUENCE ON EUROPEAN LAW: THE WORK OF ART HISTORIANS

Through the data gathered from the biographies of Italian jurists at the CJEU, our objective is to 'trace' rather than 'measure' the Italian influence on Europea

[52] See D Dellora, *Michael Kirby: Law, Love and Life* (New York, Penguin House, 2012); J Dawur A Kuenyehia, G Mcdonald (eds), *International Courts and the African Woman Judge: Unveil Narratives* (Oxfordshire, Routledge, 2018).

[53] See Bobek (n 22).

[54] See J H Merryman, *The Civil Law Tradition: An Introduction to the Legal Systems of Weste Europe and Latin America* (Stanford, Stanford University Press, 1985) defining a legal tradition as 'set of deeply rooted, historically conditioned attitudes about the nature and role of law, about th organization and operation of a legal system, and about how the law is or should be made, applie studied, perfected, and taught'.

law. By tracing, we intend to discern the ways, attitudes and elements through which Italian judges and Advocates General contributed to shaping the Court's jurisprudence and the working culture in Luxembourg during the different periods marked by three generations we called pioneers, innovators and EU constitutionalists.

Comparative law, akin to an 'umbrella term for a discipline with multiple dimensions', involves traversing various realms.[55] Comparative lawyers embark on a journey that begins with describing foreign law, proceeds to comparing different legal systems, and culminates in explaining them by reevaluating their own. In this comparative expedition, they must trace the evolution of laws or judicial doctrines across legal systems. Tracing therefore necessitates the meticulous study and mapping of legal transfers,[56] often referred to as legal transplants in mainstream discourse.[57] Additionally, it involves a more contextualised examination of receptions, diffusion, or translations, aiming to understand how laws migrate from their original environments and transform in their new ones.[58] Such transformations are influenced by a myriad of factors including geopolitical considerations, colonial ties, and the exercise of prestige or influence by one legal system over another.[59] Examining legal influence alongside historical, political, and material contexts therefore offers a framework to understand the mechanisms by which the hybridisation of laws occurs, facilitated by lawyers, judges, or politicians who serve as agents of transfer. This process involves the integration of foreign elements into relatively autonomous legal systems that, much like the layers of a building, have stratified over time.

Consider an architectural metaphor that traces elements of the Italian style, akin to examining the church of *Santa Maria sopra Minerva* in Assisi. This Italian baroque church stands atop a Roman temple that dates back to the 1st century BC, which itself combines elements of Greek and Etruscan architecture, featuring six Corinthian columns, an architrave, a cornice, and a tympanum. Inside, the baroque architecture of the 17th century captivates the observer with its theatrical flair and opulent golden decorations. The heightened and ornately

[55] See M Reimann, 'The Legal Systems of The World Their Comparison and Unification' (2020) *International Encyclopedia of Comparative Law* 8.

[56] See G Frankenberg, 'Legal Transfer', in MC Foblets *et al.* (eds), *Oxford Handbook of Law and Anthropology* (Oxford, Oxford University Press, 2022) 333; G Frankenberg, *Comparative Law as Critique* (Cheltenham, Edward Elgar Publishing, 2016).

[57] See A Watson, *Legal Transplants: An Approach to Comparative Law* (Edinburgh, Scottish Academic Press, 1974) and for a critique P Legrand, 'The Impossibility of 'Legal Transplants' (1997) *Maastricht J. Eur. and Comp. L.* 111.

[58] See MM Prado, 'Diffusion, Reception, and Transplantation', in P Cane et al. (eds), *The Oxford Handbook of Comparative Administrative Law* (New York, Oxford University Press, 2020) 254. Merry, 'Legal Transplants and Cultural Translation: Making Human Rights in the Vernacular', in Goodale (ed) *Human Rights: An Anthropological Reader* (Hoboken, Wiley-Blackwell, 2009) 265.

[59] See M Graziadei, 'Comparative Law as the Study of Legal Transplants', in M Reimann and Zimmermann (eds), *The Oxford Handbook of Comparative Law* (Oxford, Oxford University Press, 2006) 441; FG Nicola and G Frankenberg, *Comparative Law: An Introduction to a Critical Practice* (London, Edward Elgar, 2024).

adorned columns were strategically utilised by the Catholic church to awe and inspire the faithful, countering the influence of the Reformation.[60]

In *Santa Maria sopra Minerva*, the Italian architectural style undergoes evolutions and witnesses stratifications of architectural styles. The eclectism of this church retains specific traits that persist through the centuries, discerned and described by art historians rather than measured.[61] Similarly, within the architecture of the Court's case-law and of the CJEU itself, an art historian can illuminate the continuity of Italian architectural traits and their evolution and integration over time. The focus thus lies not on measurement but on delving into contextual, structural, and historical descriptions of the Italian style. This approach aims to elucidate the genesis of each 'legal building', the creativity of the architects involved, and to compare their judicial styles and reasoning across three different generations. Our starting point is the recognition that architects represent the 'human factor'[62] central to the shaping and creation of legal doctrines, culture, and style within European law. Similarly, art historians play an equally crucial role in demonstrating that law transcends mere abstract technique; it is the product of the lives, creativity, and reasoning of judges and Advocates General in Luxembourg.[63]

In particular, the case-law emerging from the jurisprudence of the CJEU embodies the transfers and hybridisations of legal doctrines, principles, and styles originating from the diverse legal traditions of the Member States.[6 Judges interpret this body of law through a comparative law method that aim to synthesise and apply general principles or interpretation techniques from various legal systems to reach decisions.[65] Our starting question was how the changing Italian legal tradition played any role in shaping EU law including it legal style, its doctrines and narratives.[66] In doing so, we have sought to isolate the elements or traits of the Italian influence that have shaped directly or indi rectly the institutional culture, the judicial style, and the jurisprudence of the Court over time.

[60] See CS Wood, *A History of Art History* (Princeton, Princeton University Press, 2019).

[61] Differently from Bobek's metaphor in his chapter in this volume (n 9), likening the study c European judges and Advocates General to that of a marine biologist observing fishes in an aqua ium, we find the metaphor of art historians more fitting. Art historians breathe life into the wor of architects, illuminating the foundations upon which European law is built. See Lecture by W Phelan, Robert Lecourt: ECJ Judge and Constitutional Architect, Boston University (27 April 2023

[62] See L Clément-Wilz, 'An Institutional View on the Influence of Italian Judges and Advocat General', in this volume.

[63] See I Rowland and N Charney, *The Collector of Lives: Giorgio Vasari and the Invention of A* (New York, W.W. Norton & Company, 2017).

[64] See Rodin (n 19).

[65] See K Lenaerts, 'Interlocking Legal Orders in the European Union and Comparative Law' (200 52 *The International and Comparative Law Quarterly* 873.

[66] See FG Nicola, 'National Legal Traditions at Work in the Jurisprudence of the Court of Justi of the European Union' (2016) 64 *American J of Comp Law* 865.

This type of comparative work on the influence on European law from domestic law is not new. Indeed, it was pioneered by David Edward, the former Scottish judge appointed by the United Kingdom, who wrote at large on how the British lawyers deeply influenced the procedure, the culture and the style at the Court.[67] Additionally, one of us has called the 'Luxembourg judicial style'[68] a set of practices and procedures that have characterised the style of the CJEU often influenced by the judges of new Member States, or their national courts through the preliminary reference mechanisms.[69] More recently, the edited volume by Graham Butler and Adam Łazowski, entitled 'Shaping EU Law the British Way: UK Advocates General at the Court of Justice of the European Union', while differing in scope and methodology from this volume, continues this research path by tracing the influences of Member States on EU law and *vice versa*.

5. FOUR TRAITS IN THE ITALIAN INFLUENCE ON EUROPEAN LAW: STYLE, PROFILE, TRANSFER AND EFFECTIVENESS

What emerges from the rich biographies collected in Part I, bolstered by the heoretical contributions in Part II of this volume, are four traits of the evolving talian influence in European law, also referred to as *Italian-ness, Italian essence* or (the) *Italian way*. In drawing upon key findings from the volume, employing he metaphor of art historians who elucidate the pivotal role of architects in naking nuanced choices in designing their buildings, we trace four traits – style, profile, transfer and effectiveness – that are emblematic of the enduring attitudes owards the law among a cohort of Italian jurists who helped to shape the archiecture of European law.

The first trait, viewed through a comparative law lens, discerns the changng Italian style within European law.[70] Despite the overshadowing presence of French and German jurists in Luxembourg, the Italian legal tradition offers ignificant contributions often underplayed in the shaping of the architecture of he European jurisprudence. These include its adeptness in navigating diverse ontinental legal traditions, notably through the incorporation of Roman law rinciples. The Italian legal style is marked by a reliance on scholarly writings o address legal *lacunae*; the strategic deployment of formal legal reasoning, rticulated through elegant legal formulas; and the view that despite its folklore

[67] See D Edward, 'The British Contribution to the Development of Law and Legal Process in the ıropean Union', in BS Markesinis (ed), *The British Contribution to the Europe of the Twenty-First entury* (Oxford, Hart Publishing, 2002) 25.

[68] FG Nicola, 'Luxembourg Judicial Style With or Without the UK' (2017) 40 *Fordham Intl LJ* '05.

[69] See G de Búrca, 'The Mutual Judicial Influence of National Courts and the European Court of stice through the Preliminary Rulings Mechanism Evidence from the UK' (2020) *NYU School of ıw, Public Law Research Paper No. 20–25*.

[70] See JH Merryman, 'The Italian Style I: Doctrine' (1965) 18 *Stanford Law Review* 39.

of strict separation between legislative and judicial power, judges could make laws when they interpret creatively or 'evolutively'.[71]

A second trait revolves around the profile of the Italian jurists, and encompasses the educational, geographical, linguistic, and professional backgrounds that influenced their nomination to the CJEU. This focus enables us to elucidate both their overall profile and the type of symbolic capital they amassed through their legal careers, linguistic proficiency, international experience, and proximity to political power – whether initially in the Ministry of Foreign Affairs or later in the Prime Minister's Office – that ultimately propelled their nomination to the Court.

A third trait utilises insights from comparative law and contextual legal analysis to illustrate how Italian jurists played a pivotal role in transferring European legal thought into the framework of Italian law. Indeed, the robust network of Italian jurists at the Court facilitated the transmission of their knowledge back home, where legal professionals – particularly judges, lawyers, and academics in Italy – were keen to understand the legal innovations emerging in Luxembourg. This network served as a potent transmission belt for reintegrating European law and its principles into the judicial and academic fabric of Italian law.

A final trait emerges in the doctrinal trend promoted and expanded by almost the majority of Italian judges and Advocates General in advancing the protection of individual rights through doctrines of direct effect and effectiveness of EU law. This doctrinal trait shows the ability of the Italian jurists in Luxembourg to move beyond the formal logic of Italian judicial interpretation as mere application of statutes and to instead use creatively procedural tools to favour the effective protection of individual rights as a core Italian influence on European law.

5.1. First Trait: The Italian Style

Our collective biographical endeavour highlights traits that emerge in the *Italia[n] style*, defined by John Henry Merryman as a 'set of deeply rooted, histori[-] cally conditioned attitudes about the nature of law, about the role of law in th[e] society and the polity, about the proper organization and operation of a lega[l] system, and about the way law is or should be made, applied, studied, perfecte[d] and taught'.[72] The Italian style, particularly in a transnational setting, serves a[s] an archetype to comprehend not only the origins of civil law rooted in Roma[n] law but also the adeptness of Italian jurists in navigating between distinct cont[i-] nental legal traditions. Caught between the French positivist attitude and th[e]

[71] See JH Merryman, 'The Italian Style III: Interpretation' (1966) 18 *Stanford Law Review* 58[3–] 597; C Crea, 'What Is to Be Done? Tullio Ascarelli on the Theory of Legal Interpretation' (2015) *The Italian Law Journal* 181.

[72] See JH Merryman (n 70) 39.

German scholarly ambition, the *Italian style* has ingeniously walked a tightrope to reconcile the two.[73] Much like the French language, the Italian language offers some elegant legal formulas. However, akin to German, it also provides ample space for framing abstract legal concepts through the use of metaphors and other legal fictions borrowed by judges from the highly esteemed legal scholarship, known as *la dottrina*.

One hallmark of the Italian legal style lies in its eclectism in using or departing from a formal legal reasoning, expressed through refined legal formulations and Latin maxims, while also moving through a '*stratum* above which school, method, condificatoons and legal orders flow in the course of time'.[74] A good example of such eclecticisms emerges from the chapter on Alberto Trabucchi, in which the President of the Court, Robert Lecourt's speech in 1976 reveals his central involvement with his Italian colleague in the groundbreaking *Van Gend en Loos* judgment.[75] Lecourt explains that Trabucchi's 'thorough knowledge of Roman law, has been the basis […] of the clarity and the precision of some of the most famous grounds for our judgments, which have become the classic "selected passages" of Community law. […] Here too you have remained the vigilant guardian of civil law, the '*juris civilis custos*' as Cicero put it'.[76] This ability of the Italian jurists to use Roman law and precise juridical formulae to revolutionise European law through the creation of the doctrines of direct effect and primacy stems from the eclecticism of the Italian legal style.[77] Italian jurists navigate between the French tradition, the German tradition, and the revival of the Roman legal tradition in Bologna during the XII century, demonstrating an insatiable curiosity for other legal experiences, for example the pragmatic Anglo-American or the politicised Soviet legal traditions in the aftermath of World War II.[78]

However, during the Fascist era, Italian scholars deployed legal formalism and positivism to resist the political pressures of the regime in the adoption of the Italian Civil code of 1942. As Bianca Gardella Tedeschi explains, in the 1930s: 'Formalism became a trait of Italian scholarship, especially in private law, during the fascist era. The decision to detach law from society and shared values, has been later read as a way for bourgeois and non-Fascist lawyers and

[73] See L Lacchè, 'On the Italian Style: The Eclectic Canon and the Relationship of Theory to Practice as key-elements of Italian Legal Culture (19th-20th Centuries)' (2017) 34 *Journal of Constitutional History* 263, 266.

[74] Id., 269.

[75] NV *Algemene Transport- en Expeditie Onderneming van Gend & Loos v Netherlands Inland Revenue Administration* Case 26/62 ECLI:EU:C:1963:1 [1963].

[76] See E Perillo, 'Alberto Trabucchi: the Defender of the European citizens' rights and the *Van Gend & Loos* ruling of the Court of Justice', in this volume.

[77] G Marini, 'L'Italian Style fra centro e periferia, ovvero Gramsci, Gorla e la posta in gioco del diritto privato' (2016) 7 *Rivista Italiana per le Scienze Giuridiche* 95, 96.

[78] See F Vassalli, ''Estratatualita' del Diritto civile', in *Studi in Onore di Antonio Cicu* (vol II, Milano, Giuffre, 1951), 481–490 that promotes greater opportunities for continental jurists to study Anglo-American law.

judges to be able to be good jurists and at the same not embrace fascist values and projects'.[79] While Italian jurists adeptly employed formalism and deductive legal reasoning to resist politicisation during the Mussolini regime, by the late 1950s, this formalist structure came under criticism from civil lawyers. Scholars like Rodolfo Sacco began to employ comparative legal tools to challenge the rigidity and abstract nature of formulas employed by private lawyers.[80]

A second controversial aspect of the Italian style that emerges from Merryman's writing in the 1960s, is the frustration with the legislative folklore as the strict separation between legislative and judicial power. The Italian style was characterised by the orthodoxy of its legal sources above all legislation while judge-made law was discarded. However, such propositions were continuously challenged by scholarship, the jurisprudence of the Italian Constitutional Court and the nascent law of the European Communities.[81] Italian judicial interpretation was therefore in constant competition with doctrinal and authentic interpretations provided by scholars and legislators, respectively. Tullio Ascarelli (1903–1959) and Piero Calamandrei (1889–1956) were among the most prominent scholars who challenged the folklore of Italian judicial interpretations. Ascarelli was a Roman commercial lawyer and the son of Jewish lawyers and so had to leave Italy in 1939 because of the Mussolini Racial laws.[82] He was also a scholar of comparative law (open to the interplay between civil law and common law) and a fine scholar of legal hermeneutics. Hence his great 'openness':[83] indeed, when he came back to Italy from Brazil in 1949, he became a towering figure through his publications that advocated for 'the need to go 'beyond legal concepts', the ongoing 'quest of value judgments', and the aware ness that interpreting law is 'a creative and not simply a declarative activity'.[84]

Piero Calamandrei was a Florentine civil lawyer who participated in the drafting of the Italian Civil Code of 1942 as a leading scholar of civil proce dure despite being an Anti-Fascist. Later, Calamandrei was elected to the Italian Constituent Assembly in 1946 as a member of a liberal socialist party His positon on judicial interpretation was that statutes could be interpreted creatively through an evolutive interpretation, through general principles o

[79] See B Gardella Tedeschi, 'Italian Comparative: A Trait of the Legal System' (2024) *FI* (forthcoming).

[80] See R Sacco, 'Prospettive della scienza civilistica italiana all'inizio del nuovo secolo' (2005) 5 *Rivista di Diritto Civile* 417.

[81] See N Lupo and M Cartabia, *The Constitution of Italy: A Contextual Analysis* (London Bloomsbury Publishing, 2022).

[82] See T Amico di Meane, *Sulle Spalle dei Giganti. La questione metodologica del diritto compar ato e il suo racconto* (Naples, Editoriale Scientifica, 2022).

[83] Its 'cultural manifesto' can be found in T Ascarelli, 'Antigone and Portia' (2015) 1 *The Italian Law Journal* 167 (translated with notes by C Crea).

[84] See Crea (n 71) 187, which explains that 'The evolution of Ascarelli's thinking – as far as the complexity and the unity of the legal experience is concerned – originate from his background in commercial law, with its attention to empirical data and from the perceived inadequacy of codi fied law'.

through analogy because these are 'windows which open the word'. Therefore by using them 'the judge can, within the limits of the law, keep the law abreast of changing times'.[85] Calamandrei's view on the creative potential of judicial interpretation, through an 'evolutive interpretation', was also shared among many of our second generation of jurists – that we called the innovators – beginning with Alberto Trabucchi and his Florentine *référendaire* Paolo Gori.

Not surprisingly, Gori's contribution to the 50th anniversary of *Van Gen en Loos* addresses the pragmatic conception of Calamandrei, which doesn't entail the partiality of the judges, but rather the notion that judicial decision-making includes the application of both formal logic and also some meta-juridical elements, such as 'values', that are part of the human experience.[86] Gori further elaborates that, in light of Trabucchi's emphasis on safeguarding individual rights, he advocated for an evolutionary interpretation. This entailed expanding the indirect application of the preliminary reference procedure. Simultaneously, Trabucchi aimed to ensure equal and effective protection of these rights within the internal legal systems of the Member States by fostering cooperation among national judges.[87]

A third element of the Italian legal style in the EU law context is the reliance on scholarly writings, *la dottrina*, to address the legal *lacunae* of the codes and the statutes. First it is important to highlight that this reliance on scholarly writings serves to understand what Merryman calls doctrinal folklore, that is the reliance on legal science by which only the scholar provides guidance to the judge.[88] Yet, differently from the folkloristic Italian style in which citing *la dottina* for judges is severly prohibited by the Italian Civil code, the Italian judges in Luxembourg, especially those coming from an academic rather than judicial background, have made extensive use of this practice.

An example of this reliance on scholarly opinions, combined with the creative role of judicial interpretation, is evident in many of the Opinions of the Italian Advocates General featured in this volume. This is particularly notable in the third generation of jurists as articulated in the Opinions of Antonio La Pergola, Federico Mancini, Antonio Saggio and Giuseppe Tesauro, who were innovators in constant discussion with *la dottrina italiana*. However, tracing such reliance of the Advocates General on *la dottrina*, is not always an easy task, due to the challenge of translation and its inherent ambiguities.[89]

[85] See Merryman (n 71) 602.
[86] See Gori (n 8) 32.
[87] ibid., 33.
[88] See Merryman (n 71) 586, as Merryman critically puts it, '[t]he scholar is the scientist, and the judge, at best, merely the engineer. The scholar provides systematic, scientific legal structure that the judge accepts and applies. The work of the scholar is creative and exalted; that of the judge is, although important, on a lower plane'.
[89] See K McAuliffe, 'Translating Ambiguity' (2015) 9 *Journal of Comparative Law* 65; and McAuliffe, 'Behind the Scenes at the Court of Justice', in Nicola and Davies (n 26) 35.

Take, for instance, the case of *Simone Leitner*,[90] in which Advocate General Antonio Tizzano, later followed by the Court, interpreted Directive 90/314 on package travel, package holidays and package tours as allowing for the compensation of the non-material damage for a spoiled vacation. While this type of compensation was a 'trend prevailing across the Member States favouring the reparations of the non-pecuniary damage for spoiled holidays',[91] Tizzano, in footnote 13 of his Opinion, cites the towering civil scholar Guido Alpa as 'authoritative legal opinion that liability for non-material damage or *danno morale* is a subject marked by extremely diverse and confused assessment criteria. Heads of liability vary greatly from one system to another, being classified in one system as material damage and in another as non-material damage'.[92] Rather than a simple comparative assessment, Tizzano relies on Alpa's expansive notion of *danno morale* or moral damage. This model, as he explains, is hard to export outside Italy because it encompasses a broader category of non-pecuniary harm allowing a plaintiff to recover for the non-economic harm to a person based on a violation of a constitutionally protected individual right.[93] Even though Tizzano concludes his Opinion by stating that 'enjoyment of a holiday is treated as an asset worth protecting', he does so by returning to the notion of the effectiveness of the judicial protection of individual rights.[94] All the elements of the Italians style – eclectism, creative judicial interpretation and reliance on Italian scholarly writings – emerge from this Opinion.

5.2. Second Trait: The Profile of the Italian Jurists

The provenance, legal education and the professional backgrounds of our protagonists before arriving in Luxembourg are varied and diverse, apart from the fact that they were all 'male lawyers'.[95] Such geographical and professional differences were a 'richness' for the CJEU and contributed to the creation of a 'legal melting pot', which enabled the Court to be a 'genuine European judiciary'.[96]

[90] See *Simone Leitner v TUI Deutschland GmbH & Co. KG* Case C-168/00 ECLI:EU:C:2002:16 [2002].

[91] See M Graziadei (n 10) 10, attributing this position of AG Tizzano to a comparative method applied in this case.

[92] In footnote 13 of his Opinion, Tizzano cites G Alpa, 'Il danno alla persona nella prospettiva europea', in A Tizzano (ed), *Il diritto privato dell'Unione europea* (Vol I, Turin, Giappichelli, 2000) 787, 803.

[93] See G Alpa, 'Il Danno non Patrimoniale Rivisitato' (Altalex, Wolters Kluver, 2020); G Alpa, *danno biologico* (2nd ed, Padua, Cedam, 1993).

[94] *Simone Leitner v TUI Deutschland GmbH & Co. KG* Case C-168/00 ECLI:EU:C:2001:47 [2001], Opinion of Advocate General Tizzano, para 44.

[95] See A Vauchez, 'Italian Ways of EU Law: Rooting Italy in European Legal Integration', in this volume.

[96] LS Rossi, 'Working at the Court of Justice of the European Union, in the experience of a judge' in this volume.

From a geographical point of view, for example, the Italian members of the Court represented almost the entire Italian peninsula, from the northern regions – such as Lombardia, Veneto, Liguria and Piemonte –[97] to Campania, Puglia and Sicilia,[98] and through Emilia-Romagna, Umbria and Lazio.[99] As for their legal education, all of them earned a Degree in Law – the highest academic degree at the time –[100] from an Italian university, not rarely one that was territorially close to the place where they were born and/or grew up in.[101] This does not mean that they lacked knowledge of the 'outer world'.[102] In fact they were all fluent in multiple languages including French, but also German and English as many of the future members of the Court spent some research periods abroad as young scholars. For instance, Federico Mancini spent study periods in Vienna, Bordeaux, Paris and Chicago, Giuseppe Tesauro spent a period of study at the Max Planck Institute in Heidelberg, and La Pergola at the University of Edinburgh and at the Harvard Law School in the US.

In terms of professional backgrounds, members of the national judiciary and university professors were appointed as Italian judges and Advocates General at the CJEU. This demonstrates that, unlike in other Member States, such a role was not exclusive to either profession. However, after the 1990s there was a predominance of the Italian legal academics – as the majority of them were full-time university professors,[103] especially from the 'second generation of innovators' onwards–,[104] with a protagonist role played in this context by the School of International Law at the University of Naples.[105] It should be noted, however,

[97] See, respectively, the chapters on Rossi, Trabucchi, and Monaco: A Arena, '"Notre Nestor, Monsieur le Juge Rossi" (1889–1974): an Internationalist's Contribution to the Making of a Supranational Legal Order', in this volume; Perillo (n 76); E Greppi, 'Riccardo Monaco and the Doctrine of Supranationality in International Institutional Law', in this volume.

[98] See, respectively, the chapters on Capotorti, Bosco, Tesauro, Saggio, Catalano and La Pergola: Daniele, 'Francesco Capotorti: the Man, the Academic, and the Avocate-General at the Court of Justice', in this volume; J Ziller, 'Giacinto Bosco, a rather well-known politician in Italy, and one of the lesser-known Italian members of the Court of Justice of the European Communities', in this volume; R Mastroianni and M Condinanzi, 'Giuseppe Tesauro – Advocate General at the ECJ – 1988–1998: A paladin of effective judicial protection', in this volume; A Aresu and C Iannone, 'Antonio Saggio: A Major Contributor to the European Integration', in this volume; Pavone (n 15); and Amalfitano and F Croci, 'Antonio La Pergola: The Idea of Europe as an Objective to be Pursued, between Founding Values and Fundamental Principles', in this volume.

[99] See the Chapters on Mancini and Pilotti: E Greppi, 'Riccardo Monaco and the Doctrine of Supranationality in International Institutional Law', in this volume; and Fritz (n 2).

[100] The PhD Degree was introduced in Italy by Law No. 28/1980 and finally established by a Ministerial Decree of 15 June 1982.

[101] Yet, some exceptions certainly exist. For example, Catalano, born in Apulia, graduated in Law from the University of Rome; Rossi, born in Chiavenna (Lombardia), graduated from the University of Bologna.

[102] As we are about to see, all of them conducted postgraduate research activity or gained international experience *before* joining the Court.

[103] Rossi (n 96).

[104] Cf. Part I.

[105] See Vauchez (n 95).

that the professions of judge or professor were not completely separate, nor are they an exhaustive list. In fact, many Italian jurists have exercised more than one profession, working also as civil servants and/or combining academic positions with their membership of the national judiciary,[106] or with legal practice as private attorneys, as in the case of Giuseppe Tesauro. The scenario is not uniform either when we look at their field of specialisation. While the majority have been professors of international law,[107] the careers of others have been more focused on civil or labour law, often with a 'comparative approach'.[108] It should also be stressed that such a varied but equally prestigious professional background before arriving in Luxembourg comes at a price. The other side of the coin is that it is not uncommon for Italian judges and Advocates General to be appointed to the ECJ at a fairly advanced stage in their careers. About half of the members under investigation were appointed when they were over sixty.[109] This age factor can certainly play a role during their time at the Court – in acquiring or not a certain degree of symbolic capital –[110] and afterwards, in influencing their ability to play their role as agents of transfer.[111]

The scenario is heterogeneous even with regard to their 'political affiliations' or 'political areas of reference', which vary considerably in colour, form and degree as not all of them were formally close to a political party. While many of them had links with the Christian Democratic Party or *Democrazia Cristiana* (DC) Party, others were closer to the Italian Socialist Party.[112]

Notwithstanding this diversity in their backgrounds, the analysis carried out in the eleven chapters that make up Part I of this volume, allows us to isolate three major, and to some extent interrelated, common features: (a) 'international standing', (b) 'professional proximity', and (c) 'political proximity' that characterise the career trajectories of Italian judges and Advocates General prior to their appointment to the CJEU.[113]

[106] See, eg, Nicola Catalano, who, albeit being a judge, had worked, inter alia, as an assistant lecturer of international law at the University of Rome; Monaco, who combined the academic career with several experiences in the Italian judiciary; or Saggio, who, albeit being a judge, had worked, inter alia, as a lecturer and professor and always maintained close ties with academia.

[107] For instance, Giuseppe Tesauro was professor of both International and Community Law.

[108] For instance, Rossi, a member of the Italian judiciary, authored many publications on foreign and comparative law; Trabucchi, a professor of private law, also taught comparative private law for some years; Mancini, a professor of labour law, has a deep interest for comparative law; and La Pergola was professor of constitutional law and general and comparative public law and also taught American public law.

[109] In chronological order, Massimo Pilotti was 73, Rino Rossi 69, Giacinto Bosco 71, Giuseppe Federico Mancini 61 and Antonio La Pergola 68.

[110] Cf sections 5 and 6.

[111] See section 5.3 below.

[112] Nonetheless, these two areas shall not be considered as completely detached from one another nor as an exhaustive representation of those areas of reference, as pointed out below.

[113] Further 'common features' or 'traits' of the Italian members of the CJEU that concern their period in Luxembourg and also the period after the end of their mandates are illustrated in other paragraphs of this chapter, see also Vauchez (n 95).

Two preliminary clarifications seem necessary at this stage. First, as is well known, the appointment of judges depends on many factors and contingencies, which have recently attracted attention in the academic literature in relation to the 'European judges'[114] and which are highly sensitive issues in light of the search for greater clarity and transparency in the functioning of the CJEU.[115] This is also true at the national level: the appointment of Italian judges and Advocates General has long been characterised by an opaque system, dominated by the governments of Member States.[116] With just one exception,[117] this is still the case today, although the power to propose candidates, which for decades was in the hands of the Italian Ministry of Foreign Affairs, has now shifted to the Government under the Office of the Prime Minister in coordination with the Minister for European Affairs. In particular, Article 17 of Law No. 234/2012 requires the Government to inform the Italian Parliament as soon as it 'proposes or appoints' the Italian members of the CJEU (or other EU institutions and bodies), by indicating the procedure followed to reach this decision, the reasons for this choice, and the curriculum vitae of the persons proposed or appointed.[118] Secondly, it is worth emphasising that the features of continuity we have identified have been 'touched' (and partly shaped) by the passage of decades. In other words, 'continuity' does not mean 'immutability': these features are 'in motion' like the rest of the European integration process.[119]

By 'international standing', we are referring to the fact that the professional trajectories of all the Italian members under investigation are not merely characterised by an unquestionably high level of competence.[120] In addition, they all

[114] Bobek explains this with three main factors: the exponential growth in their dockets over the last decades, the eastern enlargement, and the changes in the academic reflection as well as in the political environment in Europe See M Bobek, 'Prologue: The Changing Nature of Selection Procedures to the European Courts', in Bobek (n 22) 1.

[115] See L Clément-Wilz (n 62).

[116] L Clément-Wilz, *La Cour de justice de l'Union européenne* (Paris, LGDJ, 2020) 57.

[117] In October 2018, a public competition was opened by the Italian Prime Minister for the selection of two new judges to the General Court. According to the call published in the Official Journal of the Republic of Italy, the candidates had to fulfil the requirements set out in 254 TFEU and the applications would have been examined by a five-member Panel – appointed by the Prime Minister upon consultation with the Minister of Foreign Affairs – who were in charge of presenting a list of six candidates, preferably selected on the basis of the principle of gender equality and having the power to interview candidates. See Concorso 'Procedura di selezione dei candidati per l'elezione a giudice del Tribunale dell'Unione europea', GURI No. 80, 9 October 2018.

[118] As noted in the literature, the content of such information has been calibrated to meet the requirements of the 255 Panel. In this vein, see C Favilli, 'Il Regno Unito apre una selezione pubblica per la designazione del giudice del Tribunale dell'Union dell'Unione europea: una buona prassi anche per l'Italia?', in *Eurojus.it* (12 February 2015), available online.

[119] With regard to the developments concerning the appointment of CJEU's members, it is worth mentioning the creation of the evaluation panel established pursuant to Article 255 TFEU (aka the 255 Panel) following the Lisbon Treaty, which has been one of the most important developments about the appointments of members of the CJEU.

[120] This high level of competence was often explicitly or implicitly acknowledged by their peers. For instance, Pilotti was referred to as '*premier magistrat d'Italie*' or Italy's most distinguished judge; Mancini had been put forward as a candidate to become one of the five judges of the Italian

arrived at the Court after having gained some experience at the international level, which made them stand out. This applies both to members of the judiciary and to university professors. With regard to the members of the judiciary, it is worth mentioning the following examples: Massimo Pilotti had participated in the Paris and Brussels Conferences on post-war measures, had been involved in the activities of the League of Nations, was appointed as a judge at the Permanent Court of Arbitration in The Hague, and had been President of the International Institute for the Unification of Private Law (UNIDROIT); Nicola Catalano was appointed as Italy's agent in the conciliation commissions created by the 1947 Peace Treaty that followed the end of World War II, had served as chief legal adviser to the Tangier International Zone, was a member of the Legal Service of the High Authority of the European Coal and Steal Community (ECSC), and had taken part in the *groupe de rédaction* of the Treaty of Rome; Rino Rossi had worked at the District Court of Rhodes and the Consular Court at Cairo, and had taken part in the drafting of the rules of procedure of the ECSC Court of Justice; Riccardo Monaco was a member of the Italian delegation to the Rome Conference for the creation of a European Political Community and took part in the 1955 Messina Conference; and finally, Antonio Saggio had worked as *référendaire* in the Chambers of Francesco Capotorti, when he was appointed Advocate General at the end of the 1970s.

Such an international standing was also the prerogative of many university professors. In fact, Francesco Capotorti had taught two courses at the Academy of International law, in The Hague, in 1963 and 1971. Giacinto Bosco had been elected as a member of the Institute of International Law, founded in 1873 in Ghent (Belgium); as a member of the Italian Parliament, he had taken part in the Italian delegation to the European Parliament's sessions; and, as a member of the Italian Government, he was involved in several meetings at the international level (within the Council of Europe, the United Nations, and the EC Council). Antonio La Pergola was Minister for European Affairs under two different Governments (1987–1989) and was a member of the European Parliament for one term (1989–1994).

Let us now turn our attention to the twofold 'proximity' mentioned above which should be understood as sometimes converging or overlapping. By 'professional proximity', we mean the *direct* and *formal* link between the future Italian member of the CJEU, in his professional capacity, and the Italian public administration, in particular – though not exclusively – the Ministry of Foreign Affairs. As Vauchez points out, this is particularly evident in the case of the first generation of 'pioneers,' ie, Pilotti, Catalano, and Rossi. While Pilotti worked as legal adviser to the Italian Foreign Ministry after the end of the First World War, he also played a central role in the so-called 'purges' by participating in a

Constitutional Court elected by Parliament but was ultimately not appointed for political considerations; La Pergola, instead, had been judge of the Italian Constitutional Court before his appointment to the CJEU, serving as its President during the last year of his mandate.

ad-hoc commission set up by the Government to remove fascists from both the State bureaucracy and the liberal professions.[121] Catalano, as well as working as an agent of the Italian Government, was a legal expert on the Italian delegation for drawing up the Treaties of Rome; Rossi had worked at the Italian Ministry of Foreign Affairs and had good contacts with Monaco, at the time Secretary General of the Diplomatic Disputes Service of the Ministry, who played a major role in his appointment.[122] In addition to Monaco, for whom such a proximity *ça va sans dire*,[123] also Capotorti, Bosco, and, for a shorter period, Tesauro served as legal advisers in the same Ministry. There are however examples of other professional experiences with (and ties with) the Italian public administration: Saggio, for example, worked in the *Ufficio Legislativo del Ministero di Grazia e Giustizia* that is the Legislative Office of the Ministry of Justice.

Finally, by 'political proximity', we are referring to the personal connections of the Italian jurists with the political majorities in power at the time of their nomination to the CJEU, such as with the ministers and/or the *Presidente del Consiglio*,[124] and, more generally, with a particular 'political area' or 'political family'. Two aspects deserve attention. First, although the *Democrazia Cristiana* Party (DC) and the Italian Socialist Party (PSI) were the primary political areas from which the vast majority of the Italian jurists were nominated to the CJEU, it is important not to view them as providing an exhaustive representation of the entire political spectrum.[125] Second, as noted above, such connections with a political area vary considerably in shape and degree. Indeed, while some future Italian judges and advocates general were 'formally' connected to a political party – such as Bosco,[126] Mancini,[127] and La Pergola –,[128] others had instead 'informal connections' with a political area. Members of the Court such as Trabucchi, Capotorti, and Tesauro had informal yet powerful connections with their governments while remaining formally independent jurists or technocrats.[129]

[121] See Fritz (n 2).

[122] See Arena (n 97).

[123] See Greppi (n 97), which states that Monaco worked in three different offices at the Ministry of Foreign Affairs, namely the Treaties Office, the Diplomatic and Treaty Litigation Office, and the Legislative Affairs Office.

[124] These elements are among those that it is necessary to take into consideration according to Vauchez (n 95).

[125] For instance, Vera Fritz's chapter in this volume illustrates Pilotti's hostility towards the abolishment of the monarchy, see Fritz (n 2).

[126] Bosco was a member of the DC Party. Elected for five consecutive legislatures to the Italian *Senato* since 1948, he was close to the DC leaders, especially to Amintore Fanfani and Arnaldo Forlani, and served as a member of most governments from 1953 to 1972.

[127] Mancini was a member of the Central Committee of the Italian Socialist Party and supported the renovation of the Party led by Bettino Craxi.

[128] La Pergola was a member of the Italian Socialist Party. He served as Minister for European Affairs under two different DC-led governments and, once elected at the European Parliament, he joined, at European level, the Party of European Socialists.

[129] In a nutshell, Alberto Trabucchi was the younger brother of the Italian Minister of Finance, Giuseppe Trabucchi, who, in turn, was close to Antonio Segni, Minister of Foreign Affairs (see

However, it should be emphasised that the affiliation of Italian jurists with the political sphere has traditionally been relatively weak. Their appointments were often based on familial or social networks, and showcased their elite status or networking abilities rather than a strong political affiliation with the Christian Democratic or Italian Socialist Party. This is evidenced, for example, by the fact that, although Capotorti belonged to the political area of the Socialist Party, his appointment to the CJEU was solely the initiative of Prime Minister Aldo Moro, who was a prominent political figure of the Christian Democratic Party.[130] In a similar way, La Pergola, although a member of the Italian Socialist Party, served as Minister for European Affairs under two different Christian Democratic governments.[131] Within the biographical context provided in this volume, while the nominations of Italian jurists may have originated from their connections with or proximity to a particular political area or party, this factor represented merely the final element that propelled their nomination. Their ability and overall character to mobilise their social and legal networks, as well as to showcase their professional international careers and multilingual skills, played pivotal roles in their appointments.

5.3. Third Trait: Agents of Transfer of European Law Back Home

A background that includes holding a teaching or professorial position at a university is a prevalent characteristic among numerous Italian judges and Advocates General, starting from the second generation of jurists 'the innovators' onward. This background is also manifested in their function as agents of transfer or disseminators of the CJEU jurisprudence back home. We refer to the evident inclination, more pronounced in certain members but nevertheless observed across many of the biographies scrutinised in this volume, to bring back home (as much as is possible) the outcomes of their endeavors at the Court along with their firsthand insights gained from being immersed in the *Kirchber* environment as insiders.

The vocation of agents of transfer becomes more apparent in the biographies of individuals who had previously engaged in teaching activities at their respective universities, compared to those who had previously held different roles such as national judges, diplomats, or attorneys. Not surprisingly, these agents of transfer traditionally maintained the appellative of 'Professors' inside the Court and among the members of their *cabinet*. Unlike in other Membe

Pavone (n 15)); Capotorti was a good acquaintance of Aldo Moro, a prominent politician for DC they had been colleagues at both the University of Bari and the Sapienza University in Rome; ar Tesauro was born into a family of prominent academics and politicians who were close to leadi politicians from the Christian Democratic Party.

[130] In this vein, see Daniele (n 98).

[131] See Amalfitano and Croci (n 98).

States, for the Italian members the position at the CJEU is incompatible with any other activity, including university teaching.[132] Consequently, Italian jurists in Luxembourg were relieved from lecturing obligations during their tenure. However, this did not stop Italian judges and Advocates General from maintaining some responsibilities akin to that of university lecturers, such as publishing legal works (articles, case notes, or handbooks of Community law) or participating in conferences and giving *lectiones magistrales*.

This 'dual authoritative influence' continues to shape both the Italian academic discourse and the development of young scholars in Italian universities. To give just one example, the publication of the first edition of Giuseppe Tesauro's Handbook 'Diritto comunitario' in 1995, which was published at he end of his first term of office as an Advocate General, filled a clear gap in the andscape of university manuals because it was the first to be devoted to both the nstitutional and substantive part of Community law. As regards publications hat follow the end of their term in office, scholarly studies on the operations of he Court of Justice, which encompass procedural aspects and rules governing actions, have long gravitated towards a seminal work authored by Francesco Capotorti, featured prominently in the most prestigious Italian Encyclopedia of law.[133]

It is worth underlining that the Italian members of the CJEU played this role of agents of transfer both during the years spent in Luxembourg and in the time ollowing the end of their mandates. This shows that many of them considred themselves as 'witnesses' and contributors to the European legal tradition. Throughout their tenure, academia sought their presence (or they promoted hemselves) not only from their home universities but also from other academic nstitutions. Their purpose was to disseminate the outcomes of the Court's case aw to legal audiences because, as a result of geographical distance or the chalenge of accessing direct sources, the Court was still perceived in some academic ircles as being remote and of lacking a significant impact on national law at hat time.

The Italian universities organised, and still organise, conferences in which the alian members of the Court would be invited to systematically carry out this ask.Often, the dates of these events coincided with the dates of the *semaines blanches* at the Court, in order to facilitate their physical presence. Among these vents, it is worth mentioning, for example the *Tavole rotonde di diritto comunitario* or Round tables of Community law, which was organised by the Catholic niversity of Milan in the 1980s at the initiative of Professor Giuseppe Biscottini. dditionally, the annual conferences of the Italian Society of International Law r *Societá Italiana di Diritto Internazionale* (SIDI), often devoted to Community

[132] See *Decree of the President of the Republic*, No 382 of 11 July 1980, Article 13, 'Compulsory ave for situations of incompatibility'.
[133] F Capotorti, 'Processo Comunitario', in *Enciclopedia del Diritto* (Vol XXXVI, Milan, Giuffrè, 87) 837.

law,[134] and, more recently, the annual conferences of the new Italian association of scholars in European Union law, known as *Associazione Italiana Studiosi di Diritto dell'Unione Europea* (AISDUE), initiated its activities in 2018 under the leadership of Giuseppe Tesauro and Antonio Tizzano. This role of agents of transfer found the conferences and events organised by academic groups in a university setting to be a transmission belt. This trend was amplified by new events that were organised by the Bar Associations or by the judiciary, particularly by the Italian Constitutional Court, where some of its members were more inclined than others to entertain a dialogue with the judges of the CJEU.[135]

As demonstrated in our volume, the Italian members of the Court continued to serve as agents of transfer even after the conclusion of their tenure in Luxembourg. While in some instances, the return to Italy occurred after reaching the retirement age for university teaching – as was the case with Francesco Capotorti or Antonio La Pergola – or coincided with assuming other prestigious institutional positions, such as Giuseppe Tesauro's appointment to the Italian Constitutional Court, it remains true that in all cases Italian members of the Court continued to play leading roles, whether through engaging in European academic debates or through their legal practice as Euro-lawyers.[136]

The role of agents of transfer that was fulfilled by Italian jurists in Luxembourg significantly contributed to a deeper understanding of the original EU law system of 'integration through law'.[137] Particularly during the 1970s and 80s, EU law struggled to garner the attention it deserved not only from practitioners and judges,[138] but also from Italian academic circles, despite its decisive impact on the practice of law within the country. Through the biographies of individuals who served as architects in constructing the foundations of CJEU jurisprudence, this volume illustrates how they established a substantial and enduring bridge that connected Luxembourg with the various legal professions within the Italian legal context.

[134] Until recently, in the Italian Law Schools European Community law was considered as a branc of International law, so it is not surprising that it is in that circle that the members of Italia academia were more sensible to the developments in the ECJ jurisprudence.

[135] This is the case, for instance, of the seminar held at the Constitutional Court that was dedicat to the relationship between Comminuty law and national law, in which Giuseppe Tesauro gave th keynote speech. The proceedings of that seminar are published in the volume *Diritto Comunitar Europeo e Diritto Nazionale. Atti del Seminario Internazionale – Roma, Palazzo della Consul 14–15 luglio 1995* (Milano, Giuffré, 1997).

[136] The exemplary case of Nicola Catalano, in T Pavone, *The Ghostwriters, Lawyers and the Po tics behind the Judicial Construction of Europe* (Cambridge, Cambridge University Press, 2022).

[137] See M Cappelletti, M Seccombe, and JHH Weiler (eds), *Integration Through Law, Europe ar the American Federal Experience-Vol 1 Methods, Tools and Institutions* (Berlin, De Gruyter, 1985

[138] See A Bartolini and A Guerrieri, 'The Pyrrhic Victory of Mr. Francovich and the Principle State Liability in the Italian Context', in Nicola and Davies (n 26) 338, which shows how the Itali judges confused the Strasbourg Court with the Luxembourg court when they referred to the we know *Francovich* case.

5.4. Fourth Trait: Effectivess in the Protection of Individual Rights

This section examines, from a doctrinal standpoint, the common thread linking the collective biographies of the Italian judges and Advocate General analysed in this book. Most specifically, in light of the chapters in Part I of our volume, we shed light on an *Italian way, Italian-ess* or *Italian essence* that emerges with specific reference to the principles and doctrines established over the years in the CJEU jurisprudence. To this end, our focus is primarily on the Opinions deliv-ered by Italian Advocates General, the judgments for which Italian judges were *juges rapporteurs*, and their writings published before and or after their tenure n Luxembourg.

The judicial biographies of the eleven members of the CJEU reveal two prominent features that transcend their diverse legal or professional back-grounds, and which encompass specialisations in international, domestic, and European or Community law.[139] The internationalists[140] were primarily scholars of international law or senior state officials,[141] particularly but not exclusively coming from the Ministry of Foreign Affairs.[142] Italian law specialists were either cholars or judges with backgrounds in private law, civil procedure and labour aw.[143] Finally, European or Community law experts dedicated their careers to he European integration project within the European Economic Community nd later the European Union.[144]

The first feature highlighted in the biographies compiled in this collection – lbeit with varying degrees of persuasiveness – is the unanimous support for European integration among all judges and Advocates General from 1952 to 000. Both during their service and post-tenure in Luxembourg, they fervently hampioned European integration efforts, acknowledging its distinct challenges, specially regarding the participation of citizens in the European legal system as ndividual subjects of law.

[139] Many of the Italian judges and Advocates General, of course, have diverse 'souls' in terms of gal background. For instance, Rossi was an official and judge; Monaco was an academic and idge; Capotorti was an academic and member of the Diplomatic Litigation Council at the Minis-y of Foreign Affairs; Bosco was an academic and public official; Mancini was an academic and a ember elected by the parliament to the national Judiciary Council; La Pergola was an academic, onstitutional judge, and minister; Tesauro was an academic and an attorney; and Saggio a ministry fficial, judge, and academic.

[140] With the caveat of what stated in footnote n 139 above, see, eg, Monaco, Capotorti, Bosco, esauro, and Saggio.

[41] With the caveat of what stated in footnote n 139 above, see, eg, Rossi, Capotorti, Bosco, Mancini, a Pergola, and Saggio.

[42] For instance, Saggio worked at the Legislative Office of the Ministry of Justice.

[43] For instance, Pilotti, Rossi, and Saggio were judges. Trabucchi and Mancini, instead, were niversity professors specialising in civil and labour law, respectively. See Fritz (n 2), Arena (n 97), esu and Iannone (n 98), Perillo (n 76) and V Di Bucci, 'The Contribution of Giuseppe Federico ancini as Advocate General (1982–1988) and Judge (1988–1999) to European Constitutionalism', this volume.

[44] Catalano has been chief legal adviser to the Tangier International Zone and a member of the oupe de redaction charged with drafting the Treaty text in late 1956 and early 1957. Yet even within e group, Article 177 was debated and drafted 'without awareness of this innovation's importance',

The second characteristic relates to the pivotal role of judicial rights protection as the essence of the European Treaties, centered around two key concepts: direct effect and effective judicial protection. These two doctrines of EU law – particularly when linked to the principle of effectiveness/*effet utile*, the preliminary ruling procedure under Article 267 TFEU, the teleological interpretation of EU law and the State liability remedy – occupy a fundamental position in the practice of European law by Italian judges and Advocates General, albeit to varying degrees among them.[145]

Concerning the doctrine of direct effect, the inaugural judgment by what was then the ECSC Court underscored the autonomous nature and direct applicability of a primary law norm.[146] This was established in the *Fédération Charbonnière* case of 1956,[147] presided over by Pilotti, which specifically addressed Article 4 of the ECSC Treaty. The reasoning behind this rulinig was based on both the principle of *effet utile* and a systematic and teleological interpretation of the ECSC Treaty, in which it was stated that its rules should be interpreted with the aim of 'giv[ing] the provisions of the treaty full effect' and 'must be considered as a whole and applied simultaneously'.[148]

Similarly noteworthy is Trabucchi's role as the staunchest advocate for the rights of European citizens. Utilising a thought-out *note en délibéré* and drawing on his mastery of private law, he stood out within the CJEU for advocating the advancement of Commumity law beyond the conventional categories of international law. Specifically, he championed the direct effect of the norms of the EEC Treaty, particularly Article 12, more vigorously than any of his peers.[149] Trabucchi's approach, which centred on the effectiveness of EEC law thanks to the activism of the individual, also an agent of the European legal order, is also reflected in the Opinions rendered as Advocate General, particularly in *Rewe Zentralfinanz*,[150] and, regarding horizontal relationships, in *Defrenne II*.[151]

Furthermore, the strategy proposed by Trabucchi, while ostensibly in contrast to Rossi's stance – who typically hesitated to recognise the unique character of the EEC legal order in comparison to international law – was, in reality backed by Rossi himself.[152] In fact, in the *Van Gen en Loos* ruling, Rossi played

see P Pescatore, 'Les Travaux du 'Groupe de redaction' dans la Négociation des Traités de Rome (1981) 34 *Studia Diplomatica* 159, 173, referred to in T Pavone (n 15).

[145] As can be seen from the previous chapters of this volume, Trabucchi, Tesauro and Saggio can be considered examples of 'paladins' of direct effect and effective judicial protection, while Rossi Capotorti and Bosco attribute less centrality to these concepts.

[146] See Fritz (n 2).

[147] *Fédération Charbonnière de Belgique v. High Authority of the European Coal and Steel Community* Case 8/55 ECLI:EU:C:1956:7 [1956].

[148] ibid., 195.

[149] See Perillo (n 76).

[150] *Rewe-Zentralfinanz eGmbH v Direktor der Landwirtschaftskammer Westfalen-Lippe* Case 39/73, ECLI:EU:C:1973:98 [1973], Opinion of Advocate General Trabucchi.

[151] *Gabrielle Defrenne v Société anonyme belge de navigation aérienne Sabena* Case 43/ ECLI:EU:C:1976:39 [1976], Opinion of Advocate General Trabucchi.

[152] See Arena (n 97).

a pivotal role in securing the 4-3 majority within the Court for the direct effect ascribed to Article 12 of the EEC Treaty. This apparent ambivalence, which gives way to Rossi's eclectic and pragmatic interpretative style, is a recognition of the uniqueness of Community law. As Amedeo Arena highlights, according to Rossi, the 'practical assessment' of Community law was to be considered as the 'most meaningful way to really understand the raison d'être of the Communities and the concrete goals they pursue'.[153]

Aligned with Trabucchi's approach on the protection of individual rights, Catalano theorised and implemented this approach in a more developed and committed manner than Rossi, initially serving as an agent of the High Authority oefore becoming a judge of the EEC Court. Catalano was instrumental in the nclusion of Article 177 in the EEC Treaty, an article that was modeled on the eferral procedure to the Italian Constitutional Court for questions of constitu-ional legitimacy, as stipulated in the Italian Constitution.[154] The preliminary ulings procedure assumes pivotal significance, enabling the full realisation of he principles of primacy and direct effect. Together, these principles and the oreliminary reference procedure form the 'magic triangle' or *triangle magique*[155] hat has, over the years, transformed Community law, thereby distinguishing it rom international law and guiding the process of integration. This is evident rom both Catalano's commentary on *Van Gend en Loos*, published in *Il Foro adano* in 1963, and his report for the *Federation Internationale Pour le Droit uropéen* (FIDE) in the same year.[156]

The principle of effective judicial protection, which emerges from several udgments issued by the Court to which Monaco contributed to, perfectly aligns vith his theory of supranationality as described in his academic writings.[157] This theory enabled Monaco to challenge established beliefs of the time, well-ooted in the international law reflection, including those prevalent in Italian egal academia. Ultimately, his work played a significant role in softening the olkloristic or clear-cut distinction between EU supranational law and domestic aw, particularly in how the norms of these legal orders impacted individual ights. The *International Fruit* case,[158] delivered when Monaco was Chamber resident, demostrated a significant softening of the rigidity that character-ed the *Plaumann* judgment,[159] which regarded the definition of the standing

[153] R Rossi, 'Recensione a "Manuale di Diritto delle Comunità Europee" di Nicola Catalano' 962) 29 *Rivista di Studi Politici Internazionali* 649–650, recalled in Arena (n 97).
[154] See Pavone (n 15).
[155] See A Vauchez, 'Judge-Made Law: aux origines du modèle politique communautaire (retour r Van Gend en Loos et Costa c. ENEL)', in O Costa and P Magnette (eds), *Une Europe des élites? éflexions sur la fracture démocratique de l'Union européenne* (Bruxelles, Editions de l'Université Bruxelles, 2007) 139.
[156] See Pavone (n 15).
[157] See Greppi (n 97).
[158] *NV International Fruit Company and others v Commission of the European Communities* ined Cases 41-44/70 ECLI:EU:C:1971:53 [1971].
[159] *Plaumann & Co. v Commission of the European Economic Community* Case 25/62 CLI:EU:C:1963:17 [1963].

conditions that private parties must satisfy to bring annulment proceedings against a European Community act.

In the chapters on Capotorti and Bosco,[160] while the analysis of their role in shaping the CJEU jurisprudence does not specifically address direct effect and effective judicial protection, it is evident that their scholarly contributions accentuate the uniqueness of the European legal system. For both of them, this system – through its focus on the protection of individuals – successfully emancipated EU law from traditional international law categories.

Both direct effect and effective judicial protection are at the centre of Mancini's activity, as judge *rapporteur* and as Advocate General.[161] The landmark *Bosman* judgment[162] stands out for its clear and well-substantiated recognition of horizontal direct effect by the CJEU, with specific reference to the free movement of workers. In this seminal ruling, triggered by a free movement of workers provision, the CJEU recognised the doctrine of horizontal direct effect to protect an individual against private entities with regulatory power in which the individual was the weaker party of the dispute, underpinning the preliminary reference from the Belgian court. This commitment to protecting individual rights is further exemplified by Mancini's Opinion as Advocate General, in *Les Verts*.[163] In this case, the Advocate General's position on the potential annulment of a decision by the European Parliament was fully endorsed by the Court in its final judgment.

Tesauro significantly influenced the principle of effective judicial protection within the European Union's legal order. In his Opinions as Advocate General he emphasised strengthening this principle through its nexus with the doctrine of direct effect. Many of the cases he was involved in have guided the CJEU jurisprudence in subsequent years. Even in instances in which the Court did not adopt his views, his contributions have been profoundly impactful on academic research and scholarship. Several examples of Tesauro's influence can be found in his *Brasserie* Opinion,[164] with reference to the possible combination between State liability remedy and direct effect; in the *Hermès* Opinion,[165] which regards the possible attribution of direct effect to WTO norms; and finally in the *Factortame* Opinion,[166] which ensured the protection of fundamental rights

[160] See Ziller (n 98) and Daniele (n 98).

[161] See Di Bucci (n 143).

[162] *Union royale belge des sociétés de football association ASBL v Jean-Marc Bosman, Royal club liégeois SA v Jean-Marc Bosman and others and Union des associations européennes de football (UEFA) v Jean-Marc Bosman* Case C-415/93 ECLI:EU:C:1995:463 [1995].

[163] *Parti écologiste "Les Verts" v European Parliament* Case 294/83 ECLI:EU:C:1986:166 [1986].

[164] *Brasserie du Pêcheur SA v Bundesrepublik Deutschland and The Queen v Secretary of State for Transport, ex parte: Factortame Ltd and others* Joined cases C-46/93 and C-48/93 ECLI:EU:C:1995:407 [1995], Opinion of Advocte General Tesauro.

[165] *Hermès International (a partnership limited by shares) v FHT Marketing Choice BV* Case C-53/96 ECLI:EU:C:1997:539 [1997], Opinion of Advocte General Tesauro.

[166] *The Queen v Secretary of State for Transport, ex parte: Factortame Ltd and others* Case C-213/89 ECLI:EU:C:1990:257 [1990], Opinion of Advocte General Tesauro.

through an interim relief in case of directly effective EU law norms and capable of generating, thanks to the principle of primacy, the duty to disapply national laws in conflict with EU law.

In line with the Italian style and the use by judges of *la dottrina* in their evolutive interpretation, in relation to *Factortame*, it is no coincidence that Tesauro strategically referenced to the works of eminent Italian civil law and procedural aw professors. He leveraged these authoritative sources to persuade the CJEU o adopt the positions he outlined in his Opinion, successfully influencing the Court's approach[167] – a testament to the integration of the Italian style in shaping the jurisprudence of the CJEU within the EU's legal framework. Indeed, Tesauro, during the 1980s and 1990s, mirrored the approach Trabucchi took in he 1960s and 1970s. Trabucchi, serving as a mentor to Tesauro, undoubtedly played a fundamental role in shaping Tesauro's views on the EU legal order. However, it was Tesauro who continued to promote the legacy of the *Van Gend n Loos* judgment as embodying a commitment to the 'culture of defending the ights of individuals'[168] through the EU legal order.

Regarding La Pergola, his nature as an eclectic and atypical constitutional urist is clearly evidenced from the significant contribution he made during is tenure at the Italian Constitutional Court. His work was instrumental in he construction of the *Granital* doctrine,[169] which, for the first time, fully mbraced the *Simmenthal* ruling[170] by the CJEU that had been, until then, more r less explicitly opposed by the same court. With his tempered dualist vision nd thesis of 'federalism by analogy',[171] La Pergola addressed European law vith extreme openness, rather than suspicion, as many of his constitutionalist olleagues at the time did (and some still do today).[172] This suspicion among alian Constitutional Court judges is articulated in *Granital* and is rooted in the onviction that, due to primacy and direct effect, the widespread disapplication f Italian law by ordinary judges was a natural consequence inherent in the relaon between the European and the domestic legal order.

An emphasis on the judicial protection of rights, and the effectiveness thereof, evident in several Opinions delivered by La Pergola. For instance, in the *Smits* ase,[173] significant attention is dedicated to safeguarding and exercising the rights f free movement, which arise directly from the Union's legal order.

67 See Mastroianni and Condinanzi (n 98).

68 G Tesauro, 'Alcune riflessioni sul ruolo della Corte di giustizia nell'evoluzione dell'Unione euroa' (2013) 18 *Il Diritto dell'Unione europea* 483, 500.

69 Italian Constitutional Court, Judgment No. 170/1984.

70 *Amministrazione delle Finanze dello Stato v Simmenthal SpA* Case 106/77 ECLI:EU:C:1978:49 978].

71 See Amalfitano and Croci (n 98).

72 D Gallo, 'Challenging EU constitutional law: The Italian Constitutional Court's new stance on rect effect and the preliminary reference procedure' (2019) 25 *European Law Journal* 434, 454–455; Gallo, 'The Taricco Saga: When Direct Effect and the Duty to Disapply Meet the Principle of gality in Criminal Matters', in P Craig and R Schütze (eds), *Landmark Cases in EU Law* (Oxford, art, 2024, forthcoming).

73 *Smits and Peerbooms* Case C-157/99 ECLI:EU:C:2001:404 [2001].

The Opinions by Advocate General Saggio align with the trajectory set by the other ten Italian jurists.[174] Particularly in *Portugal v Council*,[175] in which he clarifies, prefiguring the *Kadi* legacy,[176] that certain EU norms and principles are inviolable even by norms and principles of international law. Furthermore, in his Opinion in the *Océano* case,[177] then endorsed by the CJEU, Saggio clearly delineated the central role attributed to the principle of effective judicial protection in the realm of consumer protection.[178]

A further evidence supporting the assertions in this section can be found in Tizzano's reflections, as articulated in his concluding remarks. He discerns a common thread that runs through the activity of Italian judges and Advocates General in Luxembourg, irrespective of their legal backgrounds as international, domestic or European lawyers, and the career paths they pursued prior to their appointment to the CJEU. This common thread is rooted in the conviction that the Community, now the Union, represents an extraordinary positive phenomenon. This positive uniqueness is especially articulated in the centrality of the individual subject of law, which lies at the core of the EU Treaties. This centrality of the individual strengthens principles of effective judicial protection and direct effect that are functional to the effectiveness/*effet utile* of EU law.[179]

6. CONCLUSION: THE ITALIAN ARCHITECTS IN EU LAW

This volume aims to re-centre the research in European legal scholarship on collective judicial biographies from one Member State to show the relevance of a domestic legal tradition to the fabric of EU law. The focus on individual members at the CJEU has allowed us to expand beyond a jurisprudential analysis of the case law and to extend our gaze to other contextual, institutional, legal narrative and structural features that shape the Court's jurisprudence

[174] See Aresu and Iannone (n 98).

[175] *Portuguese Republic v Council of the European Union* Case C-149/96 ECLI:EU:C:1999:9 [1999], Opinion of Advocate General Saggio.

[176] *Yassin Abdullah Kadi and Al Barakaat International Foundation v Council of the European Union and Commission of the European Communities* Joined cases C-402/05 P and C-415/05 ECLI:EU:C:2008:461 [2008].

[177] *Océano Grupo Editorial SA v Roció Murciano Quintero (C-240/98) and Salvat Editores SA v José M. Sánchez Alcón Prades (C-241/98), José Luis Copano Badillo (C-242/98), Mohammed Berroane (C-243/98) and Emilio Viñas Feliú (C-244/98)* Joined Cases C-240/98 to C-244/98 ECLI:EU:C:1999:620 [1999], Opinion of Advocate General Saggio.

[178] It is interesting to note in this regard that the extension of the scope of consumer protection under the relevant European directives, inaugurated by the Opinion delivered by Advocate General Saggio in *Walter Rechberger, Renate Greindl, Hermann Hofmeister and Others v Republik Österreich and*, case C-140/97 ECLI:EU:C:1998:321 [1998], and confirmed, as for the procedural guarantees with the Opinion delivered in *Océano*, was maintained by his successor Antonio Tizzano, as an ideal passage of the baton, in his Opinions like the one delivered in *Simone Leitner v TUI Deutschland GmbH & Co KG* Case C-168/00 ECLI:EU:C:2001:476 [2001].

[179] In this regard, see D Gallo, *The Direct Effect of EU Law* (Oxford, Oxford University Press, forthcoming 2024).

thus providing further insights on the broader and more nuanced struggles that unfold beyond the literal text of the law.

Each judicial portrait thus illuminates how these individuals shared their local knowledge to varying degrees of success in a transnational setting. We trace how Italian jurists, once in Luxembourg, have influenced the shaping of European law not only through their participation in judicial deliberations but also through involvement in institutional processes. Profound believers in European integration, they contributed to shaping the Court's jurisprudence and the working culture in Luxembourg during the different periods marked by three generations we called pioneers, innovators and European constitutionalists. While at the Court they acquired varying degrees of symbolic capital and occupied elite roles, such as the Presidency of the CJ and GC, as well as the Vice-Presidency of the CJ, and as Chamber Presidents.

We used the metaphor of the Italian architectural style that undergoes evolution over time, yet retains specific traits that persist through the centuries, which are discerned and described by art historians rather than measured. Similarly, within the architecture of the CJEU jurisprudence and of the CJEU itself as an institution,[180] a legal historian can illuminate Italian architectural traits and their evolution, mismatching or integration over time. The focus lies thus not on measurement, but on delving into contextual, structural, and historical descriptions of the Italian style. This approach aims to elucidate the genesis of each legal 'building', the genius and creativity of the architects involved, while mapping the changes across different eras.

In our work as 'art historians', we uncovered the background and intellectual aspirations of a selected group of architects who designed the jurisprudential edifice of EU law and the institutional edifice of the EU judicial system. Four defining traits – style, profile, transfer, and effectiveness – emerge as the essence of Italian influence on European law. Through the biographies of eleven individuals who served as judges or Advocates General in Luxembourg, we have traced these collective traits and have highlighted their roles as enduring and evolving ties between the European and Italian legal contexts.

[180] See the 'institutional view' adopted by Laure Clément-Wilz in her chapter in this volume (n 62).

Epilogue

National Judges and the ECJ: Looking Back, Looking Forward

JHH WEILER

1. FRAMING

THE IMPORTANCE OF this book goes well beyond the light it pours on both the personalities and judicial orientation of several generations of Italian judges and Advocates General at the ECJ as well as their nfluence on, and contribution to, the European Community (EC)/European Jnion (EU) legal order. It is a remarkable example of biographical historiography at a very high level. The book as a whole, in its design and execution could, longside a few similar (though far from identical) exercises,[1] serve as a model or other national endeavors.

The prospect for success for those engaged in such an endeavor is not self-vident. There is a risk in singling out just one chapter in a volume which abounds ith excellent contributions. I will take such a risk. Michal Bobek's chapter, oncise yet penetrating, highlights the methodological challenges, refers to the levant literatures as well, and of course offers his own unique take on such xercises. The conclusion by the editors' addresses many of the methodological hallenged posed in the second part of the volume by well-known European law holars. It should be obligatory reading for any scholar embarking on similar ntures.

To give but one example, Bobek highlights some features of the ECJ, which nder this exercise particularly challenging. Famously, there are no separate or ssenting opinions by the judges, making individual analysis difficult if one is rely only on the official record, to individuate the specific contributions of dividual judges in specific cases. (In this respect, the Advocates General are a privileged position). For sure, in the *délibéré* of the Court, separate and

[1] Bobek in his notes provides a useful survey and bibliography on the state of the field, see Bobek, 'Judicial Biographies and Judicial Decision-Making: A Fish Reflects on the Work of rine Biologists', in this volume.

dissenting views are expressed. But those are eventually submerged into the final consensus based decision – not infrequently to the detriment of the clarity or coherence of the rendered decision.

Even the pioneering Copenhagen legal historians and the Paris legal sociologists[2] with their own pioneering exploration of the Courts archival material cannot fully make up for this 'notorious' black hole that makes the contribution of the book all the more remarkable.

When one finishes reading the volume (and another of its great virtues, often overlooked by book editors, is the fact that it is such a good read eschewing the formal mind numbing style of so much of Italian legal scholarship) one feels that one has a fulsome picture of the contribution of Italian members of the ECJ to the evolution of European law. And this is so despite the huge methodological challenge which Bobek and most other authors like Laure Clément-Wilz, Eleanor Sharpston, Siniša Rodin and Antoine Vauchez highlight,[3] in individuating the personal contributions in a judicial context which does not allow separate, let alone, dissenting opinions. (The inclusion of Advocates General was for this reason, too, a felicitous decision of the Editors.).

There is, however a latent 'blind spot' of which the editors were of course fully aware. If I were to make my own list of the most important and influential Italian judges and Advocates general in the shaping of European law alongside some of the names included in the book, I would have to include handful of national Italian courts and judges who played a key role in shaping the national jurisprudence which has had such an impact on the evolution of European law.

Though obvious it is worth spelling out: If one is to understand the impact of national judges, and a national judicial and legal culture on European Law the dialogue between national courts and the ECJ is as important as the role of individual Italian jurists being member of the Luxembourg court.

I should immediately add that this dimension has been endlessly studied whereas the role of individual jurists in the ECJ has received far less scholarly attention, one reason this volume is both so interesting and precious.

And yet, for reasons which will become clear, I want to address the mo classical approach (the dialogue of national courts with the ECJ) which wil additionally, if there is any merit in my analysis, have also implications for th role of national judges within the ECJ.

[2] ibid.

[3] See, respectively, L Clément-Wilz, 'An Institutional View on the Influence of Italian Judges a Advocates General', in this volume; E Sharpston, 'Comparative Legal Reasoning (Overt and Cove in the Work of the Advocate General', in this volume; S Rodin, 'Impact of the National Legal Tra tions on the Role and Activity of the EU Judges', in this volume; A Vauchez, 'Italian Ways of Law: Rooting Italy in European Legal Integration', in this volume.

2. LOOKING BACK

In looking at the past, what has been the traditional normative yardstick in evaluating the position and role of national judiciaries in the European legal order?

I think many readers would agree with me that the words loyalty and obedience overwhelmingly underlie much of this evaluative literature. And this for good reason: I allow myself to be trite and state the obvious. Much of European Law, whether primary or secondary, unlike other forms of international law, eg WTO (which addresses many similar *materiae*), is 'the Law of the Land' creating rights and obligations on national public authorities and individuals.

The European Court of Justice can climb to the top of the Mountain and sermonise on supremacy and direct effect and all the rest from here till further notice. If the national judiciaries which have the primary role in the enforcement of European Law do not listen to such 'sermons from the mount', European law would be an empty letter as is so frequently the case with other international legal obligations imposed on States.

Additionally and consequentially, if even the judiciary of one Member State were to be disloyal or disobedient, the principle of equality before the law, foundational to the Rule of Law, would be compromised.

As mentioned, this is terrain covered *Ad Nauseam* and *Ad Tedium* and it is not my intention to re-plough this terrain. There are, however, different national approaches to the exercise and manifestations of the duty of loyalty and obedience, and I do want to revisit two braces of cases, which will highlight what I consider two admirable characteristics of the Italian approach to the dialog and to the duty of loyalty and obedience.

Perhaps you will agree with me that the Italian and German legal orders and judiciaries stand out in the history of European Integration. Fiercely loyal to the underlying ethos and telos of the European construct (not surprising perhaps given their fascist past), and with somewhat similar constitutional legal orders as well as their prominence as two of the three largest Member State among the original Six. (There is a 'fierce' debate which of the two can claim credit for the preliminary reference procedure, the single most important provision in the Treaties from a legal point of view).

Let's look first at the historical *Solange* and *Frontini* cases. It was not surprising given that fascist past and the similarity of their constitutional architecture that the challenge to the supremacy of European law which, at the time, had no guarantees of protecting fundamental human rights, issued from German and Italian courts.

But there is a marked and telling difference how this challenged expressed itself in the two cases. In *Solange*, the German Constitutional Court simply asserted that it could not, and would not fully accept supremacy 'So Long As' the issue of protecting fundamental rights were not addressed. But, reading between the lines, it was clear that the German Court was happy to assert that prerogative without calling into question the position of Germany within the European legal order or what such a position would mean to the coherence of the European legal order. With a twinkle in my eyes it was a bit Panzer like: You will just have to live with us. (Mind you, without that German and Italian jurisprudence it is doubtful if and when the ECJ would understand that it had to do something about human rights if its doctrine of supremacy were to take hold within national judiciaries.).

The Italian Constitutional Court in *Frontini* was both more profound, more transparent and acted with greater legal integrity. It understood that a lega order which depended on the loyalty of national judiciaries and had to respec the principle of equality before the law of all citizens in the Member States could not tolerate this German type 'you just have to live with me' approach It thus both presented the problem starkly and honestly with no camouflage Should a European norm compromise the human rights guaranteed by th Italian constitution, it held, there would be but three options to ensure the integrity of the European legal order: Either the Treaties would have to be interprete differently or changed (to bring them in line with the Italian guarantee), or th Italian constitution would have to change (to bring it in line with the Europea norm) or Italexit! No less.

Res Ipsa Loquitur. Or, if you wish, *Patti Chiari, Amicizia Lunga*. Paradoxicall the terse and transparent Italian statement is, in my book, the most faithful an constructive expression of loyalty to the European ethos and telos.

Let us now compare two recent cases which evoked huge discussion an decimated entire forests in the number of (repetitious) publications – *Wei* and *Taricco*. It is not my intention to address the all too well-known substan tive issues underlying the two cases. But here, with yet another twinkle in m eye, one can compare the differences between the two courts to the differen between German and Italian football (or at least that elegant Italian footba as it used to be – recall as one example the 1982 final of the World Cup whi pitched Germany against Italy or the 2006 semi-final).

Most of the literature comparing the two cases, contrasts them as follow The German case is condemned as an example of a rebellious disloy Court – putting into practice the hypothetical 'you must just live with me' *Solange* vintage. The Italian case as given as an example of admirable loy cooperation and dialogue.

There is no small measure of window dressing in such a framing of the diff ences. The Italian Court was in substance no less categorical than its Germ counterpart – albeit the iron fist came covered with a typically elegant Itali velvet glove. The message to the ECJ was crystal clear: If you insist on yo interpretation of the Treaty, we will not be able to abide and we see no roo for negotiation on such a fundamental principle of the Italian legal order. T *Frontini* formula was very much in the back ground: either European law w need to change, or Italian law. But apart from the fact that a full explanati was offered to the ECJ, there was some genius in throwing the ball back to the ECJ and making it responsible for precipitating a constitutional crisis. It also offered it a way to climb down from its high tree. The European Court blinked first and a constitutional crisis was avoided.

So in effect, the underlying position was no different from the German decision. But the style of handling was what made the difference. Whoever believes that style does not matter, is someone who has never been involved in high stake negotiations or who has not walked down a Milan throughway and a Frankfurt throughway.

3. LOOKING FORWARD

f one were to articulate the Holy Trinity of the European constitutional order, ts Trinitarian elements would be the following: European law, in its sphere of pplication, is (with some exceptions) the law of the land; it is the supreme law f the land which national authorities have to respect and national courts have o enforce; and the ECJ is the final authority when it comes to interpreting this aw.

The huge success in the construction of this impressive legal edifice was ne result, *inter alia*, of the relationship of trust built between the ECJ and s national counterparts and of the general support the European construct njoyed by the major political forces across Europe. These were the political nd sociological premises, which explain the huge success of this new European vic religion.

Today both premises are under considerable stress.

As regards the legal order, there are striking data to indicate some seismic emors – surely not yet an earthquake – which prudence suggests should not e brushed aside as 'mere tremors'. I refer, as one may imagine, to a stream – rely not a river – of cases where the very foundation of the legal order, the ıthority of the ECJ as the final arbiter on issues of European (constitutional) w, has been called into question. We no longer have the luxury of dismissing ese as aberrations of one or two recalcitrant Courts from recalcitrant Member ates – the usual whipping boys being Hungary and Poland. Denmark, the zech Republic, Italy, France, Romania and of course Germany constitute a oader spectrum. But even if one takes the view, as I do, that we are not facing rue earthquake, a veritable Revolt of the Judicial Masses,[4] these cases[5] raise ues which need thinking and rethinking, even if a crisis were not looming.

[4] J Ortega y Gasset, *La rebelión de las masas* (Madrid, Revista de Occidente, 1930); see also rmuid Rossa Phelan, *Revolt or Revolution: The Constitutional Boundaries of the European nmunity* (Dublin, Round Hall Sweet & Maxwell, 1997).

[5] The most prominent is surely the *PSPP* or *Weiss* decision of the German Federal Constitu-ıal Court, BVerfGE 154, 17; the supremacy of EU law and the role of the ECJ as its arbiter have) been defied by other Member State constitutional or supreme courts: Czech Constitutional

At the political level, the phenomenon – superficially not of a constitutional dimension – which strikes me as most significant is not just the vagaries of public support for the integration project as evidenced in, say, long-term Eurobarometer data.[6] Even more significant is the normalisation and centralisation of Euroscepticism in Member State politics.[7] When we look at the map of electoral politics (the issues which even mainstream politicians and parties raise on the hustings in the hope of garnering votes[8]) we no longer have the comfort of treating Euroscepticism as epiphenomenal – the usual whipping boys, here too, being Hungary and Poland. Think Marine Le Pen in France Giorgia Meloni in Italy, the rise of AfD in Germany to give but three examples from Founding Members of the Union.[9] And of more than anecdota significance, when a mainstream politician such as Michel Barnier, a forme

Court Pl. ÚS 5/12 *Slovak Pensions XVII/Holubec*; Danish Supreme Court, Case 15/2014, *Ajos*; Polis Constitutional Court, Case K 3/21; Romanian Constitutional Court, Decision 390/2021; whereas th courts of further Member States have established the ability to review EU law on basis of nationa (constitutional) law: Belgian Constitutional Court, Case 62/2016; Hungarian Constitutional Cour Case 22/16 (XII.5); the French Conseil d'État refused to make a reference for a preliminary rulin leading to infringement proceedings, see *Commission v France* Case C-416/17 ECLI:EU:C:2018:81 [2018], and, more recently, developed a novel approach to escaping primacy and the reach of th ECJ concerning national security, see Conseil d'État, Ass., 21 April 2021, Req. no. 393099; th Spanish Constitutional Court implied it was not bound by a previously-requested ECJ prelimina ruling, STC 26/2014; the Italian *Taricco*-Saga belongs, as seen above, to this trend. see general Ana Bobić, *The Jurisprudence of Constitutional Conflict in the European Union* (Oxford, Oxfor University Press, 2022).

[6] See C E De Vries, *Euroscepticism and the Future of European Integration* (Oxford, Oxfo University Press, 2018).

[7] For an early overview see P Taggart and A Szczerbiak (eds), *Opposing Europe? The Comparati Party Politics of Euroscepticism* (Vol 1/2, Oxford, Oxford University Press, 2008); M Rooduijn a S van Kessel, 'Populism and Euroskepticism in the European Union', in W R Thompson *et al* (ed *Oxford Research Encyclopedia of Politics* (Oxford, Oxford University Press, 28 August 2019); broad perspective may be found in M Kaeding, J Pollak, and P Schmidt (eds), *Euroscepticism a the Future of Europe. Views from the Capitals* (Cham, Palgrave Macmillan, 2021). How realis an outlook is provided by the eurobarometer is disputed, see M Höpner and B Jurczyk, 'How t eurobarometer blurs the Line between research and propaganda' (2015) MPIfG Discussion Pap No 15/6, available online.

[8] N Brack and N Startin, 'Introduction: Euroscepticism, from the margins to the mainstrea (2915) 36(3) *International Political Science Review* 239; T Persson, C Karlsson, and M Mårtenss 'The influence of Eurosceptic challenger parties on mainstream party behaviour: Is oppositio behaviour contagious?' (2023) 29(1) *Party Politics* 100; the development of Eurosceptic attitude decidedly not a phenomenon found exclusively in right-wing parties, see S Wagner, 'Euroscepti as a radical left party strategy for success' (2022) 28(6) Party Politics 1069.

[9] For France see D Stockemer, *The Front National in France. Continuity and Change Un Jean-Marie Le Pen and Marine Le Pen* (Cham, Springer, 2017); G Ivaldi, 'Contesting the EU in ti of crisis: The Front National and politics of Euroscepticism in France' (2008) 38(3) *Politics* 2 regarding Italy, see A Donà, 'The rise of the Radical Right in Italy: the case of Fratelli d'Ita (2022) 27(5) *Journal of Modern Italian Studies* 775; concerning Germany, see C Dees, 'The 'Al native for Germany': The rise of right-wing populism at the heart of Europe' (2018) 38(3) Poli 295; M Baloge, 'From Brexit to Dexit? Alternative für Deutschland's Euroscepticism on Europ debates in the Bundestag' (2021) 29(4) *Journal of Contemporary European Studies* 552; genera J Sondel-Cedarmas and F Berti (eds), *The Right-Wing Critique of Europe. Nationalist, Sovereig and Right-Wing Populist Attitudes to the EU* (London, Routledge, 2022).

Commissioner, finds it expedient in his electoral bid for the French Presidency, in the context of the immigration debate, to propose a referendum in France in order, inter alia, 'no longer [to] be subject to judgments of the CJEU' one gets a feel how far the political barometer has moved.[10] The recent elections to the European Parliament confirm this trend. One should not be overly impressed by, say, the French Right coming behind the Left and Center in the tally of parliamentary seats. If one looks at the raw popular vote, Le Pen was by far the winner with no less than 37.3% of the French electorate voting for her compared to 26.9 and 22.3 respectively for the Left and Center. Euroscepticism has become mainstream.

What does this mean for the future relationship between the ECJ and the national judiciaries?

There is of course a lesson to be learnt by the European Court itself which will not outline here but the shorthand of which is simple enough: The ECJ hould, first, abandon definitively the vestiges of its Pescatorian hermeneutics More Integration is always better than less integration; and if the political institutions do not follow this path, We The Court, must step in); and second the Court has to position itself, and appear to be positioning itself, as a true 'federal ourt' the task of which is to defend the prerogatives of the Member State legal rder as much as the prerogatives of the Union.

But what role for the national judiciaries? Given the historical ethos of loyalty nd obedience one temptation would be to double down against the Eurosceptic arbarians at the Gates.

I believe this would be, paradoxically, as detrimental to the future of the uropean construct. Trust in the European judicature has to be regained, and ational courts, in the field of application of European law are as much part of e European judicature as is the ECJ. In building trust in the Judiciary, national ourts have a pivotal role to be played. They must be seen too, yes, as guardians the Treaties. But the role of guardians of the Treaties in the 20s of this century as to be understood differently than it was say, in the early decades of the EU. also means to be guardians of Member State and citizen rights in a European onstruct that truly respects the notion of United in *Diversity*.

Naturally, I am not advocating rebellion and disobedience. But I am recommending a different content and tone to preliminary references. When at issue e important issues of national constitutional law, national identitarian issues d the values of diversity, more elaborate and more 'educational' preliminary ferences must be drafted by domestic courts. Dialogue after all is meant to be -directional.

Taricco II style references should become the norm, when justified, not the ception, an Italian lesson to the European Judiciary.

[10] P Dallison and E Braun, 'Barnier the Brexiteer? French candidate gets tough with EU on npaign trail' (*Politico.eu*, 9 September 2021).

4. FUNDAMENTAL RIGHTS AND FUNDAMENTAL BOUNDARIES

By way of conclusion I wish to focus on one issue, that of EU jurisdictional creep and the limits to the competences of the Union.[11] This is of direct concern to the ECJ since it is in this context that some of the most clamorous challenges to the authority of the Court have been raised but also since it may new thinking on the relationship between the European and national judicatures.

There is little point, as mentioned above, in rehearsing in length, yet again, the all too justified laments about the unfortunate decision of the German Federal Constitutional Court ('BVerfG') of 5 May 2020 in the case of *Weiss* on the European Central Bank (ECB)'s public sector asset purchase programme.

Although dealt with in Panzer fashion, the problem the BVerfG faced was real and acute: What is a national constitutional court, which has ultimate responsibility for ensuring the rule of law, human rights, and the principles of democracy within its jurisdiction to do, when faced with an EU measure, which in its view, violates such? And what should that court do when a judgment of th Court of Justice, the guarantor of all those values within the sphere of compe tences of the EU, legitimates that EU measure in a manner which the nationa court regards as inadequate?

The matter is at its most acute when at issue is the line delimiting the respec tive competences of the EU and its Member States. After all, the EU derives it competences and powers by delegation from its Member States as enshrine in the Treaties, its *de facto* constitution. So even if procedurally the Court c Justice is the sole court empowered to pronounce, as a matter of Europea Union law, on such issues, is it not, at least partially, a matter of national law t define what could constitutionally be delegated? And it is worth rememberin that the principle of supremacy operates only within the sphere of competence of the European Union. An *ultra vires* norm does not and should not enjc supremacy. But surely one cannot allow these issues to be decided by nation courts resulting in an unequal application of Union law within its legal spa and compromising the principle of equality before the law of individuals subje to Union law. One outcome in France and another in Latvia depending on whic jurisdiction decided the case?

The matter is further complicated by several additional considerations.

[11] In the following, I borrow liberally from an earlier proposal. For the full discussion and t extensive commentary it received see JHH Weiler and D Sarmiento, 'The EU Judiciary Af Weiss', (Verfassungsblog, 2 June 2020), available at <https://verfassungsblog.de/the-eu-jud ary-after-weiss/> and JHH Weiler and D Sarmiento, 'The Comeback of the Mixed Chamb (Verfassungsblog 2 October 2023), available at <https://verfassungsblog.de/the-comeback-of-t mixed-chamber/>.

First, in its preliminary reference jurisdiction, the European Court of Justice, like several other international and national tribunals, is a court of first and last instance. There is no appeal to a higher court from its decisions. This is an uncomfortable legal situation. After all, *errare humanum est*. We live more comfortably with uncomfortable decisions if they are reviewed and affirmed by a higher court of appeal. In the European Convention on Human Rights (ECHR) system a decision of a Chamber can be appealed to the Grand Chamber with a different composition of judges.[12] But I have already underlined the untenability of each and every national court acting as a Court of Appeal in matters concerning the delimitation of EU competences.

Second, despite its fundamental and indispensable contribution to European integration, the European Court of Justice has shown itself over the years to have one blind spot. It has not proved to be a strict guarantor in policing the limits to EU competences and jurisdiction. The very limited number of cases where it has flagged a breach of competence have been the exception that proves a very general rule of broad EU competence. This is probably due to a misconceived vision of federalism, in which the federal vision is (wrongly) associated with a centralist understanding of the EU. The case-law of the Court of Justice has been interpreted, in particular by the Italian jurists, as setting a straightforward rule: in case of doubt, the competence is of the EU in order to ensure the *effet utile* of EU law, in the same way that in the logic of fundamental rights, in case of doubt, the judge must rule for the benefit of individual freedom.[13]

This is an ill-sighted approach that rightly raises the concerns of national courts, particularly of those with a more acute sense of the logic of federalism. It is aggravated by the far wider areas of EU action compared to the very limited sphere of competences and activity when the constitutional foundations of the EU were put in place more than 50 years. Not only has the sphere of competences widened and deepened but it touches today many more sensitive areas to Member State identitarian interests.

How, then, in the long run, is one to resolve the structural dilemma of a jurisdictional conflict of this nature? It seems a circle that cannot be squared. And yet with no solution the specter of *Weiss* will continue to hover and threaten the integrity of the EU.

It is for this reason that it was proposed[14] that in the Conference on the Future of Europe serious consideration be given to the establishment of a new appeal jurisdiction – a Mixed Chamber – *within the Court of Justice*, strictly and narrowly confined to *Weiss* type cases, where at issue is the delineation of

[12] See Article 43 ECHR.
[13] See F G Nicola, D Gallo, R Mastroianni, and L Cecchetti, 'Conclusion: Four Traits of the Italian Influence on European Law', in this volume.
[14] See Weiler and Sarmiento, 'The EU Judiciary After Weiss' (n 11).

the jurisdictional line between the Member States and the EU. I believe that this appeal procedure should remain within the province of the Court of Justice and the obvious forum would be its Grand Chamber.

I am fully aware that the political chances of this proposal are at best medium term or long term. But the very discussion of this idea is meant to highlight why the future of the relationship between national judiciaries and the ECJ cannot rest on inertia – that is how it was, that is how it should be. As another great Italian has taught us, everything must change if at its core it is to remain the same.

Index

www.ingramcontent.com/pod-product-compliance
Ingram Content Group UK Ltd.
Pitfield, Milton Keynes, MK11 3LW, UK
UKHW020236290926
15470UKWH00002B/576

9 781509 967